Juup Stelma, Achilleas Kostoulas
The Intentional Dynamics of TESOL

Juup Stelma, Achilleas Kostoulas

The Intentional Dynamics of TESOL

DE GRUYTER
MOUTON

ISBN 978-1-5015-2088-4
e-ISBN (PDF) 978-1-5015-1116-5
e-ISBN (EPUB) 978-1-5015-1106-6

Library of Congress Control Number: 2021932154

Bibliographic information published by the Deutsche Nationalbibliothek
The Deutsche Nationalbibliothek lists this publication in the Deutsche Nationalbibliografie; detailed bibliographic data are available on the Internet at http://dnb.dnb.de.

© 2022 Walter de Gruyter Inc, Boston/Berlin
This volume is text- and page-identical with the hardback published in 2021.
Cover image: enginakyurt11/iStock/Getty Images Plus
Typesetting: Integra Software Services Pvt. Ltd.
Printing and binding: CPI books GmbH, Leck

www.degruyter.com

Contents

List of Figures —— IX

List of Tables —— XI

List of Abbreviations —— XIII

Chapter 1
Introduction —— 1
    1.1   Our theoretical stepping stones —— 2
    1.2   A summary of intentional dynamics —— 5
    1.3   How the book is structured —— 7
    1.4   The contribution of the book —— 13

Part A: Developing the model of intentional dynamics

Chapter 2
Everything is connected: Ecological theory —— 19
    2.1   Aspects of ecological theory —— 19
    2.2   Ecological concepts —— 26
    2.3   What we take from ecological theory —— 33

Chapter 3
Everything is dynamic: Complex dynamic systems theory —— 35
    3.1   A brief introduction to CDST —— 36
    3.2   How we use CDST in this book —— 45
    3.3   What we take from CDST —— 50

Chapter 4
Meaning is primary: Intentionality —— 52
    4.1   Two complimentary definitions of intentionality —— 52
    4.2   An ecological view of intentionality —— 58
    4.3   TESOL as an intentional ecology —— 64
    4.4   What we take from intentionality —— 66

Chapter 5
A model of the intentional dynamics of TESOL —— 68
- 5.1 Looking back: The building blocks so far —— 68
- 5.2 Intentional activity and TESOL —— 70
- 5.3 The generative potential of intentional activity —— 73
- 5.4 The intentional dynamics of TESOL: A model —— 80
- 5.5 Looking forward: Our use of the model —— 84

Part B: Exemplifying the model of intentional dynamics

Chapter 6
Individual intentionality: Language teachers becoming researchers —— 89
- 6.1 The intentional ecologies of teaching and research —— 89
- 6.2 Teachers becoming researchers: A case study —— 92
- 6.3 Conclusion: Teachers doing research in TESOL —— 103

Chapter 7
Shared intentionality: Task-based activity in a young learner classroom —— 106
- 7.1 Sociocultural aspects of the Norwegian primary education context —— 106
- 7.2 The data, learners, and task —— 107
- 7.3 The initial normative consensus —— 109
- 7.4 Early non-linearity in the learners' intentional activity —— 112
- 7.5 Emergence of a new shared intentionality —— 117
- 7.6 Conclusion: The nature and role of shared intentionality —— 124

Chapter 8
Derived intentionality: A Greek private language school —— 126
- 8.1 The school, the curricular reform, and the study —— 127
- 8.2 Idiosyncratic intentional structures in the language school —— 129
- 8.3 Derived intentionality in the language school —— 133
- 8.4 Intentional dynamics of resistance —— 138
- 8.5 Conclusion: Idiosyncrasies, resistance, and curricular change —— 142

Chapter 9
Sociocultural aspects of TESOL as an intentional ecology —— 144
    9.1   Sociocultural aspects of the intentional ecology of international TESOL —— 144
    9.2   Intentional structures and language teaching approaches —— 154
    9.3   Conclusion: Intentional structures and change —— 159

Part C: Extending the model of intentional dynamics

Chapter 10
Language learning as intentional becoming —— 165
    10.1   The intentional dynamics of language use —— 165
    10.2   The intentional dynamics of language learning —— 172
    10.3   Promoting language learning as intentional becoming —— 177
    10.4   Conclusion —— 184

Chapter 11
A critical-intentional perspective for TESOL —— 185
    11.1   Being critical in TESOL —— 186
    11.2   A critical-intentional perspective —— 191
    11.3   Conclusion —— 198

Chapter 12
Researching intentional dynamics in TESOL —— 200
    12.1   A mind-set for researching intentional dynamics —— 200
    12.2   Researchable aspects and processes of intentional dynamics —— 209
    12.3   Reflecting on research design, methods, and analysis —— 217
    12.4   Conclusion —— 223

Chapter 13
Intentional dynamics and the future of TESOL —— 225
    13.1   Intentional dynamics as a contribution to TESOL —— 225
    13.2   Intentional dynamics and TESOL practice —— 228
    13.3   Intentional dynamics and new horizons for TESOL —— 235

References —— 243

Index —— 267

List of Figures

Figure 1 Intentionality, attractor states, and intentional activity —— 72
Figure 2 Model of the intentional dynamics of TESOL —— 80
Figure 3 The pedagogy of the research unit —— 94
Figure 4 The intentional dynamics of becoming a researcher —— 97
Figure 5 The shift in intentional activity across iterations of the task —— 122
Figure 6 Intentional dynamics across the language school's curriculum —— 139
Figure 7 Paradigmatic summary of international TESOL —— 154
Figure 8 Change in paradigms and teaching approaches —— 160
Figure 9 Language learning as intentional becoming —— 177
Figure 10 Researchable aspects and processes of the intentional dynamics of TESOL —— 210

List of Tables

Table 1   Dynamic properties of complex dynamic systems —— 40
Table 2   Stratification of complex dynamic systems —— 43
Table 3   Contingent intentional activity —— 74
Table 4   Normative intentional activity —— 76
Table 5   Creative intentional activity —— 77
Table 6   Purposeful intentional activity —— 78
Table 7   Typical event structure of the role-play task —— 108
Table 8   Overview of the nature of the learning materials —— 134
Table 9   A mind-set for researching intentional dynamics —— 209
Table 10   Aspects of intentional ecologies described in our own research —— 211
Table 11   Typology of researchable aspects and processes of intentional dynamics —— 217

List of Abbreviations

EFL	English as a Foreign Language
ELT	English Language Teaching
IELTS	International English Language Testing System
TESOL	Teaching English to Speakers of Other Languages
CDS/CDST	Complex Dynamic System / Complex Dynamic Systems Theory
LLS	Language Learning Strategies
MA	Master of Arts
WTC	Willingness To Communicate
L1	First Language
L2	Second Language(s)
VLE	Virtual Learning Environment

Chapter 1
Introduction

This book is shaped by our primary and enduring impression of TESOL as activity that is interconnected and dynamic, and which is generated by our unique ability to make meaning. TESOL contexts, activity, and outcomes arise from the multitude of interconnected, dynamic, and purposeful contributions of teachers, learners, and other language education stakeholders from across a wide range of international contexts. We have, ourselves, benefitted from teaching and researching English language education in settings such as Greece, Norway, and South Korea, and we have worked – as teacher educators – with English language teachers from a wide range of additional international settings. Our understanding of TESOL is international and comprises English as a Foreign / Second / Additional Language, English for Academic / Special Purposes, Content and Language Integrated Instruction, English as a Medium of Instruction, Teaching English to Young Learners, and more. Thus, our impression of TESOL, and the view that informs this book, emerges from inclusive experiences of international TESOL; some intra-personal, some classroom-situated, and some that have unfolded on a global dimension.

To make sense of meaning-making across TESOL settings, we have engaged with ideas from ecological and complex dynamic systems theories, and have used the concept of intentionality to understand the nature of meaning and meaning-making. This theoretical and empirical work has appeared in a gradually expanding corpus of publications (Fay and Stelma 2016; Kostoulas 2014, 2015, 2018; Kostoulas and Stelma 2016, 2017; Kostoulas et al. 2018; Stelma 2003, 2011, 2014; Stelma and Fay 2014, 2019; Stelma, Fay, and Zhou 2013; Stelma et al. 2015). We now feel it is time to pull together all our work and to take a larger step forward. This book is our attempt to put all that we see and believe about TESOL together into a model of the intentional dynamics of TESOL – which is our theory of the interconnected and dynamic meaning-making that shapes TESOL contexts, activity, and outcomes.

The model of the intentional dynamics of TESOL that we develop is a synthesis of ecological and complex dynamic systems theories, with the addition of the concept of intentionality. Our aim is to better understand the psychological and social processes that give shape to TESOL contexts, activity, and outcomes. We believe that our model of intentional dynamics can provide new insights into a range of TESOL phenomena, including the local activity of teachers, learners, and other stakeholders, and a better understanding of the shared and global processes through which socio-political and professional values give shape to what we do. The intentional dynamics that we describe in this book are cognitive and social, they bridge local and global phenomena, and thus enable a new, different, and holistic understanding of TESOL.

In the sections that follow, we give a brief overview of some of the theoretical stepping-stones that have led to this book (section 1.1), we outline the main features of our model of the intentional dynamics of TESOL (section 1.2), we provide an overview of the parts and chapters of the book (section 1.3), and we end with a brief discussion of the contribution we are making, and how this fits in the field of TESOL (section 1.4).

1.1 Our theoretical stepping stones

The starting point for the intellectual journey culminating in this book was our already established interest in ecological theory and Complex Dynamic Systems Theory (CDST). Ecological theory developed our appreciation of TESOL as an interconnected whole, and language teaching and learning as human-activity-in-context. Ecological theory suggests that the person and the environment are "equal partners" in a reciprocal relationship. If this relationship is disrupted, then change – good or bad – is likely to follow. CDST gave us a unique perspective on order and change. Language classroom activity may be both patterned and unpredictable. We may struggle to get a language lesson underway, but then enter a flow-like state where time seems to slip by unnoticed, or we may shift into a more deliberate mode – either rushing to the end or looking back in reflection. The longer-term personal and linguistic development of teachers and learners is similarly both patterned and unpredictable, and curricula, school management, and language policies may be sources or loci of order, change, or both. Thus, ecological and complex dynamic systems theories provided us with an appreciation of the interconnected and dynamic nature of activity and outcomes on different levels and timescales of TESOL. However, we often struggled with the fact that these theories originated in fields very different to TESOL, including biology, mathematics, physics, and more (Bocking 1994; Gleick 1987; Kauffman 1996; Rotabi 2007). Thus, the analytical affordances of ecological and complex dynamic systems theories do not easily extend to the meaning-making we want to understand.

The next stepping-stone towards understanding meaning-making, and our model of intentional dynamics, drew on the ecological work of Michael Young and colleagues (Young et al., 2002). They adopted the common position, from the field of ecological psychology (Gibson 1979; Reed 1996), that educational activity is propelled forwards by affordances, or action possibilities, present in the environment. Young et al.'s original contribution was that these affordances would be constrained by the intentions of individuals, something which led them to develop an ecological and dynamic theory of "intention formation". Inspired by Young et al.'s work, we were now able to understand how intention developed within a cascade of constraining structures. For example, we could envisage a situation where a government articulated the longer-term goal of increasing the country's economic competitiveness. "One level down", the Ministry of Education might then be tasked with developing a curriculum to make economic success more likely. The Ministry policy-makers would observe that English is the international language of business, and thus a new English language curriculum emphasising communicative competence would be developed. "Further down" in the constraints hierarchy, schools would then be expected to implement the new communicative curriculum, and on the ground teachers would be obliged to do communicative language teaching. At the same time, students would be motivated, or compelled, to study for new exams with a communicative focus. This represents a hierarchy of intentions, with intentions originating on a higher level (increasing the country's economic competitiveness) cascading down to stakeholders on all levels, which are constrained to pursue a particular set of affordances for action.

While we were intrigued by Young et al.'s contribution, including its potential for explaining how activity in TESOL is shaped, we felt that their constraints hierarchy left little room for the kind of creativity that we see so much of in TESOL. Creativity is central not only in language use, on all timescales, it is central also in generating the broader ecologies of language use we are all a part of, both inside and outside of classrooms. A constraints hierarchy seemed overly top-down and deterministic. It seemed to privilege a view of TESOL teachers and learners "falling into line", and pursuing affordances and intentions imposed from higher up in the hierarchy. This led us to Alicia Juarrero's (1999) book-length contribution, entitled *Intentional Dynamics in Action*. Juarrero suggests that human intention is an emergent phenomenon resulting from intentional dynamics that include both bottom-up and top-down processes. She suggests, then, that intentions develop from complex dynamics, including both unconscious processes and more deliberate reflection, and when an intention to do something appears in the mind of an individual, this intention constrains what action possibilities (affordances) may be pursued. Thus, in Juarrero's view, intentions can emerge bottom-up, making creativity possible. However, we were still not quite convinced that we had a theory of meaning. We had some new ideas about how the particular meaning-structure of intention might emerge and operate, but were uncertain about whether this would work for meaning and meaning-making more generally. An additional concern was that much of the work on everyday intentions seemed to focus on the activity of individuals. Our experience of TESOL suggests that what we do is just as often collaborative.

A next stepping-stone towards understanding meaning and meaning-making was work in developmental psycholinguists, which has documented the role of "shared intentionality" in child development. Tomasello and Carpenter (2007) define shared intentionality as one person having some ability to understand what another person's intention may be, and how collaborative activity may proceed based on this shared understanding. This prompted us to wonder how aware language learners might be of their teachers' intentions, how aware teachers might be about their learners' intentions, and so on. It also led us to think about the possibility of more collective intentional structures being present in the social-professional fabric of TESOL. Collective phenomena like the communicative zeitgeist of the 1980s, the popularity of task-based learning in the 1990s, the postmethod movement of the 2000s, and perhaps also the various critical turns currently appearing might all have some kind of "intentional structure". However, this did feel like a conceptual "jump", and we were still stuck with a somewhat narrow definition of meaning and meaning-making.

An important breakthrough for us occurred when we started disambiguating the different senses of the terms "intention" and "intentionality". The cognitive science literature, which is focused on intention-formation and acting with intention, uses the term "intentionality" as a noun to describe the psychological state of having a goal in mind. Thus, for cognitive scientists, intentionality is defined akin to the everyday, or ordinary, sense of intentions and intentionality. This ordinary sense of intentionality did motivate some of our earlier work, including ecological and dynamic descriptions of how TESOL activity and outcomes might be driven by stakeholders being purposeful in what they do (Stelma and Fay 2014; Stelma et al. 2015). However, the real breakthrough was our discovery of how the concept of intentionality was understood in the philosophy of mind. We discovered a different sense of intentionality, as proposed by philosophers like Franz Brentano ([1874] 2015) and John Searle (1983). In this sense of intentionality, our psychological states (e.g., hope, desire, love, fear, belief, and more) are "directed at" something, or are "about" something. So, in the philosophy of mind, intentionality is "aboutness". This was a breakthrough because "intentionality as aboutness" offered clues about how we might understand the interconnectedness of TESOL contexts, activity, and outcomes. The aboutness of our psychological states suggests a form of interconnectivity; an interconnectivity between our psychological states and the world around us. When we read books, we are connected to the author and the world she describes, and when we play games, we are connected to the imaginary world that our games create. This works for TESOL as well, where we can relate affective aspects of language education, such as curiosity, anxiety, joy, and other psychological states, to specific aspects of language and language learning, such as speaking, grammar, lexis, and more. For instance, we might hypothesise that the "aboutness" of a learner's anxiety is the grammar of the language, or talking in front of an audience. This is something we had intuitively felt as language educators, and the suggestion that psychological states have aboutness enabled us to theorise this intuition.

The sense of intentionality from the philosophy of mind was still an individual concept. In fact, this sense of intentionality, although more flexible, felt a bit like the propositional content of mental representations (Smith and Queller 2001). A final stepping-stone, then, was the suggestion made by John Searle (1983), that intentionality may be "assigned" or "sedimented" into objects of the external world around us. For instance, a materials writer will have particular beliefs about language learners and language teaching. The aboutness of these beliefs makes them intentional. The beliefs may be about particular learners that the writer hopes will benefit from the materials, they may be about language, about how content should be sequenced, and/or about how languages should be taught. Thus, as the materials writer goes about her work, the intentionality of these beliefs will be reflected in the materials that she produces. This means that a textbook, as well as any other object that is made by intentional humans, has what Searle calls "derived intentionality". With the notion of derived intentionality in place, the possibility of collective intentional structures in the social-professional fabric of TESOL seemed less of a conceptual "jump". Also, the philosophical sense of intentionality, as aboutness, began to reveal a more inclusive theory of meaning and meaning-making. We experience psychological states, such as belief, love, anger, regret, and more, quite directly. Moreover, this experience of psychological states appears real to us, and these states connect to those aspects of the world around us that are meaningful to us. We felt we had achieved "lift-off"; our intellectual journey was nowhere near finished, but the trajectory was becoming clear. We now had to show, in a theoretical clyoherent manner, how the concept of intentionality might combine with ecological thinking and CDST to understand meaning-making in the activity of learners, parents, teachers, materials writers, policy-makers, and researchers, across collective and broader contexts of TESOL. This book sets out to do just that, and our model of the intentional dynamics of TESOL is this coherent theory.

1.2 A summary of intentional dynamics

This section presents a brief summary of our model of intentional dynamics. The model stays true to our belief that TESOL contexts, activity, and outcomes are all inherently interconnected, dynamic, and have meaning-making at their heart. The model describes how all that we see, and all that learners, teachers, and other participants in TESOL do, is interconnected. The words and structures and texts that learners engage with connect them to millions of other speakers of the English language, and the language that they use connects them to their classmates, their teacher, and sometimes to culture and society. The teaching approaches that inform a teacher's thinking, and her day-to-day classroom techniques, connect to those of other teachers, whether directly (through observation) or indirectly through printed and online resources and interactions. Materials writers often work alone, but they may have been language teachers themselves, and they may well have taught hundreds of students – some successful and some not – whose experiences remain alive in their intentional minds. Policy-makers and university-based researchers may likewise be connected to the "real world" of TESOL, through their former teaching and learning experiences, having been teacher educators, or through their personal and professional networks. TESOL is a world-wide phenomenon, and it touches and connects us all.

The model of intentional dynamics also describes how TESOL is always in motion, and this dynamic nature sometimes prevents us from predicting or controlling what may happen in classrooms or staffrooms, or how curricula and policies change. This applies, in addition, to our language learners, whose linguistic resources and identities continually change, alongside them growing older and wiser. It also includes teachers, who may face their initial classroom encounters with wonder or trepidation, but as they develop may take on leadership roles to nurture junior colleagues. It includes schools, which change in character from year to year as students come and go, as teachers are hired, grow more experienced, or retire, as their physical facilities change, and as their curricula evolve or are re-interpreted. It includes the English language, which evolves – even if slowly – over generations. It includes teaching approaches, which may fall in and out of fashion. It includes technology and society, with opportunities and challenges seemingly always one step ahead of where we are. The model of intentional dynamics describes how this motion happens, whether on the micro-timescale of moment-to-moment classroom interaction, or in the form of slower-moving changes of society.

Finally, the model of intentional dynamics has meaning and meaning-making at its heart. The model details how meaning-making generates language learning, professional development, curriculum innovation, and more. It explains how language teachers make sense of past experiences, and how they may work – tirelessly – to make their language classrooms meaningful environments for their learners. The model helps us to understand how learners make meaning, and how they express this meaning through speaking and writing in the new language.

It helps us to appreciate how materials writers design materials that engage language learners in pedagogically useful ways, and how policy-makers try to make sense of the what, why, and how of language education. The intentional dynamics that we describe in this book is what generates all this activity, meaning, and meaning-making. In fact, our model of intentional dynamics suggests that the purpose of all language education activity, across all domains of TESOL, should be to enable our learners to contribute, and gain access, to diverse worlds of meaning. The model is, at the same time, a theory of interconnectedness, a theory of dynamic processes, and a theory of meaning-making. Somewhat audaciously, we suggest that our intentional dynamics may work as a meta-theory for TESOL, which can be used to understand phenomena as disparate as language teaching and language learning, curriculum design and innovation, social and contextual influences on TESOL, critical action to challenge power and injustice, and more.

1.3 How the book is structured

With the exception of the introduction and conclusion, this book is made up of 11 substantive chapters, and these are organised into three parts. The first part (chapters 2–5) develops our model of the intentional dynamics of TESOL, the second part (chapters 6–9) exemplifies intentional dynamics across different levels and domains of TESOL, and the third part (chapters 10–12) identifies two areas of TESOL where we believe the model of intentional dynamics may extend understanding and promote new action. The third part also includes a chapter that explores how we may research the intentional dynamics of TESOL.

1.3.1 Developing the model of intentional dynamics

The following four chapters develop the central contribution of this book: the model of the intentional dynamics of TESOL. The model draws on three distinct theoretical influences. We use ecological theory to understand the interconnectedness of TESOL, CDST to explain its dynamic nature, and the concept of intentionality to account for the meaningful aspects of TESOL. Each of these theoretical influences are covered by one chapter, and these lay the foundation for the full model of intentional dynamics that is presented in chapter 5.

Chapter 2 details our engagement with ecological theory. Ecological theory is most often associated with the natural world, specific eco-systems of this natural world, and sometimes also our own relationship with nature. This origin of ecological theory emphasises the interconnectedness which characterises the natural world, explains the viability of eco-systems, and describes how we as humans coexist with, change, and sometimes disrupt the natural environment. However, ecological theory has had a strong influence, also, on the social and psychological sciences, including – but to a lesser extent – education and TESOL. Ecological theory has surfaced in the well-known 20th century theories of human activity and development put forward by Kurt Lewin (1935), Gregory Bateson ([1972] 1987), Urie Bronfenbrenner (1977, 1979), and James Gibson (1979). These contributions have made visible how human activity and development relies on our reciprocal interaction with social and pedagogical environments. However, the origin of ecological thinking in the natural sciences means that we must approach ecological theory with caution; we need to ask what may be the appropriate focus for an ecological theory of a human and social ecology such as TESOL. We are unable to answer this question fully in chapter 2, but we do make the provisional suggestion that the focus must be on meaningful information and meaningful activity. In addition, chapter 2 introduces the concept of affordances from Ecological Psychology, which we define as information content that is present in the environment and which makes particular actions possible. Finally, the chapter develops a distinction between "ecology as system" and "ecology of activity", which is used to conclude that TESOL is an ecological system of meaningful information which shapes meaningful TESOL activity, and this meaningful TESOL activity may change TESOL as a meaningful ecological system.

In chapter 3, we turn to CDST to make sense of the dynamic nature of TESOL. Many years ago now, we both caught an interest in the exotics of chaos, fractals, strange attractors, bifurcation diagrams, and the unexpected impact of a butterfly flapping her wings in a far-away place. However, this book is not about the technical detail of such theoretical metaphors – we have long since recovered from the fantasy that CDST holds the "answer to the ultimate question of life, the universe, and everything". In fact, just as ecological theory, CDST originates in fields very different from TESOL, and the challenge of making this theory useful for understanding human and social systems, like TESOL, is considerable. What we have come to appreciate, then, is that some of the less exotic aspects of CDST, including the mutual shaping nature of activity and context (expanding on ecological theory), the dynamism of change, as well as the value of understanding ordered states (as opposed to chaotic ones) hold perhaps greater promise for developing new understanding of TESOL contexts, activity, and outcomes. Thus, the chapter discusses how TESOL as a complex dynamic system is interconnected, including how smaller systems are nested within larger systems, how we may identify analytical sub-systems, and how TESOL activity may be understood as a complex dynamic process. We take a closer look at the dynamic properties of complex dynamic systems, including adaptiveness, historicity, non-linearity, and self-organisation, and how these help us to understand the generative properties of TESOL activity. Finally, we introduce the concept of attractor states, to explain the potential and significance of ordered states in TESOL. Chapter 3 does get theoretical, but we try at all times to stay grounded by what we need from CDST, and we bring with us only that which is useful for developing our model of the intentional dynamics of TESOL.

Chapter 4 introduces intentionality, which is the final conceptual area that underpins our model of the intentional dynamics of TESOL. We start by reviewing the cognitive science literature, which is focused on intention-formation and acting with intention, and which adopts an everyday, or folk-psychological, sense of intentions and intentionality. We refer to this sense of intentionality as *ordinary intentionality*. The value of ordinary intentionality is argued for by the American philosopher of science, Daniel Dennett (1987), who suggested that an intentional stance (i.e., an epistemological outlook informed by intentionality) uniquely enables both understanding and prediction. However, in order to understand meaning and meaning-making more broadly, we also look at how intentionality is understood by the philosophy of mind literature. We draw on John Searle's (1983) suggestion that our psychological states, such as hope, desire, love, fear, beliefs, and more, are about something or someone. For instance, the psychological state of love may be "about", or "directed at", another person, a state of being, a situation, or an object. We call this second sense *ideational intentionality*. Ideational intentionality, we argue, is the "connective tissue" that gives us our meaningful experience of TESOL. Finally, we develop an ecological view of intentionality, including how the "aboutness" of intentionality may be shared by groups of people, present in derived form in texts and objects, and visible in the sociocultural norms and expectations of TESOL and of society. We propose, then, that there are individual, shared, derived, and sociocultural aspects of intentionality which comprise what we call the intentional ecology of TESOL.

With our conceptual foundations in place, chapter 5 presents the full model of the intentional dynamics of TESOL. This includes an initial discussion of intentional activity in TESOL. We establish that intentional activity in TESOL is shaped by individual, shared, derived, and sociocultural aspects of the intentional ecology of TESOL. We develop, also, a framework that distinguishes between four types of intentional activity – contingent, normative, creative, and purposeful – and link these to the four dynamic properties of complex dynamic systems – adaptiveness, historicity, non-linearity, and self-organisation. We also discuss the potential of the different types of intentional activity to reproduce or change the intentional ecology of TESOL. This is followed by a presentation of the full model of the intentional dynamics of TESOL, which accounts for how the intentional ecology of TESOL shapes intentional activity, as well as how intentional activity reproduces or changes the intentional ecology of TESOL. In addition to leveraging the concept of intentionality to highlight meaning and meaning-making, the analytical potential of the model is enabled by different elements drawn from ecological and complex dynamic systems theories. This includes the concept of affordances, the dynamic properties of complex dynamic systems, and the concept of attractor states from CDST. Finally, the model of intentional dynamics is presented as a meta-theory for TESOL. As we have suggested above, it is a model of interconnectedness, drawing on ecological insights; it is model of the dynamic nature of TESOL, viewing TESOL as a complex dynamic system; and it is a model of meaning and meaning-making, conceptualised as the intentional ecology and intentional activity of TESOL.

1.3.2 Exemplifying the intentional dynamics of TESOL

The next four chapters (chapters 6–9) exemplify intentional dynamics as they appear in different TESOL contexts and activity. In these chapters, we focus on the emergence and shaping influence of individual, shared, derived, and sociocultural aspects of the intentional ecology of TESOL. It also includes analysis of the generative potential of contingent, normative, creative, and purposeful intentional activity, the presence and role of affordances, and discussion of attractor states in TESOL settings. Finally, it includes discussion of how intentional dynamics are shaped by the stratified nature of TESOL as a system and TESOL as activity.

Chapter 6 looks at the intentional dynamics of practicing language teachers becoming researchers, while completing a UK-based, online MA TESOL programme. We focus on the development of the teachers' individual intentionality as researchers, whilst recognising that the intentional dynamics of becoming a researcher are nested in broader intentional ecologies. We describe how the intentional ecologies of language teaching and doing research differ, and discuss the challenges associated with succeeding in the previously unknown intentional ecology of research. The chapter highlights, also, the generative role of the teachers' purposeful intentional activity for developing their individual intentionality as researchers. Chapter 6 concludes with a broader discussion of the challenges, for language teachers wishing to engage in and with research, which the model of intentional dynamics highlights.

In chapter 7, we explore how shared intentionality emerged in a Norwegian primary English language classroom, and how this shared intentionality shaped classroom activity. We re-analyse data from Stelma (2003; 2014), documenting young language learners' interaction on a repeated dialogue-writing and role-play task across a one-year period. Our analysis establishes an initial normative consensus for how the role play-task was approached. Next, we outline how this normative consensus was challenged by the learners' contingent and creative intentional activity over time, and how this led to the emergence of a shared concern about "being entertaining". The chapter details how this new shared intentionality grew stronger over time, until the teacher determined that the pedagogical benefit of the new shared intentionality had run its course. Overall, chapter 7 provides an empirical analysis of shared intentionality, as embedded in a broader intentional ecology. The analysis shows that shared intentionality acts as a local, in time and place, "social structure", which enables and constrains activity.

Chapter 8 discusses the intentional ecology of a private language school in Greece (see also Kostoulas and Stelma 2017). There is a particular focus on sociocultural aspects of the intentional ecology of the school, on the derived intentionality evident in the learning materials used, and on how the interplay between sociocultural and derived aspects of intentionality constrained the success of an attempted curricular reform. We first explore the sociocultural aspects of the intentional ecology, including the presence of both international socio-professional influences and local idiosyncratic intentional structures. Next, we analyse the derived intentionality of the learning materials in terms of what affordances for teaching and learning activity they appeared to promote. Finally, we look at how the international and idiosyncratic intentional structures combined with the derived intentionality of the learning materials. We show how the interplay of sociocultural and derived aspects of intentionality resulted in attractor states, constituting intentional dynamics of resistance to the attempted curricular reform. Thus, chapter 8 demonstrates how our model of intentional dynamics can be used to generate nuanced understandings of the intentional ecology of specific TESOL settings, including also the suggestion that every language education setting will have idiosyncratic features, and that any attempt at change must include an appreciation of such idiosyncratic features of local intentional ecologies and intentional dynamics.

Lastly, chapter 9 takes a "step back" to look at how TESOL contexts, activity, and outcomes may be shaped by sociocultural aspects of the broader intentional ecology of TESOL. The chapter explores what we perceive to be the most salient sociocultural aspects of international TESOL, today. Consistent with the discussion of sociocultural aspects at play in a private language school, in chapter

8, we understand the sociocultural aspects of international TESOL as intentional structures. Following Kostoulas (2018), we categorise these intentional structures along linguistic, pedagogical, and political dimensions. Next, we explore how these intentional structures shape, or are reflected in, broadly defined teaching approaches in TESOL. More specifically, we suggest that sets of teaching approaches, including form-focused, communicative, and critical approaches, may be shaped by particular configurations of sociocultural intentional structures. Finally, we discuss the change we see, or would like to see, in these sociocultural aspects of international TESOL.

1.3.3 Extending the model of intentional dynamics

The three chapters that make up the last part of the book (chapters 10–12) extend our model of intentional dynamics by discussing how it may be used to gain a new perspective on language learning (chapter 10) and being critical in TESOL (chapter 11). Thus, these first two chapters reconceptualise existing fields of study in TESOL, and suggest new understanding and new action that the model of intentional dynamics may promote. The extension in the third chapter is more pragmatic; it is an outline of a mind-set, as well as a typology of researchable aspects, that may guide research to understand the intentional dynamics of TESOL.

Chapter 10 uses the model of intentional dynamics to reconceptualise language learning as intentional becoming. Our starting point is existing CDST views of language use and language learning. These existing views are extended to incorporate the insights of our model of intentional dynamics. We develop a CDST view of language use and language learning that includes, as defining parameters, the individual, shared, derived, and sociocultural aspects of intentional ecologies, and the dynamic properties of contingent, normative, creative, and purposeful intentional activity. Finally, we discuss the practical implications of viewing language learning through the lens of our intentional dynamics. This includes three sequenced principles for language education, suggesting that (a) language education should promote a diverse intentional ecology for our learners, which would enable (b) learners to engage in a diversity of intentional activity, and thereby (c) support them to become intentional users and learners of English as a L2.

Chapter 11 develops a critical-intentional perspective for TESOL. The chapter starts by reviewing existing perspectives on being critical in TESOL, including criticality defined by rationality, criticality foregrounding context, and criticality focused on challenging normative assumptions and unjust orders in TESOL.

Next, the critical-intentional perspective that we develop includes discussion of how normative assumptions emerge from intentional dynamics, and how the model of intentional dynamics changes our understanding of power, freedom, and agency. We also examine how the ecological notion of diversity and the CDST concept of emergence may challenge normative assumptions and the unjust orders that such normative assumptions seem to underpin. The critical-intentional perspective suggests that we harness the collective power of individuals and groups across all domains of TESOL, and that doing so is our best chance to challenge normative assumptions in TESOL. We must all seek to extend our understanding, to the limits of our knowing, and we must all engage in, and encourage in others, creative and purposeful intentional activity. When this happens, we will enhance the diversity of the intentional ecology of TESOL, the diversity of affordances and activity, and allow for the emergence of less restrictive outcomes.

The final chapter in this part (chapter 12) has a more pragmatic focus on how we may research the intentional dynamics of TESOL. We argue that for such research work to yield its maximum potential, it needs to be grounded in a mind-set that is attuned to the interconnectedness and dynamism of TESOL, as well as an appreciation of the ways in which TESOL is permeated by meaning and meaning-making. We also outline a taxonomy of researchable aspects and processes that would generate understanding of the intentional dynamics of TESOL. We also include a discussion of how our own research, as reported in other chapters of this book, has been guided by the mind-set we have advocated, and the taxonomy that we have outlined.

In the concluding chapter of this book (chapter 13), we revisit what are the contributions of the model of intentional dynamics to TESOL scholarship, review the practical implications of the model that the previous chapters have argued for, and explore what we believe are promising future directions for TESOL scholarship.

1.4 The contribution of the book

The primary contribution of this book is our model of intentional dynamics, which we believe may act as a meta-theory for understanding TESOL contexts, activity, and outcomes. We accept that our model restates some conventional wisdoms in the social sciences and humanities. The model suggests that context, with both local and global characteristics, shapes the activity of individuals and groups, and that the activity of individuals and groups will either reproduce or change local and global contexts. This is a re-statement of many previous contributions in TESOL, Education, and the Social Sciences. Our unique contribution is the focus on meaning and meaning-making, using the concept of intentionality. To our mind, using the concept of intentionality in this way has not yet been attempted by previous authors, either in TESOL or in any other field. The only previous contribution that hints at the direction we have taken is that of Kubanyiova and Feryok (2015), who have suggested that intentionality is "a feature common to different mental processes and related to purposeful actions" (p. 436), and that a philosophical approach to the concept of intentionality might allow research to focus on "all mental processes or states that are about something" (p. 440). Our model of the intentional dynamics is consistent with the suggestion made by Kubanyiova and Feryok. However, we take this further, by combining ecological and complex dynamics systems theories with the concept of intentionality to develop a unique understanding of meaning and meaning-making in TESOL. This includes understanding TESOL contexts as intentional ecologies, TESOL activity as soft-assembled by the dynamic properties of complex dynamic systems, and TESOL outcomes as morphogenetic processes of change. These contributions are brought together, as a coherent whole, by our model of the intentional dynamics of TESOL.

We believe, in addition, that our conceptualisation of the intentional ecology of TESOL, as well as our theoretical discussion of intentional activity, may represent distinct contributions. The intentional ecology of TESOL, which we conceptualise in chapter 4, brings together the meaningful contributions of individuals and groups, the shaping influence of material resources and sociocultural aspects of TESOL, and allows an analysis of TESOL as a meaningful "whole". This is a contribution which could be used in ways that are distinct from our full model of the intentional dynamics of TESOL. Likewise, our discussion of different types of intentional activity leverages CDST in a new way. As will be outlined in chapter 5, each type of activity is associated with a distinct dynamic property, and therefore also a distinct potential to reproduce or change TESOL contexts and outcomes. These two distinct contributions, we believe, could be used without adopting the full model of intentional dynamics. However, and crucially, it is the integration of these two contributions – the intentional ecology and intentional activity – that unlocks the full potential of what we propose. The full model of intentional dynamics, as informed by both ecological and complex dynamic systems theory, offers a new way of understanding how TESOL contexts shape meaningful activity, and how TESOL activity either reproduces or changes the meaningful ecology of TESOL.

The book also makes a meta-theoretical contribution. We address the lingering concern with the use of ecological and complex dynamic systems theories in both TESOL and broader Applied Linguistics and Education scholarship.

A number of authors have argued for the analytical and practical potential of these theories for TESOL (e.g., Kramsch 2012; Larsen-Freeman and Cameron 2008a; van Lier 2004) and the field of education (e.g., Davis and Sumara 2006; Mason 2008; Osberg and Biesta 2010). However, the potential relevance of these theories is hampered by their origins in the mathematical, physical, and biological sciences. This is echoed by Larsen-Freeman and Cameron (2008a: 201), who suggest there is a "material difference between applied linguistics [and, we might add, TESOL] and the natural sciences with respect to objects of inquiry". Our response to this critique is guided by Kramsch's (2008: 403) suggestion, that "both teachers of English and teachers of foreign languages are not teachers of a linguistic code but teachers of meaning." By leveraging the concept of intentionality, we have reconceptualised TESOL as an ecological and complex dynamic system of "meaning" and "meaning-making".

Finally, we must recognise that our contribution has been shaped by previous research and scholarship, in Applied Linguistics, TESOL and other related fields. Most prominently, perhaps, we have benefited from the seminal work of Diane Larsen-Freeman and Lynne Cameron, most clearly evident in their monograph *Complex Systems and Applied Linguistics* (2008a). This monograph brought CDST to the attention of the wider TESOL and Applied Linguistics communities. This was not a one-off contribution; we know personally that these authors spent decades coming to understand the "complexity paradigm", and we have benefitted greatly from their mentorship. Staying in TESOL, we have always admired the ambitious theoretical work of Leo van Lier, best expressed in his book-length synthesis (2004) of ecological and complex dynamic systems theories to understand the relationships between agency, activity, and contexts in language education. van Lier's combination of ecological theory, CDST, and focus on agency resonates with our own use of ecological and complex dynamic systems theories, and the addition of intentionality. Looking beyond TESOL, we have benefitted greatly from a number of authors making dynamic systems theory relevant to the social sciences (e.g., Byrne 1998; Byrne and Callaghan 2014) and education (e.g., Davis and Sumara 2006). Finally, we need to recognise the steady stream of new uses of CDST appearing in TESOL and Applied Linguistics journals, conferences, and book publications (e.g., Herdina and Jessner 2002; Hiver and Al-Hoorie 2020; Sampson 2016; Ortega and Han 2017, and others). These have further raised our awareness of the potential of CDST to inform the field.

It is useful, also, to point out how our interdisciplinary journey, outlined in the broadest terms by this introduction, compares with existing theories and trends in both TESOL and the informing field of Applied Linguistics. Recent scholarly work in TESOL and Applied Linguistics increasingly draws on postmodern sociolinguistics, with language use reconceptualised as translingual practice (Canagarajah 2013) or translanguaging (García and Wei 2014), and with discussions of context and society that seek to transcend colonial and post-colonial perspectives (Kubota 2016), adopting instead critical, cosmopolitan, and posthumanist perspectives able to describe an expanding set of ethical and political concerns about TESOL policy and practice (Holliday 2011; Pennycook 2018a and 2018b). We do not seek to undermine this scholarship, and our work addresses many of the same themes. However, we do develop a different way forward. Our understanding of TESOL, viewed abstractly, includes both more traditional perspectives of language education, which draw on monolingual ideologies (Gogolin 2002), and perspectives that draw on plurilingualism (C. Benson 2014; T. Lamb 2015), and as will become clear, we centrally seek to understanding how TESOL may transition from one way of thinking about language education to another. Thus, we are charting a new trail along which we may explore TESOL. This is a trail that is informed by a novel combination of social, scientific, and philosophical theories, and it provides us with a different set of affordances. The trail follows the English language education activity that we see taking place across the TESOL settings that we have experience of, and for this reason the book – we believe – has real-world relevance to the people that inhabit this world that we call TESOL. Moreover, our contribution includes the development of an ecological ethics, and a view of context and society informed by ecological and complex dynamic systems theories, which we believe is both more broadly focused and less judgmental than some of the recent post-modern scholarship in TESOL and Applied Linguistics.

Finally, this introduction can only provide a very general account of what we seek to achieve. An in-depth understanding of our model of the intentional dynamics of TESOL, including what has shaped this model and what it contributes, requires a committed engagement with the chapters of this book. The reward, we suggest, is a meta-theoretical understanding of TESOL. It is an understanding that may be used to integrate a variety of insights, which is non-ideological (although we are sure that resourceful readers will find new ways to employ it), which offers a unique understanding of meaning and meaning-making in TESOL, and which, for all of these reasons, may offer promising new avenues for research, scholarship, and practice. More than anything, we intend for this book to help us all – learners, teachers, parents, teacher trainers, materials developers, policymakers, and many more – to become intentional. Becoming more connected, more dynamic, and more meaningful, by way of diverse intentional activity, is how the intentional ecology of TESOL can become a better place for all of us.

Part A: **Developing the model of intentional dynamics**

Chapter 2
Everything is connected: Ecological theory

This book develops the view that TESOL contexts, activity, and outcomes are all inherently *interconnected* and *dynamic*, and that they have human *meaning-making* at their heart. In this first substantive chapter, we use ecological theory to help us to understand how everything in TESOL is *interconnected*.

Our look at ecological theory is tailored to support the overall argument of the book. A first section (2.1) provides an introduction to three aspects of ecological theory that need consideration, before we use this theory to inform the development of our model of the intentional dynamics of TESOL. This includes a discussion of what is the appropriate focus for an ecological account of human and social activity like TESOL, a suggested distinction between *ecology as system* and *ecology of activity*, and finally an explanation of how human and social ecologies are stratified, with different layers of social structure and multiple domains of activity. The next section (2.2) looks at three specific, conceptual contributions of ecological theory, each of which will shape, also, the later development of our model of intentional dynamics. The first is the concept of *affordances* (Gibson 1979), which is increasingly being used to understand language use and learning, the second is the notion of *molar activity* (Tolman [1932] 1949), which we use to shift the focus towards the kind of meaningful activity that we are particularly interested in, and finally, given our aim of understanding meaning-making, we explore steps taken by early ecological scholars (Bateson 1987; Blumer 1969; Vickers 1968) towards the conceptualisation of an ecology of meaning. A final section (2.3) provides a brief summary of the insights and concepts of ecological theory that we take with us to the later chapters of this book, including specific reference to chapters where the insights and concepts will be particularly relevant and visible.

2.1 Aspects of ecological theory

We start our discussion by introducing three aspects of ecological theory that we feel need consideration, and which will be important in the later outline of our model of intentional dynamics. First, given that ecological theory was originally developed within and for the natural sciences, we will take a closer look at what is the appropriate focus for an ecological account of a human and social field like TESOL. We will conclude that an ecological account of TESOL needs to focus on the distribution and flow of meaningful information and meaningful activity – somehow defined. Next, as we seek to understand TESOL both as context and as activity, a second sub-section makes a distinction between what call the "ecology as system" and "ecology of activity" perspectives. Finally, the third sub-section outlines how we understand the stratified nature of TESOL, including its multiple layers of meaningful information, or structure, and multiple domains of meaningful activity.

2.1.1 Natural versus social ecologies

Ecological theory originates in the natural sciences. It was first suggested as an area of inquiry by Ernst Haeckel, in the 19th century, to denote "the whole science of the relations of the organism to the environment" (Stauffer 1957: 140). Even today, the notion of an ecology is most often associated with organisms and habitats of the natural world, such as biologists studying the distribution and evolution of different species, or environmental scientists investigating human impacts on natural ecologies. However, the core meaning of "ecology", as suggested by Haeckel 150 years ago, has gradually permeated the social sciences.

The differences between natural and social ecologies are profound. According to Bateson (1987), natural ecologies of interconnected wholes, such as forests or oceans, seek to understand the distribution and exchange of biological forms of "energy". In Bateson's own words, these are ecologies where:

> it is natural and appropriate to think of units bounded at the cell membrane, or at the skin; or of units composed of sets of conspecific individuals. These boundaries are then the frontiers at which measurements can be made to determine the additive-subtractive budget of energy for the given unit. (Bateson 1987: 466)

It would be fool-heartedly, and certainly un-ecological, to think of a social system, such as TESOL, as (having) an "additive-subtractive budget of energy". Rather, we need to shift our attention to what Halliday (1978: 8) calls "the other part of our environment, that which consists of people". Moreover, as we shift our attention, we must avoid conceiving of individual learners, teachers, or other TESOL practitioners as units "bounded by their skin", or for that matter, schools as units "bounded by their school gates". Bateson, who is a central figure in the development of ecological theory for the social sciences, suggests that social ecologies are more fundamentally information-based (1987: 466). TESOL researchers who have adopted the ecological metaphor have echoed Bateson's advice. For instance, van Lier (2000: 246) has suggested that, "from an ecological perspective, the learner is immersed in an environment full of potential meanings". Thus, in seeking to understand TESOL as an ecology, we need to focus on meaningful information, including the meaning-making that we, as human beings and TESOL practitioners, are continually engaged in. Moreover, rather than focusing on units bounded by physical membranes of any kind, including the tempting boundaries afforded by our bodies, our classrooms, and our schools, an ecology of the social – and of TESOL – must identify boundaries (of systems or activity) that allow an investigation of the distribution and flow of meaningful information and activity.

The remainder of this chapter will incorporate this central insight of what we believe is the appropriate focus for an ecological account of a field such as TESOL. This includes, particularly, a sub-section at the end of this chapter that considers steps taken, by past ecological scholars, towards conceptualising social systems as an ecology of meaning (section 2.2.3). The full implications, however, of our determination to develop an ecological theory of meaningful information and activity, will become clearer in chapter 6, where we outline our model of the intentional dynamics of TESOL.

2.1.2 Moving between ecology as system and ecology of activity

In this book, we wish to understand both TESOL contexts and TESOL activity, and this motivates us to make a distinction between what we refer to as the "ecology as system" and "ecology of activity" perspectives. We believe that such a distinction has analytical affordances, especially in terms of what it reveals about the relationship between our activity, as participants in TESOL, and the TESOL contexts that we inhabit.

The "ecology as systems" perspective is intuitively close to the everyday observation that "everything is connected". Clearly, everything in TESOL, and probably also in the Universe, is somehow connected. However, it is more practical to evoke this interconnectedness for smaller, more immediately meaningful wholes. Thus, in the natural ecological literatures we find studies of more manageable ecological entities as interconnected wholes, such as life in a body of water, a forest, or some other natural habitat. In the social sciences we may study interconnected wholes such as a language and its users (Garner 2004; Haugen 1972), communities or society as ecological phenomena (Barker 1968; Bateson 1987), or human development as an ecological system (Bronfenbrenner 1979). In TESOL, this includes studies such as those by Pennington and Hoekje (2010), focusing on a foreign language programme as an ecological system, Peng's (2012) ecological investigation of language learners' Willingness to Communicate (see MacIntyre et al. 1998) in a Chinese University context (discussed in more detail in the following sub-section), and Hornberger's (2002, 2003) ecological framing of educational policy and practice in multilingual settings. Finally, this focus on an ecological system – of some kind – explains the intuitive appeal of phrases such as "the ecology of nature", "the ecology of a city", and closer to our own interests, "the ecology of a language classroom" and our own "ecology of TESOL".

A second mode of thinking and theorising ecologically is motivated by Lewin's (1935: 241) observation that behaviour is a *function* of both the affective and cognitive state the person is in, and the environmental situation in which the person finds herself. We refer to this as the "ecology of activity" perspective. The ecological aspect, here, is the insistence that activity is mutually determined by both the person and the environment, as specified by a particular situation (Good 2007). Looking across ecological work in the social sciences, Gibson's (1979) work on affordances is the prototypical example of ecology of activity research. The concept of affordances, which we will unpack in greater detail in a later part of this chapter, broadly refers to opportunities to act in particular situations. In TESOL, van Lier has drawn on the concept of affordances. His "headline grabbing" claim is that "language learning is not a process of representing linguistic objects in the brain on the basis of input received" (2000: 253); rather, van Lier (2004: 62) suggests, "when we are active in a learning context, affordances become available for further action. The world around us reveals its relevance for us and begins to offer affordances because of who we are and what we are doing". Thus, in van Lier's explicit ecological view, we may learn language "in the same way that an animal 'learns' the forest, or a plant 'learns' the soil" (2000: 259). Note, though, our earlier discussion of what is the appropriate focus of an ecological account of TESOL activity. We are not animals in a forest, and this poses a challenge, also, for how we use the affordance concept, or how we understand the ecology of activity. We will return to this challenge in a later part of this chapter.

Finally, the distinction between ecology as system and ecology of activity, while useful analytically, is not an attempt to recreate the divide between the structural and functional approaches, so dominant in the 20th century social sciences (see Giddens 1976). Rather, having distinguished between "ecology as system" and "ecology of activity", we can begin to explore how the ecological system shapes activity, and conversely how activity may change the ecological system. Thus, there is an inevitable and profound interplay between the "ecology as system" and "ecology of activity" perspectives, and it is this interplay that we seek to understand with our model of the intentional dynamics of TESOL. At this juncture, this interplay may be summarised as follows: *TESOL as an ecological system shapes TESOL activity*, and TESOL *activity may change TESOL as an ecological system*.

2.1.3 The stratified nature of ecological systems and activity

Building on what may be the appropriate focus of an ecological account of social systems, and the distinction between "ecology as system" and "ecology of activity", this next sub-section looks at the inevitably stratified nature of social ecologies, including also TESOL. We will suggest that social ecological systems include multiple layers of meaningful information, or structure, and conversely that social ecologies are constituted by multiple domains of meaningful activity. Moreover, these two ways of being stratified are very different, as the following discussion will make clear.

In the following, we will make reference to Bronfenbrenner's (1979) original *ecological systems theory of human development*. We will not use Bronfenbrenner's theory in any direct way to inform our own work; however, his theory is a particularly clear example of how an ecological system may be stratified, and it offers clues as to what our own theory of TESOL contexts, activity, and outcomes needs to achieve. Bronfenbrenner defined his theory as "a theory of environmental interconnections" (1979: 8), and he conceived of it visually as "a nested arrangement of concentric structures, each contained within the next" (1979: 22). This includes an inner "circle" called the microsystem, followed by further circles that he refers to as the mesosystem, exosystems, and the macrosystem (Bronfenbrenner later introduced the notion of a chronosystem, representing time in the model; for an overview, see Tudge et al. 2009). In chapter 3, we will return to the notion of nested systems, but then in the context of discussing stratification from the perspective of CDST. The *forces* that directly impact on human development are located within Bronfenbrenner's microsystem, which represent the immediate settings of the developing person, such as their family, a class, or a group of friends. Ignoring the mesosystem for a moment (but see below), exosystems are settings where the developing person plays no direct role, but which indirectly affect her or him. For instance, activity in a classroom microsystem may benefit from the class teacher having a particularly supportive microsystem of professional colleagues. The microsystem of these teachers is, through the linkage provided by the particular classroom teacher, an exosystem for the children in her classroom. Note, here, that micro and exosystems are similar in "scale", and their positioning in the model is a matter of perspective. This is a point we return to, also, in later sections and chapters. That is, all activity is local, and potentially equally interconnected and dynamic. Moreover, the power and scope of activity is often a matter of perspective (see chapters 3, 5, and 11). Bronfenbrenner's macrosystem, by contrast, refers to "the overarching institutional patterns of the culture or subculture, such as the economic, social, educational, legal, and political systems" (1977: 515) we experience, and thus carries the "information and ideology that, both explicitly and implicitly, endow meaning and motivation to particular agencies, social networks, roles, activities, and their interrelations" (1977: 515). We will, in chapter 4, develop our own conceptualisation of a "macrosystem" based on an ecological view of the concept of intentionality. Finally, the mesosystem is not a concrete layer of the stratified ecology. Rather, it is an altogether more abstract structure that defines the linkages – either singular and weaker or multiple and stronger – between two or more microsystems. For instance, if the developing person, herself, is the only person taking part in two microsystems, the linkage would be singular and weaker. If more people share the experience of two microsystems, such as school classmates together joining a football team, or parents visiting a child's classroom, then the linkage is considered multiple and stronger. Thus, Bronfenbrenner's mesosystem encourages analysis beyond the microsystem, highlighting possible pathways of influence flowing between different microsystems, and potentially across the wider stratified ecology. In some ways, which will become clear in chapter 5, Bronfenbrenner's mesosystem resembles aspects of our own intentional dynamics.

Once again, we will not be using the above stratified ecological model in our work. Also, Bronfenbrenner's model has only a limited presence in the TESOL literature (but see Peng 2012). However, it usefully illustrates the possibly stratified nature of social ecological systems, and as we have pointed out, some of the features resemble those of our model, to be developed in subsequent chapters. Turning to TESOL, the idea that language education is a stratified ecology is a common one. For instance, Pennington and Hoekje's (2010) conceptualisation of a "language program as ecology" highlights multiple layers of meaningful information and structure. They highlight how the organic whole of a language programme emerges out of a "multiplicity of interconnected components or resources and their mutual relationships and dependencies" (p. 214). Guerrettaz and Johnston (2013) provide a similar conceptualisation of the classroom as an ecology, seeing it as a "complex, interlocking set of elements and relationships in which any one element can only be understood in the light of its interactions with other elements" (p. 783). Another ecological systems contribution, we believe, is Graves' (2008) social contextual perspective on language curricula. Graves argues that the classroom "is not an isolated environment; it is embedded in specific, complex and overlapping cultural, social, educational and political contexts" (p. 153), and that these contexts "are communities of people, enmeshed in social systems that operate according to tacit and explicit norms, hierarchies and values" (p. 154). Finally, Peng (2012) has provided a rare explicit use of Bronfenbrenner's theory in TESOL. She used Bronfenbrenner's stratified ecological theory to understand English language learners Willingness to

Communicate (WTC) (see MacIntyre et al. 1998) in a Chinese university context. Employing a mix of semi-structured interviews, learning journals, and classroom observation, Peng was able to identify not only a range of microsystem (classroom) factors affecting students WTC, but also mesosystem linkages (students' past classroom experiences, extracurricular activities), exosystem effects (course schedules and course evaluation criteria that originated in the microsystems of "others"), and macrosystem influences, including students' awareness of the rising importance of the English language, the relative unimportance of speaking skills in national examinations, and the (claimed) Chinese cultural trait of other-directedness.

Whilst ecology as system is stratified into multiple layers of context, information, or social structure, the ecology of activity is stratified rather differently. The suggestion that *one person's microsystem is another person's exosystem* is an important one for understanding how activity may be stratified. Again, Peng (2012) observed what she called exosystem effects in her Chinese TESOL research setting; exosystems being the activity of others, and these others had an influence on the microsystem of Peng's research participants – through mesosystem linkages. Crucially, the exosystem of others was comprised of activity, and for these "others" this activity was microsystem activity. The impact of the activity of other TESOL stakeholders, in parts of TESOL other than that which we may be observing, may be somewhat of a "blind-spot" in TESOL research. TESOL researchers have spent a lot of time and work to understand so-called local, or microgenetic, activity in the language classroom or elsewhere, and then adding discussion of how the broader context shapes this local activity. This approach, we suggest, fails to make transparent the shaping influence of other domains of activity in TESOL. There is activity in classrooms that may be described ecologically, but there is activity also in staff rooms, in offices, in libraries, in our homes, and in offices of curriculum designers and policy makers. Activity in each of these domains is all inherently *interconnected* and *dynamic*, and all constitutes unique human *meaning-making*. Existing TESOL literature includes very few references to the interaction of such different domains of activity, or how activity in other domains may affect the activity that is being observed. Guerrettaz and Johnston (2013), cited above, deserve specific mention in this regard. They studied textbook use in a language classroom, and proposed that "although the teacher and the students in the classroom were clearly the primary participants in the classroom ecology, there is a sense in which the designers of the materials could also be seen as participants by proxy" (p. 792). On the whole, however, the shaping influence of the activity of others – even as "participants by proxy" – is not something that TESOL research and theory has addressed. Thus, we believe that the suggestion that "one person's microsystem is another person's exosystem", or the manner in which TESOL includes multiple domains of activity that are all interconnected, is an additional manner in which the social ecology of TESOL is stratified.

In sum, later parts of this book will make reference to how TESOL as an ecological system, as well as TESOL as ecological activity, is stratified. There are "layers" of meaningful context, information, or structure in TESOL as an ecological system, and there are multiple domains of meaningful TESOL activity that are interconnected, dynamic, and have meaning-making at their heart. Thus, in our determination to understand how *TESOL as an ecological system shapes TESOL activity, and TESOL activity may change TESOL as an ecological system,* we need to consider, also, the stratified natures of both TESOL contexts and TESOL activity.

2.2 Ecological concepts

This section looks at three concepts from ecological theory which we draw upon in the later development of our model of the intentional dynamics of TESOL. The first is Gibson's (1979) concept of affordances, which provides an ecological account of how activity arises in the relationship between a person and the environment. However, the affordance concept is, at least in its original incarnation, neutral as to the "value" of activity. There is, within the core definition of an affordance, no sense of more or less meaningful affordances. For this, the second sub-section looks at the notion of *molar activity*, as distinct from *molecular activity*, as proposed by Tolman (1949). Molar activity describes the more purposeful activity that we are particularly focused on when exploring the intentional dynamics of TESOL. The final sub-section extends on the earlier discussion of what might be the appropriate focus for an ecological account of a social system such as TESOL; looking at steps taken, by previous ecological scholars, towards the conceptualisation of an *ecology of meaning*.

2.2.1 From Gibson to social affordances

The first ecological concept that has shaped our thinking is "affordances", which is a theoretical expression of how activity is a function of *both* the person and the environmental situation that the person finds herself in. Gibson defined an affordance as what the environment "offers the animal, what it provides or furnishes, either for good or ill" (1979: 127). Reading this definition 40 years on, the reference to "an animal" may feel odd, but Gibson intended it also to mean human beings – his research was focused on human visual perception. What the environment offers the human, then, is "information". Humans *perceive* information present in the environment, this information specifies affordances to act in some way for the human, and this gives rise to activity. Moreover, activity sets both the person and the environment in "motion", and this motion may lead to a new, different person-environment equation, and additional or new affordances for action.

We are quite fond of the concept of affordances. It offers a unique view on how ecological interconnectedness may lead to activity, and in turn how activity may change the ecology itself. However, we are not convinced that Gibson's original definition of affordances is consistent with what is the appropriate focus of an ecological account of TESOL, as reviewed in a previous part of this chapter. Gibson stressed that affordances arise from a person's "direct perception" of the environment, and thus precludes any role for the experience, knowledge, beliefs, or intentions of individuals. Gibson originally studied the challenges US air force pilots faced in World War 2, and his focus was on understanding pilots' visual perceptual field. Thus, the information Gibson looked at was that which could be picked up by the eye – i.e., surfaces, distances, and depth. Moreover, the actions of pilots are often instinctual, rapid, and there is no immediate value for conscious deliberation. Present-day research in Ecological Psychology, the discipline that Gibson initiated, reveals a similar focus on more sensory types of perception, and there is little or no attention to what role cognitive processes, or meaning-making, may play in the perception of affordances.

A great many authors, however, insist that Gibson's affordances can be extended to social situations. Costall (1995: 478) states that "any ecological psychology worth the name has to include living beings within the natural order of things, and recognize the difference they make", and Chemero (2003: 185) suggests that "affordances are features of whole situations", with situations representing a dynamic coming together of a range of individual and socio-contextual shaping influences. Once you allow for the possibility that complex, social forms of information specify affordances to act, you then also need to treat the person in the person-environment relationship as a thinking person, whose ability to "pick up" complex/social meanings from the environment depends on experience, knowledge, beliefs, and intentions. A possible resolution is offered by Neisser (1994), who has suggested that there are three interacting systems underlying our action in the world. This includes: (a) Gibson's direct perception, (b) interpersonal perception/reactivity, and (c) recognition/representation. Neisser suggests that the first system requires no cognitive mediation, the second only a basic cognitive awareness that another person is engaging with you, whilst the third system relies on cognitive processes.

The use of the concept of affordances is gradually gaining visibility in the TESOL literature. In TESOL, van Lier's (2004) work stands out. Again, van Lier has suggested that language learning consists of discovering affordances of relevance to us, in the classroom or beyond. However, just as Neisser, van Lier believes affordances work on different levels, which require no cognition, less cognition, or more cognition. van Lier (2002) suggests that in child language development there is a progression of phases, respectively characterised by mutuality, indexicality, and predicality. Mutuality is a basic, but intimate, contact between a young child and a caretaker, and this may involve touch and simple sound/meaning events. In the indexicality phase, sounds turn into words, and the child learns that words can have communicative effect. Finally, predicality is the use of language, increasingly grammatical, to express emotions, wishes, and other psychological states. Thus, van Lier suggests that there is a movement from more primitive, instinctual, and direct perceptual processes, governed by what van Lier (2004) calls "immediate affordances", to more complex, social, and cognitive processes that involve what he calls "mediated affordances".

Accepting, then, that affordances may describe the opportunities that thinking individuals have to act in social situations, the affordance concept can provide ecological understanding of a great deal of TESOL activity. We may, for instance, talk about the affordances that language furnish us in given situations (Aronin and Singleton 2010; Gorniak and Roy 2007). As children grow older, they are gradually able to do more with language, and as we study and develop competence in additional languages the range of affordances for linguistic action expand. We may also look at affordances for language learning in a classroom. Kordt (2018) suggests that some language learners may be *affordance optimists*, believing that most tasks given to them are "easily approachable", and others may be *affordance pessimists*, who may be more sceptical about their ability to succeed with tasks. Kordt also suggests that, ideally, affordances and motivation should work together in the language classroom "as a perpetuum mobile as the use of affordances leads to the emergence of new affordances that invite exploration" (2018: 141). Jessner (2014) proposes that there may a cumulative multilingualism-factor in language education, suggesting that multilingual learners are more able to benefit from the affordances of particular types of linguistic instruction. Affordances may be useful, also, for teachers. For instance, J. Anderson (2015) presents a critique of traditional lesson planning pro formas, and offers an alternative ecological approach. He suggests that we may change "learning aims/outcomes" with "learning opportunities", the "aims" of specific lesson stages with "reasons" as a less outcomes-based justification for what we hope to do, and the common "anticipated problems" section with "possible occurrences and responses" – as consistent with the affordance concept. However, the relationship between "how much language" we know, how aware learners are about their own learning, or how perceptive teachers may be in terms of pedagogical opportunities in the classroom, will depend, also, on the social environment and its situational dynamics, including complex social, cultural, and political dimensions. These are the ecological processes that our model of intentional dynamics seeks to understand.

2.2.2 Goal affordances and molar activity

The concept of affordances has provided us with a unique view on how the mutual relationship between a person and a particular environmental situation may give rise to activity. What we are missing, though, is any sense of what affordances, or what type of activity, may be more useful, and what affordances and activity may be less so, for learning, teaching, or other TESOL activity. The suggestion by Neisser (1994), that there are different interacting systems underlying our activity in the world, including direct perception, interpersonal perception/reactivity, and recognition/representation, as well as van Lier's distinction between immediate and mediated affordances (see section 2.2.1), offers some clues, but does not get us all the way to understanding the value of different types of activity. In this sub-section, then, we take a closer look at existing conceptualisations of activity in ecological scholarship, including what may be the value of different types of affordances and activity.

The ecological literature does include a great deal of discussion of different types of activity. An early distinction, proposed by Tolman (1949), was between molar and molecular activity (for a more recent account, see Baum 2002). Tolman defined molar activity as "more than and different from the sum of its physiological parts", as well as "an 'emergent' phenomenon that has descriptive and defining properties of its own" (1949: 7). Molecular activity, by contrast, comprised the more observable and easily measurable actions that behavioural scientists focused on. The distinction between molar and molecular was used widely in the years after Tolman proposed it, among others to signify the difference between phenomenal essences (molar) and non-phenomenal realities (molecular), ecological (molar) versus reductive (molecular) explanations, socially urgent (molar) versus socially non-urgent (molecular) phenomena, as well as temporally more durable action units associated with individual choice (molar) versus spontaneous acts not associated with intention (molecular) (see Littman and Rosen 1950). The definition of molar that includes a level of choice, or intention, resembles Bronfenbrenner's (1979) later use of the same distinction in his ecological work. Bronfenbrenner defined molar activity as "ongoing behaviour possessing a momentum of its own and perceived as having meaning or intent by the participants in the setting" (1979: 45). By contrast, molecular activity, according to Bronfenbrenner, is more momentary, unintentional, and more easily interrupted.

In more recent ecological theorising, rather than classifying activity directly, different authors have attached labels to different types of affordances. For instance, Scarantino (2003) distinguishes between goal and happening affordances. Scarantino (2003: 958) explains that goal affordances are associated with *things we do* with intention, and happening affordances are associated with *things that happen to us*, and therefore lack such a level of awareness. Kordt (2018: 139) exemplifies the distinction as follows: "Reading a foreign-language text with students in order to teach them about a new grammatical item can lead to the emergence of the affordance deduce-grammatical-rules-from-able, which would be a goal affordance; for some pupils, the affordance get-bored-to-death-by-able might emerge – clearly a happening affordance".

Our attempt to make sense of what may be the value, for TESOL, of different types of activity has been influenced, also, by Young et al.'s (2002) suggestion that affordances for the activity of learners in education are shaped by what they refer to as "intentional dynamics". Young et al., thus, was one of the sources of our original use of the term "intentional dynamics" (see Kostoulas 2015; Stelma 2011). Young et al. also provided a more elaborate explanation of how the affordances for activity might relate to intention. They describe a hierarchical model of how affordances and intentions are constrained, broadly consisting of (a) the most general level of all possible worlds (with an unconstrained set of possibilities), (b) physical and natural worlds (with affordances and intentions constrained by the physics and biology of nature), (c) the world of humans (with affordances and intentions constrained by social-cultural factors), and finally (d) actual situations (where affordances and intentions are constrained by situational dynamics). This cascading constraints hierarchy results in particular activity when the "degrees of freedom are gradually squeezed out from all possible actions to only those that meet the constraints of the moment, given the intentions of the learner" (Young et al. 2002: 52).

A central theme, then, in the ecological literature is that an affordance, or an action, which is prompted by intention (i.e., molar activity and goal affordances), and which results from broader ecological processes (Young et al.'s contribution), is "somehow" more deserving of our attention. In fact, our early work on intentional dynamics in educational and TESOL contexts adopted this view. We argued that more purposeful action was especially generative for learning and development (Stelma 2011; Stelma and Fay 2014). In the present book, however, our in-depth engagement with CDST (see chapter 3), and the concept of intentionality (see chapter 4), will move us beyond the above view of only, or simply, valuing purposeful activity more than, e.g., spontaneous activity. Thus, Ecological Theory has been of benefit, but does not provide us with our more final answer as to what may be the value of different types of activity in TESOL. Our final understanding of different types of activity, and their respective contribution to the intentional dynamics of TESOL, will be presented in chapter 5.

2.2.3 Steps to an ecology of meaning

The title of this section borrows from Bateson's (1987) major work, *Steps to an Ecology of Mind*, as well as his thesis for this work, which he summarises as follows:

> The questions which the book raises are ecological: How do ideas interact? Is there some sort of natural selection which determines the survival of some ideas and the extinction or death of others? What sort of economics limits the multiplicity of ideas in a given region of the mind? What are the necessary conditions for stability (or survival) of such a system or sub-system? (p. vxii)

Bateson attributes his notion of "ecology of ideas" to Vickers, who suggested that "the dreams of men [sic] spread and colonize their inner world, clash, excite, modify, and destroy each other, or preserve their stability by making strange accommodations with their rivals" (Vickers 1968: 32). This is a salient description of an inner ecology of ideas, metaphorically ascribing agency to these ideas as they are *cast in battle with each other* in the mind. Bateson extended on this notion by suggesting that once ideas are given a real, or ontological, status, then a less bounded view of the ecology of ideas might be possible. Ideas may then extend beyond the minds of individuals, and as they do, they may supervene on the life and thoughts of individuals. Bateson gives the following example of a less bounded ecology of ideas:

> The very meaning of "survival" becomes different when we stop talking about the survival of something bounded by the skin and start to think of the survival of the system of ideas in circuit. The contents of the skin are randomized at death and the pathways within the skin are randomized. But the ideas, under further transformation, may go on out in the world in books or works of art. Socrates as a bioenergetic individual is dead. But much of him still lives as a component in the contemporary ecology of ideas. (Bateson 1987: 467)

Looking more broadly at the literatures available to us in the social sciences, there is additional theorising that focuses on how ideas or meanings structure human activity and experience. For instance, Blumer (1969: 2) outlines three premises that define the field of *symbolic interactionism*, including: (a) that "human beings act toward things on the basis of the meanings that the things have for them", (b) that "the meaning of such things is derived from, or arises out of, the social interaction that one has with one's fellows", and (c) that "these meanings are handled in, and modified through, an interpretative process used by the person in dealing with the things he [sic] encounters" (for a more recent account of symbolic interactionism, see Denzin 2004). This resembles our argument, so far in this chapter, that there is an ecological system of meaning (Blumer's first premise), which both shapes and is shaped by the meaningful activity of people in the ecology (Blumer's second and third premises).

In the TESOL literature, van Lier, whose work on affordances we referred to in this chapter, has suggested that the language classroom "provides a 'semiotic budget' (analogous to the energy budget of an ecosystem) within which the active learner engages in meaning-making activities together with others, who may be more, equally, or less competent in linguistic terms" (van Lier 2000: 252). van Lier further suggests that this semiotic budget specifies the affordances for meaningful action for learners. The implication for teachers is that they should strive "to provide a rich 'semiotic budget' [. . .] and to structure the learner's activities and participation so that access [to the semiotic budget] is available and engagement [with the semiotic budget is] encouraged" (van Lier 2000: 253). This resonates, in addition, with other ecological research in TESOL. For instance, in research on young language learners' interaction in virtual communities, D. Zheng et al. (2009) observe that when children perceive and act in virtual environments they "seem to pick up language [. . .] through making the world their own" (p. 490), thus suggesting that language learning is closely linked to children creating and becoming part of a new world of meaning.

Kramsch (2006) takes the ecological view of meaning-making one step further, adapting it to the plurality of cultures, contexts, and linguistic practices mixing in the post-modern world. She suggests "it is no longer appropriate to give students a tourist-like competence to exchange information with native speakers of national languages within well-defined national cultures" (Kramsch 2006: 250). Instead, to cope with the diversity of today's societies, students of language "have to understand the practice of meaning making itself" (p. 251). Moreover, Kramsch (2006, 2008) suggests that meaning is subjective, reflexive, relational, and multidimensional, it is mediated by a great variety of other symbolic systems (including new media), it is contingent on, and rich with, historicity of individuals and situations, it is emergent and at times unpredictable, and it is reflective of society more generally. Finally, Tudor argues for the value of recognising these characteristics of TESOL, pointing out that "taking any one perspective on a situation as canonical entails the neglect, trivialisation or, worse still, the stigmatisation of others. Accepting that the reality of a situation has multiple interpretations, or that there are several rationalities at play in this situation, opens the door to improved mutual understanding and sharing of insights" (2001: 33).

In sum, we believe there is support in the literature for a conceptualisation of TESOL as an ecology of meaning, including multiple layers of meaningful information, or structure, and multiple domains of meaningful activity. We will develop this conceptualisation of TESOL – as an ecology of meaning and meaning-making – in greater detail in chapter 4, where we focus on the contribution of the concept of intentionality, and where we will start referring to TESOL is an "intentional ecology".

2.3 What we take from ecological theory

In this chapter we have explored different aspects and conceptual contributions of ecological theory. Here we summarise what we take with us to the later chapters of this book, and the development of our model of the intentional dynamics of TESOL. In addition to the broader point about everything being connected in TESOL, we take with us:

- **The appropriate focus for an ecological account of TESOL**
  We have argued that the appropriate focus for an ecological account of a social/human system, such as TESOL, is *meaningful information* and *meaningful activity*. This point helps guard against the possible ill-informed use of ecological theory and concepts, originally developed in and for the natural sciences, to describe the agentive and social contexts and activity of TESOL. Chapter 4 will outline what we refer to as the intentional ecology of TESOL, which is our conceptualisation of the meaningful information and structure of TESOL. Chapter 5 introduces intentional activity, which is how we understand meaningful activity.
- **The distinction between ecology as system and ecology of activity**
  In order to understand TESOL both as context and activity, we need to distinguish between *ecology as system* and *ecology of activity*, whilst recognising that these two perspectives interact. In short: *TESOL as an ecological system shapes TESOL activity*, and *TESOL activity may change TESOL as an ecological system*. Chapter 3, which turns to complex dynamic systems theory to understand the dynamic nature of TESOL, provides a more detailed account of how ecology as system and ecology of activity mutually shape each other.

- **Ecological systems may be stratified**
  We need to consider the possibly *stratified nature of TESOL*, including both multiple layers of meaningful information, and multiple domains of meaningful activity. Chapter 3 includes a more detailed discussion, informed by CDST, of the different ways that systems, including TESOL contexts and activity, may be stratified.
- **Affordances provide an ecological explanation of activity**
  We have introduced the concept of *affordances*, which express the possibilities for taking action in situations. These affordances are an outcome of the mutual relationship between persons and their environment. We have explored, also, the distinction between *immediate* and *mediated* affordances, as well as how affordances and activity may be associated with less individual awareness, in which case they describe *things that happen to us*, or they may be associated with more awareness, cognition, and intent, thereby giving rise to *things that we do more deliberately*. The concept of affordances will reappear in chapter 5, where we develop our understanding of meaningful activity in TESOL, or what we will refer to as "intentional activity".
- **TESOL may be described as an "ecology of meaning"**
  The possibility that we may conceptualise TESOL as an ecology of meaning is central in our effort to develop a theory of meaning and meaning-making. We will return to this possibility in chapter 4, where we use the concept of intentionality to propose that TESOL is an intentional ecology with multiple aspects.

The next chapter turns to complex dynamic systems theory to develop the view that TESOL contexts, activity, and outcomes are inherently dynamic. Ecological theory, and the key points rehearsed in this chapter, will – on occasion – feature in this next chapter. However, ecological theory will be most visible in chapter 4, where we develop our understanding of TESOL as an intentional ecology, and chapter 5, where we outline our full model of the intentional dynamics of TESOL.

Chapter 3
Everything is dynamic: Complex dynamic systems theory

This chapter draws on Complex Dynamic Systems Theory (CDST) to understand the dynamic nature of TESOL contexts, activity, and outcomes. We believe that the holistic and interdisciplinary outlook of CDST is particularly helpful for understanding this dynamic nature, while remaining sensitive to the interconnectivity of TESOL, which we discussed in the previous chapter.

Our rationale for including CDST, alongside ecological thinking, is two-fold. First, CDST helps us to bring together, in a theoretically coherent way, the two perspectives of ecological thinking that we described in chapter 2; namely "ecology as a system" and "ecology of activity". As will become clear in this chapter, in a complex dynamic system, structure and activity continuously shape each other. This theoretical insight will help us develop our model of intentional dynamics, which describes how the intentional ecology of TESOL and intentional activity (to be defined in chapters 4 and 5, respectively) are mutually shaped. Furthermore, whilst ecological theory highlights the synchronic states of ecologies, as well as in-the-moment activity by way of the concept of affordances, CDST helps us to understand how TESOL context, activity, and outcomes develop over time. This is consistent with our model of intentional dynamics, which aims to understand processes ranging from microgenetic activity to the long-term activity of larger social structures. More generally, CDST represents a fundamental break with analytical thinking – the epistemological tradition that builds knowledge by segmenting problems into their constituent parts and examining them separately (Descartes [1637] 1966; see also P. W. Anderson 1972; Kostoulas 2018; Miller and Page 2007; van Riel and Van Gulick 2019). We agree with Cilliers (1998) that such a reductivist outlook risks losing sight of the interconnections between the phenomena that interest us, and in doing so "destroys what it seeks to understand" (p. 2). The holistic perspective provided by CDST offers a promising way to overcome this limitation. We believe, finally, that the ways in which CDST uses concepts that cut across disciplines is particularly relevant to the interdisciplinary nature of TESOL, which we view as a synthesis of Applied Linguistics, Psychology, and Education theory (Kostoulas 2019b).

We begin the chapter by articulating an understanding of CDST that is compatible with our analytical needs (section 3.1). This overview of the theory introduces core principles and concepts that will recur throughout the book. A second section (3.2) positions our thinking in relation to alternative ways in which CDST has been used in TESOL, and in adjoining disciplinary areas. In the final section of the chapter (3.3), we outline what we consider to be the main insights from CDST that we will carry forward to the model of intentional dynamics.

3.1 A brief introduction to CDST

Language educators would probably not be surprised if we described classroom interaction and language learning as complex, messy, and unpredictable. Two language lessons are unlikely to be identical, even if they are taught by the same teacher using the same lesson plan (Coughlan and Duff 1994). Sometimes even modest learning outcomes fail to materialise, even though a lot of effort is invested in their achievement. Conversely, valuable learning opportunities may arise spontaneously, leading to lasting learning effects. Attempts to explain this unpredictability as the product of motivation, aptitude, or methodological choices can all yield useful insights into psychological and social aspects of language teaching and learning. However, these explanations often feel too simple to capture the complexity and dynamic nature of language education (Larsen-Freeman 2017: 11).

CDST is a way of thinking, and a set of theoretical concepts, designed to capture the complexity, dynamics, and interconnectedness of contexts and activity. It does so by taking a holistic perspective on the entities (e.g., a school, a class, a learner) and processes (e.g., learning, teaching, curriculum innovation) that we wish to understand. These entities and processes are construed as complex dynamic systems. CDST has been increasingly used in TESOL and Applied Linguistics , especially since the publication of Larsen-Freeman and Cameron's seminal monograph *Complex Systems and Applied Linguistics* (2008a). Such CDST-informed work includes research into L1/L2 language development (e.g., de Bot, Lowie and Verspoor 2007; Tomasello 2003), bilingualism (e.g., Herdina and Jessner 2002), language attrition (e.g., Jessner 2003), motivation (e.g., Dörnyei 2009; Sampson 2016), education theory (e.g., Osberg and Biesta 2010), teacher education (e.g., Davis and Sumara 2012), and language ecologies (e.g., Larsen-Freeman 2018; van Lier 2004).

We will develop a more precise definition of CDST as we progress through this chapter, but for the time being we will provisionally view it as an attempt to understand how simple elements and processes organise themselves "into a collective whole that creates patterns, uses information, and in some cases evolves and learns" (Mitchell 2009: 4). We will refer to this "collective whole" as a Complex Dynamic System (CDS), which we understand as an interconnected assemblage of diverse elements. Much like the ecologies described in chapter 2, CDSs may describe physical or biological entities or processes, or they may describe abstract entities and processes, such as ideas, cultures, languages, education, and ideologies. In the following sub-sections, we add some detail to this general definition. We will do so by discussing, first, the complex *structure* of CDSs; next, we will discuss the dynamic properties that explain the *activity* of CDSs; and finally, we will discuss the interconnectivity of CDSs and their *context(s)*. The scope of this discussion is limited to the concepts and insights of CDST that we need for developing our model of the intentional dynamics of TESOL; for more comprehensive overviews of CDST we would suggest some of the sources that have shaped our own thinking, including Byrne and Callaghan (2014), Cilliers (1998), and – for a more domain-specific perspective – Larsen-Freeman and Cameron (2008a).

3.1.1 The structure of complex dynamic systems

We begin our more detailed discussion of CDST by exploring the question: *what makes up a complex dynamic system?* To answer this question, we look into the constitutive elements of a system, their connections, and their boundaries.

Within a CDS, we will likely find a very large number of diverse and interacting elements. Descriptions of CDSs in TESOL (e.g., Sampson 2016), typically describe these systems as comprising elements which belong to different ontological categories: these may include people with different roles (e.g., teachers, learners, and administrators), beliefs and ideologies, curricula, rules and habitual patterns of classroom interaction, buildings and books, and more. On the whole, such diversity does not stand in the way of developing theoretically coherent accounts. In fact, Larsen-Freeman and Cameron (2008a) argue that heterogeneity is a core property of CDSs. However, the diversity of a CDS does not imply that its elements are just random assortments. For these elements to constitute a system, they need to be connected in ways that generate and explain the phenomena that we seek to understand. Thus, the elements of a CDS constitute a web of relationships that generate structure (context) and processes (activity). The reason why a L2 language class may be considered a CDS is because the participants in such classes together generate the behaviour, as well as structured expectations, associated with the roles of teachers and students (e.g., asking for permission to speak, providing feedback).

When reflecting on what comprises a CDS, the question of what is the "boundary" of the system arises. Cilliers (2001: 141) argues that the boundaries of a system are "simultaneously a product of the activity of the system itself, and a product of the strategy of description involved". His further "gloss" is that we may "frame the system by describing it in a certain way (for a certain reason) but we are constrained where a frame can be drawn". At times, the boundaries of a CDS may overlap with those suggested by the physical and social world. For example, a language learning class is spatially bounded by the walls of the classroom, temporally bounded by the start and end of lessons, and bounded in terms of membership (whether individuals are either enrolled in the class or not). However, in chapter 3 we warned against 'conceiving of individual learners, teachers, or other TESOL practitioners as units "bounded by their skin" and schools as units "bounded by their school gates". Drawing on Bateson (1987), we suggested that social ecologies are more fundamentally information-based, and that TESOL as an ecology required a focus on meaningful information and meaningful activity. Thus, the boundaries of systems are not entirely unambiguous. In the example above, aspects of teaching and learning that are located beyond the physical boundaries of the system (e.g., homework, teaching preparation, school policy, or the language policy of the country where the class takes place) all generate some "fuzziness" at the borders of the system (see also Kostoulas 2019a). Again, the decision about the boundary of a system may include consideration of what elements contribute to the system's generative potential; i.e., the elements that contribute to the generation of either the structure (context), or the processes (activity), that we seek to explain.

We need to draw attention, also, to how a CDS, once defined, is an open system. Somewhat counter-intuitively, the boundary that we define for a system may be said to act as an interface; an interface that allows the system to remain open to its broader environment (Byrne and Callaghan 2014). Thus, the elements that make up the system are connected in ways that allow for the exchange of information. These connections to the broader environment may be direct, or they may involve intervening elements. In TESOL, for instance, language policy might be enacted in language classrooms directly, through centralised examinations, or through the mediating influence of teachers. This kind of mediation means that the influence of one set of elements on system processes may be "enhanced, suppressed or altered in a number of ways" (Cilliers 1998: 4). As a result, it is difficult to connect events and outcomes to each other in linear ways, and this can make the activity of the system difficult to predict (Byrne 1998). For instance, if a language learner receives repeated praise from a teacher, for her unexpectedly good performance, this could alternatively reinforce good learning practices, lead to complacency, or perhaps both at different times. However, while the activity of a CDS is not entirely predictable, it is constrained by the system's structure and, thus, not completely random either. For example, although we cannot predict in detail what may happen in any specific L2 classroom, there is commonality in the activity we observe across classrooms, and although it is impossible to accurately predict what individual students will learn, and at what rate, increased effort will typically lead to enhanced linguistic proficiency. In section 3.1.3, we will introduce the notions of nested system structures, and sub-systems, and this will offer further theoretical detail on how one CDS may interconnect with other CDSs.

One last thing that needs to be noted about CDSs is their abstract nature. A CDS may describe either physical or social entities and/or processes, such as classrooms, learners and teachers, or language learning, but crucially, the systems themselves do not exist in an ontologically concrete way (Hiver and Al-Hoorie 2020). The elements of the CDS may be observable, but the CDS as a whole "exists only in the interaction *between* things and is therefore not *itself* a thing" (Osberg 2008: 146, original emphasis). Some theorists have therefore argued that a CDS is the product of an analytical move, which comes into existence when an analyst defines, or *frames* it, in relation to the phenomenon they are interested in studying (Cilliers 1998). In a different sense, which is closer to our own analytical needs, a system is "real" as long as it has generative structure and properties, i.e., structure and properties that shape(s) activity, and activity that may change structure. This feature of CDSs will be central, also, in our model of intentional dynamics, to be outlined in chapter 5.

In the paragraphs above, we described CDSs with reference to their structural features. Our own model of intentional dynamics, which we present in chapter 5, draws on the discussion provided here, including the observation that TESOL may be a CDS that includes heterogeneous elements, and that interacts with wider environments. Specifically, in chapter 4, we will suggest that the concept of intentionality may be used to "integrate" otherwise ontologically diverse elements, in the form of a CDS that we will refer to as the *intentional ecology of TESOL*.

3.1.2 The activity of complex dynamic systems

A complete description of a CDS should address not just what a system *is*, which was the focus of the previous sub-section, but also needs to address also what the system *does*. We believe that the activity of CDSs can be usefully summarised in terms of four dynamic properties, and that these may be used to describe the dynamic nature of TESOL. A first dynamic property is *adaptiveness*, which explains how the activity of a system adjusts to changing conditions, thereby "helping" to maintain its equilibrium. The second dynamic property is *historicity*, and this explains how past and present structure and activity is connected. The third dynamic property is *non-linearity*, which explains how activity, as well as outcomes, in a CDS may be disproportional to their triggers and/or outcomes. The final dynamic property is *self-organisation*, and this explains both how the structure of a system shapes its activity, and how the activity of a system may change its structure. Table 1 summarises these four dynamic properties of a CDS, and how they are expressed in activity.

Table 1: Dynamic properties of complex dynamic systems.

Dynamic properties	This means that . . .
Adaptiveness	Activity constantly adjusts to changing conditions of the environment
Historicity	Activity is influenced by its past states
Non-linearity	Activity may be disproportional to its triggers and/or outcomes
Self-organisation	The structure of the system shapes activity (soft-assembly) and the activity of the system may change structure (morphogenesis)

The first dynamic property – adaptiveness – is the constant adjustment that a system makes to compensate for a changing environment. Thus, CDSs may be said to "absorb" change by reconfiguring their internal structure. In fact, CDSs are alternatively described as Complex Adaptive Systems (e.g., Miller and Page 2007). On the whole, CDSs tend to remain in some kind of equilibrium, or within a "preferred" set of conditions, which is called an "attractor state". However, since a system's environment may be constantly changing, maintaining equilibrium requires CDSs to also be in a state of constant adaptive flux (Byrne and Callaghan 2014). When a system is dislodged from its attractor state, it will be aided by the dynamic property of adaptiveness to return to equilibrium (Larsen-Freeman and Cameron 2008a; Miller and Page 2007). At the same time, however, the constant adaptive flux of a system also means that the system is able, if sufficiently perturbed, to change into a new state or trajectory. Thus, adaptiveness maintains the potential for both stability and change in a complex dynamic system. Adaptiveness may be observed in a variety of TESOL activity. For instance, an experienced teacher will continually receive direct and indirect feedback from her learners, and she may adapt in flexible ways to achieve her lesson objectives; globalisation and the global spread of English will continually prompt educational authorities around the world to adapt the TESOL provision in their national curricula, thereby preserving their relative competitiveness. Thus, CDSs in TESOL may "absorb" change by reconfiguring their internal structure (Mitchell 2009), provided – of course – that the CDS has the requisite internal resources to be an adaptive system (Holling 2001).

The second dynamic property – historicity – refers to the interconnectivity between the present state of a system and its past and future states (Semetsky 2008). Historicity sometimes appears as a conserving influence. If we view a school as a CDS, for instance, it will be possible to trace activity of this system back and forward in time, sometimes over decades, even after all its students have graduated, and all its teachers have been replaced, and possibly even if it relocates to new premises. The reason for why a school may be such a conserving system is because some aspects of the CDS, such as sociocultural beliefs or educational policy, tend to change at relatively slow rates, and may then have a pervasive influence on the activity of the school over time (see also section 3.1.3). In addition to connecting the present state of the system to its past, historicity also explains how future activity in a system may emerge from its current structure. Although the complex structure of a CDS means that it is hard to connect outcomes with specific causes, the historicity of CDS means that "no complex system [. . .] can be understood without considering its history" (Cilliers 1998: 107).

The third dynamic property – non-linearity – explains how the activity of a system may be disproportionate to its triggers and/or its outcomes. Since a CDS is made up of intricate webs of relationships, activity within a system may be shaped by complex flows and effects of information. Information may be intensified by similar information, information may be cancelled out by competing information, or information may loop back to its origin where it either disappears or gets amplified. This means that "small causes can have large results and vice versa" (Cilliers 1998: 4), or the combined effect of two different causes may be qualitatively different from "the effects of each cause taken individually" (Nicolis 1995: 1). Non-linearity may be observed, also, when systems undergo dramatic restructuring, perhaps as a result of small perturbations pushing a system past some metaphorical "tipping point" (Larsen-Freeman and Cameron 2008a: 62). In TESOL, we witness non-linearity in a range of domains. For instance, in language learning the investment of considerable effort may fail to produce visible outcomes, or – on occasion – seemingly little effort can lead to noticeable and positive learning outcomes.

The final dynamic property is self-organisation. We distinguish between two aspects of self-organisation, including the *soft-assembly* of activity (Thelen and Smith 1994) and the *morphogenesis* of structure (Archer 1995). Larsen-Freeman and Cameron (2008a: 169) describe soft-assembly as "an adaptive action in which all aspects of context can influence what happens at all levels of activity". More generally, soft-assembly is not what an agent does with information picked up from the environment; rather, soft-assembly is a distributed process that is shaped, also, by how we are connected to our environment (Clarke 1997: 42–45).

For our purposes, we use soft-assembly to express how multiple meaningful aspects of TESOL contexts, including also the psychological states of the individual, constitute affordances and activity in situations. The second aspect of self-organisation, morphogenesis, explains how "structure is the *result* of action in the system, not something that has to exist in an *a priori* fashion" (Cilliers 1998: 14, original emphasis). This does not necessarily mean that activity is context-free, or that there are no structural constraints on activity (as that would negate historicity), but it does mean that structures are constantly re-shaped (reinforced or challenged) by the activity of the system. In more practical terms, activity which is repeated over time will tend to generate "attractor states" (i.e., patterns of preferred activity), which over time may change the structure of the CDS. In TESOL, a repeated and predictable sequence of learning activities will tend to create expectations and social routinisation (Prabhu 1992), and may eventually become sedimented in curricular documents and the content of learning resources, and may become a sociocultural norm. In such cases, the teaching and learning activity generates structure, which then feeds-forward to change the form of later teaching and learning.

When distinguishing between these dynamic properties of CDSs, we should remain aware that all four of these properties will be evident in all activity. The differentiation we make is one of degree and prominence. We will make further reference to the four dynamic properties of CDSs in chapter 5, where we discuss how the properties may be used to understand different types of activity in TESOL. For now, we continue our description of CDST, turning our attention to the ways that different CDSs may interconnect to each other and to their broader environment.

3.1.3 The context of complex dynamic systems

We have already noted the challenge associated with drawing the boundaries of a system, since their elements are interconnected to entities outside the system, and systems themselves are connected to other systems. In this sub-section, we extend this discussion by exploring how multiple systems may form meaningful larger "wholes". We do so by looking at three ways that CDSs may be stratified. First, we discuss how systems might exist within larger systems, or what we call *structural stratification*; next, we discuss how complex phenomena can be described from different analytical perspectives, or in other words how they may be *analytically stratified*; and finally we describe how systems may be stratified in terms what *type of activity* we are attempting to understand. Table 2 summarises these three types of stratification.

Table 2: Stratification of complex dynamic systems.

Stratification	System constituents
Structural	Nested systems
Analytical	Sub-systems
By activity	Domains

The relationship between multiple CDSs sometimes resembles a hierarchy of *nested* systems, with structurally similar smaller and larger systems describing different "layers" of a context. For example, if we view a L2 class, a school, and the national school system as three different CDSs, these constitute hierarchically nested systems. Similarly, an individual's cognition about teaching and learning, as a CDS, may be nested in a larger-scale CDS describing sociocultural norms focused on teaching and learning (e.g., methodological paradigms). However, when thinking in terms of such structurally stratified systems there are a few things that we need to keep in mind. The first one is that complexity and dynamic properties apply even if we "jump levels", from smaller- to larger-scale systems. The mind of an individual learner, a L2 language class, a school, and a whole school system are all complex and dynamic. However, Holling (2001) makes the intriguing suggestion that larger-scale systems may "move" at slower speeds than smaller scale systems (see also Davis and Sumara 2006; Kostoulas 2018). Moreover, he suggests that within such a hierarchy, "each level is allowed to operate at its own pace, protected from above by slower, larger levels but invigorated from below by faster, smaller cycles of innovation" (Holling 2001: 398–399). Thus, although every nested system level is complex and dynamic, there may be "scale effects", as well as analytically interesting interactions between nested systems of different scales. A second thing we need to keep in mind is that nested CDSs are rarely as neatly hierarchical as we have suggested so far. For example, Holliday (1994) describes a "culture complex" as a system of multiple cultures (classroom, institutional, academic-professional, and more) that are manifest at different levels, but which may intersect in non-hierarchical ways. Thus, it may be more accurate to think of nested systems as interpenetrating systems with webs of interaction and causation running in all directions (Byrne and Callaghan 2014). In sum, thinking of CDSs as structurally nested systems, whether more or less hierarchical, provides analytical affordances to explain how activity in a smaller-scale system may reproduce or change the structure of a larger-scale system, or how the structure of a larger-scale system may enable or constrain the activity of a smaller-scale system.

A second way in which CDSs may be stratified is in terms of the analytical perspective they enable. In this form of relationship, an overarching system (e.g., TESOL) may be examined by delineating a number of sub-systems, with each sub-system looking at the overarching system from a different analytical perspective. The benefit of this kind of relationship between CDSs is to integrate diverse theoretical perspectives into coherent wholes. Davis offers the following justification for this type of interconnectivity between systems.

> The discourses that support and are supported by the various disciplines are commonly seen as incompatible, if not flatly contradictory. Complexity thinking provides a means around this apparent impasse, and it does so by emphasising the need to study phenomena at the levels of their emergence, oriented by the realization that new stable patterns of activity arise and that these patterns embody emergent rules and laws that are native to the systems. (Davis 2008: 52)

TESOL has a range of "native" analytical perspectives to describe language learning, teaching, curriculum design, and so on. Sampson (2016), in his description of a language learning setting as a composite of multiple systems, illustrates such a use of analytical perspectives. Some of Samson's sub-systems relate to aspects of the teachers' and learners' personalities, including beliefs, affect, motivations, and more; other sub-systems encompass aspects of social organisation, such as peer-groups, classes, small cultures, national and transnational cultures; yet other sub-systems describe the structures of education, like lesson plans, curricula, and policies. Thus, the psychological, social, and educational aspects of Samson's CDST description of a language learning setting are analytically defined sub-systems. However, it is not always straightforward to decide which analytical perspectives to include in an integrated theoretical account. We can infer, however, from Davis (2008) – quoted above – that an integrated CDST account, such as we have described here, needs to be made up of as many analytical perspectives, or sub-systems, as are needed to explain the "patterns of activity" and "emergent rules and laws" that we seek to explain.

A third way to understand how systems interconnect focuses on the way in which activity may appear across different domains. In TESOL, this may include language learner or language teacher activity, curriculum design activity, policy-making, and more. This perspective also raises questions about the power and scope of the activity we seek to describe as a CDS. Stratification according to domains of activity encourages us to distinguish between activity that is meaningful only to the individual, activity that is relevant to a local context, or activity that has more wide-ranging repercussions. This is slightly different from the suggestion that systems are structurally stratified. Again, a meeting of faculty staff and a meeting of senior policy planners are both complex and dynamic, and may both be considered as "local" activity. However, the activity of the group of senior policy-makers may have potentially greater power and scope to change whatever may be the overarching system.

Our model of intentional dynamics, which we will present in chapter 5, will draw on the above described ways that CDSs may be stratified. The model will rely on the analytical perspective provided by intentionality, which we discuss in detail in chapter 4. However, we will develop an ecological view of intentionality, and in our model we will connect different structural levels of TESOL with analytical levels of intentionality.

3.2 How we use CDST in this book

So far, our outline of CDST has looked into three features of complex dynamic systems: their structure, their activity, and their interconnections to each other and their context. We will now take a step back from this description, and make some more general comments about how we understand and use CDST in this book, and in the model of intentional dynamics that we are developing.

In the previous section, we have described CDST as if it were a single, clearly defined theory. The reality, however, is that the "complexity paradigm" (Larsen-Freeman 2017) includes a wide range of approaches. While these approaches share a common epistemological ground, they also differ in a number of potentially confusing ways. We believe it is necessary to clarify some of these differences, and to position our own thinking in relation to them. In our discussion of this complexity paradigm, we will – for the moment – eschew the distinctions between structure, activity, and context which we made in the previous section. Our purpose, here, is to highlight how we use CDST to understand TESOL, and to develop our model of the intentional dynamics of TESOL. We do so in two sub-sections. The first sub-section is structured by Holling's (2001: 391) three criteria for the use of theory to understand social ecologies. Holling argues that theory should: (a) be as simple as possible, but not simpler than necessary; (b) remain sensitive to the dynamic nature of the ecologies, and open to the possibility of structural change; and (c) be epistemologically open to the possibilities of unpredictability and uncertainty. The second sub-section examines two "faultlines" within the complexity paradigm; one concerning the theoretical orientation of CDST, and one concerning the relationship between CDST and the phenomena we seek to explain.

3.2.1 CDST as a way of thinking

The view of CDST which informs our work represents an attempt to reconstruct the scientific endeavour that has been deconstructed by postmodernism, without falling back to positivist thinking (Price 1997). We approach this task by viewing CDST as *a way of thinking* about the social world, as opposed to a rigidly defined epistemology or set of methodological procedures (see also chapter 12).

There is an influential strand of CDST that subscribes to a postmodernist epistemological perspective (e.g., Cilliers 1998; Davis and Sumara 2012). We find such an approach attractive, since we wish to remain sensitive to the socially constructed nature of the many aspects that are important to language education (e.g., ideology and power). CDST allows us to do this, as – in common with postmodernism – it rejects the idea of "a static universe describable by nomothetic, universally deterministic laws" (Larsen-Freeman 2017: 14). At the same time, we are uncomfortable with the pragmatic implications of a complete break with the empirical in language education. Negating the "external real" may release us from the bonds of structural determinism, but it complicates purposeful change. If we were, for instance, to axiomatically accept that the reality of learners is fundamentally different from that of teachers, and both differ from the reality of researchers and theorists, we would accentuate difference, it would be challenging (or impossible) to reach shared understandings, and we might struggle to propose common courses of action. We believe that our view on CDST, which draws extensively on Byrne (1998) and Byrne and Callaghan (2014), provides a workable alternative. We are focused on whatever may be the generative processes in TESOL (e.g., the role of meaning-making in language learning; the role of power in language teaching), what are the outcomes of these generative processes (e.g., L2 learning outcomes; teacher professional development), and how these processes and outcomes are contingent social phenomena and amenable to change.

We also wish to differentiate our position from a research tradition, often carried out under the designation of *Dynamic Systems Theory*, which describes aspects of language education using mathematical tools inspired by Dynamic Systems Theory, Chaos Theory, and the legacy of mathematicians like Henry Poincaré and Benoit Mandelbrot (de Bot 2017). Such work often focusses on discovering longitudinal patterns in phenomena, such as linguistic development (e.g., de Bot et al. 2007; Peltzer-Karpf 1990; Verspoor, Lowie, and van Dijk 2008; Y. Zheng 2016), language attrition (e.g., Jessner 2003; Köpke 2017; Meara 2004), and language learning motivation (e.g., MacIntyre and Serroul 2015). This strand of CDST research continues to helpfully foreground issues such as the non-linear developmental trajectories that are typical of linguistic development, and the unpredictability of learning outcomes in language education. We also acknowledge that such a mathematical perspective has "decomplexified" complexity, by revealing something about the emergence of linguistic competence, L2 motivation, and so on. However, we are conscious, also, that complexity is, ultimately, "incompressible" (Cilliers 1998: 24). We are therefore concerned that attempts to describe complex social phenomena as outcomes of relatively simple generative rules might be producing "restricted" (Morin 2006) accounts of complexity in the social world, and this would be incompatible with the first of Holling's (2001) three criteria (see p. 45). We also agree with Byrne and Callaghan (2014: 56), who note that "any general complexity science has to get beyond micro-determined emergence. It has to allow for structures with causal powers and it has to address human agency as capable of transcending narrow rules for behaviour". With the above in mind, we are not entirely convinced that the mathematical formalism sometimes evident in the above tradition always allows sufficient scope for the unpredictability of the social world, and we are concerned that, when taken to its extreme, a mathematical approach could represent a form of "hard science imperialism" within the social sciences (Byrne and Callaghan 2014: 40).

The way we will be using CDST in our theorisation of intentional dynamics is closer to what has been described as a "generalised" (Morin 2006) approach to complexity. In our view, activity is not just an epiphenomenon to be described, but rather a constitutive element of the CDS itself (Cilliers 1998). The task we set ourselves, then, is to understand the recursive processes through which activity and structure are generated. This motivates us to view intentional dynamics as a CDS, and to posit that within this system (a) activity generates structure, and (b) structure generates activity. Moreover, we will conceptualise intentional dynamics as constituted by loosely nested systems, *as well as* analytical sub-systems, of intentionality, which we will outline in chapter 4. These systems are connected to each other by complex causal powers, both top-down and bottom-up, both unidirectional and recursive, and which fluctuate dynamically depending on local contingencies. We do acknowledge that such a generalised approach, focusing on understanding the whole system of TESOL, may appear "softer" in terms of algebraic rigour, but we believe that what we sacrifice in this regard we gain in theoretical scope.

3.2.2 CDST as a meta-theory

The other point that we wish to clarify concerns the relation of CDST, as used in this book, with the phenomena that we seek to explain. In line with Larsen-Freeman (2017), we view CDST as a *meta-theory*, a property which it shares both with ecological theory, as outlined in chapter 2, and our model of the intentional dynamics of TESOL, to be presented in chapter 5.

Overton (2007: 154) defines meta-theory as a "coherent set of interlocking principles that both describes and prescribes what is meaningful and meaningless, acceptable and unacceptable, central and peripheral as theory [. . .] and as method". We distinguish this from "object" theories about TESOL, which are sets of theoretical constructs and propositions that relate directly to observations about language, language teaching, language learning, and so on. Such object theories may either be entirely native to TESOL, or – of interest to our present discussion – they may be informed by CDST. Larsen-Freeman (2017) offers an extensive list of object theories that have employed some type of "systems thinking" in language education, including theories of cognition, corpus and systemic-functional linguistic theory, theories of emergent grammars, usage-based theories of language learning, constructivist theory, and more. By contrast, we use CDST as meta-theory to integrate the object theoretical accounts that interest us into a conceptually coherent frame.

Within linguistics, there have been a number of meta-theoretic uses of CDST, aimed at achieving theoretical integration. Two of the most notable contributions include the "Five Graces" position paper (Five Graces Group 2009) and a theoretical chapter by de Bot, Lowie, Thorne, and Verspoor (2013). The first was authored by a group of ten linguists, who suggested that language can be viewed as a complex adaptive system, and that such a perspective "reveals commonalities in many areas of language research, including first and second language acquisition, historical linguistics, psycholinguistics, language evolution, and computational modelling" (Five Graces Group 2009: 1). The theoretical chapter by de Bot and colleagues argues that CDST can function as an umbrella theory connecting several "middle level" theories of second language acquisition, "which [. . .] are theories that attend to different levels of granularity and different time scales" (de Bot et al. 2013: 216). Looking beyond language education, a notable attempt to use the meta-theoretical potential of CDST is that of Davis and Sumara (2006), and further elaborated in Davis (2008). These publications describe a nested hierarchy of systems representing multiple levels of mathematical knowledge, including subjective understandings, collective understandings, curriculum structures, and mathematical objects (Davis and Sumara 2006). Each of the levels in this hierarchy may be studied individually, using an appropriate object theory. For example, one might want to focus on the genetic predisposition of learners, their personal experiences, social interaction, and cultural tools, all the way up to "an ever-unfolding conversation of humans and the biosphere" (Davis 2008: 50). However, Davis and Sumara's multiple nested systems add up to an overarching CDS of mathematical knowledge. This is achieved by tracing meaningful interconnections between each nested system, and thus discover how the complexity and dynamics of each nested system contributes to the overall system.

In one of our own publications (Kostoulas and Stelma 2016), we have provided a similar multiple systems account of language education. Adopting a holistic outlook, we described language education as a composite of three analytical sub-systems: a linguistic system, an intentional system, and a pedagogical system. We also noted that each of these analytically defined systems could be structurally stratified, and studied as nested individual, small-group, or wider societal levels. For example, at the individual level, pedagogical practice manifests itself as "habits" or "strategies"; at a small-group level, pedagogical practice gives rise to "professional practices"; and at the level of the society, the pedagogical practices may be referred to as "methodological paradigms". The same structural stratification applies to the other analytically defined systems as well. When we empirically studied each of these analytically stratified and nested systems (e.g., the shared intentions of small groups of leaners), we could use CDST as an object theory to help us to understand how classroom phenomena developed, spread, and died out. However, CDST also served a meta-theoretical function that helped us to connect the insights generated by looking at different structural layers, or looking from different analytical perspectives.

In sum, we find that the view of CDST as a meta-theory is helpful in several ways. First, it potentially enables meaningful transfer of information across disciplines, such as psycholinguistics, language education pedagogy, curriculum planning, and language education policy. In addition, it may help to trace connections between sub-systems that have been analytically defined (see section 3.1.3). Most importantly, perhaps, using CDST as a meta-theory foregrounds the reciprocal relationship between agency and structure (Byrne and Callaghan 2014). Moreover, it highlights the role of structural and/or analytical stratification in shaping agency, activity, and outcomes. For example, it helps us to see how language learning activity in a nested system like the classroom can change the structure of, e.g., TESOL as a larger-scale system, as is the case when a new teaching practice becomes established as methodological orthodoxy. Conversely, it can also offer insights into how activity in larger scale systems (e.g., the introduction of a new curriculum) might constrain the activity of smaller scale systems, such as L2 classrooms. Finally, the possibility of using CDST as a meta-theory will carry forward to our model of the intentional dynamics of TESOL. We will construe TESOL as an intentional system, or an intentional ecology (see chapter 4), which gives rise to intentional activity (see chapter 5), and our model of intentional dynamics – we will argue – is a "coherent" and "interlocking" meta-theory to understand TESOL contexts, activity, and outcomes.

3.3 What we take from CDST

This chapter has explored CDST, which adds key building blocks to be used in the development of our model of the intentional dynamics of TESOL. We have discussed CDST from the perspectives of structure, activity, and context. Moreover, we have explained our preference for a generalised form of CDST, and the promise of using CDST as a meta-theory. In the paragraphs that follow, we outline the most important building blocks that we will be carrying forward to the subsequent chapters.

- **A CDS is an interconnected whole**
  The conceptualisation of systems is one of the most visible ways in which our thinking draws on CDST. This conceptualisation goes beyond the one offered in the chapter 2 discussion of ecological theory. In this chapter, we have argued that systems bring together multiple, and potentially very diverse, elements, which – together – form an analytically *meaningful whole*. We have discussed, also, how we may draw *system boundaries* to capture those processes that generate the phenomena that we wish to investigate. We develop this thinking further in chapter 4, where we will propose what are the boundaries of what we will refer to as the "intentional ecology of TESOL".

- **The dynamics of CDSs include adaptiveness, historicity, non-linearity, and self-organisation**
  We have distinguished between four different dynamic properties of CDSs: *adaptiveness, historicity, non-linearity*, and *self-organisation*. These dynamic properties are what explain activity in a CDS, as well as the generative potential of this activity. We will refer back to these four properties in chapter 5, where we describe four types of intentional activity and their generative potential in our model of intentional dynamics of TESOL.

- **CDSs may be stratified by structure, analytical perspective, or domain of activity**
  Another key insight that will inform later chapters is the ways in which systems may be stratified. We have distinguished between *structural stratification, analytical stratification*, and *stratification by activity domain*. The notion of stratification will inform our model of the intentional dynamics of TESOL. Specifically, chapter 4 develops a view of TESOL as an intentional ecology, and this intentional ecology includes both structural and analytical stratification. In chapter 5, we develop our understanding of what we will call intentional activity, and this is activity that is stratified across different domains of TESOL.

- **Within a CDS, activity and structure generate each other**
  Chapter 2 suggested that TESOL as an ecology shapes TESOL activity, and TESOL activity may change TESOL as an ecology. CDST provides additional theoretical detail of how activity and structure generate each other. We have described how the diverse elements of the system shape activity through the process of *soft-assembly*, and how new system structure may be generated by activity through the process of *morphogenesis*. This additional detail will be reflected in the model of intentional dynamics, which we will present in chapter 5. We will argue that the intentional ecology of TESOL, through the process of soft-assembly, shapes intentional activity, and intentional activity, through the process of morphogenesis, may change the intentional ecology of TESOL.

  Related to above, we also take from CDST the concept of *attractor states*, which are preferred states of a system that are produced by activity, and which – once produced – tend to constrain activity within them. Chapter 5 will revisit the concept of attractor states, including a detailed discussion of the distinction between affordances, which we introduced in chapter 2, and attractor states.
- **CDST can be used as a meta-theory**
  The final key insight that we bring with us is the observation that CDST may be used as a *meta-theory*. As a meta-theory, CDST can be used to integrate different perspectives. This informs chapter 4, which develops a conceptualisation of TESOL as an intentional ecology, and chapter 5, which presents our model of the intentional dynamics of TESOL. This model is will be a meta-theoretical description of TESOL contexts, activity, and outcomes.

In the next chapter, we turn our attention to the concept of intentionality, thereby addressing how TESOL has meaning and meaning-making at its heart. The insights of CDST will be less visible in chapter 4, but will resurface again in chapter 5, where we present our full model of the intentional dynamics of TESOL.

Chapter 4
Meaning is primary: Intentionality

In chapter 2, we argued that the appropriate focus for an ecological account of human and social activity, like TESOL, is meaningful information, or structures, and meaningful activity. Moreover, we explored steps taken by the existing ecological literature towards a conceptualisation of an ecology of meaning, including also how meaning is central in a body of ecologically-inspired TESOL literature. In this chapter, we draw on the concept of intentionality (Searle 1983) to develop, further, the notion that TESOL is an ecology with "meaning at its heart". Thus, this chapter represents the third, and final, conceptual chapter building the theoretical foundation for our model of the intentional dynamics of TESOL.

We start the chapter by distinguishing between two senses of intentionality, which, together, capture how we conceptualise meaning within the intentional dynamics of TESOL (section 4.1). The first sense is the everyday meaning of intentionality – or what we will refer to as *ordinary intentionality*. This sense of intentionality is consistent with notions such a being goal-directed, or being purposeful. The second sense of intentionality, common within the philosophy of mind, describes the manner in which our individual psychological states tend to *be about* or *directed* towards something, including others and the world around us – and this we refer to as *ideational intentionality*. We conclude the first section by bringing these two senses of intentionality together, thus defining how we use the concept in our model of the intentional dynamics of TESOL. The next section (4.2) focuses on how meaning – now conceptualised as intentionality – may appear across the layers of the stratified ecology, or complex dynamic system, of TESOL (see chapters 2 and 3). This includes definitions and explanations of individual, shared, derived, and sociocultural aspects of intentionality. Then, in a third section (4.3), we combine these different aspects of intentionality into our final view of *TESOL as an intentional ecology*. Just as we did in chapters 2 and 3, we conclude with a summary of key insights and concepts that we take with us to the later chapters of this book (section 4.4).

4.1 Two complimentary definitions of intentionality

This section outlines our understanding of the concept of intentionality, and how this informs our model of the intentional dynamics of TESOL. A continuing challenge, in this regard, is the presence, in philosophy, psychology, education, as well as TESOL itself, of an array of different ways to understand intentionality.

In this section, we explore what we believe to be two main understandings of the concept; the *ordinary* and the *ideational* senses of intentionality. We conclude by explaining how our final understanding of intentionality draws on both the ordinary and ideational senses of the concept.

4.1.1 Ordinary intentionality

The phrase *ordinary intentionality* is our own, and we use it to express the everyday meaning of the word, including its derivatives. In this ordinary sense, intentionality is akin to "being purposeful", and acting with intention is akin to having a goal, an aim, or a purpose in mind when doing something. A prominent advocate of the analytical affordances of this ordinary sense of intentionality is the philosopher Daniel Dennett. In his book-length contribution *The Intentional Stance* (1987), Dennett argues that a focus on human intentions – as in what people aim to do – can help us predict what may happen next. In this manner, ordinary intentionality is particularly able to generate understanding of human affairs. Dennett contrasts this "intentional stance" (of a philosopher or researcher) with a "physical stance", which encourages description of physical processes, and a "design stance", which suggests architectural or mechanistic descriptions of situations. These other stances, Dennett points out, fail to go beyond description and explanation. Only the intentional stance affords prediction. Moreover, by looking at intention across time, thus making sense of the extended intentional structure of activity, the intentional stance also affords an understanding of the coherence of intentional human activity, as expressed by Jerome Bruner's functional account of intention: "An intention is present when an individual operates persistently towards achieving an end state, persists in developing means and corrects the development of means to get closer to the end state, and finally ceases the line of activity when specifiable features of the end state are achieved" (Bruner 1981: 41–42).

The ordinary sense of intentionality has been used, also, in cognitive science. Cognitive science focuses on how intentions are formed in people's minds, as well as how intentions appear in action. Thus, there are two perspectives on intention: (a) cognition that generates intentions, and (b) intentionality in action (Malle, Moses, and Baldwin 2001). This means that ascribing intention to an agent, which may precede action of any kind, is different from making a judgment about the intentionality of action. This cognitive perspective on intention and intentional action is rooted in the folk-psychological tradition, which is particularly concerned with how ordinary people explain the antecedents of their own actions, and ascribe intentionality to the actions of others.

The ordinary sense of intentionality also appears, with some regularity, in the TESOL literature. In TESOL, intentionality is used to describe deliberate, or conscious, engagement in the L2 learning process (as opposed to incidental or unconscious L2 learning), and such deliberate or conscious engagement is considered a beneficial attribute. This use is evident in studies of incidental versus intentional learning of L2 grammar; Boers (2018: 1) defines intentional learning of L2 grammar as that which results from "a deliberate focus on the language code". Similarly, in L2 vocabulary learning research the consensus seems to be that if learners' approach to the study and use of L2 vocabulary is deliberate, strategic, and self-regulated (i.e., involves intentional learning or action) then the consolidation, expansion, and productive use of L2 vocabulary will be more successful (Fuster and Neuser 2019; Pauwels 2018). Finally, there are studies of the broader benefits of ordinary intentionality for making L2 classroom, task-based interaction, and language use pedagogically more valuable (Awwad, Tavakoli, and Wright 2017).

L2 motivation research is another part of TESOL scholarship where reference to ordinary intentionality appears. Motivation research focuses on what drives or energises language learning, and one candidate driver, borrowed from cognitive psychology, is the focus on intention-formation and intention-implementation. For instance, the process model of L2 motivation (Dörnyei and Ottó 1998) outlines phases of activity that are structured by the formation, implementation, and evaluation of intentions. This includes a pre-actional phase, where intention-formation is central; a "crossing the Rubicon" phase, where intention is converted into action; an actional phase, where the intention to act is implemented; and a final post-actional phase, where the intention and its implementation are evaluated. Another theory of motivation that includes a focus on intentionality, and which is used for understanding L2 motivation, is self-determination theory (Deci and Ryan 1980, 2008; Noels et al. 2000). Self-determination theory describes motivation as determined either by expectations external to the learner, or – provided that activity satisfies a learner's psychological needs for competence, autonomy, and relatedness – by the interests and concerns of the learner herself. The goal of education, then, is to encourage learners to become self-determined, or intentional.

Finally, some of our own work has drawn on the ordinary sense of intentionality. This includes Stelma (2011), who explored how doctoral candidates in TESOL developed researcher intentionality, in the ordinary sense, in their PhD projects, as well as a study of how language teachers, attending a UK-based MA TESOL programme, developed the same sort of researcher intentionality (Stelma and Fay 2014). The ordinary sense of intentionality will play a role, also, in our model of the intentional dynamics of TESOL. However, before we explain this in more detail, we need to introduce the second sense of intentionality, which we do in the next sub-section.

4.1.2 Ideational intentionality

Ideational intentionality, which is again our own terminology, expresses how ideas, whether held by individuals, or as expressed by groups or society more generally, have "aboutness". As individuals, we have ideas that express something about others, events, objects, and more. As language teachers we may have ideas about our learners, about the curriculum we are asked to follow, or about our Head Teacher or Director of Studies. Thus, ideational intentionality is a "measure" of what our thoughts, both individual and collective, are about.

The starting point for our understanding of ideational intentionality is the original definition of intentionality, in the modern era of the philosophy of mind, by Brentano (2015). In the late 1800s, Brentano sought to define the scope of the emerging field of psychology. At the time, Wilhelm Wundt was developing the building blocks of experimental psychology, which relied on observable features of human behaviour (see Titchener 1921). Brentano, however, insisted that the domain of psychology was the mental world of individuals, and he evoked the concept of intentionality to describe how particular psychological states, including love, anger, belief, and more, are "about" or "directed at" an object (Benetka and Joerchel 2016; Moran 2000). This object, however, was not an object in the real world. Rather, Brentano's phenomenology stressed how the object of a psychological state was, itself, a mental representation. In his words, "every mental phenomenon includes something as object within itself" (Brentano 2015: 92). Thus, and consistent with later phenomenological accounts, Brentano's intentionality describes how the world appears to, and within, the human mind.

We are committed to the "aboutness" of intentionality, and the "directed" nature of psychological states, or ideas, that we have. However, the phenomenological view of intentionality as fully mental, and centred on individual lived experience, does not cohere with our commitment to undercover the "generative processes" that constitute TESOL as an ecology and complex dynamic system. In chapter 3, we stressed the need to delineate complex dynamic systems that capture those aspects and processes that we believe generate activity and outcomes in TESOL. More specifically, we seek to understand the ecological and dynamic processes of meaning and meaning-making across multiple layers of TESOL as an ecological system, and across multiple domains of TESOL activity. Thus, we need ideational intentionality to connect us, as individuals, to the world of TESOL. For this, we turn to the work of John Searle.

Searle (1984: 87) defines intentionality as "that feature of certain mental states and events that consists in their [. . .] being directed at, being about, being of, or representing certain other entities and states of affairs". Searle's "mental states" – which we refer to as psychological states – are similar to those of Brentano (2015), and thus include love, anger, belief, and more, and are similarly "about" or "directed" at something. However, Searle's "other entities and states of affairs" includes, in addition, people, objects and events in the external world. Thus, for Searle, the intentionality of psychological states is what meaningfully connects us not only to our own thoughts, experience, and aspirations, as phenomenology suggests, but also to other people and the world around us. The ideational intentionality of language learners' curiosity may be directed at previously unknown features of language, and their anxiety may be about, or directed at, speaking the L2 in public. The ideational intentionality of a language teacher who believes that a particular sequence of vocabulary learning activities works well likely includes, as part of this belief, real language learners in a real classroom, and language teaching as an ontologically real state of affairs. Thus, the position that we develop here is that ideational intentionality, as a multi-layered and multi-faceted phenomenon, is what provides the "connective tissue" that enables our meaningful experience of TESOL.

An area of TESOL scholarship that we think resonates with our ideational intentionality is the long-standing focus on how teachers and learners make sense of what happens in L2 classrooms. For example, Kumaravadivelu (1991) has looked at what are the sources of mismatch between teachers' intentions, when organising activities in classrooms, and learners' interpretation of these activities. Similarly, Breen (1989: 188) points out that when teachers and learners engage in classroom tasks, the original task-as-workplan "is metamorphosed into a task-in-process during which teacher and learners redraw the plan in terms of their own 'frames' and their own knowledge and experience". Tudor (2001: 33) also reminds us of the agentive role of learners, suggesting that "students are not 'simply' language learners. They are all individuals, each of whom has his or her own psychocognitive make up, personal history and life goals, and his or her own experience of education in general and possibly of language education in particular". Tudor continues to suggest that both students and teachers have their own "rationality" of language learning and teaching, composed of their beliefs, knowledge, and experience. These rationalities resemble our notion of ideational intentionality.

Ideational intentionality is central to the overall argument of this book. In later sections of this chapter, we will develop our understanding of ideational intentionality to include, also, shared, derived, and sociocultural aspects, and how these combine to constitute an ecology of meaning, or what we call the intentional ecology of TESOL. Thus, ideational intentionality, and the intentional ecology that it constitutes, will be fundamental in our model of the intentional dynamics of TESOL, which is presented in chapter 5.

4.1.3 The relationship between ordinary and ideational intentionality

We believe that it is possible, while remaining ecological, to explore the value of ordinary intentionality on its own (see Stelma 2011; Stelma and Fay 2014), or to focus more singularly on ideational intentionality (see Stelma 2014). In the current book-length contribution, however, we wish to keep both these senses of intentionality in mind. We do consider ideational intentionality to be more fundamental, but seek to retain, also, the affordances of ordinary intentionality as a guiding concept. Consistent with Dennett's intentional stance (1987), we believe that being purposeful, both in what we ourselves do, and as an analytical lens to understand what others do, contributes to the ecological validity and epistemic potential of the analysis of intentional dynamics that our work aims to achieve.

A closer look at the ideational intentionality of *the psychological state of ordinary intention* illustrates something more about how we understand the relationship between the two senses of intentionality. Beliefs, anger, or love are, for the most part, directed at things that are already known, or present, within ourselves or in the world. By contrast, when a teacher intends to change how she teaches a particular feature of language, or a particular group of learners, the change that is an ideational part of this ordinary intention is not yet fully known to, or present in, the world (Searle 1980). Thus, ordinary intentions have ideational intentionality that, in part, is not yet realised. This means that the psychological state of intention has, within it, both ordinary intentionality – having intentions is akin to being purposeful – and ideational intentionality – it is "about something". In addition, the cognitive and social antecedents of an ordinary intention will include a range of other psychological states with ideational intentionality. Thus, ordinary intentionality not only has its own ideational intentionality, it is inherently intertwined with the ideational intentionality of other psychological states. Thus, to understand a teacher's or learner's ordinary intentions we need to understand, also, a range of other psychological phenomena.

Our developing position, then, is a hybrid understanding of intentionality, with ideational intentionality as more fundamental, but keeping alive the analytical affordances of ordinary intentionality. This hybrid understanding is evident in our own later work (see Kostoulas 2018; Kostoulas and Stelma 2016, 2017;

Stelma and Fay 2019). We are not alone, however, in trying to tap into the combined analytical potential of these two senses of intentionality. Kubanyiova and Feryok (2015) have made a similar suggestion. These authors focused on L2 teacher education, and they lamented that that existing cognitivist perspectives privilege a top-down approach, with *a priori* established definitions of psychological states, such as beliefs, knowledge, emotions, and more, and *a priori* conceptualisations of their role in teacher cognition. A more fruitful approach, they argued, is to examine "the links among teachers' actions, reasons, and impact on students [. . .] in light of intentionality, a feature common to different mental processes and related to purposeful actions" (p. 436). Specifically, and in addition to ordinary intentions, they emphasise the need for a broader philosophical approach to intentionality (i.e., our ideational intentionality) because this allows teacher cognition research to focus on "all mental processes or states that are about something" (p. 440).

In sum, in this section we have introduced the ordinary and ideational senses of intentionality. We consider ideational intentionality to be fundamental, as the connective tissue for our meaningful experience as TESOL practitioners. Ideational intentionality will be more fundamental, also, in our model of the intentional dynamics of TESOL, to be outlined in the next chapter. However, as consistent with ordinary intentionality and Dennett's (1987) intentional stance, we continue to believe in the overall value of being purposeful, both in what we ourselves do, and as an analytical lens to understand what others do. We might say, then, that we value the ideational intentionality of ordinary intentions more than the ideational intentionality of any other psychological state.

4.2 An ecological view of intentionality

A defining feature of the above reviewed uses and definitions of both ordinary and ideational intentionality, in philosophy, psychology, or TESOL, is the focus on the intentions and intentionality of individual agents. When cognitive scientists study the antecedents to ordinary intentions, how intentions translate into activity, how intentions structure this activity, and how intentions may change during and after activity, the unit of analysis is the individual (Malle et al. 2001). Thus, being purposeful is most clearly an individual achievement. Brentano's (2015) use of intentionality to describe the directed nature of psychological states likewise treats it as an individual psychological construct. Finally, the individual is the starting point of Searle's account of intentionality (but see the following sub-sections covering derived and shared intentionality). The focus on individual agents is a strong feature, also, of TESOL research on language learning and motivation, which we briefly reviewed in an earlier part of this chapter, with the intentions and intentional actions in question being unambiguously those of individual L2 learners.

This individual character of intentionality is critiqued by Gibbs (2001), who suggests that "many aspects of intentional meaning [. . .] are products of dynamic social interactions and not solely the result of privately held, internalized mental representations" (2001: 122). He points out that "when a second person responds to the act of a first, and thus acts in a way that depends on the first person's act, the activities of the second person cannot be counted as wholly his own" and, hence, that "many individual actions are best characterized in collective, rather than purely individual, terms" (2001: 113). Gibbs also suggests that the focus on individuals may be a western folk-psychological view, and points out that in the folk-psychology of some non-western cultures the ascription of intentionality, and associated responsibility, is often far more situational and collective. We agree with Gibbs; we believe that intentionality – both ordinary and ideational – is often a collective achievement. In fact, in order to develop our ecological and complex dynamic systems view of TESOL we need a collective, or ecologically inclusive, view of intentionality. Thus, in this section we take a closer look at aspects of intentionality that go beyond the individual.

4.2.1 Shared intentionality

Tomasello and Carpenter (2007: 121) suggest that "what makes human cognition different [from that of other primates] is not more individual brainpower, but rather the ability of humans to learn through other persons and their artifacts, and to collaborate with others in collective activities". They suggest that what enables learning through others, and collaboration, is "shared intentionality", i.e., sharing psychological states with others whom you engage with. Searle (2002: 105) has, similarly, suggested that the "the biological primitive sense of the other person as a candidate for shared intentionality is a necessary condition of all collective behavior", and adding, also, that this is the kind of thing that philosophers mean when they say humans are "social animals". Moreover, Tomasello et al. (2005: 680) offer empirical evidence that the ability to recognise shared intentionality develops in the first two years of children's lives, with the goals and intentions of one individual including "as content something of the goals and intentions of the other".

Shared intentionality may be explained, also, using the notion of intersubjectivity, which Rommetveit (1976: 202) has defined as "whatever is shared, presupposed, or assumed to be known already [. . .] within a temporarily shared here and now". The "here and now" element of intersubjectivity is instructive. Shared intentionality, as intersubjectivity, should not be understood as two or more individuals sharing mirror-like ideas. Rather, the level of shared intentionality in the "here and now" only needs to be sufficient for joint attention to take place, and then for coordinated action (action guided by complementary individual intentionality) to transform into collaborative action (action guided by shared intentionality). On a basic level, then, shared intentionality is the alignment of two or more individuals' individual intentionality. This may explain situations such as when a language teacher, after a particularly good lesson, says: "I really connected with my students today". However, we would like to highlight a more dynamic understanding of shared intentionality. When individuals recognise the potential for shared intentionality in a situation, this may change their individual agentive contributions. In moments of collaborative activity, shared intentionality may supplant individual intentionality, in both the ordinary and ideational senses (Searle 2002), and the shared intentionality that emerges may be something more than the simple sum of the individual intentionality of those involved.

We believe that shared intentionality is a *de facto* focus in much recent TESOL research. For instance, L2 classroom research has focused a great deal on patterns of talk, or interaction, and this research includes, we suggest, a focus on the role of shared intentionality. Neil Mercer's (1995: 104) empirically established distinction between disputational, cumulative, and exploratory forms of talk between learners illustrates the point we are trying to make here. Learner disputational talk is "characterised by disagreement and individualised decision-making", and therefore involves only limited shared intentionality (perhaps a shared sense of proximity and disagreement). Learner cumulative talk describes talk where a learner builds "positively but uncritically on what the other has said", and this suggests a slightly higher level of shared intentionality (perhaps a realisation that they each add something to the other's ideas). Finally, learner exploratory talk describes situations where "knowledge is made more publicly accountable and reasoning is more visible", and this presupposes shared intentionality that, more directly, shapes the agency of the individuals involved. It is noteworthy that the most highly prized pattern of interaction – exploratory talk – is the pattern defined by more pervasive shared intentionality. Looking at the theoretical underpinnings guiding some of the recent research on classroom interaction in TESOL offers additional clues to how researchers are, in fact, focusing on shared intentionality. Conceptualisations of collaborative activity often draw on Vygotsky's (1978) sociocultural theory, and include the claim that individual learners internalise concepts that first appear within "interpersonal processes". This sociocultural view of L2 learning highlights the social origins of knowledge and development (Antón and DiCamilla 1998; Gibbons 2003; Kowal and Swain 1994; Swain 2000). In our view, for concepts to be internalised, learners need to identify with, or value, the shared intentionality that they experience, thereby allowing this shared intentionality to alter, or enrich, their own individual intentionality.

In sum, shared intentionality describes the here-and-now intersubjectivity that participants in TESOL may experience in the classroom, or elsewhere. This shared intentionality is distinct from individual intentionality, and, thus, is another aspect of the ecology of meaning, and meaning-making, that our model of the intentional dynamics of TESOL aims to understand.

4.2.2 Derived intentionality

Searle (1983) considers individual intentionality, or "intrinsic intentionality" as he calls it, as the most basic form of intentionality. However, he also suggests that our individual activity, as shaped by our intrinsic intentionality, will "assign" or "sediment" intentional content to the external world in forms that may be either more ephemeral, such as speech, or which may have permanence, such as texts, objects, and perhaps also routinised practices. Thus, ideas that appear embedded in speech, texts, and objects have an intentional aspect, and Searle refers to this aspect as *derived intentionality*. Stelma (2014: 122) puts this slightly differently; he suggests that individual intentionality "describes the domain of thinking; derived intentionality describes the externalised 'products' of thought – including speaking, writing and other observable ways to encode meaning".

Indeed, language is a prototypical case of derived intentionality. When we speak or write, a stream of words become auditory or visible to others, and when comprehended this speech or text directs attention to aspects of ourselves or the world around us. Using the terminology associated with speech acts (Austin 1975; Searle 1969), the individual intentionality that generates speech may be equated with the illocutionary act of utterances – i.e., the intended meaning of the speaker. Moreover, the derived intentionality of the speech may be compared with the locutionary force of the utterance – i.e., its ostensible propositional content (Kissine 2008; Searle 1979). Speech act theory also leaves room for interpretation by interlocutors. Thus, the manner in which derived intentionality is interpreted can be compared to the perlocutionary force of an utterance – i.e., the interpretation that the speech act prompts in others (Kissine 2008). By contrast, the act of writing commonly results from a great deal of mental deliberation, its purpose is to represent ideational content, and written texts may, therefore, be dense with derived intentionality. This derived intentionality may also have more permanence, and may be susceptible to repeated interpretation by many readers over time. The derived intentionality of written text may be understood as propositional content that may be evident to an analyst. Alternatively, the derived intentionality of written text may be understood using the concept of intertextuality, which describes the linguistic (words and phrases) and extra-linguistic (ideas and structure) overlaps with other texts (Kristeva 1986; Pecorari and Shaw 2012). In other words, intertextuality highlights possible overlaps between separate instances of derived intentionality. Finally, the derived intentionality of written texts may be understood as indexicality, which Hughes and Tracy (2015: 788) define as "the function by which linguistic and non-linguistic signs point to aspects of context". An exploration of the indexicality of written texts would be more interpretive, and thus an attempt to link the derived intentionality of a written text with broader sociocultural aspects of contexts (see discussion of sociocultural aspects of intentionality in the next sub-section).

In sum, derived intentionality is generated by our individual, shared, and sociocultural intentional activity in the world. This can include either the deliberate assigning, or the less deliberate sedimenting, of ideational content into the design and performance of speech, texts or objects. Moreover, once assigned/ sedimented into the real world around us, derived intentionality becomes a part of the ecology of meaning, and meaning-making, which we seek to understand.

4.2.3 Sociocultural aspects of intentionality

In addition to derived and shared intentionality, there are a range of ideas in TESOL, as well as in society, which are temporally and socially more distributed. This may include educational policies that determine what schools can or cannot do, school rules and expectations that shape teachers' and learners' views and activity, or teaching approaches that enable and constrain teaching and learning. Being schooled in the British educational system includes the requirement to read Shakespeare for your English A-levels exams. In China, the experience of middle and high school students is often dominated by the next high-stakes examination, including English language as one of the key subjects. In all parts of our lives, including within TESOL, we align ourselves to a range of traditions, rules, and expectations that we perceive to apply to us (Stelma 2011). We refer to these more permanent features of contexts as sociocultural aspects of intentionality. Sociocultural aspects of intentionality, thus defined, are distinct from shared intentionality (section 4.2), as the latter is usually temporally and spatially constrained. Although it is possible for teachers who have worked together for a long time to experience shared intentionality that is more permanent, shared intentionality is still limited to a small number of individuals. By contrast, sociocultural aspects have a permanence and force that cannot be explained by the moments of joint attention, or collaborative activity, that defines shared intentionality.

In TESOL, a great deal has been written about the shaping influence of sociocultural aspects of contexts. In an earlier section, we cited Tudor's (2001) suggestion that language learners and teachers have individual rationalities that shape their classroom activity. Tudor's ecological view extends, also, to include broader, non-agentive parts of classroom contexts. He suggests that there are methodological rationalities at play in the classroom, including assumptions and expectations about language, language learning, and pedagogy, and institutional rationalities, such as the ethos, local culture, and aims of a school. Moreover, Tudor suggests that these methodological and institutional rationalities are expressions of expectations, beliefs, and behavioural norms of society more generally. This closely resembles how we understand the sociocultural aspects of intentionality in TESOL. Our view of the sociocultural resonates, also, with the notion of normative assumptions (Pennycook 2001, 2004). Normative assumptions may be described as implicit theories shared by some decisive majority of stakeholders (see chapter 11 for additional discussion). For instance, a normative assumption in TESOL is the belief that native speakers of English are better teachers of the English language, and the related belief that particular "native speaker" English varieties (e.g., North American or British standard varieties) are more legitimate as "target language" for learners (Holliday 2006). Thus, the intentionality, or aboutness, of this normative assumption is directed at the linguistic origins of language teachers and target language varieties, and at some perceived "inherent value" of different target language varieties. Moreover, normative assumptions, and thus sociocultural aspects of intentionality, can have a strong influence on activity and outcomes in TESOL. For example, "non-native" English teachers may, notwithstanding their pedagogical qualities, or their possibly superior understanding of their learners' dispositions and aspirations, feel deficient as English language teachers (Shin and Kellogg 2007), and English language learners may "despair in view of a native-speaker ideal they are not likely to attain" (Kordt 2018: 144). Finally, normative assumptions, and therefore also sociocultural aspects of intentionality, may appear as derived intentionality across TESOL contexts. Textbooks may be written in a high status, native variety of English language; language assessment criteria may award higher marks for responses that adhere to the high-status variety of English; and L2 teacher job advertisements may specify that applicants must be "native" English speakers.

In some later chapters, we will refer to these sociocultural aspects as *intentional structures* – thereby aligning it with the more common references to *social structures* in TESOL and related literatures. We will discuss how sociocultural aspects, or intentional structures, alongside individual, derived, and shared aspects of intentionality, shape the intentional dynamics of TESOL. As for the present chapter, we have now concluded our discussion of the different aspects of intentionality that we believe shape TESOL contexts, activity, and outcomes. In the next section, we will bring these different aspects together, and thereby conceptualise what we call the intentional ecology of TESOL.

4.3 TESOL as an intentional ecology

We are now ready to define what we, henceforth, will refer to as an intentional ecology, and what we mean when, in later chapters, we refer to *the intentional ecology of TESOL*. In chapter 2, we reviewed existing ecological scholarship, as a first step towards conceptualising TESOL as an ecology of meaning. The current chapter has used the concept of intentionality to develop this conceptualisation further. We are now able to define the meaningful context of TESOL as the intentional ecology of TESOL. This intentional ecology includes the individual, shared, derived, and sociocultural aspects of intentionality that we have outlined in the previous section. Individual intentionality characterises our agentive contribution to the intentional ecology, shared intentionality is the collaborate aspect, derived intentionality resides in the texts and objects that we use, and the sociocultural aspects describe the temporally more permanent and socially more distributed ideas and meanings that comprise TESOL.

Whilst the core meaning of intentionality, as ideational aboutness (see section 4.1.2), defines how we understand meaning, and defines the interconnected nature of the ecology that we are investigating, the individual, derived, shared, and sociocultural aspects of intentionality define the ecology as a whole. Significantly, as we understand it, the intentional ecology of TESOL is stratified both structurally and analytically. Each aspect of intentionality is a nested part of the overall intentional ecology. Individuals have ideas about each other, about what they do, and what is possible or not in their own domains of activity, as well as more broadly. Shared intentionality is a different structural part of the ecology, representing ideas shared among individuals, and occasionally collaboratively generated ideas that, by way of the interactional dynamics of situations, are "more than the sum" of individuals' respective intentionality. Derived intentionality is yet another stratum, with, e.g., teacher and learner talk being about target language, pedagogy, motives, or social relationships, and the derived intentionality of textbooks valuing particular activities or perspectives on language over others. Finally, sociocultural aspects of intentionality are a temporally more stable and socially more distributed part of the intentional ecology that we are all affected by, and contribute to. At the same time, the four aspects of the intentional ecology may also comprise analytical sub-systems. We can take an individual perspective on a situation, focus on collective aspects, attempt to describe the derived intentionality of learning materials, or seek to understand sociocultural influences on TESOL. Finally, both of these forms of stratification are needed to understand intentional activity (to be defined in chapter 5). An analysis of activity consistent with our intentional dynamics would focus on the interplay between individual, shared, derived, and sociocultural aspects of an intentional ecology, and understanding this interplay requires understanding of both "scale effects" (see section 3.1) and how the different aspects of an intentional ecology are analytically different.

As suggested already, the ideational intentionality of the different strata of an intentional ecology is, by way of the activity of participants in TESOL, in continual dynamic interplay. In later chapters, where we look at the intentional dynamics of particular TESOL activities and contexts, we are sometimes able to identify the belief or desires of individuals, a set of ideas or expectations that are shared across individuals, ideas evident in learning materials, or a societal value that appears to act as a sociocultural constraint or enabling factor. However, these later chapters will show, also, how individual, shared, derived, and sociocultural aspects of intentionality "work" together. In the moment of activity, sociocultural intentionality may appear as shared intentionality, shared intentionality may at the same time be individual intentionality, or individual intentionality may overlap with derived intentionality. Moreover, just as there is a continual interplay between the different aspects of intentionality, sometimes there will be multiple intentional ecologies at play in any one situation. There may be an intentional ecology particular to a class, but the teacher's activity may – at the same time – be shaped by other intentional ecologies. For instance, a teacher doing Action Research will, through her activity, be integrating the intentional ecology of the classroom with an intentional ecology of (practitioner) research. How we define an intentional ecology, or ecologies, will depend on what we are trying to understand.

An intentional ecology is primarily meaningful to the participants in TESOL situations. In fact, only individuals can fully recognise and interpret the meaningful information that constitutes an intentional ecology. We may, on occasion, attribute agency to a class of learners ("the class liked the lesson"), a school ("the school wants to . . ."), a government ("the government aims to . . ."), and so on, thereby suggesting that such entities are capable of human agency, or interpretation of meaning. Although a particular argument can be made about dyads or small groups of individuals exercising shared agency, we must remind ourselves that only individuals are true agents. Thus, the ideas comprising the intentional ecology will play out in our individual minds, and this interplay of different aspects of intentionality in our minds will prompt our activity. This also means that an intentional ecology may be experienced differently by each individual. This must be the case because our unique individual intentionality is a part of the ecology, and the intentionality and psychological states of each of us will be different. It must also be the case because we each engage slightly differently with situations, and as such perceive and interpret ongoing activity differently. However, when we teach, learn, manage, design materials, and otherwise act in TESOL, the ideational intentionality extends far beyond our own mental selves. The intentional ecology of TESOL, which we all relate to, is continually realised through the interplay of individual, shared, derived, and sociocultural aspects of intentionality, across time and place, and it makes us all part of something much greater than ourselves.

In sum, this intentional ecology, including individual, derived, shared, and sociocultural aspects, is an ecology as system conceptualisation of the meaningful context of TESOL. It is a stratified conceptualisation of TESOL, uniquely meaningful to individuals, with the different aspects of intentionality in continual interplay across sometimes multiple intentional ecologies. This definition of the meaningful context of TESOL – the intentional ecology of TESOL – underpins the presentation of our model of intentional dynamics in chapter 5.

4.4 What we take from intentionality

In this chapter we have introduced the concept of intentionality, including its ordinary and ideational senses. We have, also, defined and discussed individual, shared, derived, and sociocultural aspects of intentionality. Finally, we have brought these senses and aspects together in our definition of the intentional ecology of TESOL. As in the previous two conceptual chapters, we conclude by outlining the key concepts from this chapter that we carry forward to our subsequent thinking.

- **Senses of intentionality**
  We have made reference to the ordinary and ideational senses of intentionality. *Ideational intentionality* describes how ideas, which may be individual, shared, derived, or sociocultural, are "about", or "directed at", objects,

events or states of affairs in TESOL. This sense of intentionality is how we understand meaning in TESOL; the aboutness of ideas is fundamental to our view that TESOL is an interconnected ecology of meaning. In later chapters, we use the terms "intentionality" and "intentional" to refer to ideational intentionality. By contrast, *ordinary intentionality* represents the everyday meaning of the term, and we will use the terms "intention", "purpose" or "purposeful" to denote this ordinary sense of intentionality. On occasion, when we need to make a more precise point about one or the other sense of intentionality, we will make overt reference to either "ideational" or "ordinary" intentionality.

- **Aspects of intentionality**
  We have discussed individual, shared, derived, and sociocultural aspects of intentionality. *Individual intentionality* is the "aboutness" of the ideas, or psychological states, of individuals; *shared intentionality* arises in situations, and represents the aboutness of ideas that two or more individuals share; *derived intentionality* is a form of ideational intentionality that has been assigned to (more deliberately), or sedimented into (less deliberately), speech, texts, or objects; *sociocultural aspects of intentionality* include traditions, conventions, and normative assumptions, and hence are temporally and socially distributed aspects of ideational intentionality.

- **Intentional ecology**
  We refer to the ecology of meaningful information that constitutes TESOL as the *intentional ecology of TESOL*. This intentional ecology is, by nature, an ecology of ideational intentionality, and its structure includes individual, shared, derived, and sociocultural aspects of intentionality. This is an "ecology as systems" view of TESOL, or an aspect of TESOL, that may be uniquely experienced by individuals.

The next chapter presents our full model of the intentional dynamics of TESOL. The starting point for our presentation of this model is the conceptualisation TESOL as an intentional ecology, or TESOL settings and situations as intentional ecologies. In addition, the presentation of the full model will use the ecological and complex dynamic systems insights that we generated in chapters 2 and 3.

Chapter 5
A model of the intentional dynamics of TESOL

The contribution of this chapter is our model of the intentional dynamics of TESOL. We start the chapter with a look back at what we have achieved in the three preceding conceptual chapters, and thus presenting the building blocks – so far outlined – for our model of intentional dynamics (section 5.1). This is followed by a section that develops our understanding of *intentional activity*, which is yet to be defined and discussed (section 5.2). We outline how the affordances for intentional action are shaped by the intentional ecology of TESOL, and how, in turn, intentional activity may change subsequent affordances, attractor states, and the future of the intentional ecology itself. We also include a section (5.3) where we argue that intentional activity may be *contingent*, *normative*, *creative*, and/or *purposeful*. This includes reference to the four dynamic properties of complex dynamic systems, introduced in chapter 3, so to explain how each of the four types of intentional activity reproduce the intentional ecology of TESOL, change this ecology, or both. With our understanding of intentional activity in place, we bring the various conceptual building blocks together to present the full model of *the intentional dynamics of TESOL* (section 5.4). A final section (5.5) looks forward to subsequent chapters and parts of the book. We outline how the different dimensions of our model of intentional dynamics are used, in the chapters that exemplify the model (in chapters 6 through 9), and in the chapters where we extend the model further (chapters 10 through 12).

5.1 Looking back: The building blocks so far

The overarching message of chapter 2 was that "everything is connected". However, we emphasised that this is an interconnectedness of meaningful information, and argued that the appropriate focus for an ecological account of TESOL is meaning and meaning-making. Moreover, in order to understand TESOL both as context and activity, we distinguished between the "ecology as system" and "ecology of activity" perspectives, whilst recognising that these two perspectives interact. This led us to the conclusion that *TESOL as an ecological system of meaningful information shapes meaningful TESOL activity*, and *meaningful TESOL activity may change TESOL as a meaningful ecological system*. In chapter 2, we also suggested that TESOL is a stratified ecology, including both multiple layers of meaningful information, or structure, and multiple domains of meaningful activity. Finally, chapter 2 introduced the concept of affordances as an ecological explanation of the emergence of activity in TESOL. We also suggested that both affordances for activity, and activity itself, may be associated with less individual awareness – describing things that *happen to us* – or associated with more awareness, cognition, and intent – describing things *we do* more deliberately.

Chapter 3 turned to CDST, and added theoretical detail to the ecological account of chapter 2. We discussed how drawing the boundary of a complex dynamic system represents an analytical move, and that our own approach is to draw boundaries that reveal those generative processes that we seek to explain. Thus, the complex dynamic system of interconnectedness – sometimes of multiple heterogeneous elements – that we need to identify is that which comprises the meaning-making that we focus on in research, scholarship, or practice. We also discussed the stratified nature of complex dynamic systems, further developing the observation, in chapter 2, that the ecology of TESOL is stratified in terms of layers of meaningful information, or structure, and in the form of multiple domains of meaningful activity. We suggested that a complex dynamic system can be stratified structurally, with nested systems such as the classroom, the school, the profession, country, and so on. Alternatively, a complex dynamic system may be analytically stratified into, e.g., psychological, social, and/or political sub-systems. Both structurally nested systems, and analytically defined sub-systems, comprise interpenetrating systems, with webs of interaction and causation running in all directions (Byrne and Callaghan 2014). Chapter 3 also suggested that activity in any domain of TESOL is, in principle, complex and dynamic, but may vary in scope and power depending on our perspective. We suggested that the dynamic properties of complex dynamic systems include historicity, adaptiveness, non-linearity, and self-organisation. These four dynamics work together, either in a process of soft-assembling affordances for activity, or to effect morphogenetic change in the structure of the complex dynamic system. This left us with the following fine-tuned view of TESOL: *The complex dynamic system of TESOL, through the process of soft-assembly, gives rise to affordances, activity, and attractor states, and TESOL activity, in turn, gives rise to morphogenetic change in TESOL as a complex dynamic system.*

Finally, chapter 4 turned to the concept of intentionality to outline our ecology as systems view of the meaningful context of TESOL. We introduced ordinary and ideational intentionality. We argued that ideational intentionality is the appropriate focus for understanding a human and social ecology such as TESOL, but we explained our reasons, also, for retaining the analytical affordances of ordinary intentionality. Next, we presented an ecological view of intentionality, leading to the distinctions between individual, derived, shared, and sociocultural aspects of intentionality. Depending on our perspective and what we seek to understand, these aspects of the intentional ecology, or ecologies, of TESOL may be understood as a structural stratification of TESOL contexts, analytical sub-systems, or both. Intentionality, and its multiple aspects – we suggested – forms the "connective tissue" that make our experience of TESOL meaningful.

The current chapter brings these conceptual contributions – from chapters 3, 4, and 5 – together in the form of our model of the intentional dynamics of TESOL. First, however, we need to present the last building block for our intentional dynamics; that is, our understanding of intentional activity.

5.2 Intentional activity and TESOL

The most basic definition of intentional activity in TESOL is *activity that is shaped by individual, shared, derived, and sociocultural aspects of the intentional ecology of TESOL*. In this section, however, we want to be more precise about how our intentional activity differs, not only from mainstream accounts of activity in TESOL, but also definitions of activity in the field of Ecological Psychology.

Existing scholarship tends to suggest that activity is shaped either by psychological, contextual, or situational factors. In TESOL, psychological constructs, such as beliefs, emotions, intentions, values, and motivation are often argued to be "driving" our activity (Borg 2003; Golombek and Doran 2014; Peng 2015). More contextually oriented accounts point to environmental factors, such as peers, authoritative figures, school settings, normative assumptions, and more (Chang 2010; Dörnyei 2019; Johnson 2009; M. Lamb 2007; Ushioda 2009). Finally, situated perspectives focus on the contingencies that govern the moments of activity that we find ourselves in. The latter position is not developed, in much detail, by TESOL researchers (but see van Lier 2004). However, this position is developed in detail in the field of Ecological Psychology, which subscribes to the direct perception account of affordances (Gibson 1979; Reed 1996; see also section 2.2.1). While we may appear to suggest, here, that existing scholarship tends to favour one factor over the others, we nevertheless believe there is general agreement that psychological, contextual, and situational factors act in concert to shape what we do. Furthermore, we believe that a social-reinterpretation of Ecological Psychology (Chemero 2003; Costall 1995; Good 2007; Pedersen and Bang 2016), and the concept of affordances, has the *potential* to reveal, in more coherent detail, how cognitive, environmental, and situational factors combine to prompt action. Affordances rely on our perception of information, and we have argued that this needs to be meaningful information. If the meaningful information that we perceive, in a particular situation, "adds up" to an affordance, then we have an opportunity to act. Our action will, in turn, change both ourselves, the environment, and hence also what information is available to be "picked up" in the next situation that we encounter. Ecological Psychologists refer to this ongoing mutualist process as the *action-perception cycle* (Young et al. 2002); our perception of information gives rise to affordances for action, and action gives rise to further perception.

However, in order to reveal how psychological, contextual, and situational factors act in concert, we need to focus on the shaping influence of the intentional ecology as a whole. This, then, is a focus on how intentional activity comes about, or may be encouraged, within TESOL. In chapter 4 (section 4.3), we argued that only human beings can interpret the various forms of intentionality at play in situations. Thus, psychological processes are certainly involved in mediating our perception of the different aspects of intentional ecologies. Our understanding fits with Neisser's (1994) and van Lier's (2004) "mediated affordances", reviewed in chapter 2, rather than Gibson's (1979) original formulation of affordances, which rely on unmediated direct perception. Theoretically, we do not reject direct perception, but the action-perception cycles we seek to understand go beyond doorknobs being "turn-able", chairs being "sit-on-able", or teachers' voices being "listen-to-able".

Action-perception cycles, affordances, and activity in TESOL are linguistic, semiotic, cultural, and political; action-perception cycles in TESOL are enabled by the intentional ecology of TESOL, and how we as individuals perceive *and* interpret situations. Thus, we are adding intentionality to the action-perception cycle, and we are "replacing" physical forms of information, which Gibson suggested specifies affordances, with intentionality as the information that specifies affordances. Although sounds, images, smells, taste, and touch do play a role, our analysis is motivated by more meaningful types of information. We suggest that the human capacity for intentionality enables our perception and interpretation of semiotic forms of information, such as is needed to understand language, to interact in classrooms, to teach, to design lessons and materials, and to generate language and education policies. What is interesting about TESOL is not the sounds we hear in a classroom, or that there is a lot of text about; what is interesting is what the sounds mean to us, and what may be the meaning of all that text. These semiotic forms of information are what we call ideational intentionality – and in chapter 4 we outlined how there is a whole ecology of ideational intentionality in TESOL.

Figure 1 visualises this mutualist relationship between ourselves and TESOL. The figure summarises how the intentional ecology of TESOL shapes affordances for activity, our intentional activity, as well as how our intentional activity may change the intentional ecology of TESOL.

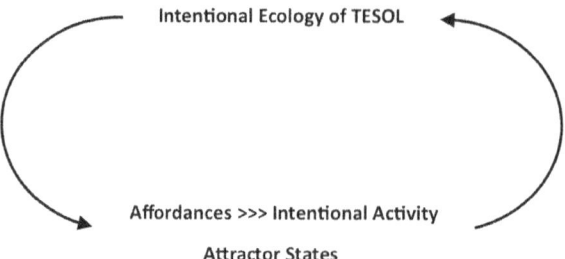

Figure 1: Intentionality, attractor states, and intentional activity.

Figure 1, and the present focus on intentional activity, includes reference to both affordances and attractor states, and this needs clarification. Affordances precede activity in a "causal chain"; the intentional ecology shapes affordances, and affordances give rise to activity. Attractor states, however, work slightly differently. In chapter 3, we defined attractor states as the equilibric state of a system (Larsen-Freeman and Cameron 2008a; Miller and Page 2007). If this is a system of activity (see section 3.1), then attractor states are "produced" by activity. At the same time, once present, attractor states tend to constrain activity within them. Thus, attractor states may either follow, precede, or co-occur with activity in the "causal chain".

Affordances and attractor states also differ in their theoretical exposition. Affordances arise from action-perception cycles (see section 2.2), and are specified by the meaningful information that we, as individuals, perceive and interpret to apply in a particular moment. Attractor states, however, are defined as outcomes of the dynamic properties of complex dynamic systems, which we introduced in chapter 3 – historicity, adaptiveness, non-linearity, and self-organisation. In addition, whilst affordances are shaped by the unique, in-the-moment interconnectedness of different forms of intentionality, attractor states are not commonly evoked to describe a unique, in-the-moment possibility or event. Rather, attractor states tend to signal possibilities and events that are repeated, and potentially more "permanent". That is not to say that attractor states are fixed over time. In chapter 3, we also stressed that attractor states are constantly re-shaped (reinforced or challenged) by activity, and attractor states may over time become more stable, less stable, or may even disappear altogether. Finally, attractor states provide a conceptual link to the ecological system of intentionality. Once formed, through activity, attractor states do more than constrain activity within them. In the same way that a popular shortcut across a green lawn will turn into a visible path (a common sight on US and UK university campuses) – attractor states will "imprint" new configurations of ideational intentionality into the intentional ecology of TESOL.

In sum, intentional activity is shaped by the intentional ecology of TESOL, including a pervasive interplay of individual, shared, derived, and sociocultural aspects of intentionality. In turn – as suggested by Figure 1 – our intentional activity may change this intentional ecology, including its individual, shared, derived, and sociocultural aspects. This highlights that there is always a broader picture; there are always different aspects of intentionality that combine in particular ways – in situations – to shape in-the-moment possibilities for action (i.e., affordances) and the potentially more permanent and generative – but even so changing and dynamic – attractor states to which activity tends. This explanation, based on the concept of intentionality, recognises that psychological, contextual, and situational factors all play their part. In our view, these psychological, contextual, and situational factors all have intentionality, and hence all have the potential to shape our intentional activity.

5.3 The generative potential of intentional activity

We have argued that activity that is shaped by an intentional ecology is intentional activity. However, we believe that there are different types of intentional activity, and that these different types vary in their potential to either reproduce and/or change the intentional ecology of TESOL. This possibility is, in part, motivated by the observation we made, in chapter 2, that both affordances for activity and activity itself, may be associated with less individual awareness – describing things that *happen to us* – or may be associated with more awareness, cognition, and intent – describing things we do more deliberately (Scarantino 2003). To develop this observation in more detail, this section employs the four dynamic properties used to describe activity in CDST (see section 3.1). In chapter 3, we suggested that complex dynamic systems had the following four dynamic properties:

- **Adaptiveness:** the activity of the system constantly adjusts to changing conditions in the environment;
- **Historicity:** the activity of the system is shaped by the past states of the system;
- **Non-linearity:** the activity of the system is not predictable or proportional to its triggers;
- **Self-organisation:** activity is shaped by the structure of the system (soft-assembly), and activity may change the structure of the system (morphogenesis).

In the following sub-sections, we argue that the interplay between different aspects of intentionality, or the interconnectedness that shapes affordances and attractor states for intentional activity, varies in terms of the above four dynamic properties of complex dynamic systems. Thus, we explore four types of intentional activity which we believe are foundational for understanding the intentional dynamics of human/social ecological systems, and hence also the intentional dynamics of TESOL. We explore *contingent* intentional activity, which we believe is fundamental for both stability and change; *normative* intentional activity, which tends to reproduce existing intentionality; *creative* intentional activity, which represents a search for new possibilities; and *purposeful* intentional activity, which we suggest has a unique potential to generate change.

5.3.1 Contingent intentional activity

We believe that much of our everyday activity simply happens, without much deliberate or conscious consideration. We often find ourselves doing things, and then not quite remember doing it. This includes common activities such as walking or driving to work, doing the dishes, or even participating in conversations. In terms of affordances, introduced in chapter 2, contingent activity results from Scarantino's (2003) "happening affordances" (see section 2.2). Moreover, the lack of conscious deliberation means that contingent activity may be explained, also, by van Lier's (2004) "immediate affordances" (see section 2.2).

We believe that the immediacy and unconscious quality of contingent intentional activity is common in TESOL. This includes activity that unfolds with automaticity, in classrooms or elsewhere in TESOL. We do not include daydreaming, or being distracted, although these may be contingent. Rather, we are interested in activity of professional and pedagogical relevance where teachers, learners, and other TESOL participants appear to be on "auto-pilot", with no deliberate attempt to alter or direct events. This contingent activity still includes an interplay of different aspects of intentionality, but this interplay is "filtered" by situational dynamics rather than our conscious minds. Table 3 summarises this type of intentional activity.

Table 3: Contingent intentional activity.

Typical situations	Interplay of intentionality	Prominent dynamic property	Outcomes
Everyday; spontaneous	Unconsciously experienced	Adaptiveness	Maintains the potential for both stability and change

In terms of CDST, Table 3 suggests that the prominent dynamic property of contingent intentional activity is *adaptiveness*. There may, inevitably, be some historicity as well. The individual intentionality involved in contingent intentional activity will include the aboutness of psychological states that has been shaped by our past experience, and which may define our habitual ways of thinking and acting. Thus, the dynamics of situations may generate normative ways of acting (see Rietveld 2008). However, the defining characteristic of our contingent intentional activity is its unreflective and responsive nature; responding as we do is an adaptive response to situational dynamics.

The nature of contingent activity may be exemplified by Larsen-Freeman and Cameron's (2008a: 204–215) observed adaptive behaviour of teachers and learners in a L2 classroom. In data from a Norwegian young learner L2 classroom, originally collected and analysed by Cameron (2001), Larsen-Freeman and Cameron observed that teacher-learner "elicitation-response" sequences began with a larger differential – between what the teacher's elicitation expected of the learners, and what the learners' responses actually provided. The teacher might start with an open-ended question that expected quite a lot from the learners. In response, the learners might give either very short answers, or offer no answer, thus resulting in a wide differential between what was expected and what was provided. However, as the elicitation-response sequence unfolded, the teacher would adapt her elicitation, and ask questions that expected less complex responses. The learners, then, were more able to offer appropriate, but still limited, responses. Thus, the adaptive behaviour of the teacher and learners, together, would follow a trajectory of "starting with a wide differential and quickly narrowing down to a stable attractor of a sequence of teacher elicitations followed by limited learner responses" (Larsen-Freeman and Cameron 2008a: 209). Using our ecological terminology, the learners' in-the-moment affordances to provide responses may have been shaped by their ability to perceive meaningful information in the teacher's questions. Thus, the more demanding questions generated limited affordances for student answers, but the less demanding questions provided enhanced affordances to respond. Thus, both the teacher and the learners engaged in contingent intentional activity, adapting to shape the trajectory of the elicitation-response sequence.

Finally, Table 3 suggests that contingent activity maintains the potential for both stability and change. We suggest that our unique ability to continually adapt to the idiosyncrasies of situations may, at times, shift our activity into an attractor state, such as represented by the eventual pattern of elicitation and response that Larsen-Freeman and Cameron observed (see above). At the same time, our ability to adapt means that we are always "primed" to respond, with flexibility, to new situations. In fact, we suggest that our ability to adapt is a crucial determiner for our ability to both *fit in* and to *change* as human beings. Thus, the dynamic of adaptiveness, as expressed by contingent intentional activity, is what preserves the possibility for both stability and change.

5.3.2 Normative intentional activity

Normative intentional activity is most clearly shaped by sociocultural aspects of the intentional ecology of TESOL. Thus, normative activity may be described as a situation where: (a) we experience some sense of "this is what normally happens in situations like this", (b) we "act according to this norm", and possibly also (c) we "do not question the norm" that shapes our activity. Learners may feel that it is normal for them to be listening quietly to the teacher, only to speak when called upon, and to do so without question. Teachers may feel it is expected of them to be knowledgeable, to act as experts, and do so without question. Normative activity may extend, also, beyond the short timescale of classroom situations. We may, as teachers, be asked to "deliver" a curriculum that values a particular target language variety. If we do not question the preference for the target variety, and our activity espouses this preference, then our implementation of the curriculum may constitute more extended normative intentional activity. Table 4 summarises the features of normative intentional activity.

Table 4: Normative intentional activity.

Typical situations	Interplay of intentionality	Prominent dynamic property	Outcomes
Conventional and/or defined by authority	Predictable	Historicity	Reproducing the intentional ecology

Table 4 suggests that normative intentional activity is associated with the dynamic property of historicity, as outlined in section 3.1.2. This historicity is often provided in the form of sociocultural aspects of the intentional ecology, which may have emerged from repeated and widely distributed TESOL activity. This may include a variety of sociocultural values, expectations, and norms, may receive intentional force from voices of authority, such as teachers or school managers, of may appear as derived intentionality in tasks, textbooks or teaching approaches. Thus, normative intentional activity may be both familiar and compelling, and aided by our adaptive instincts (i.e., associated contingent activity) the influence of sociocultural aspects of TESOL may quickly compel our activity into a stable attractor state. When this happens, normative activity reproduces the prevailing intentional ecology of TESOL. In fact, normative intentional activity is not easily perturbed; historicity can be a strong dynamic, and escaping the attractor state of normative activity may require a lot of effort.

5.3.3 Creative intentional activity

Creative intentional activity may include doing tasks that conventional wisdom deems to be creative, such as play or games, art-projects, problem-solving, as well as free or imaginative writing. However, we are equally interested in less conventional forms of linguistic and social creativity (Carter 2004). For instance, in terms of language, creativity may be an "utterance that a learner produces that does not conform to the linguistic norms of a language but is nevertheless appropriate to context" (R. Ellis 2016: 33). In terms of language teaching, we may focus on whether teachers' behaviour is creative or normative. However, we are reminded, also, of Stevick's (1980: 20) warning that "we should judge creativity in the classroom by what the teacher makes possible for the student to do". Thus, creative activity may include a much broader range of activity than conventional wisdom would suggest, including also classroom and other TESOL activity.

Our understanding of creativity is informed, also, by our ecological outlook. Although being creative is most often associated with individuals, we believe, in addition, that creative intentional activity – especially in language classrooms – may be a social achievement (Chappell 2016). Being ecological also makes us mindful of different perspectives, across cultural and social divides. As Tudor (2001: 161) points out, "most classroom behaviours are perceived to be more or less "exotic" by one group of observers or another". With the above caveats in mind, we are, however, willing to define creativity as having particular dynamics, and particular generative potential. As defined by our ecological and CDST perspectives, we view creative intentional activity as a search for new ideas, new affordances, and new possibilities. Table 5 summarises these features of creative intentional activity.

Table 5: Creative intentional activity.

Typical situation	Interplay of intentionality	Prominent dynamic property	Outcomes
Open-ended	Novel	Non-linearity	New possibilities

In CDST terms, the prominent dynamic property of creative intentional activity is non-linearity. Thus, creative intentional activity does not neatly follow from its triggers, and its outcomes are unpredictable. As viewed from the perspective of non-linearity, we can think of creative intentional activity as a *context-free* search for possibilities. This search may be constrained by our perceptual and interpretive horizons, but not by history (see Juarrero 1999: ch. 9). Of course, we cannot, as teachers, learners, or materials developers completely free ourselves from the influence of history. Dominant individual, shared, derived, and sociocultural aspects of the intentional ecology of TESOL will always weight on our minds. However, a teacher may encourage her learners to deliberately engage with a wider range of ideas, or to challenge their habitual ways of perceiving and interpreting. This may perturb otherwise normative ways of behaving, and encourage novel new ways of doing and thinking. Alternatively, in group-work tasks, learners' interaction may unexpectedly engage with a wider range of ideational intentionality, resulting in creative activity. The outcome of creative intentional activity, then, is the possibility of unexpected affordances for action, and on occasion the "discovery" of new ways of thinking, acting, or solving problems.

5.3.4 Purposeful intentional activity

The final type of intentional activity that we need to introduce is purposeful intentional activity. Contingent activity is governed by situational dynamics, normative activity is constrained by sociocultural aspects of the intentional ecology, and creative activity represents an exploration of new possibilities. Purposeful intentional activity, by contrast, is shaped by Scarantino's (2003) goal-affordances (see section 2.2). Purposeful intentional activity, then, is governed by the notion of ordinary intentionality, which we introduced in chapter 4. Table 6 summarises the features of purposeful intentional activity.

Table 6: Purposeful intentional activity.

Typical situation	Interplay of intentionality	Prominent dynamic property	Outcome
Planned; strategic; deliberate	Ordinary intentionality is dominant	Self-organisation	Changing the intentional ecology

Using our CDST terminology, the dynamic property associated with purposeful intentional activity is self-organisation. Self-organisation describes the process by which new attractor states, or new orders, emerge in a complex dynamic system. Crucially, self-organisation relies on the other dynamic properties of complex dynamic systems. Self-organisation is made possible by historicity, adaptiveness, and non-linearity. In the same manner, purposeful intentional activity is made possible by associated contingent, normative, and creative activity. This means that the goals we set for ourselves in language education are difficult to achieve, and will involve a range of other types of intentional activity over time, some of which may be beyond our own control. Yes, simple goals, such as intending to go to class, or completing a task, may predictably result in the purposeful acts of attending the class and finishing the particular task. However, a learner's goal to pass a difficult examination, or a teacher's goal for all her students to pass that same examination, will be uniquely enabled and constrained by a range of different intentional activity, and may require a great deal of effort to achieve. We suggest that this difficulty – of achieving meaningful goals – is what makes purposeful intentional activity uniquely generative. Self-organisation is perhaps the "pinnacle" dynamic property of CDST. It is the process that leads to new attractor states, new emergent orders, and new future trajectories.

We need to note that, at times, achieving difficult goals may not visibly change the broader intentional ecology of TESOL, or the change may be quite incremental. Also, the goals we work hard to achieve may simply satisfy expectations, thus suggesting a normative dimension to purposeful intentional activity. However, even though individual success may leave the broader intentional ecology of TESOL unchanged, the dynamic property of self-organisation may result in significant change on the individual level. Such individual change is, in fact, also a change in the intentional ecology; individual intentionality is – for the individual involved – a crucial part of their intentional ecology. This is something we will explore in greater depth in chapter 10, where we look at individual language learning as intentional becoming.

Finally, our emphasis on the generative potential of purposeful intentional activity is consistent with our earlier stated determination to retain a focus on ordinary intentionality in our work. As argued in chapter 4, we believe in the overall value of being purposeful, both in what we ourselves do, and as an *analytical lens* to understand what others do. Our association of purposeful intentional activity with the dynamic property of self-organisation is this analytical lens.

5.4 The intentional dynamics of TESOL: A model

We are now able to present our model of the intentional dynamics of TESOL. This is bringing together the conceptual contributions from ecological and complex dynamic system theories, as well as our understanding of intentionality, intentional ecologies, and intentional activity, as reviewed in the preceding chapters and sections. Our model of the intentional dynamics of TESOL is composed of the following dimensions:
- TESOL is an intentional ecology, with individual, shared, derived, and sociocultural aspects that – taken together – comprise a complex dynamic system of ideational intentionality;
- The intentional ecology shapes affordances and attractor states for intentional activity;
- Intentional activity may be contingent, normative, creative, or purposeful;
- Intentional activity generates the intentional ecology of TESOL.

Figure 2 is a visual representation of the model. The contextual dimension in the figure includes the four aspects of intentionality – individual, shared, derived, and sociocultural – which comprise the intentional ecology of TESOL. This dimension also represents a stratification of the ecology of TESOL. This stratification suggests a more concrete structuring of TESOL in which each aspect of intentionality represents a smaller-scale system nested in the ecology of TESOL. Thus, individual intentionality is associated with the agentic contribution of individual TESOL participants; shared intentionality is associated with small collectives in L2 classrooms and other TESOL settings; derived intentionality represents external or material resources in TESOL; and sociocultural aspects of intentionality are associated with the norms and expectations of TESOL

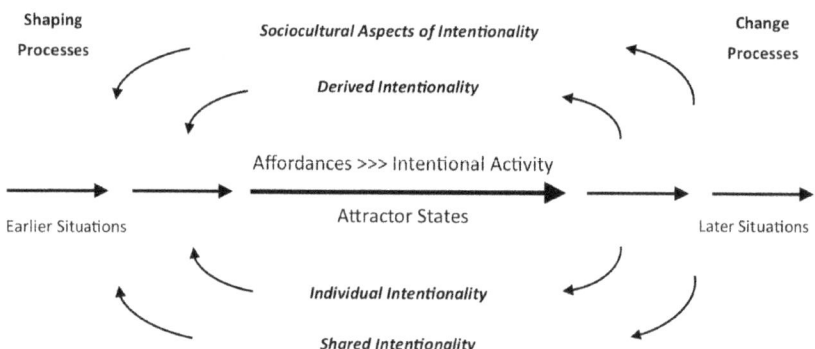

Figure 2: Model of the intentional dynamics of TESOL.

as a profession and society more generally. At the same time, this is an analytical stratification, with individual, derived, shared, and sociocultural aspects each representing a different sub-system of TESOL as an overarching intentional ecology.

Affordances, intentional activity, and attractor states are at the centre of the model. The model suggests that the four aspects of intentionality all shape affordances, our intentional activity, and possible attractor states. This includes the ideational intentionality of our psychological states (beliefs, intentions, and more), whether as individual or shared intentionality, as well as the derived and sociocultural aspects of ideational intentionality present in TESOL contexts. Thus, the various aspects of intentionality "come together" in situations, to soft-assemble (see section 3.1) affordances, intentional activity, and attractor states. This part of the model captures the human-environment mutuality of Ecological Psychology (Good 2007), with derived and sociocultural aspects of the intentional ecology (in the upper half of the figure) coming together with individual and shared intentionality (in the lower half of the figure) to shape affordances and activity. As distinct from Ecological Psychology, our mutualism includes the possibility of both individual and collaborative agentive configurations. Thus, the agentive contribution that specifies affordances, and which shapes intentional activity, may at times be individual, and at times be collaborative.

The right-hand side of the figure suggests how intentional activity changes the intentional ecology of TESOL. Intentional activity reproduces, or changes, individual, shared, derived, and sociocultural intentionality, and hence also the intentional ecology of TESOL as a whole. Moreover, the different types of intentional activity act differently to change the different aspects of the intentional ecology, with,
- contingent activity ensuring the possibility of both stability and change;
- normative activity reproducing the intentional ecology;
- creative activity representing a search for new possibilities; and
- purposeful activity having the potential to change the intentional ecology.

The model of intentional dynamics applies to activity in all domains of TESOL, whether this be learners' classroom activity, teachers' lesson planning or actual teaching, material designers doing needs analyses or writing textbooks, or decision-makers creating policy. As pointed out in chapter 3, all activity is local, all activity is complex and dynamic, and each domain of activity in TESOL is, therefore, subject to the intentional dynamics depicted in Figure 2. That said, the perspective we adopt is important. The activity of particular TESOL stakeholders is governed by action-perception cycles, and will be shaped, therefore, by the perceptual and interpretive resources and horizons of such particular stakeholders. In this respect, the activity of each learner in a classroom will be shaped by a slightly different intentional ecology, and the activity of teachers will be shaped by a different intentional ecology as compared to the activity of a policy-maker. The role of power, and how this affects agency, may complicate the picture further, and this will receive separate attention in chapter 11. In sum, according to the model, the activity of stakeholders across all the domains of TESOL will be shaped by intentional dynamics, and all stakeholders' activity has the potential to either reproduce or change aspects of the intentional ecology of TESOL.

The model of the intentional dynamics of TESOL is a model of context (the nested systems/sub-systems of the intentional ecology), a model of activity (the soft-assembly of affordances and intentional activity), and a model of outcomes (attractor states and a continually changing intentional ecology of TESOL). As a model of context, it suggests how different aspects of TESOL are interconnected. In CDST terms, the model draws boundaries that highlight those aspects of the intentional ecology that give shape to activity, it focuses on the types of activity that generate stability and change in the intentional ecology, and it focuses on those aspects of TESOL that may change – over time. As a model of activity, the model highlights how affordances for activity arise, through the soft-assembly of different aspects of intentionality in situations. The model also captures how intentional activity in earlier situations (the horizontal arrows on the left of the figure) *feeds forward* to shape current affordances and intentional activity, and how the current intentional activity will *feed forward* to shape the affordances for activity in later situations (the horizontal arrows on the right of the figure). As a model of outcomes, it suggests that intentional activity may settle into attractor states, and it highlights, then, how intentional activity may change the individual, shared, derived and sociocultural aspects of the intentional ecology of TESOL.

It is pertinent at this point to comment on our use of the term "intentional dynamics". Although the term is not new, *how we define intentional dynamics is new*. Two previous uses of the term, which have been influential for us, are those of Young et al. (2002) and Juarrero (1999). These authors have focused on what we have called ordinary intentionality (see section 4.1). Young et al.'s ecological analysis of intentional dynamics focuses on how intentions may cause the selection of one affordance over another, and Juarrero's complex dynamic systems analysis focuses on how human intentions emerge, and how they may be recognised. Our "intentional dynamics", by contrast, describes an intentional ecology comprised of a continual interplay of individual, shared, derived, and sociocultural aspects of ideational intentionality, how this interplay gives rise to affordances and intentional activity in situations, possible attractor states, and how, in turn, intentional activity may change the intentional ecology of TESOL. We must recognise, also and again, the contribution that Searle (1983) has made to our work. Searle provided what for us was a pragmatic re-interpretation of the aboutness of intentionality, and this enabled us to understand the interconnectivity of meaningful information in TESOL (see section 4.1). Searle, however, was not explicit about the ecological interplay of different aspects of intentionality, and he did not address our more abstract sociocultural aspect of intentionality.

Finally, the model of the intentional dynamics is a model of both meaning and meaning-making. The model suggests that meaning resides in the great variety of intentionality present in the intentional ecology of TESOL. Individual TESOL stakeholders will experience this meaning directly, through the ideational intentionality of psychological states, both cognitive and affective, in particular situations. Teachers may *believe* that what they see happening in a classroom is useful for their learners; learners may *desire* that the teacher changes what she is doing; a parent may *hope* that their child does well on a test; and a Director of Studies may *intend* to introduce a new curriculum to her school. The psychological states of *believing*, *desiring*, *hoping*, and *intending* all have ideational intentionality; they all represent ideas about ourselves, others, or the environment. Taking a broader perspective, language teaching as a meaningful activity has both historical and geographic reach. Over decades, and in some places centuries, people have engaged in language education, and from their language education activity the recognisable field of TESOL has emerged. This includes people doing language teaching together, and thus developing shared intentionality; it includes people beginning to refer to themselves as materials writers, managers, and policymakers focused on teaching and learning languages; and it includes the appearance of teaching and curricular materials, and policies and practices, with the meaningful information of TESOL assigned/sedimented into derived intentionality for the profession. The interplay between individual, shared, and derived intentionality, as well as emerging sociocultural aspects, constitutes TESOL as an intentional ecology and a complex dynamic system. Moreover, this meaningful ecology is, as any complex dynamic system, always in motion. Our intentional activity is meaningful because it is shaped by the intentional ecology of TESOL, and intentional activity is meaning-making because it reproduces and changes the intentional ecology. In sum, the model of intentional dynamics suggests that meaning (the intentional ecology of TESOL) enables meaning-making (our intentional activity in TESOL) and that this meaning-making reproduces, and sometimes changes, the meaningful information of the intentional ecology of TESOL.

5.5 Looking forward: Our use of the model

We wish to conclude with a look at how we will be using the model of intentional dynamics to explore TESOL contexts, activity, and outcomes. This is both an initial statement about how we operationalize the model, and a look forward to later chapters, where we make use of the model to make sense of a number of TESOL situations.

One dimension of the model of intentional dynamics is the four aspects of the intentional ecology (see section 4.2). In the four chapters that follow, we will focus on the emergence and shaping influence of individual, shared, derived, and sociocultural aspects of the intentional ecology of TESOL. Chapter 6 will look at the intentional dynamics of practicing language teachers becoming researchers, while attending a UK-based distance Masters programme. Thus, we focus on the individual intentionality of the teachers – the researcher intentionality that they develop. In chapter 7, we focus on the emergence and shaping influence of a shared intentionality among learners in a Norwegian primary English language classroom. In chapter 8, we discuss derived and sociocultural aspects of the intentional ecology of a Greek young learner context, and how these aspects appeared to shape and constrain curricular innovation. Finally, chapter 9 takes a step back, and offers a broader discussion of the shaping influence of sociocultural intentional structures of the intentional ecology of TESOL. Each of these chapters, then, has a specific focus on one aspect of the intentional ecology of TESOL. At the same time, however, each chapter recognises the other aspects of intentionality that comprise intentional ecologies, and thus that there are broader intentional dynamics at play in every TESOL context.

Another dimension of the model of intentional dynamics is the different types of intentional activity (see section 5.3), and how these generate stability or change. Chapter 6, which focuses on practicing language teachers developing individual intentionality, also includes a specific focus on purposeful intentional activity in generating the teachers' individual researcher intentionality. Chapter 7, which primarily addresses the emergence and impact of shared intentionality, in addition discusses the interplay of normative, contingent, and creative intentional activity. Later chapters also make reference to the generative potential of different types of intentional activity. Chapter 10, where we reconceptualise language learning as "intentional becoming", makes extensive reference to how contingent, normative, creative, and purposeful intentional activity contributes, in different ways, to the language learning process. Finally, chapter 11 looks at how creative and purposeful intentional activity may support what we call a "critical-intentional perspective", leading to action focused on challenging normative assumptions, as well as unjust orders of power and inequality, in TESOL.

Affordances and attractor states are a further dimension of the model of intentional dynamics. Chapter 7, which explores the emergence and shaping influence of shared intentionality among a group of Norwegian young language learners, suggests that the shared intentionality that emerged in this classroom acted as local-in-time attractor state. Chapter 8 provides a detailed analysis of the affordances associated with the derived intentionality of the learning materials used by a Greek language school. The chapter suggests that these affordances constituted an "affordance landscape" (Kostoulas 2018) that shaped teaching and learning. Moreover, the chapter explores how this affordance landscape appeared to combine with idiosyncratic intentional structures in this setting, comprising a form-focused attractor state that shaped teaching and learning in the school. Chapter 9 explores sociocultural intentional structures in international TESOL, and how the morphogenetic change of international TESOL appears to be governed by an overall transactional attractor state. Finally, as part of chapter 11, which develops a critical-intentional perspective for TESOL, we suggest that normative assumptions, which underpin unjust social orders, may be attractor states.

Part B: **Exemplifying the model of intentional dynamics**

Chapter 6
Individual intentionality: Language teachers becoming researchers

This is the first chapter that exemplifies intentional dynamics in TESOL contexts and activity. In this chapter, we look at the intentional dynamics of practicing English language teachers "becoming researchers", while completing a UK-based, online MA TESOL programme. We focus on the developing individual intentionality (see chapter 4) of these teachers, whilst recognising that becoming a researcher involves other aspects of intentional ecologies. Thus, we will make reference, also, to various shared, derived, and sociocultural aspects (see section 4.2) of the teachers' professional intentional ecology, the intentional ecology of the world of research, as well as the intentional ecology for teacher development created by the pedagogy of the online MA TESOL programme.

The first section of this chapter (6.1) establishes how the intentional ecologies of language teaching and research, respectively, may differ. The next section (6.2) presents a case study of a small group of language teachers becoming researchers whilst attending the UK-based online MA TESOL programme. The case study draws on our model of intentional dynamics (see chapter 5) to understand the teachers' developing individual intentionality focused on doing research. There is a particular focus, also, on the contribution of purposeful intentional activity (see section 5.3) in the teachers becoming researchers. A final section (6.3) provides a more general discussion of the challenge associated with teachers bridging between the potentially distinct intentional ecologies of teaching and research.

Before we proceed, we must recognise that much of this chapter, and the case study in particular, relies on continuing joint research and professional collaboration with Dr Richard Fay, of the University of Manchester (see Stelma and Fay 2014; Fay and Stelma 2016). Richard Fay's name appears in this chapter, as one of the two tutors on the MA TESOL course unit that we explore.

6.1 The intentional ecologies of teaching and research

Examining the experience of practicing language teachers becoming researchers, as we will do in the coming section, reveals differences between the worlds of teaching and research. Thus, we first want to outline how we view this difference from the perspective of our notion of intentional ecologies. In doing this, we are conscious of, and will return to, the many attempts to align the worlds of teaching and research into a more unitary "mind-set", whether as Action Research (Carr and Kemmis 1986; Edge 2007; Edwards and Burns 2016), teacher or practitioner research (Cochran-Smith and Lytle 1990; Reis-Jorge 2005), or – as native to TESOL – Exploratory Practice (Allwright 2003; Allwright and Lenzuen 1997; Hanks 2015). Given the focus on individual intentionality, we are concerned with teachers as agents, engaging with particular situations of teaching, development, and research. For this reason, we use Donald Schön's ([1983] 1991) conceptualisation of reflective practice, and – as we proceed – we draw some parallels between Schön's work and our own framework of intentional dynamics. Using both Schön and our framework, we argue that teaching differs from the activities of teacher professional development (to a lesser extent) and research (to a greater extent), and that each of these activities is associated with distinct intentional ecologies, which may place very different demands on language teachers.

Teaching as a distinct agentive activity, shaped by professional aspects of the intentional ecology of TESOL, may be understood using Schön's (1991) notions of *action-present* and *appreciative systems*. Schön's reflecting-in-practice is bounded by the action-present of the teacher, including the preparatory activity, classroom, learners, and teaching that constitutes the teachers' present experience. This action-present only loosely refers to "present-time"; in fact, Schön suggested an action-present could stretch over weeks or months. In our own view, the more significant meaning of Schön's "present" is the "presence" of activity and situations defined by a particular appreciative system that frames the teacher's professional context. Schön was not precise in his definition of appreciative system, but he appears to have viewed it as a type of "self-reinforcing system of knowing-in-practice" (1991: 282). Crucially, Schön (1991: 272) emphasised the need for constancy of the appreciative system.

> Constancy of appreciative system is an essential condition for reflection-in-action. It is what makes possible the initial framing of the problematic situation, and it is also what permits the inquirer to reappreciate the situation in light of its back-talk [. . .] If [. . .] there were a sudden shift of appreciative system, inquiry would no longer have the quality of a reflective conversation with the situation.

We believe that teachers' experience of an action-present, with their thinking-in-action shaped by a particular appreciative system, resembles our intentional dynamics, with situations of intentional activity shaped by a particular professional intentional ecology. This situated view of teaching and teacher thinking, defined by an action-present and a familiar appreciative system, may be contrasted with situations of *teacher development* that "remove" teachers from their action-present, allowing them to take a step back to focus on methods, their own teaching, or the relationship between their teaching and learning outcomes. Such "out-of-context" teacher development activity is rightfully framed in terms of reflection *on* practice (Edge 2011; Farrell 2014, 2016). Following Schön, reflection *on* practice involves a shift in appreciative systems. In our own terminology, out-of-context teacher development will be shaped by a different intentional ecology than that of teaching itself, and will have its own unique technical vocabulary to highlight specific aspects of pedagogy and teacher thinking. In fact, out-of-context teacher development often asks teachers to engage with theories (i.e., derived intentionality) that may originate in the intentional ecology of academia.

Doing research involves yet another shift of appreciative system. The world of research has its own intentional ecology (or ecologies), with epistemologies that differ a great deal from those of the world of teaching. The difference is particularly clear in the case of university-based TESOL researchers attempting to make contributions to the knowledge-base of TESOL (e.g., what we are doing as we write this book). However, the difference is evident, also, for some approaches to research originally intended to be "for" teachers. For instance, when Wallace (1998: 4) defines Action Research as "systematically collecting data on your everyday practice and analysing it in order to come to some decisions about what your future practice should be", we see terminology that feels unconnected to the day-to-day activity of teaching, including "systematically collecting data" and "analysing" this data.

One possible conclusion is that a teacher wishing to do all three – teaching, teacher development, and research – needs to be attuned to three different appreciative systems – or three different intentional ecologies. The teacher must be "fluent" in teaching, "fluent" in the jargon of teacher development, and "fluent" in the concepts and approaches of research. Clearly this is problematic, and again there are a number of efforts in TESOL to understand teaching, teacher development, and teacher research as something more unified. At this point in the chapter, however, we will "run with" the suggestion that if teachers wish to do research, or to become researchers, it means that they have to move between their own familiar professional intentional ecology, and the potentially new and unfamiliar intentional ecology of research. This move between two distinct intentional ecologies, perhaps bridged by an overlapping intentional ecology of teacher development, is – we suggest – a non-trivial challenge.

6.2 Teachers becoming researchers: A case study

This case study explores a group of practicing language teachers' developing individual intentionality as researchers (see also Stelma and Fay 2014). The teachers' experience was in the context of a research course unit on a UK-based MA TESOL programme, which the participants did through online study, whilst continuing their language teaching jobs in their respective international contexts. We start by describing the intentional ecologies that the participants had to relate to, and what was the rationale for, and pedagogy of, the research unit. This is followed by the actual case study, detailing the challenges that the participants faced in developing their individual researcher intentionality.

6.2.1 The intentional ecologies at play in the course unit

The participant language teachers were doing a UK-based MA TESOL programme in a "distance" or "online" mode of study, in part relying on an online Virtual Learning Environment (VLE). The 13 teacher participants were experienced professionals, and all worked as language educators in different contexts around the world whilst doing the MA part-time. Thus, the participants had at least two distinct intentional ecologies that they needed to relate to. On the one hand, as English language education professionals, they had to relate to the shared, derived, and sociocultural aspects of the intentional ecologies of their workplace contexts. This included national contexts as diverse as Japan, Qatar, Italy, and the UK, and institutional contexts ranging from public schools and universities, private institutes teaching students of different ages, as well as non-school settings such as online language education. Most of the participants were doing the UK-based MA degree for professional development purposes, and the MA curriculum had been adjusted, where possible, to recognise this professional development motive. However, a UK Masters programme is also considered an academic qualification, and it should therefore prepare participants for further advanced study (e.g., doctoral study). Thus, the curriculum showed a concern, also, with the academically-located intentional ecologies of theory and research, thereby going beyond what might be optimal for the teachers' needs as language education professionals.

6.2.2 The pedagogy and data

Here, we focus on a research course unit on the UK-based MA TESOL programme. It was the last unit in the taught part of the participants' MA programme, and was designed to prepare them for more independent research in the subsequent MA dissertation stage. Thus, the development of their individual intentionality as researchers was a key focus of this unit. The unit included introductions to different forms of "teacher research", such as Action Research and Exploratory Practice. However and again, the MA also served as preparation for individuals who might wish to proceed to further academic study. Thus, whilst attempting to remain relevant to the participants' professional contexts, the pedagogy of the unit was designed to give the participants opportunities to develop individual intentionality as defined by the intentional ecology of research.

The actual progression of the participants through the unit was shaped by an experiential model of learning (Whiteman and Oliver 2008; Winn 1995), with the participants doing a small pilot study that trialled a data gathering method, and a form of data analysis that the participants might be using in their later independent dissertation work. More generally, the small pilot study was conceived by the derived intentionality present in the course unit materials, VLE postings, and email messages as a "developing researcher competence" experience (see Stelma and Fay 2014). In the present chapter, we refer to this "developing researcher competence" dimension as the participants' *developing research intentionality*. Figure 3 provides a "bird's eye view" of the pedagogy, and how it sought to balance the dual focus on professional relevance and researcher competence/intentionality. The figure captures movement along two dimensions. The vertical dimension in the figure represents the – already mentioned – distinction between the intentional ecologies of teaching and of research. The other dimension captures the distinction between "becoming a researcher" and "being a researcher". Finally, the figure as a whole describes the overall intentional ecology of the MA course unit, and it alludes to possible intentional dynamics (to be discussed in subsequent sections) that the course unit pedagogy encouraged.

As shown in Figure 3, the experiential process started with a "professional puzzle" framed by the intentional ecology of the participants' own workplace (north-east quadrant in the figure). Next, the participants responded to their puzzles through doing a small pilot study. Doing the small study was supported by a systematic series of pedagogical steps, including refining the focus, formulating a research question, designing a data gathering instrument, gathering data, and then processing, analysing, and interpreting this data (see Stelma and Fay 2014). By keeping the study small, including a single research question, a single research method, and gathering only a small amount of data (e.g., a single interview), the pedagogy ensured that the participants had ample time for in-depth engagement with the intentional ecology of research, thereby developing their intentionality as researchers (south-east quadrant). Towards the end of the

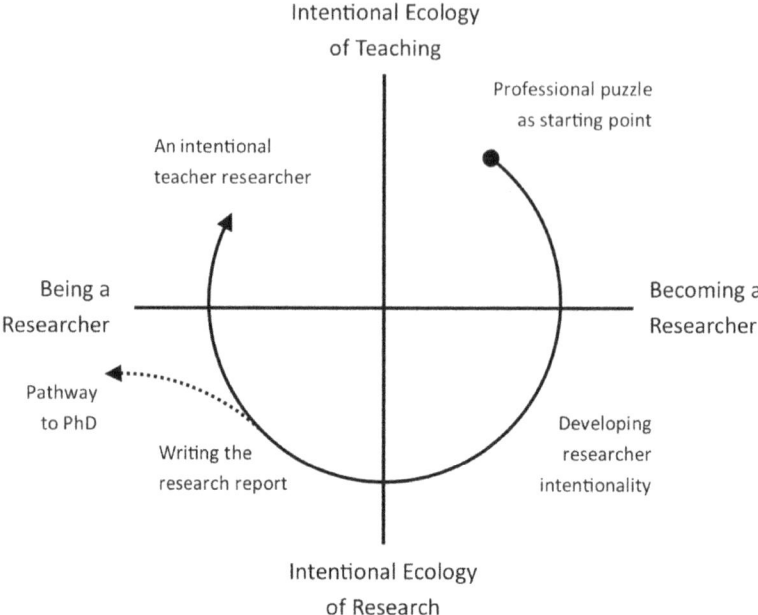

Figure 3: The pedagogy of the research unit.

course unit, the participants had to write an assignment (south-west quadrant). The main component of this assignment was a research report, but also asked for a reflective part where the participants discussed their developing researcher intentionality, looked forward to their MA dissertations, and considered what might be the value of doing research as part of their further professional development as teachers (north-west quadrant). This process represented a sequence of purposeful activity. The initial identification of a puzzle was purposeful from a professional standpoint. Next, the purpose shifted to developing researcher intentionality. This was followed by the assignment writing stage, which purpose was to display their newly developed researcher intentionality. Finally, the additional reflective piece of writing provided opportunities to make purposeful connections to future academic and professional situations.

The following sub-sections analyse the actual experiences of the teacher participants on this MA course unit. The data that we use was gathered, with all the participants' permission, from the VLE discussion forum, from email exchanges, as well as from the assignments that the participants wrote. Real names have been used for those participants who gave their explicit permission for this; for the remaining participants we have used pseudonyms.

6.2.3 Participants' professional intentional ecology as starting point

As encouraged by the pedagogy, the participants' starting points were indeed shaped by their own professional intentional ecologies (north-east quadrant in Figure 3). Extracts 1 through 3 illustrate the types of professional starting points that the participants adopted, including reference to how the puzzles were experienced in their teaching contexts, and alluding to the professional significance of researching the puzzles.

Extract 1: Marco's puzzle
I want to investigate how middle school students at an international school acquire art-related vocabulary and apply to in their discussions about art [. . .] I want to investigate this topic is because I am currently teaching art to middle school students at an international school, and I have noticed that, while my students seem to "acquire" art-related vocabulary and apply it in structured situations with relative ease, they often do not use this vocabulary when discussing art outside of these focused sessions [. . .] I want to better understand their vocabulary acquisition processes so that I can improve the way that I teach, with the ultimate goal of enabling students to talk about a piece of art eloquently, critically and in depth.

Extract 2: Paul's puzzle
I am interested in exploring how and why students use L1 when completing tasks in groups in my oral English classes [. . .] I work in a High School in Japan and am constantly battling to get the kids to speak English. I have begun to consider that the students speaking Japanese may not actually be quite the negative thing I once thought. I would also be interested in how different types of task affect the language produced (Japanese) and whether the teacher actually has any influence over this in terms of task introduction and presentation.

Extract 3: Caroline's puzzle
What strategies, if any, do Arab learners use in reading IELTS text? [. . .] for a long time now, I have puzzled as to why my students (mostly of Arab nationalities) have difficulty with reading comprehension where reading is achieved through a meaning-construction process [. . .] My hunch to the reason for this problem is that they probably lack good reading strategies. A rough survey of IELTS results at the [name of institution] revealed that a higher number of candidates do not get the required band in mostly the reading section compared to the other [sections].

In sum, there were clear professional purposes provided for the participant starting points. Next, the pedagogy suggested that the participants interrogate their puzzles, so as to delineate in more detail what they wished to research. This interrogation was meant to culminate in a specific research question that had to be "answerable by research". The interrogation of the puzzles was also meant to surface any hunches that a participant had in relation to their puzzle, something which would aid reflexivity at later stages of the research process. In this way, formulating a research question acted as an early "bridge" between their professional intentional ecology and the intentional ecology of research, which they were asked to enter into. However, there was a "competition" of purposes here – what Young et al. (2002) refer to as "dynamics of intentions" – with the participant teachers wishing to do more professionally focused reading on the puzzles. This wish appeared to be guided by their belief that a researcher should know a lot about the topic of the research, including being able to identify a "gap" in the literature. By contrast, the pedagogy of the research unit encouraged the participants to move on to the research process itself. This was, in part, because the participants had written multiple professionally focused assignments, already, as part of their MA TESOL programme. Thus, this was an instance where the idiosyncratic intentional ecology of the course unit itself, and the MA programme, constrained the participants' activity.

6.2.4 Developing researcher intentionality

The participant teachers now moved to the purposeful activity of developing their researcher intentionality, as structured by the intentional ecology of research (south-east quadrant in Figure 3). In an early posting, Tutor 1 (Juup Stelma) gave the following summary of what was expected.

> Extract 4: Instructions to the participants for the becoming researcher stage
> [The pilot study is] an opportunity to develop your competence as a researcher. This process of development has already started, and each posting here in [name of VLE] and each of your own diary entries (for steps 1, 2, 3 etc.) are data to understand your development. This process must include a great deal of time and space for reflection [. . .] So, the pilot study is not about designing a study that will guarantee good findings. The dissertation will be more about findings, so there will be an opportunity later for this. At this point you have an opportunity to take some risks, experiment with a research method, and things that work less well are opportunities for reflection/learning [. . .] Ideally, you want a clear manageable focus, a single research question and one research method that is capable of generating a bit of data that you can use to respond to your one research question.

In other words, having identified a puzzle from their own professional context (see section 6.2.3), the pedagogy now expected the participants to shift intentional ecologies – to that of the world of research. Figure 4, which mirrors the model of intentional dynamics presented as Figure 2 (see p. 80), shows the flows of meaningful information and learning that we sought to encourage. The participants were expected to engage with the derived intentionality of the research methods literature, as well as the broader sociocultural aspects of research (the top half of Figure 4). This, then, should shape their research and learning activity at this stage of the course unit (middle part of the figure). In turn, their activity would generate, through the process of morphogenesis (see section 3.1), new individual and shared intentionality as researchers (bottom half of Figure 4). The purpose of this stage of the pedagogy, therefore, was to develop the participants' individual and shared intentionality – to encourage them to become intentional researchers. Finally, at the start of the process, the participants' embryonic individual or shared researcher intentionality would have a smaller impact on activity – hence the dotted "lines of influence" in the bottom left of Figure 4. However, as the following discussion will show, this changed as the participants began to develop their own intentionality as researchers.

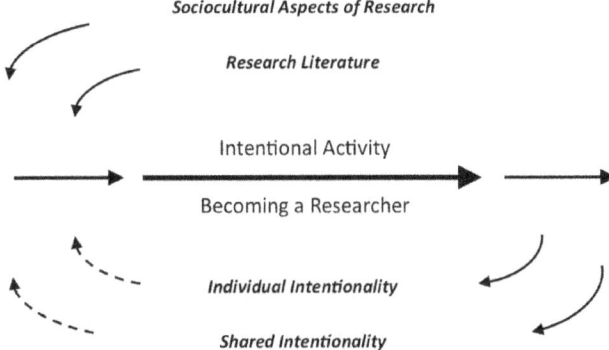

Figure 4: The intentional dynamics of becoming a researcher.

In addition to the continuing instinct to engage with the professionally-focused literature, the participants struggled with the advice that the pilot study was "not about designing a study that will guarantee good findings" (see extract 4). They seemed attracted to different intentional dynamics, seeking to "solve" the puzzles they had identified, to answer their research questions as fully as possible, and for their research to make a contribution to the world of teaching. However, in the spirit of "learning to walk before learning to run", the message emphasising developing researcher intentionality – i.e., keeping things small and using the research methods literature to problematize their use of research methods – was repeated with regularity. The participants, though, countered with repeated requests for clarification, as exemplified by extract 5 – to which both tutors, one after the other, responded "Absolutely".

> Extract 5: Anthony
> So, should the research method produce limited or even no data regarding answering my research question, even though I might have argued it as being a research method I feel might best provide relevant data regarding my research question, is that still okay for the purposes of this pilot study?

The advice to keep it small, and that the purpose of the course unit was to develop researcher intentionality, was also rehearsed in relation to the specific research activity that the participants were engaged in, as is evident from the exchange initiated by Paul in extract 6. Paul's small pilot study focused on the use of L1 in task-based learning (see extract 2), he had audio-recorded two language learners, and only 80% of his 8 minutes of recorded data was "on task".

> Extract 6: Paul
> With only about 80% of about 8 minutes of video data, is this really sufficient? The students only use Japanese a handful of times during the recording so I really only have very limited examples to work with. Can I draw any kind of conclusions based on such a limited amount of data?

The tutors' response followed quickly (extract 7), and again emphasised that the purposeful activity that the participants were expected to engage in was to develop their intentionality as researchers.

> Extract 7: Tutor 1
> If you video-record classroom interaction, the potential richness of the data is enormous. Coming to grips with this as a data gathering method, including the many ways in which to analyse the data, will then be an important outcome of your pilot study (in terms of developing researcher competence). To allow space and time for this learning to occur I suggest video-recording one, or maximum, two task performances (even if the tasks are quite short).

When enough of the participants seemed to understand the purpose of this stage of the pedagogy, they started to offer advice to each other, contributing to a shared intentionality focused on becoming researchers. Thus, what was being created by the course unit was a pedagogical space, or a local-in-time intentional ecology, that facilitated purposeful intentional activity focused on becoming researchers. Extracts 8 and 9 illustrate the intentional dynamics that this local-in-time intentional ecology enabled. Extract 8 shows Ralitza describing her intention to use two different research methods – questionnaires and diaries. This is followed by Marco's response to Ralitza (extract 9), echoing the tutors repeated advice about keeping it small, and recognising that the diary method was more central in Ralitza's thinking.

Extract 8: Ralitza
I've decided to gather the data through questionnaires that might lead to discussions and diaries. Students will be asked to keep a diary of their learning difficulties/feeling [. . .] I will also be keeping a diary of the experience of doing the learner training session, which at the moment I am contemplating as a dedicated lesson a day for the first month and then 15–20 mins a day of reflection and planning for the remaining of the course. Any comments?

Extract 9: Marco
I guess one question that comes to mind is, for the pilot study, do you need to have questionnaires also? Or would you be using those more for the dissertation? I don't know, but it might be simpler just to stick with one [method] for the small-scale Pilot Study [. . .] just a thought:)

Over time, the pedagogical interactions allowed the participants to demonstrate increasingly sophisticated researcher intentionality. Such more sophisticated individual intentionality is exemplified by Chloe's carefully crafted response (extract 11) to Philip's concern about "representativeness" and being able to "generalize" findings (extract 10).

Extract 10: Philip
As for the research method, I'm most swayed by using a semi-structured interview with a small sample of student volunteers from about 50 students who are studying in this class (in 2 separate sections), and doing an audio recording of the interviews. I'd probably settle for 6–10 students [. . .] I do however recognize drawbacks with the method I'm considering, for example [. . .] such a small sample may not present any generalisable findings.

Extract 11: Chloe
I noticed from your questions that you were slightly concerned about representativeness re. your interview sample. If it helps, I'm only interviewing one person for my pilot, I expect it to take about an hour, and because I'm only interviewing one person, there's no way that person can be "representative" of the broader context. It's still a valid contribution to the pilot – it helps you to assess the use of an interview as a research tool, and will still (hopefully) produce some valuable data – and help to inform you about possible interesting directions you might be able to follow for the dissertation in terms of content. I'm not expecting my one interview to produce any "generalisable findings" at all.

In sum, the pedagogy asked the participants to engage in purposeful pedagogical interactions. Moreover, the "learning-by-doing" model gradually shifted the participants towards increasingly purposeful research activity, thereby developing their individual intentionality as researchers. This purposeful activity extended across formulating their research question, designing their small pilot study, deciding on their data generation method, gathering, processing and analysing their data, as well as interpreting the value of their findings.

6.2.5 Writing the research report: Being intentional researchers

As they came to the end of their pilot studies, the teacher participants were asked to write an assignment, whose main component was a research report. This represented a shift to "being researchers", engaged the participants in assigning derived intentionality to paper, and was an opportunity to demonstrate their newly developed researcher intentionality (south-west quadrant in Figure 3). However, as the participants worked on this report, the "becoming a researcher" focus was still "alive", with a great deal of discussion about how to "report" on research. For instance, in extract 12, Chloe is wondering about how much of her transcript (of an interview) to include in the research report, and in extract 13 Tutor 2 (Richard Fay) responds by – again – emphasising being purposeful.

> Extract 12: Chloe
> I was planning to include my entire transcription as an Appendix – this is very long, 24 sides of A4 – and there are others to include as well – is this okay?

> Extract 13: Tutor 2
> You should have a good rationale for including the whole thing. Why isn't the inclusion of a sample of your transcription work sufficient? [. . .] As in all things, purposefulness and transparency are the best guides here. Have a good reason for including things and re interview transcripts, a sample surely makes transparent your transcription work to your reader? What is gained by giving it them all?

Similarly, in extract 14 Paul can be seen wondering about how to represent the bilingual aspect of his research.

> Extract 14: Paul
> When transcribing Japanese I used the original Japanese script in order to maintain authenticity and also make it really clear where Japanese is being used. It really stands out from the Roman alphabet. In terms of a final copy I was thinking of writing phonetic reading underneath (Roman alphabet) and then a translation under that. Is this going to make my transcription messy? Would it be okay to omit the phonetic transcription or would it be better to get rid of the original Japanese script as it is unreadable by most?

Tutor 2's response again stressed purposefulness ("depends on the purpose of the transcription") and transparency ("they need to be able to see exactly what is what from your work"). The teacher participants, now acting as researchers, also demonstrated independent decision-making, showing that their engagement with the intentional ecology of research had resulted in a great deal of individual intentionality focused on doing and writing about research, as evident from Miriam's perfectly intentional comment about the use of graphs in extract 15.

> Extract 15: Miriam
> Before I started writing, I thought I would add a bunch of them [graphs] to make the finished product look spiffy and impressive. Now that I have a near final draft, I've noticed I've only used two graphs [. . .] One depicts the differences in the use of LLSs [Language Learning Strategies] between male and female students (one bar for each of the six strategies). The other depicts the differences in male/female usage for particular questions on my survey which I show raised a red flag of concern for me [. . .] I could go back and sprinkle the assignment with some more graphs, but to be honest, the writing doesn't really call for it and it may come off looking like party sprinkles.

In sum, the participants' assignment writing was an exercise in "being intentional researchers", as shaped by the individual intentionality that they had developed, by intentionality shared with their classmates, and by the derived intentionality present in the research literature that they were consulting and citing in their reports.

6.2.6 Navigating different intentional ecologies

At the start of this chapter, we quoted Schön (1991: 272), who argued that "constancy of appreciative system is an essential condition for reflection-in-action". The course unit deliberately engaged the teacher participants with the appreciative system, or intentional ecology, of research. When experiencing becoming a part of this intentional ecology, the participants' reflection will have been *in-action*. We believe this was a successful experience of becoming researchers. The end-state of this process – individual researcher intentionality – was on display in the reflective comments of the participants, such as Paul's comments in extract 16.

> Extract 16: Paul
> By the very practice of conducting research, my view changed from that of an outsider with little appreciation of the steps involved, to that of an insider, aware of the difficulties that arise when one tries to investigate and understand human behaviour. Reflecting on the process enabled me to develop my researcher competence, and this pilot study represents the author's first tentative steps into the exciting but challenging world of educational research.

However, the participants were also asked to look forward, to the dissertation and their own future professional practice (north-east quadrant in Figure 3). The question, then, is whether the constancy of appreciative systems, which Schön emphasised, were compromised when "looking forward". We need to make a distinction, here, between the participants' reflections on their later dissertation, and their reflections on their future professional practice. Creating a sense of constancy between the small pilot study experiences, which we have described in the previous sections, and the participants' upcoming MA dissertation, may have been more achievable for the participants. The assumption, then, is that the small pilot study and the later dissertation were parts of the same academically-located intentional ecology of the MA TESOL programme. Using Schön's terminology, the participants may have been able to view the two activities as belonging to the same action-present. By contrast, creating constancy between the pilot study experiences and their later professional practice may have posed a greater hurdle for the participants. The possible disconnect, between the worlds of research and teaching, was suggested by a late reflective comment by Miriam (extract 17); note the distinction between the "big plunge", which is experienced with "wide-eyed wonder", and the reference to teaching as her "daily routine".

> Extract 17: Miriam
> TESOL Research is similar to a ride in a glass-bottom boat. Everyone is very excited before the big plunge, full of wide-eyed wonder in the midst of the journey, and a bit disappointed to return to our daily routine when it's all over.

However, there was also a great deal of evidence that meaningful connections were made across these different intentional ecologies. For example, in extract 18 Marco comments on how the pilot study experience shed light on "my students' learning processes" and "caused" him to see his "students and curriculum from a different angle". In the same extract, he is able, in addition, to set out concrete plans for his upcoming dissertation, saying "I will probably pursue the same topic for the dissertation, but in greater depth". Thus, Marco was able to make connections between the intentional ecology of research, his professionally-located intentional ecology, as well as the academically-located (future) intentional ecology of his MA dissertation work.

> Extract 18: Marco
> I felt that the outcomes of my pilot study were quite meaningful in terms of going some way toward answering my research question and shedding some light on my students' learning processes. They have caused me to see my students and curriculum from a different angle, and already I have made some changes to the way I teach as a result of this project [. . .] So I'm thinking I will probably pursue the same topic for my dissertation, but in greater depth – that is, I want to learn more about how my students learn the vocabulary they need to discuss and evaluate art, and how I can get them to move beyond understanding to application of the language they have learned.

We would like to believe, then, that the pedagogical intentional ecology of teacher development, created by the MA TESOL programme, and in this instance the research course unit, did help to connect between the intentional ecologies of research and teaching. Extract 19, showing Caroline's reflection on her developing understanding of her learners' strategy use while reading, provides further evidence of such connecting.

> Extract 19: Caroline
> By knowing what strategies EFL readers actually use when reading, as opposed to what I think they do, I will not only improve my understanding of reading as a communicative act but also my understanding of how it might be taught.

Finally, there was evidence, also, of the teacher participants leveraging what they gained, in terms of individual researcher intentionality, for later professional career progression. This is visible in extract 20, where Anthony suggests that the insight gained from doing research may help him make more informed career choices.

> Extract 20: Anthony
> As I am looking at finding employment in the area of online learning in this country in the future, conducting research in this area would be of value to myself in helping to develop my understanding of the practical issues and problems with using such tools with learners and to better understand and maximize the learning potential of such technology.

In conclusion, whilst there were ample opportunities for the participants to make connections between their professional contexts and research, and some of the participants made such connections, we must emphasise once again that the worlds of teaching and research will, in many cases, represent two distinct intentional ecologies. Using Schön's terminology once again, for some of the participants the two intentional ecologies may have remained distinct, or unconnected, appreciative systems.

6.3 Conclusion: Teachers doing research in TESOL

With ever more being expected of language teachers, we believe that the above case of language teachers becoming researchers, discussed from the perspective of our intentional dynamics model, is of interest to the language teaching profession. Freeman (2016) suggests that the expectations on teachers, in terms of the sorts of thinking they should be engaging in, and in terms of their role in knowledge production, has changed markedly over time. In the 1960s, knowledge and thinking were defined by codified ways of behaving in the classroom (e.g., audio-lingual teaching). In the 1970s, teachers were expected to work faithfully within a method, and the knowledge-base of language teaching was defined by this method (e.g., communicative language teaching). From the 1980s onwards, teachers were increasingly expected to consider the "who" and "where" of language teaching, and thus contribute to the context-specific knowledge of teaching. More recently, Freeman argues, teachers are expected to engage with the purposes of teaching language, and thus contribute to the critical movement in TESOL. Given this gradually expanding role of language teachers, both in terms of modes of thinking and knowledge contribution, the intentional ecologies and intentional activity that language teachers have to engage with, and in, have multiplied.

Alongside the changing expectations on teachers that Freeman describes, there have been a number of more concrete suggestions for how teachers can get involved in doing research. The notion of Action Research, first proposed by Lewin (1946: 35) as research leading to social action rather than "research that produces nothing but books", is frequently evoked. In an earlier part of this chapter, we suggested that Action Research is sometimes described using terminology unconnected to the day-to-day activity of teaching. However, some TESOL scholars have challenged this view of Action Research. For instance, Edge (2007) argues passionately for Action Research as something that teachers can do for their own purposes, and thus not informed by, or seeking to inform, external or generalisable truths. We believe Edge was trying to position Action Research within the intentional ecology, or action-present, of the language teacher and the language classroom. A number of other authors have proposed conceptualisations of teacher research that similarly position such activity within the professional intentional ecology, or action-present, of teachers. Writing for a broader education audience, Carr and Kemmis (1986: 162) have suggested that Action Research is "a form of self-reflective enquiry undertaken by participants in social situations in order to improve the rationality and justice of their own practices, their understanding of these practices, and the situations in which these practices are carried out".

Within TESOL, the most radical proposal may be Exploratory Practice (Allwright 2003; Allwright and Lenzuen 1997; Hanks 2015, 2017). Allwright (2003) argues that it is unrealistic for teachers to engage in "extra" activity that relies on the vocabulary and knowledge of the world of research. In its place, Allwright (2003: 121) suggests that teachers might find "classroom time for deliberate work for understanding, not instead of other classroom activities but by exploiting normal classroom activities for that purpose". Thus, the aim of Exploratory Practice is to develop situated understandings, something which Allwright argues is the basis for a more sustainable model of teacher research. We have a lingering question, though. We strongly agree that teachers' own reflection and knowledge generation is integral to TESOL. Moreover, if we believe that the world of research has no value whatsoever for TESOL, then clearly Edge's and Allwright's positions are the way forward. However, by shielding language teachers from the academically-located intentional ecology of research, we may be throwing out the "baby with the bathwater". We wish to remain open to a variety of options, including adding a research dimension to the intentional ecology of teachers, as suggested by the above-cited authors, as well as valuing the outcomes of research shaped by an intentional ecology distinct from teaching. Thus, our question going forward is how different language teachers, in particular contexts, may engage with, benefit from, and contribute to research differently (see Barkhuizen 2009; Borg 2010). We believe that our conceptualisation of these two worlds, of teaching and of research, as potentially distinct intentional ecologies and with possibly distinct intentional dynamics, may help us to address this question going forward.

Chapter 7
Shared intentionality: Task-based activity in a young learner classroom

In this chapter, we continue to exemplify intentional dynamics in TESOL contexts and activity. Here, we focus on the emergence and shaping influence of shared intentionality among learners in a Norwegian primary English language classroom. In chapter 4, we defined shared intentionality as "sharing psychological states with others whom we engage with". The engagement we will discuss, in this chapter, is Norwegian Year (Grade) 6 learners' repeated engagement with a dialogue-writing and role-play task sequence. This chapter will focus, also, on the role of normative, contingent, and creative intentional activity, as defined and discussed in chapter 5.

Similar to chapter 6, the analysis here is based on empirical data, and we begin with a brief introduction to sociocultural aspects of the intentional ecology of English language education in the Norwegian primary education sector (section 7.1). This is followed by a description of the dialogue-writing and role-play task that the learners did five times over the course of a ten-month period (section 7.2). Next, we document the presence of what we call the "initial normative consensus", or initial shared intentionality, that guided the learners' intentional activity in this Norwegian classroom (section 7.3). We also highlight the contingent and creative activity, and thus adaptive and non-linear dynamic properties, associated with this initial normative consensus (section 7.4), as well as how these adaptive and non-linear properties of the learners' intentional activity prompted a change in the shared intentionality, replacing the initial normative consensus with a shared concern for "being entertaining" (section 7.5). Finally, we consider the nature and role of shared intentionality more broadly, as a social structure that may have pedagogical implications (section 7.6).

7.1 Sociocultural aspects of the Norwegian primary education context

English language teaching in Norway is long established, and for the most part an uncontested element in the curriculum. Norway has a well-established linguistic policy, aimed at preserving its own linguistic heritage, but including also an open attitude to foreign languages. English is the only compulsory foreign language in the school system. At the time the data that we report on here was gathered – in 2002 – English was compulsory from Year 4 in the Primary level. However, soon after this data collection took place, the starting age for English language study was lowered to the first year of Primary school. Most children also study one additional foreign language – usually German, French or Spanish – for a shorter period of time. Thus, the Norwegian education system is effectively operating an "English plus one other foreign language" policy. The English language is commonly viewed as the language of historical friends and allies (older generations), and the language of international exchange, culture, and media (younger generations). Overall, both parents and children view the English language in a positive light, and there is ready access to a variety of educational and social media in the English language. Finally, the particular primary school context we explore in this chapter is government funded, and it tends to be shaped by national curricular norms rather than those of TESOL. For this reason, the sociocultural aspects of the intentional ecology of international TESOL represent a relatively minor influence on this Norwegian context. However, there is certainly a social turn in Norwegian primary education, and a valuing of learning in groups, and these represent intentional structures that mirror some of the broader developments in international TESOL (see chapter 9).

7.2 The data, learners, and task

The data we will look at in this chapter was generated by a larger project aimed at understanding the emergence and pedagogical value of different patterns of learner interaction (Stelma 2003). The identification of shared intentionality in the learner interaction data happened in a later re-analysis (Stelma 2014). The present account is a further look at the emergence and shaping influence of shared intentionality in this data, leveraging the link we have made between different types of intentional activity and the dynamic properties of complex dynamic systems (see chapter 5).

The data was generated through fieldwork in a Year 6 class of a semi-rural Norwegian government primary school. The learners were in their third year of English, and they had two consecutive 45-minute English language lessons every week. In addition, most of the learners had extensive exposure to English through various media (music, television, the internet, and games), and travel. The approximate age of the pupils was 11 years when fieldwork began, and there were eight girls and nine boys in the class. At the end of the fieldwork, the class had moved to Year 7, the English teacher had changed, and they had three non-consecutive

45-minute English language lessons each week. Both the Year 6 and Year 7 English teachers were qualified to teach the English language in the Norwegian primary school system. The Year 6 English teacher had been in the school for three years, and she had previously lived and worked in English-speaking environments. The Year 7 English teacher had worked in the school for several years, and had about 25 years of experience in the Norwegian school system.

We will focus on the emergence and shaping influence of shared intentionality in this class over a ten-month period, focusing on five iterations of the already mentioned dialogue-writing and role-play task sequence. The task sequence asked the learners to work in pairs to compose a dialogue between two fictional people in a pre-determined scenario, and then together perform their dialogue as a role-play in front of the whole class (see Table 7). The data collection included audio-recording of the teacher's instructions, the talk of three learner pairs while writing their dialogues, as well as the subsequent role-play performances. The participants' informal talk in-and-around the task sequence was also recorded (subject to the limitations of a total of three recording devices). The fieldwork was done by one of us (Juup Stelma), who was a minimal participant while observing the classroom, did brief post-observation interviews with the learners and the teacher, and had access to all relevant hand-outs and textbooks (Stelma 2003). We should note that there was no data collection during the fourth iteration – see explanation in a later section.

Table 7: Typical event structure of the role-play task.

Activities
1. Pupils return from their break and settle down
2. Teacher hands out the task sheet and gives instructions
3. Pupils form pairs and find places to work
4. Pairs compose their role-play dialogues
5. Pairs rehearse their role-play dialogues
6 Pairs perform role-plays to the whole class

In each of the five iterations of the task sequence, the role-play scenarios were copied from, adapted from, or more loosely based on exercises in the *Scoop 6* and *Scoop 7* textbook series (Lothe Flemmen and Sørheim 1997, 1998, 1999a, 1999b). The scenarios commonly included a first few lines of dialogue, which the learners could use as a starting point. For instance, the first iteration of the task used the following scenario:

Teacher:	Why have you not done your homework?
Pupil:	I didn't do my homework because I overslept.
Or	I didn't do my homework because I put my books in the barn and the cow ate them. etc.

You can do the same for being late for school.

Teacher:	Why are you late for school today?
Pupil:	I am late for school because I got on the wrong bus.
Or	The doctor told me I was ill.

The Year 6 teacher routinely used English in her instructions to the class, and in the first iteration of the task sequence she went through the task sheet and read the sample dialogue. Then she added: "and it can be a million different reasons why the teacher is upset, right? So it is really up to you guys to figure out what it's all gonna be about". The teacher repeated this point, using different words, to individual learner pairs as they got started with their writing. Thus, the task was open-ended in terms of the meaning-making the learners might engage in.

The following analysis of the emergence of, and change to, shared intentionality across the five iterations of the task focuses on the intentional activity of three learner pairs: (a) Veronica and Karen, (b) Tim and Morten, and (c) Marcus and Dennis (the names are pseudonyms). We begin with a description of a normative consensus, or initial shared intentionality, which seemed to govern the first iteration of the task sequence. Next, we look at contingent and creative aspects of the learners' intentional activity, and we explore how these adaptive and non-linear dimensions of the learners' activity may have contributed to the emergence, over the repeated iterations of the task sequence, of a new shared intentionality. Finally, we look at how the new shared intentionality was questioned by the Year 7 teacher, and his attempt to re-establish a shared intentionality for the task that resembled the original normative consensus.

7.3 The initial normative consensus

In this section, we document a normative consensus that governed the intentional dynamics of the task sequence at the start of the 10-month long period. We consider this consensus "normative" because it appeared to cohere with what was expected by the textbook, the teacher, as well as apparent, although unspoken/unwritten, expectations about how to act in this Norwegian primary classroom (something akin to a "small culture"; see Holliday 1999). When doing the task, the learners were expected to be creative in formulating their own dialogues, but they were also expected to use their English language resources to formulate "good" English dialogues, with attention to lexical and grammatical accuracy. They were expected, also, to complete the task fully and in a timely manner, and at the end to perform their dialogues in front of the whole class with fluency and accuracy. In the following paragraphs, we describe how this normative consensus acted as the initial shared intentionality, including discussion of "agreeing roles", "writing with accuracy", "task completion", and "displaying linguistic competence".

When starting to work together, all three learner pairs that we discuss in this chapter immediately negotiated who would take on which role in the dialogue and the later performance, as exemplified by extract 21. Sometimes the allocation of roles included humour, such as in extract 22, where another anonymous learner joked that Veronica might want to be "neither". Note how in these and later extracts, the central column is an intonation unit-based, bilingual transcription (see Stelma and Cameron 2007) of the learners' original speech. Contextual comments appear in curly brackets, period marks represent shorter pauses, numbers in parentheses represent longer pauses (in seconds), overlapping speech is marked by square brackets, incomplete words are marked by a hyphen, and incomplete utterances by a double hyphen. The right-hand column provides necessary translation (not including pausing, notes or paralinguistic features).

Extract 21
Dennis: Okay
             da er du ehm læreren   then you are the teacher
             {speaking to Marcus}

Extract 22
Veronica: hva er jeg?   what am I?
Anonymous: du er ehm .. enten lærer eller elev   you are either teacher or pupil
             hv hva vil du være?   what do you want to be?
             (2.0)
Anonymous: ingen av dem?   neither?

Another normative element, which all the learner pairs seemed to adopt, was to spend time and attention on writing their dialogues in accurate English. In all the pairs, both learners wrote down the entire dialogue (and not only their own lines), something which encouraged discussion of vocabulary and grammar, as exemplified by extracts 23 and 24.

7.3 The initial normative consensus — 111

Extract 23
Marcus: should- --
(1.0) not shouldn't
(1.0) you shouldn't
. . . vi kan'ke skrive not shouldn't   we can't write 'not shouldn't'
vi må skrive .. you shouldn't --   we have to write 'you shouldn't'
.. vi kan'ke skrive not shouldn't lissom we can't write 'not shouldn't' kind of

Extract 24
Tim: ka er det du skriver nu?   what are you writing now?
Morten: Erik
        . . . how .. did .. you
Tim: å ska vi se åssen skal vi skrive   and let's see how should we write
        det a?   that then?
        .. how skrives ikke det [H O W]?   "how" isn't that written H O W
Morten: [nei det skrives] W H O   no it is written W H O
        (1) nei gjør det ikke det a?   no isn't it like that?

A further element of the normative consensus was a concern with completing the task fully, exemplified by Marcus pointing out that they need to write "something more" in extract 25, and in a timely manner, as exemplified by Tim and Morten asking the teacher how much time there is left in extract 26.

Extract 25
Dennis: nei vi tar det her a   no let's take this
Marcus: Okay
         (1.0) too expensive
         (1.0) ehm vi må skrive noe   but we have to write something
         mer da   more

Extract 26
Tim: ja kor lang tid har vi igjen?   ok how much time do we have left?
          . . .
Morten: ehm ganske mye   quite a lot
Teacher: fem seks {minutes}   five six
Tim: Okay

A final normative element that seemed shared amongst the learner pairs was a wish to get the language of the performance right. It seems, then, that the role-play performances were viewed as a "display" of competence. This was evident both from their talk whilst composing the dialogue, as exemplified by extract 27, and from the eagerness with which all the pairs rehearsed, in pairs, the dialogue before performing to the class. For instance, Morten and Tim went to an adjacent room – the school library – and managed to rehearse their role-play twice. Marcus and Dennis rehearsed their role-play in the classroom, and they had just started their second rehearsal when the teacher stopped them because the performance stage was about to start (see Table 7). Karen and Veronica were late finishing their writing, but managed to rehearse their dialogue once, quietly, whilst the teacher was getting the performances underway.

Extract 27

Marcus:	åssen skrives therefore a?	how is "therefore" written?
Teacher:	Therefore	therefore
Marcus:	derfor? {the word sounds similar in Norwegian}	therefore {in Norwegian}
Teacher:	nei det gjøkke det dere må prøve litt sjøl og nå dere spør om veldig mye som --	no it isn't that you have to try a bit yourselves now you are asking about a lot that
Marcus:	[jamen vi] –	but we
Teacher:	[som] dere ikke prøver på engang	that you don't even try
Marcus:	nei men hvis vi s- -- hvis vi skal ta å .. si det fram er det litt kjipt å si feil å	no but when we when we perform it is a bit sad to say it incorrectly

In sum, these elements seemed to add up to a local (in time and place) common understanding, or what we call shared intentionality (see section 4.2). This shared intentionality included elements that were normative for this task (agreeing roles; task completion), and for this context (writing with accuracy; displaying linguistic competence). Thus, the above-described learner activity constitutes what we have called normative intentional activity, which is associated with the dynamic property of historicity in complex dynamic systems (see section 5.3). This historicity was presumably shaped, also, by individual, derived, and sociocultural aspects of the intentional ecology at play whilst doing this task in this classroom. Some aspects, however, of the intentional dynamics and the broader intentional ecology, were less normative. This is the subject of the next section.

7.4 Early non-linearity in the learners' intentional activity

Alongside, or within, the normative consensus that we described in the previous section, there was, in addition, non-normative activity. This activity was non-normative because it was not encouraged by the teachers' instructions, and/or not evident across all the learner pairs. This additional activity included both contingent and creative intentional activity, which added adaptiveness and non-linearity to the task performances (see section 5.3). We will argue that

7.4 Early non-linearity in the learners' intentional activity

the adaptiveness and non-linearity of the learners' contingent and creative activity contributed to the emergence of a new shared intentionality. This additional intentional activity is exemplified with additional data from the first iteration of the task sequence, and it includes activity characterised by "acting", "formulating entertaining dialogue", and "competing with other pairs".

A first non-normative element of the learners' activity, during the first iteration of the task sequence, was a concern with how to "act" the role-play. Unlike the normative elements of "displaying linguistic competence", the concern for acting was not something that all the learner pairs showed an interest in. Rather, this element seemed to appear spontaneously from time to time, thereby suggesting that it was part of the learners' adaptive response to the task, or what we have called "contingent intentional activity". Extract 28 shows this element arising in Veronica and Karen's learner talk, with Veronica suggesting that the student, which she would be acting in the later performance to the whole class, should appear "unsure" in her response to the teacher, and Karen suggesting that the teacher, which Karen was going to be, should be "strict" (see highlighted words in the extract).

Extract 28
Veronica:	jeg var jeg var ehm ehm ehm ehm --	I was I was
	. . . jeg bare kom ikke	I just didn't come
	nei @ {laughter}	no
	. . . lissom .. være litt [**usikker**]	kind of be a bit **unsure**
Karen:	[ja]	yes
	.. ja	yes
	å så --	and then
	. . . å så etterpå så sier jeg sånn **strengt** atte	and then afterwards I say kind of **strictly** that
	nei du må gi meg et svar	no you have to give me an answer

How to act did not appear to be a concern for the two pairs of boys, with the single exception that when Tim and Morten practised their dialogue Tim did suggest that he use a "dark" (manly) voice when reading the lines of the teacher. Finally, the teacher herself appeared to index the notion of "acting" when, at the start of the performance stage, she commented: "Ja, vi er klare. Publikum er klare" [Yes, we are ready. The audience is ready].

A second element, which did not appear to be part of the initial normative consensus, was a concern with formulating entertaining dialogue. Some of the learner pairs made a lot of deliberately silly suggestions while composing their role-plays, as is evident from extract 29, where Veronica suggests that the pupil's grandmother "almost died". However, most of the learner pairs tended to revert to more conventional, or realistic, dialogues. Indeed, in extract 29 Karen pointed out that the "grandma" suggestion did not fit because the dialogue happened during school hours. Next, Karen suggests not hearing the school bell, signalling the end of recess, as a more realistic excuse for the student in the dialogue.

Extract 29

Veronica:	ehm gikk med bestemor	went with grandma
	hun holt jo på å dø idag og	after all she almost died today
Karen:	jamen det er er før timen	but it is before the next class period
	ho var ute i friminuttet	she was outside for recess
Veronica:	Ja	yes
	[ja]	yes
Karen:	[me]n da kan vi kanskje skrive atter ehm --	but then we can perhaps write that
	je- --	I
	(..) jeg spilte fotball litt lenge	I played football a bit long
	å så (1.0) hørte jeg ikke ringeklokka	and so I didn't hear the bell
Veronica:	Ja	yes

Not all the learner pairs managed to resist the temptation of formulating entertaining dialogues. In extract 30, Marcus tries to resist the dry humour suggested by Dennis – the teacher getting upset about a child wearing brown shoes – by saying "not so silly", and then later "we don't do anything too silly". Note, there are no school uniforms in Norwegian schools, and thus wearing brown shoes does not break any rules. However, a couple of minutes, later Dennis and Marcus did include the suggestion that the pupil was wearing "brown shoes".

Extract 30

Marcus:	Ikke sann oversakelig . . .	not so silly
Dennis:	øj,/	yo
	ja hvorfor har du brune sko på deg,_	why are you wearing brown shoes
	sa ikke jeg igår at du ikke skulle ha på deg brune sko idag igjen./	didn't I tell you yesterday you shouldn't wear brown shoes today?
	(..)	
Marcus:	nei vi tar bare sånn,_	no vi just do like
	why do you come for late da	{da = then}
	(2) vi tar ikke noe for oversaklig./	we don't do anything too silly
Dennis:	jamen {complaining intonation}	but

Finally, Tim and Morten managed to incorporate entertaining dialogue through fairly competent indexing of sociocultural influences. Tim and Morten were two of the "stronger" English language users in this class, and perhaps, therefore, more able to appreciate sociocultural aspects of the English language. In extract 31, Tim and Morten make reference to Eric Cartman, a character from the US animated television series *South Park*. Indexing Eric Cartman, a school boy whose behaviour is invariably subversive in this television series, made it natural, and in an adaptive manner, to include a variety of entertaining lines in their role-play dialogue. They also named their teacher "Mr Trunchball", who is a particularly strict (although originally female) school principal from Roald Dahl's story of *Mathilda*. This not only indexed humorously subversive sociocultural influences, but also that the boys were able to build on their classmates' knowledge of these characters to amplify the entertainment value of their role-play dialogue.

Extract 31
Morten: Erik
 (1.0) åsså sier du and then you say
Tim: Eric Cartman @@@ {a character
 from South Park; laughter}
Morten: @ ja,_ yes

Finally, the teacher's instructions did include repeated advice to the whole class, and individual learner pairs, that they had to "come up with their own" dialogue. Thus, being original, which perhaps could have been added to the above description of the initial normative consensus, may have contributed to the learners being tempted to formulate entertaining dialogues.

A final less normative element of the learners' activity was the sense of competition among pairs. This sense of competition surfaced from time to time, but it was again not evident in all the learner pairs. Extract 32, where Tim and Morten are heard counting how many lines they have written, illustrates this competitive behaviour. Just before the performances were to take place, Tim could be heard talking to another pair of learners about how many "lines" they had written, and later Morten joined in as well. There was seemingly an interest, then, in making some kind of comparison with "how much" other pairs had written.

Extract 32
Tim: nei kor mange replikker har dokke no how many lines do you have
 {talking to learners from another pair}
 ... vi har -- we have
 han har en to tre fire .. fem seks ... sju he has one two three four five six
 ... åtte seven eight
 du har åtte replikkar {talking to Morten} you have eight lines
 og her en to tre fire -- and here one two three four
 er fem replikker {Morten now also there are five lines
 counting}

After Tim and Morten had performed their role-play, in front of the class, Dennis and Marcus made a similar comparison, as evident from extract 33. Then later, after Marcus and Dennis had performed their role-play, and had sat down again, they concluded – whispering to each other – that although their role-play was shorter it was still "the best".

Extract 33
Dennis:	vår er kjempeliten i forhold til den der	ours is super small compared to that one
Marcus:	jamen den var -- den ekke så lett (1.0)	yes but that one was it (ours) is not so easy
Teacher:	er dere klare?	are you ready?
Marcus:	Ja	yes
Dennis:	vår -- vår ekke så lang da i forhold til den men	ours but ours isn't so long compared to that one
Marcus:	come on	

In sum, whilst overall the learners' task-based activity seemed governed by a shared intentionality, which we have described as the initial normative consensus, some of their intentional activity on this task was less normative. We suggest that this additional activity, including a concern for "acting", "formulating entertaining dialogue", and "competing with other pairs", introduced two distinct dynamic properties into the intentional dynamics of the task sequence. On the one hand, the non-normative elements appeared to represent contingent intentional activity, and thus introducing adaptiveness to the intentional dynamics. The inclusion of a performance stage may have encouraged the occasional focus on "acting", as an adaptive response, and the teacher's instruction to be original may have encouraged the inclusion of entertaining dialogue, again as an adaptive response. Finally, the sense of competition may for some, and especially 12-year-old children, be an almost inevitable contingent, or adaptive, response to classroom task situations. Finally, in chapter 5 we argued that creative intentional activity introduces non-linearity. We believe that the focus on acting, as well as the focus on formulating entertaining dialogue – when it happened – represented creative intentional activity. It was creative because it went beyond the task instructions, and engaged the learners in a search for new possibilities (see section 5.3). This creative thinking, therefore, will have introduced non-linearity into the intentional dynamics of the task performances. In the next section, we will explore how these adaptive and non-linear properties of the intentional dynamics contributed to the emergence – over time – of a new shared intentionality.

7.5 Emergence of a new shared intentionality

In this section, we will argue that the creative and contingent activity of the learner pairs, as evidenced in the previous section, gradually – over the subsequent iterations of the task sequence – shifted the shared intentionality, from the initial normative consensus to a shared concern for "being entertaining". Thus, this section documents the emergence of a new shared intentionality. We start by looking at the second iteration of the task, when ways of acting and formulating entertaining dialogue became a more central concern for the learners. This is followed by a discussion of how, across the third and fourth iterations of the task sequence, the learners did the task with only minimal teacher direction, and how this left the shared intentionality of "being entertaining" as the dominant influence on the learners' intentional activity on the task. Finally, we look at the fifth iteration of the task, when the teacher lost patience with the new shared intentionality, and attempted to shift the learners' understanding of the task back to something akin to the initial normative consensus.

7.5.1 Acting and formulating entertaining dialogue: Second iteration

The second iteration of the task sequence appeared to run in a manner similar to the first. The teacher was the same, and the instructions and messaging appeared similar to that of the first iteration. However, a focus on "being entertaining", including formulating "entertaining dialogue" and "acting", seemed to take a much firmer hold. The concern seemed to be present from the very beginning of the lesson, when two learners were asked to read the sample start to the dialogue (this time between Robin Hood and Marion). The two pupils – both boys – actually got out of their seats to "act out" the dialogue. Although the teacher pointed out that "acting" was "not the point", the two boys proceeded to give an animated performance of the sample dialogue. A possible contributing factor to the emergence of "being entertaining" as a concern may have been the theme of the suggested dialogue. The learners were at an age where the theme of "relationships and love" is often a source of embarrassment. In fact, the two boys reading the sample dialogue (see above) "acted this out" in a manner that appeared to "mock" Robin and Marion being in love. We believe that this was contingent activity, or an adaptive response to the theme. Extract 34, which depicts a spontaneous exchange taking place just as the learners were getting into pairs, shows an unidentified boy making further fun of the theme, and Karen – in effect – asking him to "grow up".

Extract 34
Boy: eh
           (1.0) Robin
           ... Robin de bobo
Karen: kan du være så snill {irritated}   can you please
Boy: oh Robin
           oh blalalbla {mockingly}
Karen: kan du være litt stille {irritated}   can you be quiet

The focus on "being entertaining", and the way it may have been shaped by the learners' adaptive response to the theme of the dialogue, was very visible in the dialogues written by both pairs of boys. Dennis and Marcus' dialogue, shown as extract 35, included "over-the-top" references to the protagonists' appearance and activity. Moreover, towards the end of their later public performance, Dennis and Marcus acted out "Robin being stabbed by Marion". This was the first use of a prop – an object vaguely resembling a knife – in the performance of a role-play.

Extract 35
Robin: I now i are sexy
Marion: you are not so sexy as well
Robin: I think we gonna haw a party together
Marion: I haw to go an soungclub in the castle
Robin: OH Marion are I not More important than your soungclub
Marion: the soungclub is more important than a unsexy man Like you me litle robbebass
Robin: you cold me a robbe your litle your litle pricess whit disgusting hair
Marion: I gonna kill you Robin My hair is not disgusting
Robin: Im so sexy you can not kill me baby
Marion: I can kill you Robin
           from that day can not Robin hood take from the rich an give to the poor but Marion take from the poor and give to rich

Despite some of the learners being awkward about the theme, all three pairs completed the writing, rehearsed their dialogues, discussed how to act, and finally performed these with enthusiasm. Thus, the task as a whole, including the creativity that the learners were able to include into their dialogues, seemed unencumbered by the theme, and increasingly also the initial normative consensus. In the case of Veronica and Karen, however, the initial normative consensus remained more evident. Although they had Robin Hood kill Marion's father at the end of their role-play, they did not "act out" this final event in their performance, and the main elements of their dialogue were more conventional and consistent with the genre of love and relationships: i.e., Robin and Marion ending up married, with four children, a dog, and "living happy ever after". They also spent considerable time practicing this dialogue, showing a greater concern for displaying their linguistic competence than the other pairs seemed to.

7.5.2 Subversive and theatrical: Third and fourth Iterations

The third iteration of the task again appeared to run in a similar manner as the first two iterations. The learners had now moved to Year 7 of primary school, and there was a new English teacher. The new teacher, when asked, was quite happy to do the role-play task. After all, these types of role-play tasks were suggested by the Year 7 textbook as well. The teacher's instructions and messaging were similar to that provided by the Year 6 teacher, but crucially, because he was less familiar with the task, he appealed to the students' own experience and gave them freedom to take a lead in how to do the task. This freedom may have contributed to learner pairs finishing the writing stage at very different points in time, thereby creating a somewhat disorganised period between the learners finishing their writing, towards the end of the fifth lesson period, and the performances of the role-plays, which took place at the start of the sixth period (enabled by a change to the students' normal schedules).

Tim and Morten were the first pair to finish their writing, about 15 minutes before the end of the lesson period. This was not surprising since they were indeed "stronger" English learners. Veronica and Karen finished roughly five minutes after Tim and Morton, and Dennis and Marcus did not finish until the very end of the period. During the writing stage, Dennis and Marcus seemed particularly concerned about the need to include entertaining dialogue, and the need to be entertaining overall, as is evident from extract 36.

Extract 36:
5 minutes into the writing stage:

Marcus	skal vi skrive det?	shall we write that?
Dennis:	Ja	yes
	Nei	No
	jo vi må finne på noe .. enda kulere	we have to come up with something even cooler

3 minutes later:

| Marcus: | det er så vanskelig å finne på noe sånn derre sprøtt | it is so difficult to come up with something wacko |

1 minute later:
Dennis: . . . we ehm
             (2) vi må finne på noe skikkelig sprøtt   we have to come up with
                                                       something really wacko
             ikke sånn derre   not like

During the period of time when the learners completed their writing, not all at the same time, there was a lot of interaction between pairs in the classroom. This interaction was always "on task", with pairs comparing their dialogues and discussing how to perform them. These on-task cross-pair interactions contributed to Dennis and Marcus taking more time to improve their dialogue. Veronica and Karen spent ten minutes outside in the hallway practicing their dialogue – much like they had done in the second iteration of the task. Finally, during the break between the fifth and sixth periods, none of the learner pairs went outside. Instead, everyone stayed inside rehearsing their dialogues, and planning their performances. Moreover, many pairs prepared props to use in their performances. The level of creativity seemed high, and the learners were clearly motivated by the task. The performances took place in the sixth period, and everyone seemed to enjoy these. Most of the pairs used props, and some even "dressed up", making creative use of items of clothing they found in the classroom or in their bags. The dialogues were also creative, although sometimes a bit "over-the-top". Afterwards, the teacher observed that the dialogues and performances had been a bit "theatrical", but he nevertheless seemed impressed. At the end of the performances, he told the learners that "he was happy to see that they mastered the task to such an extent, and that he was open to the prospect of doing it again". Finally, in a later post-observation interview, he added that he was surprised "how well the pupils knew how to do the task, and that some of the pupils that normally participated at a very low level actually seemed into the task".

The teacher, having been impressed with how motivated the learners were during the task, decided to do the task sequence again, but this time separate from the fieldwork of the larger project (Stelma 2003). We, therefore, do not have our own data on what happened during the fourth iteration. However, the teacher did give his first-hand account when the fieldwork commenced again a month later. Significantly, the fourth iteration had shifted the teacher's view on the task. He recounted how, once again, he had let the learners "get on with the task" as they knew what to do. However, this time, he said, the dialogues and the performances got entirely "out of control". He described the dialogues as "frequently inappropriate", and told how the learner pairs, with some exceptions, seemed concerned only to make their role-play more "theatrical" than those of other pairs. On reflection, we believe that the freedom that the learners enjoyed may have been significant. Without the moderating influence of the teacher, in a purposeful manner directing the activity, and with the initial normative consensus receding into memory, the main shaping influence on the intentional dynamics was the un-moderated feedback of the learners themselves. This allowed the contingent and creative intentional activity of the learners to unfold, without normative constraint, and the result was a new shared intentionality – each learner pair competing against other pairs to be as entertaining as possible.

7.5.3 Reintroducing normativity: Fifth iteration

For the fifth iteration of the task sequence (10 months after the initial iteration), the fieldwork and data collection were again taking place. The teacher had explained what had happened since the previous round of fieldwork, as described above, and explained that he would try to shift how the learners approached the task. The teacher started the lesson by asking the learners how they felt that the task had shifted over the past year. The teacher then used the Norwegian word "orntlig" ('proper/appropriate') to suggest what he expected of the learners this time. He expected the learners to write "proper" dialogues, and to perform these in an "appropriate" manner; the observational notes we have suggest that the learners understood what the teacher meant.

The subsequent dialogues and performances were less subversive and theatrical, and the shared intentionality of "being entertaining" seemed to recede somewhat. There was rehearsal and planning ahead of the performances, but none of the learner pairs prepared props. All the learner pairs seemed content and confident throughout. The teacher's intervention, to re-establish something of the initial normative consensus, seemed to have worked. However, it did require some effort by some of the learners – and perhaps especially the boys. For instance, whilst writing Marcus was reflecting on the word "orntlig" out loud. He concluded that writing something "proper" would be easier if he could do it in Norwegian first, and then to translate the ideas into English. Ironically, throughout the iterations of the task sequence, he and Dennis, as well as the other learner pairs, for the most part had been developing their ideas in Norwegian first (for a similar pattern of code-switching, see Cromdal 2005). Thus, Marcus' reflections on the shifting shared intentionality were not necessarily coherent or fully developed. However, the teacher's recent comments had indeed caught his attention.

7.5.4 The intentional dynamics of the shifting shared intentionality

We believe that the shift, from one shared intentionality to another, was the result of particular intentional dynamics. We have argued, in chapter 5, that intentional dynamics, and indeed any complex dynamic system, have four dynamic properties; these were historicity, adaptiveness, non-linearity, and self-organisation (see also section 3.1). Moreover, we have argued that these are associated with normative, contingent, creative, and purposeful activity, respectively (see section 5.3). We have already, in the above empirical analysis, hinted at the role of contingent and creative activity in bringing about the shift. Our summary of these intentional dynamics is represented in Figure 5. The figure shows how the initial normative consensus in the first iteration of the task included more normative intentional activity. Then, across the next few iterations, the normative influences weakened, and the contingent and creative intentional activity became more prominent. This, then, represents the emergence of the new shared intentionality, focused on being entertaining. Finally, in the fifth and final iteration of the task, normativity was reintroduced by the teacher. This reduced the presence of contingent and creative activity, and the shared intentionality began to shift back to the initial normative consensus.

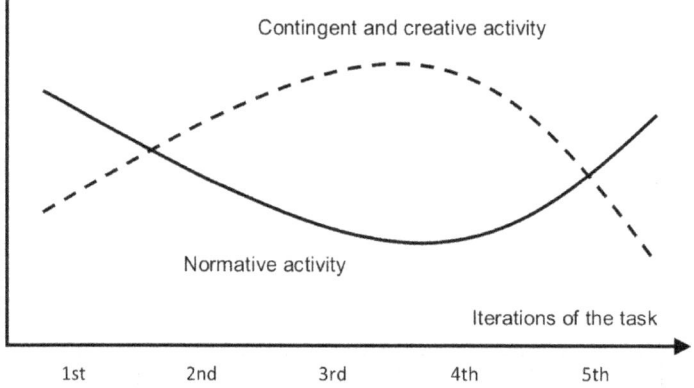

Figure 5: The shift in intentional activity across iterations of the task.

One possible interpretation of the changes to contingent and creative activity, across time, is that this was an "outcome" of the shift in the shared intentionality. However, if learner activity in a classroom is indeed a complex dynamic system, it will inherently exhibit the four dynamic properties of historicity, adaptiveness, non-linearity, and self-organisation. Again, a complex dynamic system derives its dynamism from these four properties: adaptiveness maintains both stability and the potential for change, historicity provides stability, non-linearity represents a search for new possibilities, and self-organisation is the emergence of something new. Thus, the normativity, most visible in the first iteration of the task, provided the learners with a sense of stability. Across the iterations of the task, this normative activity was gradually replaced by contingent and creative intentional activity. The learners responded in contingent ways to the affordances available to them, including the affordances associated with "having to be original" or "there being a performance at the end of the task". By themselves, these adaptive responses would not have resulted in the change we observed. However, some of the learners' creative intentional activity, including what they included in their dialogues and how they acted out the role-plays, were themselves contingent, or adaptive, responses. Thus, there was co-adaptation between contingent intentional activity and creative intentional activity; the normative and the adaptive responses were at the same time creative and non-linear. In the end, the flexibility of the adaptive responses, and the unpredictability of the observed non-linearity, provided the conditions for change to occur in the learner activity, and the shared intentionality, in this Norwegian classroom setting.

The missing part of this argument is the presence, or absence, of purposeful intentional activity, or in CDST terms, self-organisation. This may have been part of the story; while doing the task, the learners may have had the intention to make their dialogues and performances entertaining. However, we believe that, in this instance, the dynamic properties of historicity, adaptiveness, and non-linearity offer a sufficient and coherent description of the intentional dynamics that unfolded across the iterations of the role-play task in this Norwegian classroom. However, in the final iteration of the task we observed the teacher purposefully "countering" the newly-formed shared intentionality with an appeal to normativity, or historicity. He appealed to the learners' understanding of what was expected of them as pupils in the school, strategically assigned by the word "orntlig" ('proper/appropriate'). This, then, was a purposeful use of derived intentionality by the teacher – the word "orntlig" has a clear and strong meaning in the Norwegian language. This, then, shows how the Year 7 teacher's purposeful intentional activity was able to shift the task performances back to a more normative state – as represented by the right side of Figure 5.

7.6 Conclusion: The nature and role of shared intentionality

In this last section, we consider the nature and role of shared intentionality more broadly, as a "local social structure", or local-in-time attractor state for activity, that may have pedagogical implications for TESOL settings. A first observation is that shared intentionality must be understood in the context of the overall intentional dynamics of situations, and that it is overlapping and interacting with individual, derived, and sociocultural aspects of an intentional ecology. This is the same point that we made when discussing individual intentionality in chapter 6. In the Norwegian case, the derived aspects of the intentional ecology included the teacher's spoken instructions, and the use of hand-outs that originated from the textbooks used by the class. The sociocultural aspects of the intentional ecology were normative elements of this setting. This included general aspects, such as the social turn and a learner group ideal that shaped Norwegian primary classroom activity, but also more idiosyncratic aspects, such as completing tasks fully and on time. Another sociocultural aspect that we have alluded to, but not discussed in much detail, were the possibly subversive (or inspiring) influences of popular culture (e.g., *South Park* and Roald Dahl). Finally, the analysis in this chapter has not explored the influence of individual intentionality. However, our data was all generated with individual learners, working in pairs. The learners were the agents in the situations we explored, and it is reasonable to assume that the shifting shared intentionality will have been shaped, also, by the learners' individual intentionality.

Another observation is that shared intentionality may have pedagogical value. We found it striking that the learners, in this Norwegian case, through all the iterations of the dialogue and role-play task sequence, were thoroughly engaged and highly motivated. The initial normative consensus provided a clear structure for the task, and there was space within this consensus for contingency and creativity. Moreover, after a new teacher took over, the learners remained engaged and motivated by the task. In fact, as the shared intentionality shifted to "being entertaining", there may have been an even greater potential for learner meaning-making; the shared intentionality of being entertaining directly encouraged the learners to express themselves in a variety of ways. We recognise that a similar analysis of the pedagogical potential of the learner interaction might have been possible using sociocultural theory. In chapter 4, we suggested that shared intentionality resembles Vygotsky's interpersonal processes, evident in collaborative activity (Antón and DiCamilla 1998; Gibbons 2003; Kowal and Swain 1994; Swain 2000). However, sociocultural theory does not help us to understand the emergence of interpersonal processes; rather, it focuses on how these interpersonal processes may be internalised, as new knowledge and competence of learners. Our analysis of shared intentionality, looking also at the role of different types of intentional activity, offers unique analytical affordances for understanding the dynamic and emergent nature of social interaction, and hence tells us something more, we believe, about the pedagogical potential of collaborative language classroom activity.

A final observation is that this chapter has documented the emergence of local social structure. In fact, the analysis goes beyond documentation; we have explained the how and why of the emergence of this local social structure. We suggest, then, that shared intentionality is meaningful to learners, and as a local-in-time attractor state it can enable and constrain activity and outcomes. In our view, for concepts to be internalised, as per Vygotsky's (1978) explanation of learning, students need to identify with, or value, the shared intentionality that they experience. This meaningful experience is necessary for shared intentionality to alter, or enrich, their individual intentionality. This meaningful aspect suggests, in addition, that shared intentionality may explain aspects of identity and belonging in language classrooms. Some of the learners in the Norwegian classroom seemed to prosper with the shared intentionality of being entertaining, and the experience may have created a sense of belonging. However, the analysis also casts light on the opposite possibility – learners who struggle to fit in. In the Norwegian case, Veronica and Karen never fully subscribed to the shared intentionality focused on being entertaining. If this shared intentionality was allowed to develop further, they might have felt alienated by it. Thus, these two girls, and possibly also other learners in this classroom, may have appreciated the Year 7 teacher re-inserting a sense of normativity into the task sequence.

In sum, shared intentionality must be considered alongside individual, derived, and sociocultural aspects of a classroom intentional ecology. Shared intentionality is both an outcome of intentional activity, and it shapes intentional activity in classrooms. Moreover, shared intentionality is akin to a local social structure which is meaningful to classroom participants, and which may have particular pedagogical benefits. In the Norwegian classroom case, the shared intentionality of being entertaining was an outcome of the learners' own meaning-making. Thus, our analysis of shared intentionality suggests that we are indeed "social animals", and that an analysis of shared intentionality may contribute to our understanding of social forms of learning in language classrooms.

Chapter 8
Derived intentionality: A Greek private language school

In this chapter we continue to exemplify intentional dynamics in TESOL. Chapters 6 and 7 focused on individual and shared intentionality, respectively. One focus of the present chapter is to understand the shaping influence of derived intentionality, understood as the affordances for activity present in the learning materials of a private English language school in Greece. The language school is one that we have discussed in previous publications (Kostoulas and Stelma 2017; Kostoulas 2018). As we will describe in the next section, an ambitious curricular reform had been attempted at the school a few years before we conducted our fieldwork. However, despite the effort and resources that had been invested, the reform resulted in few lasting effects. We attribute this outcome not only to the derived intentionality present in the learning materials used by the school, but also to the idiosyncratic aspects of the school's intentional ecology. The chapter will therefore focus, in addition, on the role of these aspects. Overall, then, the chapter describes how the failure of the curricular reform initiative may be explained by the interplay between derived intentionality and idiosyncratic aspects of the intentional ecology of this Greek language school.

We begin this chapter with an introduction to the setting of the Greek language school, the curricular reform that was attempted, and the larger study in this setting that this chapter is based on (section 8.1). The next section (8.2) introduces the sociocultural aspects of the intentional ecology of the school, including international (TESOL) and idiosyncratic (Greek) intentional structures. In a third section (8.3), we present the analysis of derived intentionality in the learning materials of the school, including the suggestion that this derived intentionality represents affordances for activity, or an *affordance landscape* (Kostoulas 2018). Building on this data, in section 8.4, we go on to discuss the attractor states and intentional dynamics that resulted from the interplay between the derived intentionality of the learning materials and the idiosyncratic intentional structures in the language school. We suggest that the failure of the curricular reform may have been due to what may be called intentional dynamics of resistance (see also Kostoulas 2014). We conclude by arguing that the outcomes of any curricular reform, or any other innovation in TESOL, requires an appreciation that intentional ecologies will be idiosyncratic (section 8.5).

8.1 The school, the curricular reform, and the study

The school that we will describe in this chapter was a private language education provider in Greece, and the data that we will use was generated in the mid-2010s. Before we look into the intentional ecology of the school in more detail, we will provide some background information on the school, the curricular reform that was attempted, and the study into the outcomes of this curricular reform (see also Kostoulas 2014, 2015, 2018; Kostoulas and Stelma 2017).

The language school offered general English language classes to children and young teenagers, as well as examination preparation courses for (mainly young) adults. Although the Greek state school system provides extensive English language instruction throughout the curriculum, there is also a large number of private schools that offer evening language courses to young learners. The existence of this vibrant private sector may be explained by a large number of factors, including widespread scepticism about the effectiveness of state education, the fact that some private schools employ teachers who are "native speakers" of English, the use of modern and aesthetically pleasing learning materials, and aggressive marketing (Kostoulas 2018). Another idiosyncratic feature of Greek education is that qualifications are strongly valued, because of a credentialist ethos in the job market. In this context, private schools tend to be more responsive to the demand for intensive and effective examination preparation, and are therefore seen as a route to obtain language learning certificates (Matthaioudakis 2007; Sifakis 2009).

This particular language school was one of the oldest and largest in the provincial town where it was located. It had been in continuous operation since the 1970s, and at the time of our study there were several hundred learners enrolled in various language learning programmes. Typically, learners would enrol at the age of nine, and they would attend English classes over a period of several years. In somewhat simplified terms (for a more detailed account see Kostoulas 2018: 31) this learning trajectory was divided into: a two-level young learner programme called "Junior"; a recently introduced three-level intermediate programme called "New Senior" (of which only the first level was implemented when fieldwork was conducted); a three-level lower intermediate programme for older children called "Senior" (which was being replaced by the New Senior programme, so only the two higher levels were still used); and a two-level upper-intermediate programme, which we will call "Exam". The Exam programme prepared students for linguistic proficiency examinations at the Vantage (B2) and Mastery (C2) levels of the Common European Framework of Reference (Council of Europe 2001).

Over the years, the school had developed an excellent reputation as an EFL provider. Some of the strengths that teachers and parents acknowledged included emphasis on academic rigour, a strict monolingual (i.e., English-only) language policy, and a record of very high success rates at language examinations. providing internationally recognised certification. There was some concern, however, that the methods of instruction, which tended to be teacher-fronted, involved a grammar-focussed curriculum, and employed rote-learning, were out-dated. In response to these concerns, some years before the study into this context took place, the school had undergone an ambitious curricular reform initiative, including changes to both the curriculum and methods of instruction. Despite considerable investment in time and effort, however, this curricular reform appeared to have produced few lasting results. When one of us (Achilleas Kostoulas) did fieldwork the school, in the context of his doctoral studies (Kostoulas 2015), it was evident that most of the innovations associated with the project had either been silently reverted, or re-conceptualised to conform to previous established practices.

One of the main aims of the empirical work at the school, therefore, was to understand what sustained resistance to this attempt at curricular reform (Kostoulas 2014, 2018; Kostoulas and Stelma 2017). A mixed-methods approach was used, which included interviews with teachers in the school, multiple small-scale questionnaires for the students, classroom observations, and a content analysis the learning materials used by the school. When drawing on this data, we will refer to the teachers with pseudonyms, whereas the student data is anonymised. The data that was generated from these different strands of investigation was combined, using methods that were broadly consistent with grounded theory (Corbin and Strauss 2008). This produced a description of the school that contained four main components: (a) the range of linguistic, pedagogical, and political possibilities for action available to the school, (b) the sociocultural aspects of intentionality that appeared to shape these possibilities, (c) the affordances for action present in the learning materials, and (d) the actual teaching and learning sequences that took place in the school (Kostoulas 2018).

Our aim in this chapter is to theoretically refine the findings of this earlier research, and thereby to integrate them into our theoretical description of intentional dynamics. Seen from the perspective of intentional dynamics, the language school's intentional ecology was made up of two main elements: local and idiosyncratic sociocultural intentional structures, which appeared to be central to the school's intentional ecology, as well as the derived intentionality evident in the learning materials. The idiosyncratic intentional structures correspond to what we called "intentionalities" in Kostoulas and Stelma (2017). These intentional structures were generated, through morphogenetic processes, by the co-activity of broader sociocultural aspects (e.g., societal beliefs, legislation, and more), as well as the individual and shared intentionality of teachers and learners in the school. We will describe these idiosyncratic intentional structures in the next section (8.2). The subsequent section (8.3) will provide a detailed analysis of the derived intentionality, understood as sets of affordances for teaching and learning activity that were evident in the learning materials of the school. Finally, section 8.4 will explore how the interplay between derived intentionality and the idiosyncratic intentional structures seemed to generate attractor states for teaching and learning activity in the school, and how this constituted intentional dynamics that acted to resist the curricular reform that was attempted some years before.

8.2 Idiosyncratic intentional structures in the language school

The intentional ecology of the school was shaped by a large number of influences. The broader systems in which the school was nested, such as international TESOL, generated sociocultural aspects of intentionality. These included the principles of communicative language teaching and the value of English language competence. These influences were evident, also, in the teachers', learners', and other stakeholders' beliefs and expectations regarding language and education, i.e., their individual intentionality. However, there was a local dimension to the intentional ecology of the school. Although international sociocultural aspects of TESOL permeated the language school, they seemed to be idiosyncratically re-interpreted at the local level. Within the language school's "small culture" (Holliday 1999), these global influences interacted with national Greek sociocultural expectations and norms, and through the individual intentionality of the director of studies, teachers, and learners, as well as the shared intentionality that was generated by their interaction, a set of idiosyncratic intentional structures appeared to have emerged.

In Kostoulas and Stelma (2017), we empirically identified three salient local and idiosyncratic intentional structures that seemed to shape activity in the school. We called the first of these intentional structures *credentialism*, and defined it as "a strong priority attached to certifying language learning outcomes" (Kostoulas and Stelma 2017: 357). Such priority given to certification, even at the expense of actual language learning, is commonly reported in descriptions of Greek TESOL (e.g., Matthaioudakis 2007; Sifakis 2009; Tsagari and Papageorgiou 2012). In a striking example, Angouri, Matthaioudakis, and Zigrika (2010) quote a parent who explicitly instructed her daughter to focus her efforts on getting a certificate while she was at school, as "you can learn the language later" (p. 192). This intentional structure of credentialism seemed to be widespread at the language school, particularly when teachers discussed more advanced classes, which prepared learners for language certification exams. For example, in an interview that was part of our fieldwork, Martha, a highly qualified teacher who had just began working at the school, claimed that the primary motivation for many of her students was to obtain some form of certification. She described her classes as follows:

Extract 37: Martha describing her classes
I have students who don't want to come to the classes [. . .] who say "I don't like English but I have to do it in order to find a job and in order to satisfy my parents". And I think that they don't learn English just for their own sake. They learn it in order to take a degree.

In their responses to a questionnaire (also a part of the field work), students confirmed that it was important to persevere with their English courses until they had obtained at least a B2-level certificate (e.g., "you should at least take the first certificate as it is necessary for the job"), and they stressed that with an appropriate language certificate "you can find an easier job and also study in England". These views, then, appeared motivated by a form of "linguistic instrumentalism". However, the intentional structure of credentialism also appeared to be intertwined with broader sociocultural aspects of the intentional ecology, such standard language ideology (linked to the standard expected by the certification examinations), and perhaps also linguistic imperialism (the certification providers were all US- and UK-based).

The second idiosyncratic intentional structure that we identified in the language school was what we called *supplementation*. This referred to the societal expectation that private language schools should supplement the state EFL provision by "achieving learning outcomes that could not be attained in the state school system" (Kostoulas and Stelma 2017: 359). This intentional structure was pervasive in the intentional ecology of the language school, particularly when discussing learners who had transitioned from primary to secondary state education. This may have been because assessment was carried out in more systematic ways in secondary schools, including formal examinations.

One of the ways, then, that the supplementation structure manifested itself was in the form of an *accountability ethos* shared by the teachers. The teachers saw it as their duty to ensure that learners performed well academically in the state school system, even if there were differences in the curricula used by the two sectors. This led to recurring comments in interviews, where teachers expressed surprise, frustration, and indignation about the challenges involved in meeting the demands of their own syllabus *as well as* the expectations of the state school system (e.g., "if someone gets a 12 [out of 20], then it will be me who will be discussed, they [parents or colleagues] will say that my kids don't even know the basics" [Sarah Jane]).

Although these private language school teachers tried their best to meet the curricular expectations of the state education system, they also made efforts to distance themselves from state EFL, perhaps due to its perceived weaknesses. Thus, another manifestation of the supplementation intentional structure was to emphasise the difference between what they did in their private school and what happened in the state system. The state school system was generally perceived as highly ineffective, something usually attributed to low teacher motivation, large mixed-ability classes, and disruptive student behaviour (for similar conclusions, see also Angouri et al. 2010; Karavas 2010). As a result, many innovations in the state TESOL curriculum tended to be viewed with scepticism, with the teachers valuing "tried and tested" teaching practices instead. For example, the introduction of English language as a subject very early in the state primary system was questioned by the private school's teachers ("You can't have a year's worth of lessons with little songs, clapping hands and ha-ha-ha, no matter what you try" [Amy; translated from Modern Greek]), including reservations, also, about communicative and task-based teaching and learning "in which children do nothing but talk to each other" (Rose).

The third idiosyncratic intentional structure in the school was *protectionism*, which refers to a strong, if unstated, imperative to value the professional competence of local language teachers. There was a clear rationale for this intentional structure. Most of the teachers in the school were Greek, and they would often note that the Greek education system emphasised the development of metalinguistic awareness, and that teachers with this background would be especially suited to teaching Greek students. For example, Rose, a senior teacher with a degree in language and linguistics, argued that:

> Extract 38: Rose on the value of metalinguistic knowledge
> If I struggle to describe the differences between Present Perfect and Past Simple, or between Past Present Perfect Simple and Continuous, how can an Englishman or an American do this? Let's get serious. [. . .] In England they haven't taught any grammar for the last 20–30 years. (translated from Modern Greek)

Another aspect of professional competence that was valued was practical experience, with one teacher noting that "it's not the studies that turn you into a teacher; it's teaching." At the same time, academic expertise was sometimes viewed with suspicion, especially if it called established practice into question. For example, Sarah Jane, an experienced teacher, made the following remarks about a professional development event she had been encouraged to attend:

> Extract 39: Sarah Jane's views on professional development
> The theory was just too much – devastating! – multiple intelligences, affective learning, groups and tasks. [. . .] What I need is advice from someone who has experience teaching classes like mine!

Overall then, the teachers appeared to draw a contrast between their own practical, locally acquired expertise, and forms of linguistic, pedagogical, and academic expertise that outsiders might bring, including also an expressed wish to insulate the school from such undesirable influences.

These idiosyncratic intentional structures contributed to an intentional ecology that was idiosyncratic to this Greek language school. The role of the protectionism intentional structure was especially important in this regard; by dismissing the value of theory-driven professional development, the teachers at the school seemed to insulate the language school from outside influences, to some extent including, also, the (sociocultural and derived) ideational intentionality associated with communicative language teaching (see discussion in the following sections). Similarly, the supplementation intentional structure was sustained by a process of "co-adaptation" (Larsen-Freeman and Cameron 2008a: 65–69) with the state education system in Greece, i.e., an interaction between two systems where changes in one system trigger changes in the other. Thus, as the state education system introduced English language instruction for younger children, the supplementation intentional structure became a more visible feature in the intentional ecology of the private language school. However, while the intentional dynamics of the school were clearly shaped by the idiosyncratic intentional structures that we have discussed in this section, sociocultural aspects of international TESOL continued to exert some influence – at least in those domains of activity that could not be insulated by protectionism (see also Kostoulas 2014).

In describing the three idiosyncratic intentional structures that were salient in the intentional ecology of the language school, we have made reference to their interconnections with sociocultural aspects of Greek society, and to a lesser extent the international sociocultural, or professional, aspects of TESOL. We have made reference, also, to questionnaire and interview data, reflecting the learners and teachers' individual and shared intentionality. Missing from this picture is a consideration of derived intentionality. The next section takes a closer look at the derived intentionality present in the learning materials used in the school. This prepares for the later analysis of the intentional dynamics that shaped activity and outcomes in this private language school, including also the observed resistance to the above-mentioned curricular reform initiative.

8.3 Derived intentionality in the language school

In this section, we focus on the derived intentionality evident in the learning materials used by the school, and how this derived intentionality appeared to generate particular affordances for intentional activity. In chapter 4, we discussed how derived intentionality may be generated by the activity of materials developers, and noted that learning materials will include, in derived form, the producers' beliefs about language and learning. This derived intentionality may shape teaching and learning activity. For example, learning materials that cohere with a structural syllabus and a grammar-orientation will encourage practice of language forms.

We start with a brief description of the content analysis of the learning materials used by the school, thus beginning to map out the derived intentionality across the Junior, New Senior, Senior, and Exam programmes. This is followed by a discussion of the affordances associated with the derived intentionality evident in the learning materials, using the notion of *affordance landscape* suggested by Kostoulas (2018).

8.3.1 A content analysis of the learning materials

The learning materials used by the Greek school included core course- and workbooks for each of the programme levels offered at the school, as well as supplementary materials used to compensate for perceived deficiencies in the course and workbooks. All the core and workbooks were from international English Language Teaching (ELT) publishers, but were usually produced under local imprints for the Greek market. Table 8 provides an overview of the nature of the learning materials (note that we are using the names of the programmes rather than the actual textbook titles). We note again that the Junior programme was for the youngest learners. The New Senior programme was being gradually rolled out at the time of fieldwork. Although the New Senior programme course and workbook appeared to be similarly focused on grammar as the Senior programme that it was replacing, it was perceived to be less systematic in its grammar coverage, and thus was supplemented, as indicated in the table. Senior was being phased out and replaced by New Senior, but the second and third levels of this programme were still being taught. Finally, the Exam programme was not expressly marketed as an examination preparation course, but its macro-structure and the format of most activities mirrored those of major language certifications exams.

Table 8: Overview of the nature of the learning materials.

Programme	Levels	Course- and workbook	Supplementary
Junior	2	Reading stories, followed by grammar and vocabulary presentation and practice activities	In-house photocopiable resources
New Senior	3	Reading texts, followed by mainly grammar presentation and practice activities; writing activities	Dedicated grammar practice book; in-house photocopiable resources
Senior	3	Reading dialogues and texts, followed by grammar presentation and practice; writing activities; multiple revision opportunities	In-house photocopiable resources
Exam	2	Reading, grammar, vocabulary, oral skills, and writing (mirroring the language certification exams)	Practice tests; in-house photocopiable resources

A full discussion of the methodological aspects of the content analysis of these learning materials appears in Kostoulas (2018). In brief, the content of the course and workbooks was broken down into individual activities (e.g., exercises, tasks), and each activity was initially assigned to a specific category depending on its inferred learning objective (i.e., grammar, vocabulary, reading, writing, listening, and speaking). Following this, the properties of each activity were examined in finer detail, using a combination of literature-derived and inductively-generated criteria. For example, activities that focussed on grammatical awareness and/or accuracy were coded for the method used (i.e., presentation, controlled practice, free production, consciousness raising, inferring rules from context, and so on), the linguistic content focus (e.g., past tenses, conditional sentences), and whether they used metalanguage. Descriptive statistics were used to identify patterns and trends in the distribution of activities across the programme levels, and additional qualitative insights about the materials that could not be meaningfully itemised (e.g., glossaries) were also recorded.

8.3.2 The affordance landscape of the learning materials

The content analysis of the learning materials established an overview of derived intentionality. The presence of grammar activities suggested that the learning materials had been influenced by a structural understanding of language, and more process-oriented activities suggested that the learning materials had been shaped by a more communicative orientation to language education. The analysis, then, suggested that there were two salient sets of affordances in the learning materials. The first set of affordances, associated with texts modelling grammatical structures, a preponderance of presentation and practice activities, long lists of vocabulary to be memorised, and the absence of production activities, seemed to privilege *form-focused* instruction. This set of affordances was mainly present in the learning materials used by the Junior and Senior programmes, and to a lesser extent the New Senior programme. By contrast, a second distinct, but less frequent overall, set of affordances were associated with more inductive grammar activities, texts followed by activities asking learners to "process" its content, process-based writing, and occasionally more meaningful speaking and listening tasks. This second set of affordances seemed to privilege a more communicative type of language instruction. The teaching and learning activities associated with the *communicative* set of affordances were relatively more common in the Exam level programme. This content analysis suggested, then, that the derived intentionality of the learning materials represented an "affordance landscape". Kostoulas (2018: 91) defines an affordance landscape as "a metaphorical visualisation of the collective effect of the affordances that are implicit in [. . .] learning materials, and also of the probability that certain forms of pedagogy materialise in practice". The affordance landscape, then, suggested a difference between the Junior, New Senior and Senior programmes on the one hand, where the derived intentionality appeared to privilege form-focused instruction, and the Exam programme on the other hand, which derived intentionality included more communicative affordances. In the following, we take a closer look at the detail of this affordance landscape.

The dominant form-focused part of the affordance landscape included affordances associated with structuralist views of language, thereby generating opportunities for "transmissive" teaching practices. The derived intentionality associated with this set of affordances was most clearly visible in the preponderance of grammar- and vocabulary-focused activities. Grammar-focused activities formed more than one third (36.7%) of the materials in the course and workbooks used in the Junior and Senior programmes. In the newly introduced New Senior set of materials, including also the supplementary materials (see Table 8), grammar-focused activities constituted close to half (43%) of the total content. The grammar presentation activities often used sophisticated metalanguage – particularly in the Senior programme. These were typically followed by controlled practice, or quite limited production activities, with students expected to (re)produce the target structures. A large number of in-house photocopiable resources, which had been produced over time at the school, was also used across the different programmes. Typically, these elaborated on aspects of grammar and provided additional practice opportunities, usually in the form of decontextualized language (e.g., by instructing students to produce passive forms of various sentences).

Derived intentionality shaping the form-focused part of the affordance landscape was present, also, in vocabulary activities. These activities seemed similarly designed to facilitate transmissive forms of instruction. This was especially true for the Senior programme, where the learners were expected to engage with a demanding number of new lexical items (in one extreme case, learners were presented with a set of 48 new words to be memorised in a single lesson). The course books presented some vocabulary in the form of semantic sets (e.g., farm animals), and included tasks that involved practicing this vocabulary. These were supplemented with sometimes long lists of vocabulary that had been created in-house, which included English-language definitions and, possibly, derivatives and examples. In addition, teachers had access to a large corpus of vocabulary tests, which were intended to encourage rote learning of the spelling, semantic meaning, and derivatives of vocabulary items.

In addition to the above, a large number of skills-focused activities included implicit grammar objectives, and thus also contributed to the form-focused part of the affordance landscape. This was particularly the case in the Junior programme, where reading and listening tasks often used contrived texts designed to exemplify target structures or recently-taught vocabulary. The following extract, from the script of a listening activity from the Junior programme, illustrates the contrived nature of texts. Note the repetition of the "how much/many" and the present simple structures in both the question and answers across the two, structurally identical, sample dialogues.

> Extract 40: Sample listening activity (from Kostoulas 2018: 107)
>
> Shop assistant: Good morning, Danny!
> Danny: Hello! I want some red paint and some paintbrushes, please.
> Shop assistant: How much paint do you want? And how many paintbrushes?
> . . .
> Shop assistant: Hello, Flora.
> Flora: Hello! I want some red paint, some green paint, and some paintbrushes, please.
> Shop assistant: How much paint do you want? And how many paintbrushes?

Finally, the derived intentionality evident in genre-based writing tasks also seemed to constitute affordances for form-focused teaching and learning. These affordances were typically distributed across sequences of activities.

For instance, the learners might have to read a text that exemplified a writing genre (e.g., a letter of complaint), and then be required to reproduce the features of this model in a series of guided writing activities.

By contrast, the communicative part of the affordance landscape included derived intentionality, and associated affordances, in the form of more inductive, process-oriented, and production-focused activities. Overall, the activities that generated affordances for communicative language teaching were fewer than the ones that were associated with form-focused instruction. In total, the communicative affordances represented approximately one third (37%) of the activities in the learning materials. These tended to cluster in the materials used in the Exam programme, but also in the skills-development sections of the course books used by the other programmes.

Communicatively-oriented derived intentionality was found in some reading activities, where the learners were expected to engage with the propositional content of a passage. Such readings tended to be quasi-genuine passages, which mimicked the formal features of real-life texts, such as emails, newspaper articles, menus, websites, and more. These texts were less common in the programmes for the younger learners. They made up approximately a quarter of the reading activities in the Junior and Senior programmes (24% and 27% respectively); in these programmes, texts more commonly introduced target structures, or acted as model texts for writing. By contrast, two-thirds (68%) of reading activities in the Exam programme expected the learners to engage with the propositional content of texts. Derived intentionality associated with communicative language teaching was present also in process-based writing activities. These typically involved practicing various writing sub-skills (e.g., brainstorming, planning, producing a draft, editing, and proofreading). Such activities were unevenly distributed in the learning materials. They were completely absent in the Junior and Senior courses, but they formed approximately one third (36%) of the writing activities in the newly introduced New Senior programme, and two thirds (65%) of the writing activities in the Exam programme. Finally, affordances for communicative language teaching were less evident in listening and speaking activities. In fact, listening and speaking activities that encouraged actual communication, as opposed to practicing newly-introduced language, were uncommon in the learning materials. More generally, the proportion of listening activities across the programmes was relatively low (<6% of the total number of activities), and as noted above, many tended to focus on language forms. Only the Exam programme included a small number of listening activities that encouraged communicative language teaching. As for speaking activities, a similar pattern was observed. The number of speaking activities ranged from 5% in the Junior course to 15% in the Exam course, and activities tended to shift from practicing sounds, words, and target structures on the lower level programmes, to collaborative interaction activities in the Exam programme.

In sum, the derived intentionality that was present in the learning materials generated an affordance landscape (Kostoulas 2018) with two main features: a set of form-focused affordances and a set of communicative affordances. These two sets of affordances were not uniformly present across the learning materials. The set of form-focused affordances was a more prominent feature across the affordance landscape, and was present across all the programme levels. By contrast, the set of communicative affordances were mostly a feature of the Exam programme, as well as in the core course and workbooks for the New Senior programme (note again that the New Senior programme was supplemented with a separate, dedicated grammar practice book – see Table 8). Finally, we must note that the affordance landscape signifies possibilities for action, rather than actual activity in the language school. In the next section, we will look at the interplay between the idiosyncratic intentional structures, which we introduced in the previous section, and the derived intentionality and affordance landscape of the learning materials. This will reveal what we will call intentional dynamics of resistance, which we believe "blunted" the curricular reform effort that was undertaken in this Greek language school.

8.4 Intentional dynamics of resistance

In this section, we explore the interplay between the idiosyncratic intentional structures, which we discussed in section 8.2, and the derived intentionality and affordance landscape evident in the learning materials, which we outlined in the previous section (8.3). The section is informed, also, by the broader insight into the Greek language school setting afforded by the extensive fieldwork which was undertaken (see Kostoulas 2018). The section identifies two curricular attractor states (see section 3.1) that appeared to shape the intentional dynamics of teaching and learning across the four programmes of the school – including the Junior, New Senior, Senior, and Exam levels. We relate these attractor states to the curricular reform that had been attempted in the school (see section 8.1), and conclude that the intentional dynamics in this language school, as viewed from the perspective of curricular progression, exhibited an element of resistance to the attempted curricular reform.

We begin by presenting a summary figure (see Figure 6), displaying the curricular progression across the programme levels. This progression coheres with the two sets of affordances – the form-focused and the communicative

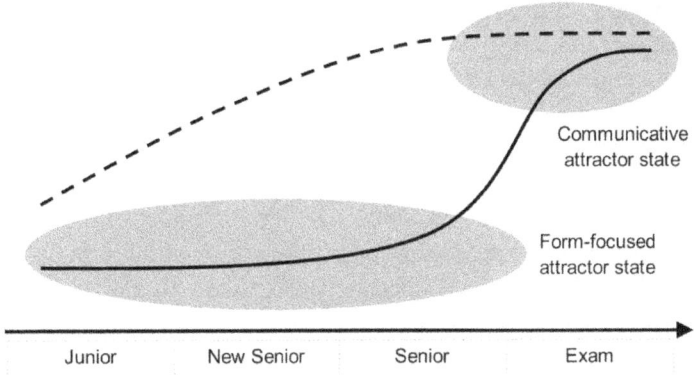

Figure 6: Intentional dynamics across the language school's curriculum.

sets – which we have argued made up the affordance landscape of the learning materials. In this section, we have reinterpreted the affordance landscape as a form-focused attractor state and a communicative attractor state, which appeared to constrain actual teaching and learning activity across the curriculum. The figure suggests that the curricular progression – the solid line – was constrained by the form-focused attractor through the Junior, New Senior, and Senior programme levels, and only in the Exam programme did the communicative attractor shape the teaching and learning. By contrast, the earlier curricular reform envisaged a progression more akin to the dotted line, with the communicative attractor shaping the teaching across all the programme levels to a greater extend. We explain this discrepancy, between the wished-for progression shaped by a communicative attractor state and the actual progression shaped mainly by a form-focused attractor state, with reference to the intentional dynamics of three parts of the curriculum: the Junior and Senior programmes, the New Senior programme, and the Exam programme.

When viewing the curriculum in the Greek language school as a complex dynamic system, the dominant dynamic property in the "old" part of the curriculum – the Junior and Senior programmes – was historicity (see section 3.1). The materials used in these two programmes were among the oldest in the language school, which meant that they fed the intentional ecology with derived intentionality that had been assigned and sedimented several years into the school's past. The idiosyncratic intentional structure of protectionism (see section 8.2) seemed to contribute additional historicity, and overall the teaching and learning activity in the Junior and Senior programmes may be described as normative activity. A key component of the intentional structure of protectionism was the value accorded to metalinguistic knowledge, both in the curriculum and as one of the strengths in the teachers' professional profiles.

The possible interplay between derived intentionality and the intentional structure of protectionism was on display, also, in the marketing texts of the published materials. The Junior and Senior course and workbooks were produced by local affiliates of international publishing houses, and contained frequent references to the particularity of Greek TESOL. For instance, the back cover of one course book highlighted that it had been "written especially for the Greek market", and the author of another course book was described as having "extensive experience working in the field in Greece". This marketing text did not index cultural references, storylines, or characters that might appeal to Greek learners; rather, it seemed to be about – as described in yet another course book – "the common grammatical and lexical mistakes that Greek students often make".

Finally, the observational data gathered by the larger study (see Kostoulas 2018: Ch. 6) confirmed that the actual teaching of the Junior and Senior programmes did indeed unfold in accordance with the form-focused attractor state. Thus, the stakeholders' individual and shared intentionality (some of which we have cited in earlier sections), the derived intentionality of the learning materials, and the idiosyncratic intentional structure of protectionism, all contributed to strengthening the form-focused attractor state in these two old programmes. Thus, these programmes were characterised by normative, form-focused teaching activity (the solid line in Figure 6), grounded in the notion that "this is how things have always been done". This deviated from what the earlier curricular reform had envisaged (the dotted line in Figure 6). In sum, this is one way in which the interplay between the learning materials and the idiosyncratic intentional structures in the setting generated intentional dynamics of resistance that emanated from the "older" programmes and "spilled over" to the rest of the system.

The intentional dynamics at play in the New Senior programme were slightly different. The New Senior programme was designed for learners who were younger than the participants in the Senior programme, which the New Senior programme was replacing. The earlier curricular reform was an original influence on the design of the New Senior programme. In fact, if the analysis of affordances in the New Senior learning materials had been limited to the core course and workbooks only, thus disregarding the supplementary component (see Table 8), then the affordance landscape for this part of the curriculum would have appeared more communicative. However, another influence on the design of the New Senior programme was the introduction of English language as a subject at a younger age in the state primary provision. The knock-on effect was that the learners in the New Senior programme were younger than those attending the older

Senior programme; the New Senior learners were in their early years of secondary education, which – in the Greek state school system – is when formal in-class and end-of-year examinations are introduced, and they therefore had less experience with such examinations. Thus, the New Senior programme design was driven, also, by the accountability pressure for the students to perform well in the state school system, as characterised by the idiosyncratic intentional structure of supplementation. Finally, the specific form which the supplementation took will have been driven, also, by the sense of protectionism shared by the teachers in the school. The relatively younger learners that attended the New Senior programme had less developed metalinguistic awareness, both in English and in Greek language. Thus, as consistent with the intentional structures of supplementation and protectionism, a dedicated grammar-practice book was added to this programme.

The observational data gathered (see Kostoulas 2018) again confirmed that the actual teaching of New Senior programme appeared constrained by the form-focused attractor state. However, and distinct from the Junior and Senior programmes, the prominent dynamic property in the intentional dynamics of the New Senior programme was adaptiveness. In chapter 3, we defined adaptiveness as the way a complex dynamic system adjusts to changes in its environment, while preserving as much of its structure as possible. In the case of the New Senior programme, the addition of a dedicated grammar practice book was an adaptation, or a contingent curricular decision, shaped by the intentional structures of supplementation and protectionism. This was a second way in which the intentional dynamics, focused on curriculum progression in the school, exhibited resistance to the earlier curricular reform initiative.

The syllabus of the Exam programme was distinct from the Junior, Senior, and New Senior programmes. The affordance landscape of the Exam programme learning materials contained communicative affordances. This difference was due to the credentialism intentional structure in the language school, and possibly, but to a lesser extent, the supplementation structure. Although certification was always present in the thinking of teachers, learners, and parents, it became more prominent as the students approached the age when they were expected to take a certification examination. These examinations, which were designed and administered by international examination boards, tended to align with the principles of communicative language teaching, and hence the broader sociocultural, or professional aspects, of international TESOL. These communicative principles were evident in the examinations, and these examinations therefore generated a "washback effect" (Alderson, Clapham, and Wall 1995: 46) on the intentional activity of the school. Thus, in the learning materials for the Exam programme, grammar activities were fewer in number and inductive in nature, reading and writing tasks focused more on meaning than on form, and there was an increase in the number of listening and speaking activities. Just as with the New Senior programme, the dominant dynamic property in the curricular decisions focused on the Exam programme was adaptiveness. That is, the observational and interview data gathered in the larger project showed no observable traces of overtly conscious or purposeful decision-making. Thus, the communicative attractor state was an outcome of adaptive intentional dynamics, involving an unconsciously experienced and particular interplay of individual, shared, derived, and sociocultural aspects of the intentional ecology of this school.

In sum, the intentional dynamics shaping the Junior and Senior programmes included historicity, and associated normative activity. This normative activity was shaped by an interplay of the derived intentionality of the learning materials, characterised by form-focused affordances, and the idiosyncratic intentional structure of protectionism. This contributed to a form-focused attractor state, constraining the actual teaching and learning activity in the Junior and Senior programmes. The intentional dynamics shaping the New Senior programme, by contrast, were characterised by adaptiveness, with the addition of a dedicated grammar practice book as a contingent response. This addition of a grammar practice book was consistent with the idiosyncratic supplementation and protectionism intentional structures, and ensured that the New Senior programme also remained constrained by the form focused attractor state. The intentional dynamics of all of these programmes, while different, both constituted forms of resistance to the earlier curricular reform initiative in the school. Thus, the idiosyncratic intentional ecology of the school exhibited a strong resilience to change, and this helps us to understand why the curricular reform initiative that we mentioned in section 8.1 appeared to fail (see also Kostoulas and Stelma 2017). Finally, the intentional dynamics shaping the Exam programme was also characterised by adaptiveness and contingent intentional activity. However, this was an adaptive response, or contingent curricular decision-making, shaped by the communicative language teaching principles of international TESOL, a different set of affordances in the learning materials, as well as the idiosyncratic intentional structure of credentialism.

8.5 Conclusion: Idiosyncrasies, resistance, and curricular change

In this chapter, we have used our model of intentional dynamics to explore how the intentional ecology of the Greek language school included idiosyncratic intentional structures, and how these reflected the individual and shared intentionality of the learners, teachers, and parents of the school. We have shown, also, how derived intentionality evident in learning materials may be understood through the lens of affordances, and following Kostoulas (2018), how derived intentionality across a school's curriculum may be understood as an affordance landscape. Finally, we have argued that attractor states for teaching and learning may arise from the interplay of idiosyncratic intentional structures present in a school context and the derived intentionality of learning materials.

Before ending this chapter, we wish to highlight three insights that the chapter has contributed. The first insight is that schools, whatever their composition, are likely to be idiosyncratic contexts. Each school will have an idiosyncratic intentional ecology shaping teaching and learning activity. In this chapter, we have used our model of intentional dynamics to shed light on such idiosyncratic aspects in a Greek private language school. Next, we tentatively suggest that the idiosyncrasies of language schools may make them "conservative" systems that tend to resist change. We accept that this suggestion is very preliminary, and additional empirical work would be needed for this to be substantiated. However, in the Greek school that we have explored, normative and contingent intentional activity appeared common, and this normative and contingent activity was shaped by the idiosyncrasies of the schools' intentional ecology. Normative and contingent intentional activity is characterised by the dynamics of historicity and adaptiveness, neither of which, by themselves, are particularly likely to generate change. Finally, our analysis suggests that a different sort of intentional dynamics may be needed for curricular reform and innovation to succeed. In this Greek language school, there was a great deal of historicity and adaptiveness, but a possible lack of creative and purposeful intentional activity. Clearly, the curricular reform initiative that preceded the fieldwork for this study may have been both creative and purposeful. Nevertheless, it may be that the teachers and learners did not share in this creativity and sense of purpose. Again, creative and purposeful activity are associated with non-linearity and self-organisation, both of which are driving forces for change in a complex dynamic system (see section 3.1). If there really was a lack of creative and purposeful intentional activity, or if it was not shared across all the school's stakeholders, this may have contributed to the resilience of the form-focused attractor across the curriculum, and hence also the limited success of the curricular reform initiative.

Chapter 9
Sociocultural aspects of TESOL as an intentional ecology

In this last in a series of four chapters that exemplify intentional dynamics in TESOL, we take a closer look at sociocultural aspects of the intentional ecology of TESOL. Our discussion in this chapter is limited, then, to the sociocultural; we do not address individual, shared, or derived aspects of intentionality (see chapter 4). We focus particularly on the international arena of TESOL, so to gain a view of global social and professional influences on TESOL contexts, activity, and outcomes. The chapter also explores how the sociocultural ecology of international TESOL appears to shape, or is reflected in, form-focused, communicative, and critical approaches in TESOL. We conclude with a discussion of the intentional dynamics of change that may be taking place in the sociocultural ecology of international TESOL.

The chapter is divided into three sections, beginning with an outline of salient sociocultural aspects of international TESOL (section 9.1). Following Kostoulas (2018), we analytically divide the sociocultural aspects of international TESOL along linguistic, pedagogical, and political dimensions, and we identify transactional and transformative paradigms that appear to define this sociocultural ecology of TESOL. The second section (9.2) looks at how the sociocultural aspects of international TESOL appear to shape, or are reflected in, broadly defined teaching approaches, including form-focused, communicative, and critical approaches. A final section (9.3) explores what may be the intentional dynamics of change in the sociocultural ecology of international TESOL. We suggest that there may be change – although slow and uneven – from the transactional paradigm, which represents an attractor state in the sociocultural ecology of TESOL, towards an alternative, future transformative paradigm.

9.1 Sociocultural aspects of the intentional ecology of international TESOL

Our discussion in this section draws on Kostoulas (2018), who provides a CDST overview of the "state space" of TESOL. Kostoulas defines this state space as "the range of possible states in which a system [TESOL] can find itself" (2018: 61). Moreover, Kostoulas analyses this state space in terms of linguistic, pedagogical, and political dimensions. In the present section, we retain this analytic division of international TESOL along three dimensions, but we replace the concept of a "state space" with our notion of an intentional ecology. This, we note, is more than a terminological substitution; it reflects the fact that an intentional ecology plays an "active role" in shaping activity, as opposed to a "state space", which is an aggregate of outcomes. The chapter also adopts the term "intentional structures" to define the sociocultural aspects of the intentional ecology of TESOL. As well as being consistent with the idiosyncratic intentional structures at play in the Greek private language school, discussed in chapter 8, we believe intentional structures resonate with the more commonly used notion of social structures, in TESOL and in other informing literatures. Finally, this section explores those linguistic, pedagogical, and political intentional structures which, based on literature review and our own professional experiences, appear particularly salient in international TESOL.

9.1.1 The linguistic dimension of international TESOL

We believe that some of the linguistic intentional structures that shape TESOL consist of relatively under-theorised beliefs about the nature of language. Language is sometimes viewed as little more than a corpus of words and a set of (grammar) rules, which come together to produce text and speech. To the extent that such beliefs can be codified, they seem to relate to structural linguistics (Richards and Rogers 2014), which attempts to describe language as a system of sounds, words, and grammatical markers, and in some cases larger units. This systems perspective on language tends to disregard any connections between the language and the social contexts where it is used. Thus, for some English is "just a language", with no consideration for the sociality of discourse, the power relations that language may index, or how language may shape social reality (e.g., Dendrinos 2009). This view may be called the *language as system* intentional structure; the belief that language is a relatively stable, decontextualised system of words and grammar (Gregg 2010). In some TESOL settings, this intentional structure may even have the status of a normative assumption – i.e., an implicit view shared by a decisive number of stakeholders. Where it is a normative assumption, therefore, the language as system structure may have a decisive influence on teaching and learning in language classrooms.

The "language as a system" intentional structure may co-exist, also, with what may be called the *standard language* intentional structure. This is a hierarchical frame of reference that ascribes value to particular (standard) varieties of the English language, i.e., the ones with the highest prestige, or what Widdowson (2003: 35, original italics) playfully described as "real English, *Anglais real*, Royal English, Queen's English, or (for those unsympathetic to the monarchy) Oxford English". In addition to the 'prestige' varieties of British English, the standard language is often defined by drawing on American English varieties, and occasionally also Australian English varieties, as long as these varieties are ideologically associated with high social status. Not infrequently, the valorisation of the standard variety co-exists with monolingual ideologies, which view linguistic variation as an aberration from an idealised linguistically homogeneous community. In contexts where the standard language view is normative, and hence will determine future opportunities, some authors suggest that it may be pedagogically undesirable, and even unethical, to teach a less prestigious variety of English. For instance, Quirk (1990: 9) argues that deviating from the standard language variety may "lock the least fortunate into the least rewarding careers".

Intentional structures relating to the function of the English language may be similarly under-theorised. This includes the intentional structure of *linguistic instrumentalism* (Kubota 2011; Wee 2008). To many people worldwide, the English language is considered a resource, or a form of cultural capital (Bourdieu 1988), that will facilitate professional and social advancement (Marginson 2006; Watts 2011). As Pim (2013: 19) remarks about primary education, "parents often consider academic excellence in English to be the number one priority in terms of access to higher education, university accreditation and economic prosperity of their children". This, then, may lead to pressure for more intensive teaching at earlier ages. In addition, English-language competence is often a requisite for participation in the global economy, provides membership in various transnational communities (Widdowson 2003), facilitates travel (Park 2014), and – in the context of the information economy – it is not just the means but also the product of professional activity (Heller 2010). In sum, linguistic instrumentalism represents a transactional view of language, learning, and communication, and is focused on maximising future opportunities. Moreover, it may sometimes coincide with the standard language intentional structure; in order to maximise future opportunities, some argue that we should be teaching the most highly valued standard variety of the English language.

Another less theorised view of the English language is what may be called the intentional structure of *English as development*. Pennycook (2001: 56) has called this the "colonial-celebratory position", or the set of beliefs that "trumpets the benefits of English over other languages, suggesting that English is superior to other languages". This intentional structure originates in the belief that the teaching of English is (or was) a "civilising influence" on colonised regions (Crystal 2003: 78). Thus, the origin of this intentional structure may seem somewhat anachronistic. However, the global spread of English continues to be discursively linked with outcomes such as economic development, poverty reduction, and democratisation (Seargeant and Erling 2018). Moreover, in many parts of the world, the English language is increasingly replacing local national languages as the medium of instruction across different levels of otherwise non-English language educational systems (Macaro et al. 2018; van Ginkel 2017; Williams 2015). Thus, the English as development intentional structure often persists alongside the standard language and linguistic instrumentalism intentional structures. From the perspective of this combination of intentional structures, English language teaching and English Medium Instruction acts to enhance individual and social development and opportunity, or conversely, it creates situations where disproportionately less power and prestige is accorded to local languages and educational systems (Stelma and Fay 2019). Despite its colonial origins, this intentional structure appears to remain to this day, in a postcolonial disguise, and in some places as a normative assumption that may have decisive impact on TESOL.

The language as system intentional structure, as well as the other linguistic intentional structures reviewed above, are frequently challenged. We may contrast the above set of structures with what may be called the *language as social action* intentional structure. This is the belief that language shapes, reinforces, and potentially also challenges social structures (e.g., Pennycook 2001). From this position, additional views of English language follow. If language shapes the social world, it follows that language is a situated phenomenon, language reflects the socio-cultural diversity of the world, and for this to be possible there needs to be linguistic diversity. This encourages a view of language as more than just words and grammar; it encourages more inclusive understandings of English, such as those provided by the fields of World Englishes (e.g., Kachru 2017) and English as a Lingua Franca (Seidlhofer 2011). These additional views are often addressed as part of political debates, and we will therefore return to these – as more fully defined intentional structures – in the later discussion of the political dimension of the intentional ecology of international TESOL.

9.1.2 The pedagogical dimension of international TESOL

We now turn our attention to sociocultural intentional structures of TESOL that pertain to language teaching and learning. The first set of intentional structures that we will examine relates to the overarching belief that, in the context of TESOL, learners' opportunities to use English must be maximised. One effect of this belief is the prevalence of strictly monolingual English language teaching programmes. We may call this the *English-only* intentional structure, and this is an intentional structure that appears across a wide range of international TESOL settings (Kerr 2016). English-only policies are often adopted by private language schools – or at least they aspire to offer such a monolingual environment, and this feature is often also exploited in marketing (Phillipson 1992). English-only programmes sometimes appear in state educational systems in the form of integrated language and content models, such as Content and Language Integrated Learning (Nikula et al. 2016), and English as a Medium of Instruction (Dearden 2014). Theoretically, this intentional structure may be related to broader policies of integration (e.g., Gunderson 2007) and monoglossic language ideologies (Flores and Aneja 2017). However, the more practical reality may be that sustained engagement with academic content in English is considered necessary for success in a competitive job market, thereby linking it to the earlier reviewed intentional structures of linguistic instrumentalism and English as development.

Another phenomenon related to maximising learners' opportunities to use English is the global trend to introduce English language instruction for increasingly younger children (see Cameron 2003; Enever 2011; Enever and Lindgren 2017; Muñoz 2006). Driving this trend, we suggest, is the intentional structure of *earlier is better*. The trend to introduce language instruction at younger ages often results from political pressure, parental beliefs, and a discourse of global competitiveness (Copland, Garton, and Burns 2013). The intentional structure appears to have some theoretical justification in L1 development research, in the hypothesis that there may be maturational constraints on second language acquisition (Long 1990; Singleton 2005), and in the calculation that if you start earlier there will be more opportunity and time to use and learn the language (Krashen, Long, and Scarcella 1979). However, the empirical findings that are used to legitimise the "earlier is better" trend seem somewhat incautiously applied to *instructed* L2 development (Snow and Hoefnagel-Höhle 1978), where "conditions regarding number of pupils per classroom, [and] exposure to appropriate input and curriculum time available" may differ from other naturalistic settings (García Mayo 2017: xiii). In fact, the empirical evidence of the impact of early English learning initiatives has been less than impressive (Muñoz 2006; Pfenninger and Singleton 2017; Singleton and Ryan 2004). Nevertheless, the "earlier is better" intentional structure seems to exert a very strong influence on TESOL worldwide.

Also related to maximising opportunities to use the English language, although more indirectly, is the intentional structure of *authenticity*. Authenticity is generally taken to mean that the classroom conditions and language use should approximate the conditions and language use of the real world (McDonough and Shaw 1993). Widdowson (2003: 112) suggests that authenticity is motivated by a desire to avoid the "confinement and routine drudgery" of contrived language, although he also cautions that classroom contexts are fundamentally different from real-life ones. The drive to achieve authenticity has also led to the creation of English language immersion programmes, which seek to maximise students' opportunities to use the English language and to replicate recognisable features of idealised English-speaking environments (e.g., Seargeant 2005). Thus, the intentional structure of authenticity often co-occurs with the standard language intentional structure, reviewed in the previous sub-section. This combination of intentional structures also explains the proliferation of students from non-English speaking contexts participating in study-abroad programmes in English-speaking countries. However, we are aware of anecdotal evidence that such programmes are also located in countries where English is a second language, although more widely used than the country where the students are from.

Another set of intentional structures is focused on the processes of teaching and learning, and these appear related to the shifting roles of the language learner. Since at least the mid-1970s, social aspects of language learning have been foregrounded, and learner roles have shifted from those of problem-solvers, engaged in solving linguistic puzzles, to those of social beings who "constructively interact with their peers and their mentors to develop their identities and communicative resources" (Canagarajah 2015: 20). This shift has given shape to what Holliday (1994: 54) has called the "learning group ideal", which he glosses as the "optimum interactional parameters [. . .] for a process oriented, task-based, inductive, collaborative, communicative language teaching methodology". Thus, following Holliday, we refer to this intentional structure, focused on the social aspects of language learning, as the *learning group* intentional structure.

However, whereas language classrooms are becoming more social, many other aspects of teaching and learning are becoming more technical. We use the term "technical" here to denote two related lines of thinking, which together constitute what we refer to as the intentional structure of *technicalisation*. The first line of thinking is influenced by discourses of modernity, which seek to maximise the professionalism of language education. This line of thinking foregrounds linguistic awareness and teaching expertise (Skela 2019), or what Tudor (2001: 7) has called the "technology of teaching". The second line of thinking is structured by a neoliberal agenda (see the next sub-section) that shifts the goal of education away from preparing citizens, and towards training a workforce (Giroux 1992). Within the context of TESOL, these twin lines of technicalisation are believed to maximize efficiency, sometimes by proposing sharp divisions of labour in TESOL. This means that activities such as curriculum planning, teaching, and the assessment of outcomes are considered separate and specialist professions. Technicalisation may also relate to the intentional structure of linguistic instrumentalism, reviewed in the previous sub-section, as well as politically informed intentional structures, which we will discuss in the next sub-section.

A final intentional structure related to teaching and learning is – following Kumaravadivelu (2006b) – what we will call the *postmethod* intentional structure. This intentional structure has emerged from the interplay between two seemingly opposing trends: the "centripetal force" of globalisation, and the "centrifugal effect" of the continuing presence of the local (Robertson 1995). In the context of TESOL, this is reflected in attempts to strike a workable balance between global trends and Western perspectives on the one hand, and the particularities of local educational traditions on the other. For instance, even though TESOL continues to be informed, at least nominally, by the communicative approach (Richards and Rogers 2014), there is a growing sense of dissatisfaction with this approach (e.g., Díaz Maggioli 2017; Pozzi 2017). The result, in some TESOL settings, is that the communicative approach is either implemented with flexibility (Kumaravadivelu 2006c) or overtly challenged (Bax 2003; Holliday 2005). Moreover, prompted by Prabhu's (1990) pronouncement that "there is no best method", the TESOL profession seems to be re-orienting itself towards contextualised teaching methodologies. Thus, the central element of the postmethod intentional structure is the co-existence of core values from international TESOL and locally appropriate instructional priorities and techniques (Holliday 2005; Kumaravadivelu 2003a, 2006c).

9.1.3 The political dimension of international TESOL

The third dimension of the sociocultural ecology of international TESOL is the political dimension. The first political intentional structure we will discuss is *English as hegemony*. This view is outlined by Phillipson in his seminal publication *Linguistic Imperialism* (1992), where he claims that "the dominance of English is asserted and maintained by the establishment and continuous reconstitution of structural and cultural inequalities between English and other languages" (p. 42). Phillipson relates this power imbalance to a range of phenomena, including the preference for monolingual instruction, the privilege of "native speakers", and the dominance of English in education. As part of his argument, Phillipson alerts us to the structural power relations of the profession (see also Pennycook 2001), and the unidirectional flow of language learning materials and methods from the Anglophone "centre" to the rest of the world (see also Block 2008). Thus, the consequence of the English as hegemony intentional structure is that English language teaching reinforces scholastic, linguistic, cultural, and economic dependence of the rest of the world on the Anglophone centre (Kumaravadivelu 2006a).

An intentional structure that is perhaps more salient in contemporary discourse, but which sometimes appears alongside the hegemonic view, is *neoliberalism*. Neoliberalism is defined by Bourdieu as "a system of beliefs and values, an ethos and a moral view of the world, in short, an *economic common sense*", which is linked to cognitive and social structures (2015: 10, original emphasis). In TESOL, Flubacher and Del Percio (2017: 6) suggest that the neoliberal agenda "has led to the development of standardized curricula, learning objectives and assessment tools that aim to transform every acquired competence into a quantifiable skill, and render workers comparable within and across national economies". More generally, neoliberalism is associated with a number of socioeconomic normative assumptions, including emphasis on individual accomplishment, free movement, privatisation, and competitiveness (Bernstein et al. 2015; Holborow 2015; Piller and Cho 2013). Such socio-economic normative assumptions have had an impact, also, on the development of other intentional structures that we have discussed, including, e.g., the "earlier is better" and the technicalisation intentional structures.

There are also intentional structures in international TESOL that emphasise more inclusive social values, and thus challenge the intentional structure of neoliberalism. One such intentional structure is *diversity*. The intentional structure of diversity values and encourages difference rather than productivity. This intentional structure is developed through a range of scholarship focused on issues such as race, speaker background, student profiles, patterns of intercultural communication, and more. For example, scholarship on race and TESOL highlights the sometimes dehumanising effects of the racial "undertones" of native-speakerism (Javier 2015; Ruecker 2011; Ruecker and Ives 2015), and thus problematizes the dominance of "native speakers" in the TESOL profession (e.g., Aneja 2016; Clark and Paran 2007; Kabel 2009; Selvi 2011). There is also a trend towards greater inclusivity with regard to students, as language education and Applied Linguistics scholarship find new ways to engage with the challenges of globalisation and migration flows (Canagarajah 2018; Schwarzl et al. 2019; Shapiro, Farrelly, and Cuddy 2018). Moreover, the focus on intercultural communication is growing (e.g., Holliday 2010; Kramsch 2011), and there are numerous pedagogical suggestions that value the multilingualism and cultural diversity of learners. Examples of such pedagogies include the Multicultural Awareness Through English model (Fay, Lytra, and Ntavaliagkou 2010), the Intercomprehension framework (Mewald 2019), and models of teacher education that aim to prepare language teachers for working with superdiverse populations (e.g., Kitsiou et al. 2019).

Also challenging the neoliberal agenda is what we call the *critical-humanistic* intentional structure (see chapter 11). The emergence of this intentional structure is symbolically indexed by Widdowson's (2004: 362) remark that "ELT has [. . .] lost its innocence". This intentional structure, then, challenges the unreflective assumption that language and language education are neutral, or innocent, and replaces it with a perspective that views them as political and contested action (Holborow 2012). According to the critical-humanistic perspective "language serves a political purpose, constructing particular meanings and signs that work to mask social conflict" (Codd 1988: 237). In more radical versions of this critical tradition, language education is not just problematised in relation to its political implications. It is reconceptualised, also, as an intervention that aims to challenge unjust social orders. For Canagarajah (1999: 2), for instance, language education "provides for the possibility that the powerless in postcolonial communities may find ways to negotiate, alter and oppose political structures, and reconstruct their languages, cultures and identities to their advantage". However, Canagarajah stresses that to oppose existing political structures, such as neoliberalism, is not a rejection of the English language, but rather an attempt "to *reconstitute* it in more inclusive, ethical and democratic terms" (1999: 2, original emphasis). Thus, the impact of the critical-humanistic intentional structure on TESOL is to develop historically situated understandings of language use, non-essentialist perspectives that foreground hybridity, and an active focus on the needs of the local context (Pennycook 2001: 68).

A final intentional structure that we believe is becoming visible in international TESOL is what we may call the intentional structure of *sustainability*. This intentional structure seems to be emerging from a nexus of some of the structures already discussed, including the diversity and critical-humanistic intentional structures. Sustainability, in this context, may be construed either in a strictly linguistic sense, or in the broader sense of global sustainability. In the first sense, it primarily refers to the preservation of local linguistic ecologies (Phillipson and Skutnabb-Kangas 1996). One area of study that focuses on such preservation is ecolinguistics, which seeks to address issues of language loss and language maintenance in the context of increased language contact (Fill 2018). Also shaped by the linguistic sense of sustainability is scholarship on linguistic human rights (Skutnabb-Kangas 2000), which has implications for national and international language planning (Kaplan 2018). In this linguistic sense, then, there is considerable overlap with the intentional structure of diversity. The second sustainability strand, by contrast, calls for a reorientation of English language education to foster a broader global sustainability. For instance, Edge (2006: xxix) argues that TESOL must be a politically-informed praxis "in which we afford to difference a great deal of the respect that we have previously afforded to conformity". Suggestions have also been made to connect language education with developing ecological awareness (Goulah 2017), there are suggestions for English language teaching to be reformed as "global education" (Lütge 2015; see also Mewald 2019; Wehrmann 2019), and for English language education to serve pro-human and pro-social attitudes in the "global civil society" (Birch 2009). Although it is too early to know what its impact will be, we believe that the intentional structure of sustainability is of potential great importance to the uncertain and changing world that we live in.

9.1.4 Paradigmatic summary

To summarise, we have explored a range of sociocultural aspects of the intentional ecology of international TESOL. We did this by looking at multiple intentional structures, analytically organised into linguistic, pedagogical, and political dimensions. We focused on intentional structures that we – based on our own engagement with the literature and our professional experiences – deem to be salient in TESOL. Taking a step back, the linguistic, pedagogical, and political dimensions of international TESOL suggest some patterns. The linguistic dimension suggests a continuum between the "language as system" and "language as social action" intentional structures; the pedagogical dimension suggests a continuum between the technicalisation and postmethod intentional structures; and the political dimension suggests a continuum between the neoliberal and the critical-humanistic intentional structures. It may be possible, then, to suggest that TESOL contexts, activity, and outcomes are shaped by a combination of intentional structures that span a continuum between (a) a nexus of "language as system", technicalisation, and neoliberal intentional structures, and (b) a nexus of "language as social action", postmethod, and critical-humanistic intentional structures. As suggested by Figure 7, we can take this one step further and postulate that there are two contrasting paradigms for TESOL. We may call the former the *transactional paradigm*; this paradigm seems to be the more dominant paradigm at present, or an attractor state in the sociocultural ecology of TESOL. The latter may be called the *transformative paradigm*; this is not (yet) an attractor state in TESOL, but it is portrayed as a desirable future state by a number of influential, if somewhat different, authors and publications in TESOL and Applied Linguistics (Holliday 2005; Kumaravadivelu 2006a; Ramanathan 2002; Rivers 2014).

Finally, Kostoulas (2018) suggests that the sociocultural aspects of international TESOL are reflected, also, in common language teaching approaches.

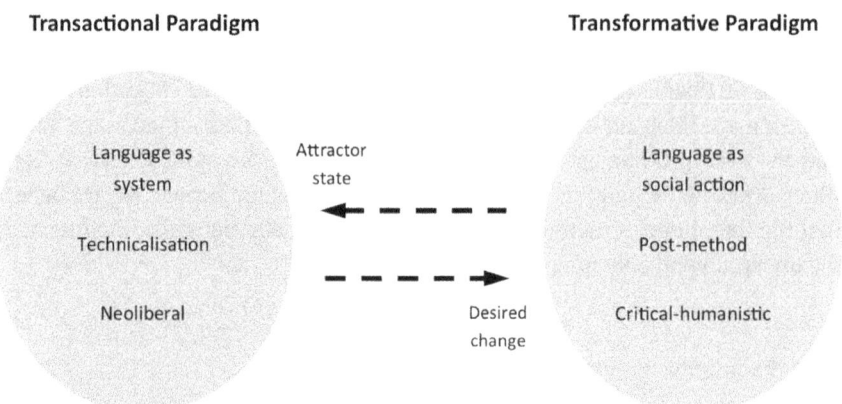

Figure 7: Paradigmatic summary of international TESOL.

In other words, teaching approaches may be shaped by the intentional structures that we have reviewed, or alternatively by the two paradigms suggested by Figure 7. In the next section (9.2), we will explore how the intentional structures that we have introduced may shape, or are reflected in, three broadly defined sets of teaching approaches: form-focused, communicative, and critical approaches. We believe that this is a useful next step, as it may help language teachers, materials writers, researchers, and policy-makers to better understand the sociocultural influences on the approaches they adopt in, or for, local TESOL settings. Finally, in the concluding section (9.3), we will return to the paradigmatic summary – shown in Figure 7 – to comment on how the sociocultural ecology of international TESOL may be moving towards the desirable alternative vision for TESOL – the transformative paradigm – while recognising that this change is constrained by the transactional attractor state.

9.2 Intentional structures and language teaching approaches

In this section we explore how the intentional structures, representing the sociocultural aspects of international TESOL, may be evident in three broadly-defined teaching approaches. We will explore *form-focused*, *communicative*, and *critical approaches*, respectively.

9.2.1 Form-focused approaches

In this chapter, we understand form-focused approaches as a broad category of transmissively-oriented teaching approaches, including among others grammar-translation, the oral methods, and audiolingualism. We accept that these approaches are quite diverse in terms of aims and the pedagogical techniques used. For instance, in the grammar-translation method learners are presented with decontextualized language, and they must use their knowledge of vocabulary and grammar to translate "meaning" from one language to another (Howatt 2004; Stern 1983). By contrast, with the direct method, the oral approach, and situational language teaching (Howatt 2004; Richards and Rodgers 2014) the emphasis shifts from the written modality to the oral one, and value is placed on maximising exposure to the target language. Finally, in audiolingualism, learners are presented with carefully selected segments of language, which they are expected to learn through memorisation and mimesis (Richards and Rodgers 2014). What these approaches do have in common, when viewed from the broad perspective of international TESOL, is an overlapping set of sociocultural intentional structures.

We believe that form-focused approaches tend to be shaped by, and reflect, the transactional paradigm, which is constituted by the "language as system", technicalisation, and neoliberal intentional structures (see Figure 7). Within form-focused approaches, this combination of intentional structures encourages a hybrid structure of standardisation and reproduction. Standardisation is evident in the way the language curriculum is conceptualised as a system of language units and rules, which are to be taught in lockstep, and to be committed to memory by learners. The reproduction element is evident in the narrowing down of the language education curriculum and the use of standardised testing – both of which are forms of technicalisation. Moreover, language learners are required to reproduce the target language units and rules from memory when needed for language use. There is also a sense of reproduction of language learning outcomes across learners, classrooms, and schools. This reproduction of outcomes may be encouraged by the neoliberal focus on competitiveness and accountability, with the outcomes presumed to be linear and measurable. The standard language and linguistic instrumentalism intentional structures are, at times, also evident in form-focused approaches. The English language may be conceptualised as a "single monochrome standard" (Quirk 1985: 6), and typically a prestige variety (Davies 1999). Such a standard language view facilitates standardised language testing, implemented through internationally recognised examinations that are designed in the English-speaking West (e.g., the UK and the US). Moreover, where this standard language view is normative, the intentional structure of hegemony may also be present, at least in indirect form. The international standardised testing regimes, and with economic and social value attached to the resulting certificates, can create an ecology that reinforces the hegemonic status and power of the English language.

Finally, we are not suggesting that all form-focused approaches are shaped by, or reflect, each and all of the aforementioned intentional structures. These sociocultural influences will appear in different constellations across the approaches, and there will be differences in their local implementation. However, when detached from the particularity of local settings, and as viewed from the perspective of international TESOL, we believe the mentioned intentional structures do underpin, and are reflected in, this set of form-focused approaches. Moreover, we believe that the intentional structures that give shape to form-focused approaches are normative in many TESOL settings across the world.

9.2.2 Communicative approaches

The second set of teaching approaches – communicative approaches – also includes a range of methods and techniques. These approaches view language and communication as interconnected, and the central aim is to foster communicative competence (Richards and Rogers 2014; Stelma 2010). There are both strong and weak versions of communicative language teaching (Littlewood 2011), as well as more and less formal versions (R. Ellis 1982). A typical feature of these diverse approaches is "classroom work which involves learners in comprehending, manipulating, producing, or interacting in the target language [. . .] in which the intention is to convey meaning rather than to manipulate form" (Nunan 2004: 4).

The communicative approaches are shaped by a less clearly defined set of intentional structures. At times, the implementation of communicative language teaching appears shaped by the same nexus of intentional structures as that which shapes form-focused approaches – thus including the "language as system", technicalisation, and neoliberal intentional structures. We have personally observed many classrooms where there is careful presentation and practice of new language, but where at the end of a lesson there is no time left for any communicative production stage, thereby depriving the learners from using the language more freely to express meaning. In such cases, the "language as system" parts of the skills-development sequence are retained, but the "language as social action" stage, designed to develop contextually flexible competence (Dekeyser and Criado 2012), is neglected. Moreover, task-based teaching approaches, with carefully prescribed pedagogical steps (R. Ellis 2003; Nunan 2004;

Willis and Willis 2007), are arguably a form of technicalisation. Finally, we have experience, also, of teaching settings where the word "communicative" is evoked for neoliberal marketing purposes, while in reality the teaching and learning is only minimally communicative.

A somewhat different set of influences on communicative approaches is the social turn in western pedagogy, and the associated emergence of the learning group intentional structure. The "earlier is better" intentional structure, with the associated need to develop teaching techniques that are suitable to the cognitive and affective needs of younger learners, is influential as well. Moreover, the value attached to authenticity, with the inclusion of classroom activities and patterns of language use of more immediate relevance to future real-life situations, have bolstered the development and the visibility of communicative approaches. However, communicative approaches shaped by this additional set of intentional structures may, even so, be consistent with the "language as system", technicalisation, and neoliberal nexus of intentional structures. Moreover, these additional intentional structures are often amplified by the norm-providing role of the English-speaking West, with innovation in teaching methodology and standards flowing from these Western settings to the rest of the TESOL world. This may, variously, implicate the standard language, "English as development", and hegemonic intentional structures.

When viewed more theoretically, communicative approaches may again point in the direction of the transactional paradigm, and its intentional structures. An early and influential definition suggested that communicative competence "is composed minimally of grammatical competence, sociolinguistic competence, and [. . .] strategic competence" (Canale and Swain 1980: 27). The inclusion of sociolinguistic competence did recognise a social action dimension. However, this sociolinguistic competence included no recognition of the diversity of English language varieties or discourse patterns one might encounter when crossing national and cultural boundaries, or when such boundaries are blurred. More generally, the "native speaker" bias in the original definitions of communicative competence in TESOL seem inappropriate for informing language education when the goal of learners is to communicate with speakers from a variety of international contexts, including many of whom may not be English native speakers themselves (Alptekin 2002).

However, communicative approaches are not inherently technicalist or neoliberal. In other words, although the history of communicative approaches tends to align with the above described nexus of intentional structures, this is not a reason to dismiss communicative language teaching (Stelma 2010). In fact, communicative approaches may also align with the contrasting "language as social action", postmethod, and critical-humanistic nexus of intentional structures.

A key ingredient for such a reorientation is a more inclusive view of communicative competence; one that can account for English language communication in an increasingly globalised world. This may include a recognition of so-called World Englishes (Kachru 2017), non-native speaker varieties and patterns of discourse, and processes of intercommunication between English language speakers from different backgrounds (Seidlhofer 2011). In place of the standard language view, emphasising Quirk's (1985) monochrome standard, World Englishes scholars tend to emphasise intelligibility, comprehensibility, and interpretability in communication between speakers of different backgrounds (Smith and Nelson 1985). Other scholars replace communicative competence entirely, preferring instead to promote alternative conceptualisations such as symbolic competence (Kramsch and Whiteside 2008) or intercultural communicative competence (Alptekin 2002; Byram 1997). This shift, towards more inclusive and situated forms of communicative competence, are consistent with the intentional structure of diversity.

9.2.3 Critical approaches

Whilst implementations of communicative approaches may reflect varying sets of intentional structures, critical approaches reflect the language as social action, postmethod, and critical-humanistic nexus of intentional structures. Compared to form-focused and communicative approaches, critical approaches are relatively harder to define in terms of how teaching and learning is structured and implemented. Rather, the defining feature of critical approaches is a view of language education as a social intervention, and the aim of making the intervention of language education both more explicit and more "just".

Critical approaches reject the value-free "language as system" view, and replace it with the "language as social action" intentional structure. Language as social action has the power to reinforce existing social orders. This may be illustrated using the concept of indexicality (Blommaert 2007; Hughes and Tracy 2015), which describes how words and discourse may "point to" existing orders of power and privilege, or may "point out" disadvantage and servitude. The classic example, which resists change even to this day, is the use of masculine pronouns to index individuals holding positions of power, authority, and expertise. Each additional occurrence of this masculine indexicality reinforces, both to individuals as well as in shared and sociocultural ways, existing social orders. Often, the standard language and hegemonic intentional structures, which often shape form-focused approaches, and sometimes also the communicative ones, will contribute to the reproduction of existing systems of indexicality.

Finally, critical approaches encourage teachers, learners, and other stakeholders to continually problematize the normative assumptions that underpin unjust social orders (Pennycook 2001). Thus, critical teaching views both language use and language education as social action with the potential to either reproduce or challenge existing, and possibly unjust, social orders. This agenda is captured by Kumaravadivelu's (2006c) postmethod proposal. At the core of this proposal are overarching principles, some of which are narrowly linguistic (e.g., integrating language skills, facilitating meaningful classroom interaction) and some of which have a more social outlook (e.g., promoting pro-social perspectives, visualising possible and desired alternatives). The actual implementation of these principles, however, is not prescribed. In Kumaravadivelu's words, a postmethod pedagogy provides "an alternative to method, rather than an alternative method as such" (2003c: 32–33). Instead, the postmethod intentional structure empowers teachers with autonomy, encouraging them to decide, on their own, what specific methods and techniques are most appropriate to their context, and most likely to enhance their learners' autonomy. This may include helping language learners to develop critical literacy skills necessary for understanding the role of the English language in politics and society, and in shaping views of race, gender, and other socially constructed divisions. It also involves teachers problematising how unjust social orders may be embedded in the discourses and practices of TESOL, and a commitment to reflexively interrogating one's own assumptions and roles in generating, sustaining, and challenging these discourses and practices.

9.3 Conclusion: Intentional structures and change

In summary, this chapter has explored sociocultural aspects of the intentional ecology of international TESOL. We have outlined linguistic, pedagogical, and political dimensions of TESOL, including a number of intentional structures that we suggest give shape to, and are reflected in, common teaching approaches in TESOL. In this section, we return to the paradigmatic summary (shown in Figure 7) and discuss what may be the intentional dynamics of change in the sociocultural ecology of international TESOL.

Figure 8 superimposes the three sets of teaching approaches, as discussed in the previous section, onto the paradigmatic summary provided in section 9.1. Figure 8 suggests the possibility of change, from the current and dominant transactional paradigm, which is an attractor state in the sociocultural ecology of international TESOL, to a possible, future transformative paradigm for TESOL. However, we accept that the transactional paradigm and attractor state is a

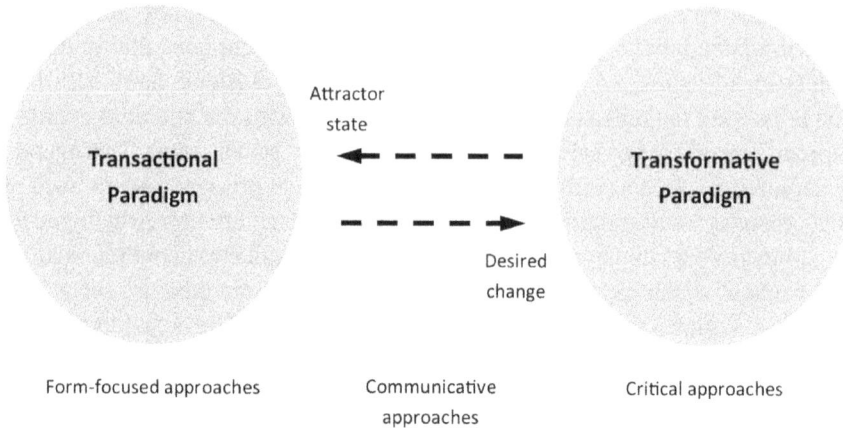

Figure 8: Change in paradigms and teaching approaches.

strong one, and that any shift to the alternative transformative vision for TESOL is slow, uneven, and may never be fully realised (but see also chapter 11). The figure suggests that form-focused and critical approaches fit with the transactional and transformative paradigms, respectively. The communicative approaches, however, seem to fall in-between the two paradigms. Communicative approaches tend to be constrained by the transactional attractor state, but may on occasion appear to bridge to the alternative transformative vision for TESOL. In the following paragraphs, we will comment in more detail on the possible change that is suggested by Figure 8, as well as the obstacles we see in the way of TESOL moving to an alternative transformative future.

At the time of writing, we believe that, on the whole, teaching approaches across the world of TESOL tend to be either form-focused or communicative. English language education has expanded world-wide during a period of rapid economic exchange and development, and this environment of economic exchange and development has been fertile ground for the language as system, technicalisation, and neoliberal intentional structures. These intentional structures are relatively restrictive in terms of language education activity (e.g., the reproduction of the standard language ideology, the reliance on memorisation and mimesis, and the instrumental role of standardised testing), and tend not to be consciously experienced by language teachers and learners (e.g., the power asymmetries associated with linguistic hegemony). Moreover, the historicity of this nexus of intentional structures are likely to produce intentional activity that is contingent or normative. Contingent intentional activity pertains when the teacher responds to situations without much conscious consideration, and normative intentional activity effectively reproduces established ways of thinking and doing (see section 5.3). A teacher may design a lesson focussing on the presentation, controlled practice, and free production of a grammar structure, either because she is following the implicit structure of her learning materials (contingent), or because past experience has convinced her that this is an efficient way to teach (normative). These contingent and/or normative intentional activities, we suggest, serve to recursively strengthen the intentional structures that they rely on, leading to intentional dynamics that resist change (see also chapter 8).

We do think that communicative approaches include, within themselves, the potential to challenge normative intentional structures. Communicative approaches, more than the form-focused ones, encourage creative and purposeful intentional activity. In particular, the learning group intentional structure may encourage creative intentional activity, with teachers or learners attempting to subvert expectations produced by historicity (e.g., by introducing new activity types), sometimes leading to unexpected, non-linear outcomes. Communicative approaches also have an inbuilt sense of purpose, as they are designed to prepare learners for communication in the real world. In the classroom, this may give rise to teachers altering intended learning outcomes (e.g., to further develop speaking skills), and implementing specific activities to realize these outcomes (e.g., by introducing more group work and by increasing the proportion of speaking activities in the classroom). From our CDST perspective, creative and purposeful intentional activity may lead to enhanced affordances for activity in the classroom and beyond. For this reason, the intentional dynamics of communicative approaches may have contributed to its swift adoption in the early 1980s. It may also have contributed to the rapid turnover of more specific communicative approaches in the decade that followed (Richards and Rogers 2014). Over time, however, as expectations regarding communicative language teaching have become more predictable, the intentional dynamics and associated intentional activity may have shifted to become more normative and/or contingent, and thus posing less of a challenge to prevailing orders in TESOL. Thus, communicative approaches today may pose a more limited challenge to the normativity of the standard language, linguistic instrumentalism, and hegemonic intentional structures.

By contrast, the intentional structures giving shape to, and reflected in, critical approaches, are uniquely constituted to encourage change. Language and language education as social action are meant to transform social ecologies; the intentional structure of diversity provides an openness to new and different perspectives; and the purpose of critical-humanism is to challenge the normative assumptions that underpin the intentional structures of standard language, hegemony, and neoliberalism. We note, however, that critically informed teaching and learning are not frequently encountered in actual practice. This is somewhat paradoxical, considering that the nexus of intentional structures that shape, and are reflected in, critical approaches are visible and continually developed in current TESOL scholarship (Edge 2006; Pennycook 1999; Ramanathan 2002; Rivers 2014). It is similarly hard to trace, in TESOL practice, the impact of many strands of research in Applied Linguistics, which have focused on plurilingual development (e.g., Cenoz and Gorter 2011; May 2014), heteroglossia (e.g., Blackledge and Creese 2014; Flores and Schissel 2014), plurilingual, intercultural, and performative competences (e.g., Byram 1997; Canagarajah 2013; Marshall and Moore 2018), the ways in which teachers and learners construct their social and cultural identities (Norton 2013, 2016), symbolic power theory (Kramsch 2015), and the (geo)political forces that are shaping multilingual institutional contexts of instruction (Phillipson 2009; Ramanathan and Morgan 2009).

In sum, we believe that the resilience of the sociocultural intentionality that views TESOL as a purely linguistic/pedagogical phenomenon that is confined to largely monolingual classrooms, and is relatively unconcerned with ethical and political implications of language contact, attests to the constraining power of the transactional attractor. We are concerned, in addition, that the bottom-up approach to change that appears to be preferred by the critical-humanistic intentional structure, whereby teachers and learners seek to change TESOL through a local-is-better mind-set, may have a somewhat limited impact on the normative and dominant neoliberal order. This is something that we will return to in chapter 11, where we argue that creative and purposeful intentional activity across *all* domains of TESOL, including *everyone* from learners to policy-makers, is our best chance to challenge and replace the neoliberal influence of the transactional paradigm.

Part C: **Extending the model of intentional dynamics**

Chapter 10
Language learning as intentional becoming

In the previous four chapters we exemplified intentional dynamics in TESOL, including a focus on the emergence and shaping influence of individual, shared, derived, and sociocultural aspects of the intentional ecology of TESOL. This is the first chapter that seeks to extend the reach of intentional dynamics to a new area of TESOL, where we believe our model may contribute to new understanding and new action. The particular focus of this chapter is a re-conceptualisation of L2 language learning as *intentional becoming*.

We use as our starting point existing conceptualisations of *language use* as a dynamic, or complex dynamic system (Elman 1995; Five Graces Group 2009) and *language learning* as an emergent phenomenon (N. C. Ellis 1998; Hohenberger and Peltzer-Karpf 2009). Thus, a first section (10.1) introduces relevant CDST perspectives on language use, and then adds our intentional dynamics to provide a conceptualisation of language use as intentional activity. Specifically, we show how language use as a complex dynamic system may be extended to include, more profoundly, the dimension of meaning, as captured by the individual, shared, derived, and sociocultural aspects of intentional ecologies. The next section (10.2) introduces relevant CDST perspectives on language learning, and then again adds our intentional dynamics. We argue that a more inclusive CDST account of language learning should recognise how language learners are becoming intentional, both as learners and users of the L2. In a final section (10.3), we discuss what new action our view of language learning as intentional becoming might promote. We present three principles for L2 language education, suggesting that (1) language education should promote a diverse intentional ecology for our learners, which would enable (b) learners to engage in a diversity of intentional activity, and thereby (3) support them to become intentional users and learners of the new language.

10.1 The intentional dynamics of language use

This section represents the first step towards reconceptualising language learning as intentional becoming. A first sub-section looks at recent conceptualisations of *language use* as a complex dynamic system. A second sub-section considers how the CDST view can be extended to incorporate meaning and meaning-making, using our model of intentional dynamics.

10.1.1 Language use as a complex dynamic system

As we have alluded to already (chapter 3), CDST has been a part of TESOL, as well as its informing academic field of Applied Linguistics, for some time already. In the 1970s, the realisation emerged that language use and learning was more than simple cognitive rehearsal. Language teachers themselves questioned the audio-lingual and translation-based approaches, which were based on behaviourist and structural linguistic traditions, as "simply not working" (Julian Edge, personal communication). Sociolinguistics saw a similar shift to more organic, ecological, and/or dynamic thinking, including social-semiotic (Halliday 1978) and communicative (Sauvignon 1983) views of language and language teaching. Soon, more explicit mentions of language as a dynamic system emerged, as in Brumfit's (1980: 3) observation that "with language, as with any other semiotic system, we construct and play, adapt and refine, stretch and twist and break the components of the system in order to create new messages, for ourselves or for others. We acquire a flexible, dynamic system; and the process of acquisition must itself be flexible and dynamic".

In its more explicit form, the view of language use as a complex dynamic system arguably originated in connectionism, a sub-field of cognitive psychology (see Elman et al. 1996). The connectionist view was presented as a counter to both Chomsky's nativist explanation of language (Chomsky 1986, [1981] 1993), as well as the mainstream information-processing alternatives (J. R. Anderson 1996; McLaughlin, Rossman, and McLeod 1983). The connectionist view of language use as a dynamic phenomenon challenged the following normative consensus (Elman 1995: 198–199).
- the commitment to word types as context-free symbolic representations, and word tokens as bound to more specific situations;
- words as the objects of syntactical processing;
- mental representations, including the complex mental representations "built" by multiple constituent parts (words, syntax, and other psychological states) as inherently static; and
- language processing described with a 'building metaphor', with words acting as "the bricks in a building" and syntactical rules "the mortar that binds them together".

Larsen-Freeman and Cameron (2008a: 79) argue that this existing normative consensus "may yield descriptive adequacy", but also that it "provides no vocabulary or concepts for the discussion of dynamic processes". The connectionist counterproposal, of the late 1980s and 1990s, was that the mind is a massively distributed network of nodes, that language use represents particular patterns of activation in this network, and that language learning is the emergence of new patterns of activation. According to Elman, rather than being objects or "bricks", words act as inputs that effect and affect the patterns of activation; conversely, syntactical rules act as attractor states for patterns of activation. Critical in this account is the notion of time; language use at any point "will be some function of the current inputs plus the network's prior state" (Elman 1995: 201). Thus, all language processing in the mind may "pass through" a number of "forks", with paths of varying probabilities that reflect *historicity*. Where past experience has strongly primed the network to follow particular activation patterns (with probabilities closer to 1.0), language use may be quite predictable. However, in the case of less familiar language (e.g., L2 learners struggling with new words or syntax), the possible paths may include minimal differences in probability, or there may be a lack of pathways altogether. In such cases, prior states will play a reduced role, and language in the mind may be more adaptive to situations, and possibly also exhibit non-linearity. Hoey (2005: 9), whose lexical priming theory resembles that of connectionism, explains this as follows (using the word "priming" to express probabilities).

> Every time we use a word, and every time we encounter it anew, the experience either reinforces the priming by confirming an existing association between the word and its co-texts and contexts, or it weakens the priming, if the encounter introduces the word in an unfamiliar co-text or context or if we have chosen in our use of it to override its current priming.

The connectionist view of language as a complex dynamic system is limited to processes that take place in the human brain. However, it paved the way for more broadly bounded CDST accounts in TESOL. An early account was that of Larsen-Freeman (1997: 142), whose purpose was to "call attention to the similarities among complex non-linear systems occurring in nature and language and language acquisition". Larsen-Freeman observed that the view that language use is shaped by a variety of system levels, and that language changes diachronically, was already well-established in the linguistic sciences. However, she also observed that the existing models did not "capture well the dynamism and variability of language in use" (p. 147), and that existing models were unsuited to explain the non-linearity of diachronic growth and change. Finally, Larsen-Freeman suggested that a CDST explanation "makes no distinction between current use and change/growth; they are isomorphic processes. Every time language is used, it changes" (p. 148). This explains how language use derives its dynamic properties from its use, by humans, to make meaning. As Slobin (1996) has argued, we need to shift our focus from "thought and language" to "thinking for speaking". In this vein, Larsen-Freeman and Cameron

(2008a: 102) refer to language in the mind as "process representations", indicating that linguistic mental representations are only meaningful when language is being used. Thus, the current CDST view of language in TESOL resembles that of connectionism, but draws wider system boundaries. For instance, the Five Graces Group (2009: 2) believe that language use as a complex dynamic system has the following elements and features.
(a) Language as a complex dynamic system includes multiple interacting agents (i.e., speakers);
(b) Speakers' language use is based on past interactions, and past and current language use affect future language use;
(c) A speaker's language use is shaped by a range of factors, including perceptual and social processes;
(d) Patterns of language use emerge from patterns of experience, social interaction, and cognition.

The first two features are aptly explained by Larsen-Freeman and Cameron's (2008a: 115) suggestion that language "is the way it is because of the way it has been used". This use of language, then, extends beyond cognitive processes, to social uses among people. On this broader social arena, as the boundary of a broader complex dynamic system, patterns of language use may exhibit greater or lesser degrees of historicity. A social situation may appear quite familiar, with a great deal of historicity informing what happens. Thus, strong attractor states (i.e., patterns of language use with probabilities close to 1.0) may result in language use that is predictable, and this may also enable the complex dynamic system to resist, or adapt to, perturbations. By contrast, in unfamiliar social situations, or when we struggle with unfamiliar language, language use may be characterised by greater degrees of non-linearity, and the adaptiveness of the system may allow language use to shift to new states. The presence of all of these dynamic properties, simultaneously, is a feature of language use, and it means that patterns of language use in any situation may be either more or less stable. As N. C. Ellis (2007: 24) suggests, patterns of language use are usually "sufficiently apparent to have allowed generations of linguists to describe their categories and rules of combination, yet obscure enough to prevent agreement".

The Five Graces Group's third feature of language use as a complex dynamic system (see above) reminds us that direct perceptual processes may also play a role. We may raise our voice to get someone's attention, or we may speak slowly for emphasis, and these are features of language use that others can perceive directly (as in Gibson's [1979] original definition of information "pick-up"; see section 2.2). However, as suggested by our earlier exploration of ecological theory, and the concept of affordances, language use will be shaped – a great deal we argue – by social motives, and by mediated affordances that rely on various forms of intentionality as information (see section 5.2). Finally, the fourth feature suggested by The Five Graces Group resonates perhaps most clearly with our own model of intentional dynamics. Language use, just as all intentional activity, is shaped by both individual and social forms of experiencing and knowing. Again, the four features, taken together, reinforce the view that language use as a complex dynamic system is intimately tied to how we, as individual and social beings, use language to make meaning.

10.1.2 Language use as intentional dynamics and intentional activity

When we use language, we are "in dialogue not only with other human beings and with ourselves, but also with the natural and the cultural configurations we lump together as 'the world'" (Alfaro 1996: 272). This view has been voiced by various researchers for a long time. For instance, Blumer (2005: 91), working within the influential Symbolic Interactionist movement, has suggested that,

> human beings interpret or "define" each other's actions instead of merely reacting to each other's actions. Their "response" is not made directly to the actions of one another but instead is based on the meaning which they attach to such actions. Thus, human interaction is mediated by the use of symbols, by interpretation, or by ascertaining the meaning of one another's actions. This mediation is equivalent to inserting a process of interpretation between stimulus and response in the case of human behavior.

Thus, language use is a central means for connecting with ourselves, others, and the world around us in meaningful ways, and thus contributes to what we refer to as an intentional ecology (see chapter 4). The CDST view of language use, which we outlined in the previous section, adopts the same broader boundaries for understanding language use. However, this CDST view lacks a theorised connection between cognitive and social processes, or language and other forms of knowledge. Individuals' linguistic processing remains the domain of psycholinguistics, and social meaning and meaning-making is the domain of sociolinguistics. Equally, individuals' epistemic meaning and meaning-making remains the domain of cognitive psychology, and the roles of social structure and interaction is in the domain of social/sociocultural theory. We suggest that our model of intentional dynamics, with its focus on individual, shared, derived, and sociocultural aspects of intentionality, offers a possible way to merge the interests of psycho- and socio-linguistics, as well as cognitive psychology and social/sociocultural theory. If we view language use as an integral part of an intentional ecology, with an interplay of individual, shared, derived, and sociocultural aspects of intentional ecologies, then a more comprehensive understanding of language use as a complex dynamic system is possible.

Beginning with *individual intentionality*, we do think that learners develop their own individual understanding of both language (words, grammar, pragmatics, and more) and intentionality (psychological states that are about themselves, others, and the world). However, distilling what is individual within a broader intentional or linguistic ecology is difficult. Language use and our psychological states are at the same time individual, shared, and sociocultural. It may be better, then, to establish – somehow – that there are aspects of language use and thinking that *point to* the existence of individual intentionality. The Piagetian perspective is helpful in this regard. Piaget's constructivism suggests that knowledge, including linguistic knowledge, is individually constructed. The individual constructs linguistic and other knowledge through the cognitive processes of assimilation and accommodation. These Piagetian processes, then, point to the existence of individual intentionality. Notions such as linguistic identity and relativity provide additional clues as to the existence of individual dimensions of linguistic knowledge and intentionality. Of course, we do not reject alternative sociocultural accounts. Individual intentionality and individual understanding of language does not exist in isolation from the broader dynamics of intentional activity. Moreover, individual intentionality is best described not as static knowledge representations, but rather as Larsen-Freeman and Cameron's *process representations* (2008a: 102), whose probabilities for activation in any next situation are shaped by both past and present intentional dynamics.

We suggest, in addition, that there is particular language use associated with *shared intentionality*. Eckert (2003: 113) argues that "language plays a key role in the creation and maintenance of social groups". It is in social groups that we experience shared intentionality. Many of us, especially those who have multiple siblings, may have, or recall having had, unique ways of using language in our families. Such intra-group language may include specific words or expressions, or in the case of multilingual families, it may include particular patterns of code-switching (Hua 2008), or what Søndergaard (1991) has called a "familylect". This extends to education as well, with Eckert (2003) suggesting that attending compulsory education can be a "social hothouse" where there is a great deal of energy that goes into negotiating relationships. Eckert (2003: 113) goes on to suggest that "by virtue of its institutional status, standard language is associated with education, institutional affiliation, homogeneity, and conservatism; vernaculars, by contrast, are associated with an anti-institutional stance, local orientation, diversity of contact, and local innovation". Finally, in his work on small cultures, Holliday (1999) evokes the notion of "discourse community" to describe intra-group language. According to Swales (1990), a discourse community has shared goals, a threshold of expertise needed for membership, and a shared vocabulary/language to intercommunicate. Thus, shared intentionality and language use are connected in discourse communities. Hymes' (1972) notion of a "heterogeneous speech community", which gives space to "expressive values, socially determined perception, contextual styles and shared norms" (1972: 59) is another way to view intra-group language. These various perspectives, then, provide clues not only to the social and individual significance of intragroup language, but also its status as shared intentionality.

Language use and *derived intentionality* exhibits what is perhaps the clearest and most direct relationship. Borrowing from Edge (1993: 46), derived intentionality in language may be understood as "the textualization of human awareness". Thus, as rehearsed in chapter 4 (see section 4.2), when language users generate speech and text, meanings become assigned or sedimented into actual and observable language use. When this happens, the derived intentionality of spoken and written language does not represent simple "subjective" or "objective" meaning structures. Bakhtin (1981) reminds us of the heteroglossic, dialogic, and polyphonic qualities of texts. Likewise, Kristeva's (1986) intertextuality, which she presented as a further development of Bakhtin's work, reminds us that texts should be understood as "differential and historical, as traces and tracings of otherness, since they are shaped by the repetition and transformation of other textual structures" (Alfaro 1996: 268). Thus, the derived intentionality of language use is created "out of the sea of former texts [and speech] that surround us, the sea of language we live in. And we understand the texts [and speech] of others within that same sea" (Bazerman 2004: 83–84). We add to this that the derived intentionality of language use, both written and spoken, includes not only dipping into the pool of other (and others') language use. It includes, also, dipping into broader ecologies of intentionality, and thus involves "the repetition and transformation" of individual, shared and sociocultural aspects of these intentional ecologies. Academic writing, with its overt and tacit reliance on previous authors' work, on whose proverbial "shoulders we stand", is a salient example of such an engagement with a broader intentional ecology of ideas, and thus intertextuality in action (Pecorari and Shaw 2012).

Finally, in chapter 4 (section 4.2) we discussed how indexicality (see Hughes and Tracy 2015) was a feature of derived intentionality. However, indexicality may also be understood as the connection between language and cultural patterns, societal structures, and hence to sociocultural aspects of intentional ecologies. In Critical Applied Linguistics, indexicality is used as "a sensitising concept that [. . .] point[s] a finger to (index!) important aspects of power and inequality" (Blommaert 2007: 118). For instance, the use of dominant (e.g., UK and US) varieties of English in TESOL curricular materials indexes (points to) how these may be of greater valuable than other varieties of English. Moreover, Blommaert (2007: 117) suggests that patterns of indexicality, whether this be dominant language varieties or specific vocabulary, represent "systemic patterns of authority, of control and evaluation, and hence of inclusion and exclusion by real or perceived others". Our view, however, is that indexicality, in-and-of-itself, is not inherently ideological, or political. Language use can index both more or less politically charged sociocultural aspects of intentional ecologies.

In sum, what we have suggested is that the complex dynamic system of language use is located within a broader intentional ecology of human experience, and that the dynamism of language use needs to be understood as part of the broader intentional dynamics that play out in situations, such as L2 classroom interaction. We are suggesting, therefore, that language use, just as all other activity we find ourselves engaging in within TESOL, is complex, dynamic, *and* intentional.

10.2 The intentional dynamics of language learning

We now move from language use to language learning. We begin by reviewing the CDST view of L2 language learning, which emphases the emergent nature of language in the mind, and then consider this view in light of our model of intentional dynamics.

10.2.1 Language learning as an emergent phenomenon

On one level, the shift in focus, from a CDST view of language use to a CDST view of L2 language learning, is theoretically uncomplicated and intuitive. If language use is a complex dynamic system, then every new situation of using language will shape us, and shape our individual and collective language resources. In connectionist terms, every linguistic input or output strengthens or weakens cognitive patterns of activation, and thus alters the complex dynamic system of language in our minds. This is what Larsen-Freeman and Cameron (2008a) meant when they suggested that current language use and change/growth of language use are isomorphic processes. Thus, just as language use emerges in situations, longer-term L2 development is itself an emergent phenomenon (N. C. Ellis 1998; Hohenberger and Peltzer-Karpf 2009; MacWhinney 1999). In fact, this view of language use and language learning as isomorphic underpins what has been called the strong version of communicative language teaching, "in the sense of a methodology in which students are always engaged in communication" (Littlewood 2011: 542). However, and particularly in the case of classroom-based L2 language learning, we believe that the CDST view of language learning needs some additional unpacking.

We suggest that L2 language learning is constituted by three analytically distinct complex dynamic processes. Each process will have its "own" dynamic properties, but all three contribute, as analytically defined sub-systems, to the overall complex dynamic system of language learning. The three processes are:
- The process (and dynamic properties) of *language use*, as reviewed in the previous section;
- The process (and dynamic properties) of *language learning activity*;
- The process (and dynamic properties) of *longer-term L2 development*, which results from successive experiences of language use and language learning activity.

We have already established how *language use*, shaped by an intentional ecology, may activate either familiar or novel patterns of activation in a language learner's mind. In the case of familiar language, the language use will be characterised by the dynamic property of adaptiveness (e.g., our ability to use vocabulary and grammar with both stability and flexibly across different situations) and historicity (e.g., repetition of previously learnt vocabulary or grammar). However, the task of a language learner includes engaging with new language, and this will introduce the dynamic property of non-linearity. Non-linearity may also be encouraged if a language teacher sets a task that deliberately asks learners to be creative with the language. Thus, the language use of a language learner will include ample opportunities for activating patterns of language use on the mind, including both familiar and new language and meanings. The problem with this view, however, is that learners in language classrooms do more than simply using the language. Thus, we need to look beyond the dynamic properties of language use only when explaining language learning. What learners actually do in L2 classrooms, or when they are studying the language in more autonomous situations, includes both experiential and analytical strategies (Littlewood 2011), and this may include memorising new words, trying to understand new grammar, practising new functions, or doing either form- or meaning-based tasks set by a teacher or textbook. We can think of this more inclusive view of language learning as a complex dynamic system of *language learning activity*.

L2 language learning researchers have focused a great deal on language learning as activity. For instance, *negotiation of meaning* research suggests that language learning, or acquisition, takes place when language classroom interaction includes rhetorical devices such as clarification and confirmation requests, comprehension checks, as well as repetitions, repairs, corrections, and completions (Doughty and Pica 1986; Long 1983; Oliver 1998). Sociocultural researchers, by contrast, suggest that learning takes place when "more knowledgeable others" scaffold the activity of the "less knowledgeable" learners (DiCamilla and Anton 1997; Donato 1994; Ohta 1995), when learners are engaged in metalinguistic talk during critical, or language-related, episodes in tasks (Kowal and Swain 1994; Swain and Lapkin 1995; Storch 1998), or when learners' talk exhibits particular participatory structures (N. Mercer 1995, 1996). Task-based researchers focus on learning that occurs when students use language that exhibits particular complexity, accuracy, and/or fluency (Bygate 1999; Skehan and Foster 1997), when the task promotes particular patterns of participation (Stelma 2003; Storch 2002), or when tasks with particular stages are used (Nunan 2004; Skehan 1996; Willis and Willis 2007).

We believe that it is analytically useful to think of language learning activity as having its own distinct dynamic properties. Language learning activity may be familiar and predictable; a teacher may be consistent in how she introduces new language, in how she provides feedback, or in the types of tasks she employs. Thus, language learning activity may exhibit both adaptiveness and historicity. Alternatively, learners may be asked to do unfamiliar tasks, and the resulting activity may exhibit non-linearity and self-organisation of unexpected outcomes. Thus, we now have two analytically defined complex dynamic sub-systems (see section 3.1); a complex dynamic system of language use and a complex dynamic system of language learning activity. These two sub-systems will be in continual interplay, both contributing to soft-assemble the intentional activity of language learning. However, as different complex dynamic systems, they are shaped by slightly different intentional ecologies, and will be characterised by different intentional activity. Whereas language use is shaped by the ecology of ideational intentionality at play in communicative or other language use situations, language learning activity is (often) a purposeful intentional activity focused on accumulating new linguistic knowledge, or the ability to perform in *future* communicative or other language use situations.

The two complex dynamic sub-systems – language use and language learning activity – together shape the complex dynamic sub-system of *L2 development*, which is what we are ultimately seeking to explain. Thus, the suggestion that language use and language learning are isomorphic processes ceases to apply. Instead, L2 development results from the interplay of both language use and language learning activity, and it will therefore have its own unique dynamic properties. Just as language use and language learning activity, L2 development may include adaptiveness, historicity, non-linearity, and self-organisation. The dynamic property of adaptiveness may be somewhat obtuse in L2 development over longer timescales. Adaptiveness describes flexible adjustment to the environment and situations we find ourselves in, and this is intuitively more applicable to the real-time processes of language use and language learning activity. L2 researchers have documented how L2 development includes a great deal of variability (Verspoor et al. 2008), and this may offer clues to adaptiveness across the longer timescale of L2 development. Historicity in L2 development seems easier to identify. This may include L1 language transfer (Odlin 1989), overgeneralisation of interlanguage features (Selinker 1972, 2013), or relying on patterns of activation that have high probabilities (see the earlier discussion of connectionism). Finally, L2 development as a form of change will, by necessity, exhibit non-linearity and self-organisation (Ke et al. 2002; Hohenberger 2002; Hohenberger and Peltzer-Karpf 2009). In fact, L2 development results from the self-organisation of new patterns of activation, or new attractor states, as defined by the broader intentional ecology and (overall) complex dynamic system of language education, and it is the job of teachers and learners to select combinations of language use and language learning activities to enable this self-organisation to take place.

Finally, the dynamic properties of the three complex dynamic sub-systems of language use, language learning activity, and L2 development will be in continual interplay, and sometimes in ways deliberately manipulated by teachers. For instance, a teacher may ask her learners to use language that is new to them, but she might use a highly familiar classroom learning activity to scaffold this experience. Thus, the historicity of the activity counters lack of historicity of the language use that is encouraged, and this may create opportunities for creative and purposeful intentional activity that affects the trajectory of the complex dynamic system of L2 development. Alternatively, a teacher may try to deepen her learners understanding of already familiar language through a deliberately creative classroom activity. In this case, the language use that is encouraged includes historicity, but this historicity is challenged by the non-linearity of the learning activity, and this may again shape the trajectory of the complex dynamic system of L2 development.

10.2.2 Language learning as intentional activity

The above CDST account of language use, language learning activity, and L2 development has not addressed meaning and meaning-making. Orr and Cappannari (1964), working in anthropological linguistics, aptly explain why meaning must be part of any account of language use and learning. They suggest that an "essential feature of language is its arbitrariness, i.e., phonemes and morphemes do not have inherent meaning", and that "for language to be arbitrary implies, among other things, that close contact and sharing between members of a group must have been present for it to have evolved" (1964: 320). Thus, an adequate theory of L2 use, learning, and development must consider the social roles of language, and how meaning is made.

CDST researchers do stress the need for a focus on meaning. Larsen-Freeman and Cameron (2008a: 79) suggest that "linguistic forms interact with non-linguistic information in the determination of meaning". Kramsch (2008), developing her symbolic interactionist version of ecological theory, overtly suggests that language teachers should be "teachers of meaning". Finally, The Five Graces Group (2009: 3) argue that "the nature of language follows from its role in social interaction", and that "the individual actions that form [. . .] joint action must be coordinated for the joint action to be carried out successfully". Drawing on Bratman's conceptualisation of "shared cooperative activity" (see Bratman 1999), they give the example of moving a piano, and how things would break down if "mental attitudes" where not shared. This, the Five Graces Group suggest, is where language comes in; language enables the requisite mental attitudes to be shared. However, these statements fall short of integrating meaning or meaning-making into a complex dynamic systems theory of language learning. In fact, we have yet to find scholarship that makes meaning and meaning-making a theorised part of a CDST view of language use, language learning activity, or L2 development.

Motivated by our model of intentional dynamics (see chapter 5), our position is that learning a new language is inherently becoming a part of a new intentional ecology, and engaging in new intentional activity. L2 development is developing individual and shared intentionality, as well as the ability to access and engage with derived and sociocultural aspects of intentionality, as defined and expressed through the new language. Thus, when we learn a new language, our "horizon" of experience and understanding may gradually expand, to include knowing, feeling, saying, and doing in the new language and with new intentionality.

Figure 9 depicts our more inclusive CDST model of language learning. The figure reflects our model of intentional dynamics, presented in Figure 2 (chapter 5). The model incorporates the three complex dynamic sub-systems of language use, language learning activity, and L2 development, which we reviewed in the previous sections. We are suggesting that the complex dynamic system of *language use* is intentional activity, and that its dynamic properties (D1 in Figure 9) are shaped by the intentional ecology of the new language, as played out in the psycho- and socio-linguistic intentional dynamics governing the classroom or other situations. This psycho- and socio-linguistic intentional ecology will include

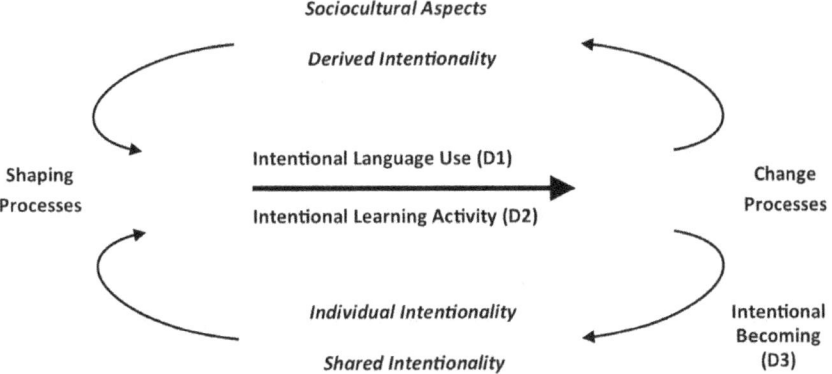

Figure 9: Language learning as intentional becoming.

individual, shared, derived, and sociocultural aspects. At the same time, the complex dynamic system of *language learning activity* is intentional activity, with analytically separate dynamic properties (D2 in Figure 9), as shaped by a pedagogically specified intentional ecology. This pedagogical intentional ecology will include individual intentionality (e.g., the learners' own habits and expectations), shared intentionality (e.g., group norms and expectations), derived intentionality (e.g., teacher and learner talk and writing, as well as text on whiteboards and in study materials), and sociocultural aspects (e.g., the normative value accorded to particular activity types or teaching methods). Finally, these two intentional activities together, as complex dynamic subsystems, constitute the complex dynamic system of L2 development across a longer timescale. Since this L2 development emerges from intentional dynamics, this developmental process will, itself, be shaped by an overall intentional ecology. In fact, we believe that the best way to understand L2 development – or at least the sort of L2 development that we describe in this chapter – is as a process of becoming intentional in the new language (D3 in Figure 9). This addition of intentional dynamics introduces meaning and meaning-making into our CDST of language learning.

10.3 Promoting language learning as intentional becoming

We believe that our model of intentional dynamics enhances the relevance of the CDST view of language learning. In this section, we present three principles for new action in language teaching, focusing particularly on classroom L2 learning, thereby addressing the "so what" of the conceptual contribution we make in this chapter. The first principle says that language education should encourage a diverse intentional ecology for the new language. This would maximise the opportunities for learners to become a part of the intentional ecology, as well as to make the new language a part of their own developing individual and shared intentionality. The second principle suggests that language learners should get opportunities to engage in a diversity of contingent, normative, creative, and purposeful intentional activity, including both language use and language learning activities, thereby harnessing all the dynamic properties of language use and language learning as complex dynamic sub-systems, including adaptiveness, historicity, non-linearity, and self-organisation. The third principle suggests that there are no short-cuts to language learning success, and that learners, teachers, researchers, and other TESOL stakeholders should come together to enable and sustain the journey of language learning as intentional becoming.

Principle 1: Encourage a diverse intentional ecology in the classroom

Experiencing and engaging with the individual, shared, derived, and sociocultural aspects of the new language is necessary for learners to appreciate the potential scope of the new intentional ecology and intentional dynamics they are becoming a part of. Thus, learners should be learners of meaning as much as they are learners of language, and teachers should be teachers of meaning as much as they are teachers of language.

One part of any ecology of intentionality, and a shaping influence on intentional dynamics in TESOL, is learners' own individual intentionality. Encouraging learners to develop their own understanding of the language, and evolving their own meaningful uses of the language, resonates with existing proposals in TESOL. This includes research on, and advocacy for, promoting learner autonomy (Noels et al. 2000; Wu 2003), learner initiative (Garton 2002; Kinginger 1994; Waring 2011), learner agency (S. Mercer 2011a, 2011c, 2012; van Lier 2007), and learner identity (Block 2009; Norton 2016). It resonates, also, with pedagogical scholarship advocating humanistic approaches (Stevick 1990) or learner-orientations in language teaching (Nunan 1990), including more specific pedagogies such as Exploratory Practice (Allwright 2003; Hanks 2015), Project and Enquiry-based Learning (Kohonen et al. 2014), and to some extent, also, communicative language teaching and task-based learning, which may encourage learners' meaning-making activity.

Aspbury (2018) describes the all too common situation in language classrooms – that we want to get away from – thereby explaining the challenge of making the L2 language classroom meaningful to our learners.

> When a person becomes a language learner, they adopt a project, *for-the-sake-of-being-a-language-learner* and enter the *language-learner-world*. This world has its own set of interrelated meanings, purposes and assignments with which learners are generally familiar. This familiarity, constructed through experience, cultural norms and so on, allows learners to interact with tasks without much cognition as they have an awareness, conscious or not, of what a task is for and what *one does* as a language learner. However, when learners act as *one does*, they lose their individuality; they act in a way undifferentiated from any other learner and this an inauthentic way to behave.
>
> (Aspbury 2018: 48, emphases original)

The situation Aspbury describes resembles what we, in chapter 6, have called normative intentional activity. Again, our normative intentional activity is characterised by a focus on "this is what normally happens in situations like this" and we "do not question the norm" (see section 5.3). Aspbury's suggested "solution" is to enable learners "choosing and acting on the possibilities unique to them as individuals" (p. 48). This emphasises the development of individual intentionality in the language classroom, which is a component of becoming intentional. Thus, our first principle suggests that learners should be given the space and time to cultivate their individual interests in, their individual understanding of, and their individual relationships to the new language.

Alongside a focus on learners' individual intentionality, there needs to be a focus also on shared, derived, and sociocultural aspects of the intentional ecology that the learners are becoming a part of. Language education needs to develop a diverse intentional ecology for learners to succeed. Starting with shared intentionality, intra-group language is an important feature of the overall intentional ecology. Intra-group language may serve as an "interpersonal space", from which new language can be internalised – as described (and proscribed) by sociocultural theory (Vygotsky 1978; see also section 7.6). In addition, shared intentionality and intra-group language will, over time, aid the development of identity and belonging, and it will make the classroom more welcoming to learners. Shared intentionality often arises quite naturally in language classrooms, but the development of intra-group language and shared intentionality is not emphasised in the existing TESOL literature. We suggest, therefore, that teachers and learners be open to shared language, even if idiosyncratic in terms of grammatical correctness or normative relevance.

In terms of language associated with sociocultural aspects of the intentional ecology, possible tensions may arise. Sociocultural aspects of language may act as a vehicle of power and ideology. Thus, the fear of dominance by powerful sociocultural forces may be a valid concern (see chapter 9). However, Canagarajah (1993: 602) suggests that the dynamics playing out in classrooms may mitigate these forces.

> The classroom is a site of diverse discourses and cultures represented by the varying backgrounds of teachers and students such that the effects of domination cannot be blindly predicted. Such classroom cultures mediate the concepts defined and prescribed by the Western academy as they reach the periphery. It is possible that various modes of opposition are sparked during this encounter.

We agree with Canagarajah; sociocultural forces, through language or other practices, do represent a shaping influence, but the intentional dynamics of classrooms will also be shaped by bottom-up processes. This will be especially the case, we believe, if there is a deliberate effort to create space and time for the development of individual and shared intentionality. Moreover, the sociocultural is not always normative; there will also be creative sociocultural influences. Whatever the nature of the sociocultural, and its expression through language, it is a part of any intentional ecology. Sociocultural aspects are integral, but not all-powerful, in the intentional dynamics of TESOL. Human and linguistic ecologies that we are part of are stratified, and as individuals we must embrace the value of both our agency – expressed through individual and shared intentionality – and social structures – expressed through (sometimes normative) sociocultural aspects of intentionality.

Thus, our first principle encourages teachers, curriculum designers, policy-makers, as well as learners themselves to create a diverse intentional ecology for the new language, including individual, shared and sociocultural aspects. In doing so, language learners, teachers and curriculum designers will have some power over the shaping of the intentional ecology they create with, and for, the new language. There is, for instance, no need to uncritically adopt any one dominant variety of the English language, the cultural and ideological values associated with this variety, or to spend time learning how to use the language within such a narrow cultural frame. At times, a dominant variety may be preferred for good reasons, but teachers and learners should always exercise critical judgment (see chapter 11) about what language and meaning is included in the intentional ecology of language use that they create for themselves.

Principle 2: Encourage a diversity of intentional activity in the classroom

The second principle again argues for diversity, but now focused on the intentional activity we encourage learners to engage in. In the present chapter, we have argued that intentional activity, including language use and language learning, as well as the temporally more extended process of L2 development, all exhibit their own dynamic properties. However, these analytically distinct complex dynamic processes exist in a continual interplay. This second principle, then, encourages teachers and learners to engage in a diversity of language use and language learning activity, including contingent, normative, creative, and purposeful intentional activity, as introduced in chapter 5. This will not only help generate a more diverse intentional ecology, it will also ensure that there are diverse intentional dynamics to propel the learners' complex dynamic system of L2 development. In the following, we will point out, also, that this applies to the distinct and interacting complex dynamics of *both* language use and language learning activity.

We have rehearsed the specific characteristics of contingent, normative, creative, and purposeful intentional activity in chapter 5. Here, these types of intentional activity are discussed in terms of language learning. Contingent intentional activity represents flexible adjustment to situations, and is characterised by the dynamic property of adaptiveness. The spontaneity of contingent language use may promote valuable communication and fluency practice. However, to maintain the contingent nature of language use in classrooms, the teacher and other learners may need to defer normative responses, such as immediate error correction. Teachers may focus, also, on contingency in language learning activities. Even if structured in familiar ways, activities should – on occasion – be allowed to become spontaneous. Normative intentional activity, by contrast, is characterised by the dynamic property of historicity. Normative activity, therefore, may provide learners with a sense of "this is what normally happens in situations like this", and this may engender a sense of stability and trust in the classroom. In terms of language use, normative activity may help learners to develop confidence in what to say in familiar or common situations, as well as what meanings and meaning-making applies in such situations. In terms of language learning activity, when we use tasks that are familiar and predictable, we may reduce the immediate cognitive demand we put on our learners, and this may allow us scope to introduce new, unfamiliar language. Managing the demands we place on learners in the classroom may be especially important for beginner and younger language learners (Cameron 2001). Creative intentional activity is characterised by less restricted interplays of the different aspects of intentionality, and it is associated with the dynamic property of non-linearity. Cook (2000) argues that creative and imaginary situations and language use are pervasive in society. This includes television and films, tabloid newspaper headlines, advertising, as well as more serious domains such as politics. We have ourselves, in chapter 7, explored the intentional dynamics of creative language use and activity among Norwegian young language learners. In the Norwegian classroom, a repeated, and thereby familiar, classroom task sequence led to learners' creative language use. Finally, purposeful intentional activity is associated with the dynamic property of self-organisation. Self-organisation describes how intentional activity may change the structure of the complex dynamic system. Thus, being purposeful in classroom language use, and in the learning activities we engage in, may have positive generative effects on L2 development as a complex dynamic system. This suggests that language use in the classroom should be communicative, and that teachers and learners need to be clear about what are the aims of learning activities.

Encouraging a diversity of intentional activity in the classroom may involve teachers and learners, together, cycling through a varied "menu" of intentional language use and learning activities, thereby encouraging intentional dynamics that include adaptiveness, historicity, non-linearity, and self-organisation. This may be facilitated by reflection, and negotiation with all involved, about what types of language use and learning activities the class should be doing, including when, how and why. This reflection and negotiation should include the learners themselves in deciding, or evolving, the mix of language use and language learning activities. This will ensure that the intentional dynamics of the classroom will be shaped, in addition, by the learners' own individual intentionality. Our view mirrors that of Brumfit (1980: 8), who has suggested that classroom language use and activities "cannot be designed in detail, because the syllabus being developed will be that of the learner, not the teacher: the syllabus designer provides and structures the major part of the input, but the learner structures all the learning".

Principle 3: Encourage language learning as intentional becoming

If language learning inherently means becoming a part of a new intentional ecology, which reflects the new language and its use, and engaging in new intentional dynamics, then L2 development is a great deal more than developing new patterns of activation, or attractor states, in the learners' minds. Rather, the task of language learners is not only "to approximate or appropriate for oneself someone else's language, but [also] to shape the very context in which the language is learned and used" (Kramsch 2008: 400). We are suggesting, therefore, that the learners' intentional becoming is what drives L2 use, learning and development. This intentional becoming is akin to a journey that language learners are on. This is a view that follows from our model of the intentional dynamics of TESOL. An emerging intentional ecology shapes language learners' intentional activity over time, and this intentional activity may change the emerging intentional ecology over time, including the learners' own individual intentionality. Thus, these intentional dynamics evolve over time, much like a journey that language learners experience over time. This third principle, therefore, suggests that teachers should be encouraging the "intentional becoming" of their language learners.

At this point we must recognise the contribution of Harvey (2017) to the development, and particularly the wording, of our language learning as intentional becoming. Harvey worked on L2 motivation, and saw the opportunity, within both the L2 and broader motivation literatures, to reconceptualise motivation as a holistic process. She drew on Bakhtin's (1981) work on *ideological becoming*, and how this becoming is mediated by language, as well as Ushioda's (2009) view of learners as "persons-in-context" who "are inherently part of, act upon and contribute to shaping the social, cultural and physical environments with which they interact" (Ushioda 2015: 48). Thus, Harvey reconceptualised motivation as ideological becoming, and defined this as "a process of learning to be in the world, of finding one's own voice through interaction with other voices" and "grow and mature in a shared story of persons-in-relation" (2017: 71). In addition to the phraseology, our intentional becoming is similarly holistic, shares the person-in-context view, and also stresses the important role for learners, as helped by their teachers, to learn "to be in the world". Where we differ is that our intentional becoming has emerged from our model of the intentional dynamics of TESOL. We are not concerned about reconceptualising L2 motivation; rather, our intentional becoming is a part of our broader metatheoretical contribution to TESOL.

Finally, language learning as intentional becoming underscores the importance of the first two principles, rehearsed in the previous two sub-sections. Promoting a diverse intentional ecology within the classroom and encouraging a diversity of intentional activity is the best way to encourage our learners' intentional becoming. Crucially, this path has no short-cuts. Employing language games, offering rewards, appealing to authority, or to trying to visualise desirable end-points may initially propel the journey. However, teachers and learners must act together, through their intentional activity, to sustain the intentional becoming of the language learning journey. More broadly, intentional becoming describes an always changing "driving force" for language use, language learning activity, and L2 development. In addition, the "aboutness" of intentionality provides "direction", and is intimately shaped by learners' developing identity and sociality. Finally, intentional becoming has its own intentional dynamics, comprising a broader complex dynamic system than their language use, language learning activity, or their L2 development. Language education is about the whole person, not only language in isolation.

10.4 Conclusion

In conclusion, we believe that extending the CDST view of language learning, in the form of our language learning as intentional becoming, adds both theoretical validity, as outlined in the first half of this chapter, and practical relevance, as developed in the last section. We have proposed that language use and language learning are both intentional activities, which shape the longer term intentional becoming of L2 development. We have proposed that teachers and learners should work towards developing diverse intentional ecologies for language use and language learning in their classrooms, including deliberately valuing individual, shared, derived and sociocultural aspects of intentionality. We have proposed, also, that language learning as intentional becoming will benefit from engaging in a diverse range of contingent, normative, creative, and purposeful intentional activity, and that teachers and learners need to work together, without short-cuts, to sustain this intentional becoming.

Chapter 11
A critical-intentional perspective for TESOL

This chapter presents a second area of TESOL where we believe the model of intentional dynamics may extend understanding and promote new action. We will outline a *critical-intentional perspective*, which by its nature cuts right across all domains of activity in TESOL. This critical- intentional perspective was first developed in earlier work (Stelma and Fay 2019; Fay and Stelma 2016), with a particular focus on how critical-intentional activity might transform broader Applied Linguistics situations. In this chapter, we outline the critical-intentional perspective in ways that fit more closely with the model of intentional dynamics that we have developed in this book, and thus with a somewhat narrower focus on TESOL as a sub-discipline of Applied Linguistics. We rely on the observation, which we developed in chapters 2, 3, and 5, that TESOL is stratified into multiple domains of activity. The intentional dynamics of TESOL is constituted by a continual interplay between the activity of learners, teachers, managers, curriculum designers, and more. The critical-intentional perspective suggests, therefore, that individuals and groups across TESOL need to be included in challenging normative assumptions and unjust orders that constrain activities and outcomes. We must all seek to extend our understanding, to the limits of our knowing, and we must all engage in, and encourage in others, creative and purposeful intentional activity (see section 5.3). When this happens, we will enhance the diversity of the intentional ecology of TESOL, the diversity of affordances and activity, and allow for the emergence of more diverse, and thereby less restrictive, outcomes.

We begin this chapter with a review of existing critical perspectives in TESOL (section 11.1), including discussion of cognitive accounts of critical thinking, the unique-to-TESOL suggestion to be critical about context, and the more ideologically oriented focus on normative assumptions and unjust orders in the field of Critical Applied Linguistics (Fairclough 2001, 2013; Pennycook 2001). This is followed by a section that develops the critical-intentional perspective in more detail (section 11.2). This includes the development of an intentional dynamics account of normative assumptions and unjust orders, and an associated reconceptualization of the notions of power, freedom, and agency. We also look at the role of intentional diversity, and the need for creative and purposeful intentional activity, in promoting innovation and change. Our conclusion (section 11.3) suggests that encouraging the emergence of diverse new ideas and activity, across all domains of TESOL, is our best chance to challenge existing normative assumptions. Moreover, if this emergence of intentional diversity gains momentum, then TESOL will be in continual forward motion, existing normative structures will lose their grip, and future dominant social structures are less likely to emerge.

11.1 Being critical in TESOL

In this section, we look at some of the many incarnations of "being critical" in TESOL, drawing also on scholarship in the broader disciplines of Applied Linguistics and Education. Building on the earlier work of Stelma and Fay (2019), we move chronologically, starting with Kant's (2013) rationalism, which we believe underpins 20th century cognitive conceptualisations of critical thinking. Next, we look at what we think is a unique-to-TESOL concern with contextual particularities, and how this concern adds a contextual dimension to being critical. This is followed by discussion of more recent views of criticality, such as Pennycook's (2001) *Critical Applied Linguistics*, including also how these recent views have been informed by Karl Marx's ([1859] 2010) political philosophy and Paulo Freire's (2005) critical pedagogy.

11.1.1 The critical-cognitive perspective

The first incarnation of being critical that we will discuss is what Stelma and Fay (2019) have referred to as the *critical-cognitive* perspective. This perspective may be traced back to Kant's philosophy of rationalism. For Kant, rationalism was integral to morality, or as Osberg (2008: 135) has argued, "for Kant, without freedom there is no choice, without choice there was no struggle and without struggle there is no genuine morality". Thus, according to Kant, the freedom to choose what we do with our lives, and the link to morality, is what makes us human. This philosophy of rationalism had a wide-ranging impact not only on the enlightenment, and (without any overt moral dimension) shaped Western scholarship on critical thinking and education in the 20th century. The influence can be seen in John Dewey's frequently cited definition of reflective thought as an "effort to establish belief upon a firm basis of reasons" (1910: 6), and his suggestion that reflective thought is "active, persistent, and careful consideration of any belief or supposed form of knowledge in the light of the grounds that support it, and the further conclusions to which it tends" (Dewey 1910: 6). It seems evident, also, in Bloom's widely used Taxonomy of Educational Objectives, originally proposed in the 1950s (Bloom 1956). Krathwohl (2002), who was involved in the development of the both the original and later revisions of Bloom's taxonomy, points out that "critical thinking" was rejected as a discrete category in the taxonomy. However, both the focus on Knowledge, Comprehension, Application, Analysis, Synthesis, and Evaluation in the original taxonomy, as well as the later revision that includes both knowledge and cognitive processing dimensions, seem closely aligned with the rationalist programme of critical thinking (see Sternberg 1986).

The focus on rationalism in this critical-cognitive perspective has been subject to a great deal of critique. Stelma and Fay (2019) suggest that the critical-cognitive perspective privileges individual cognitive categories such as knowledge, belief, and reason, and excludes any consideration of feelings, emotions, or inter-personal dynamics. Moreover, Atkinson (1997) suggests that this cognitive form of critical thinking may be difficult to teach in the language classroom. He suggests that rational critical thinking may be akin to a social practice associated with certain cultures. Thus, Kant's "freedom of thought", which through its link to morality is expressly individual, may be encouraged by some cultures, whilst other cultures may encourage more collective or emotive ways of thinking, or both. Finally, in terms of our model of intentional dynamics, the aspects of intentionality that shape critical-cognitive activity is a restricted set. The critical-cognitive perspective foregrounds individual intentionality, and sometimes has a textual bias (critical thought that relies on individuals' engagement with information and problems presented in textual form – i.e. derived forms of intentionality). Thus, the critical-cognitive perspective has less to say about shared or sociocultural aspects of the intentional ecologies we live, work, and study in.

11.1.2 The critical-contextual perspective

Another incarnation of being critical is the concern with context in TESOL and Applied Linguistics, or what Stelma and Fay (2019) have called the *critical-contextual* perspective. The focus on context in TESOL has emerged gradually over the past 40 years. In this TESOL scholarship, the argument for the importance of context has often been framed in metaphorical terms that are specific to language education (rather than in theoretical terms). For instance, Holliday and Cooke (1982), writing about English for Specific Purposes (ESP), observed early that using the same teaching method across different national contexts might be misguided. They argued that ESP might be a "somewhat temperamental hybrid plant, native to Britain" (p. 125), and thus suggested that in different national contexts ESP (the plant) might not grow very well at all. Later, Holliday (1992) offered another metaphor, comparing TESOL contexts to human bodies, and if you introduced a teaching method from another context (another human body) you might get "tissue rejection". The focus on context, therefore, appears to be a reaction against the earlier dominant focus on methods in TESOL (see Freeman 2016 for a historical overview). Stelma and Fay (2019: 53) summarise this reaction as follows:

> The critical-contextual perspective has included theorization of a variety of socio-cultural dimensions of context, and in the case of language education there is a concomitant rejection of context-independent constructions of "best methods" in favour of teachers, with their local knowledge of their socio-cultural contexts, being the arbitrators of method-in-context.

However, this shift in focus, from method to context, was neither sudden nor uncontested. Kumaravadivelu (2006b: 63) describes how there was a strong belief, in the late 1980s and early 1990s, that the communicative language teaching method could be "adapted to suit various contexts of language teaching across the world and across time". By the early 1990s, Holliday suggested that language teachers needed to seek out locally appropriate teaching methodologies (Holliday 1994), and ten years later, Bax (2003: 281) remarked that "methodology is not the magic solution, that there are many different ways to learn languages, and that the context is a crucial determiner of the success or failure of learners".

The critical-contextual perspective has implications, also, for the content-focus of language teaching and language teachers' reflective practice. In terms of the content that teaching focuses on, Soherwardy (2019: 16–17) argues that rural Pakistani language learners "are at a disadvantage because of the foreignness of the [English] language", and observes that "a group of Pakistani students sharing a similar socioeconomic background may find relevant the festival of Eid. Each individual may have a personal memory attached to the festival. The content is personally meaningful to the whole group because of the cultural norms and traditions they share". In terms of teachers' reflective practice, Ollerhead and Burns (2016: 227) remind us that "language teachers have to operate within considerable educational constraints, controlled by rapidly changing and top-down ministry policies, mandated curricula, prescribed materials, and prespecified outcomes", and Sharkey (2004) has detailed how language teachers' curricular and pedagogical decisions are mediated by their knowledge about context, and this includes reflection on shaping forces originating on multiple contextual layers.

Finally, the critical-contextual perspective resonates with our intentional dynamics account of TESOL. Intentional ecologies may be particular to specific TESOL settings. A concern with context is, in our vocabulary, a concern with individual, shared, derived, and sociocultural aspects of particular intentional ecologies. Thus, we believe, just as Sharkey (2004), that curricular and pedagogical decisions will be mediated by teachers' and other stakeholders' knowledge about context. However, if too narrowly defined, context is no more the "magic solution" than method is (*pace* Bax 2003). A critical perspective needs, in addition, to incorporate the experience of individuals and collectives of agents, whose intentional activity shapes ever more multilingual and multicultural contexts, as well as the ideological aspects of intentional ecologies, which we will consider in the next section.

11.1.3 The critical-humanistic perspective

A more recent incarnation of being critical in TESOL and Applied Linguistics is the ideologically oriented focus on social, political, and economic structures of power and inequality, and how these may constrain the affordances for activity in TESOL. Hawkins and Norton (2009) attribute this perspective to Habermas' (1976) argument that reality must be viewed not as objective and rational, but as social and subjective. Habermas' focus was on social individuals, and on the subjective experience of individuals in situations of "crisis", when they might understand "structural alterations as critical for continued existence and feel their social identity threatened" (1976: 3). This shift from the objective to the subjective, Hawkins and Norton (2009: 31) argue, enables us "to see that our ideas, interactions, language use, texts, learning practices, and so forth, are not neutral and objective, but are shaped by and within social relationships that systematically advantage some people over others, thus producing and reproducing inequitable relationships of power in society". Stelma and Fay (2019) refer to this ideological view of criticality as the *critical-humanistic* perspective. The focus is humanistic because the central motive is to empower individuals in local settings. Thus, the critical-humanistic perspective is "a search for the social, historical, and political roots of conventional knowledge and an orientation to transform learning and society" (Benesch 1993: 546), and explicitly seeks to empower the voices of participants that are otherwise suppressed (Canagarajah 1993).

The critical-humanistic perspective may be linked to the critical-contextual perspective, but with a wider social and political conceptualisation of context. Pennycook (2004: 796) has suggested that critical researchers need to "remake the connections between discourse, language learning, language use, and the social and political contexts in which these occur". Moreover, Kumaravadivelu's (2006c) proposal for a postmethod perspective aligns the focus on context with issues of human freedom and agency. Kumaravadivelu's three parameters, defining what he refers to as the postmethod condition, include (a) the *particularity* of context, (b) the *practicality* of teacher action-in-context, and (c) how *possibilities* for action may be limited given teachers' and learners' positions in applicable social orders. The first two parameters – particularity and practicality – constitute reflection on context and the intersection of context and method. However, the parameter of possibility is concerned with much broader and ideological considerations, focusing on realizing learners' full human potential – or what Kumaravadivelu calls a programme of "liberatory autonomy".

This incarnation of being critical is sometimes linked to the political philosophy of Karl Marx. Habermas attributes his use of the word "crisis" to Marx, and Gottesman (2010) goes as far as referring to it as "the critical Marxist" perspective. Marx centrally argued that "it is not the consciousness of men that determines their existence, but their social existence that determines their consciousness" (Gottesman 2010: 92). This perspective is in sharp contrast, then, with the earlier reviewed critical-cognitive perspective. With Marx's social-to-individual determinism, the critical thinking of individuals (Kant's rationalism) will be of limited importance. Rather, if social reality shapes consciousness, critical work needs to uncover the lines of power within the social world. A much-cited example of this Marxist programme is Freire's ([1968] 2005) *Pedagogy of the Oppressed*. Freire's starting point was the Brazilian context, where he observed that the working classes were subject to oppression, or dehumanization, by unjust social and economic orders. It is somewhat difficult, however, to draw parallels between the contexts of poverty which motivated Freire, or the grim realities of the industrial society that inspired Marx, and contemporary contexts of TESOL. However, there are clearly unjust orders in TESOL. We have pointed out one such order already – i.e., Soherwardy's (2019: 16) observation that rural Pakistani learners "are at a disadvantage because of the foreignness of the [English] language". This may be related, also, to the larger-scale observation by Phillipson (1992) about the hegemonic and monolingually construed position of English in the world, and how the dominance of the English language may jeopardize the future sustainability of local multilingual and multicultural communities in developing contexts. Of course, the TESOL profession is central in generating these kinds of unjust orders. An important strand within the critical-humanistic perspective, therefore, is to problematize normative assumptions that underpin unjust orders in TESOL (Pennycook 2004, 2001). We define normative assumptions as "implicit views shared by a decisive number of stakeholders". Normative assumptions are often implicitly held; Bateson (1987: 509) observes that "the survival of a frequently used idea is [. . .] promoted by the fact that habit formation tends to remove the idea from the field of critical inspection". Moreover, normative assumptions gain their power by being held by enough people to make a decisive difference to TESOL contexts, activity, and outcomes.

We fully support the aims of the critical-humanistic perspective. However, we will, in the next part of the chapter, challenge the theoretical premises upon which this critical work is based. We believe that our conceptualisation of TESOL as an intentional ecology, as generated by intentional dynamics, can provide a theoretically more inclusive account of how normative assumptions emerge and prevail, and therefore also more effective ways to challenge and transform unjust orders.

11.2 A critical-intentional perspective

In this section, we present the elements of the critical-intentional perspective, first developed by Stelma and Fay (2019). This perspective embraces the cognitive, conceptual, and humanistic perspectives on being critical, as outlined in the previous section. We recognise rational cognitive processes as intentional dynamics. However, this rationalism captures only part of the rich experience that we have, and which may contribute to being critical. Moreover, we believe that cognitive processes are not quite as reductive as suggested by, e.g., Bloom's Taxonomy of Educational Objectives (reviewed above). We also value the focus on context that has emerged in TESOL over the years, but we want to stress the role of individual and collective activity in reproducing, and sometimes changing, the contexts we find ourselves in. Finally, we wholeheartedly value the aim of the critical-humanistic perspective to problematize the normative assumptions underlying unjust orders in TESOL. However, we will conceptualise the notions of power, freedom, and agency rather differently, leading us to less ideologically-motivated and more ecologically-valid – we believe – recommendations for critical action in TESOL. It is this new and ecological understanding of power, freedom, and agency that distinguishes our critical-intentional perspective from other, recent critical, cosmopolitan, and posthumanist perspectives in TESOL and Applied Linguistics (Holliday 2010; Pennycook 2018a, 2018b).

In a first sub-section, we discuss the role of normative assumptions in the intentional dynamics of TESOL. As outlined in previous chapters (e.g., chapters 4 and 9), normative assumptions may be understood as sociocultural aspects of intentional ecologies. However, they also appear in the guise of individual and shared intentionality – sometimes imposed and sometimes espoused – as well as in the form of derived intentionality. Thus, normative assumptions are an integral part of the intentional dynamics that shape TESOL. We describe these normative assumptions, and the unjust orders that they engender, as potential attractor states in the intentional dynamics of TESOL activity. Next, we take a closer look at how power, freedom, and agency may be understood in the context of our model of intentional dynamics. We point out that stakeholders everywhere in TESOL shape its intentional ecology. Thus, we believe that TESOL is a stratified ecology where the power that shapes agency, and the agency that shapes power, is more pervasively distributed than what either Marx or Freire appear to have considered. Finally, we return to ecological thinking and CDST to argue for the generative power of diversity and emergence, respectively, to make future intentional ecologies of TESOL more inclusive.

11.2.1 Normative assumptions and intentional dynamics

In order to successfully challenge normative assumptions, and thereby the unjust orders that they underpin, we need to have a better understanding of how such assumptions appear in the first place. In this section, we will describe how normative assumptions, which may be understood as sociocultural aspects of an intentional ecology, emerge from intentional dynamics that are shaped, in addition, by individual, shared, and derived aspects of intentionality. We introduced the relationship between normative assumptions and sociocultural aspects of intentionality in chapters 4 and 9. In chapter 9, we suggested that the sociocultural aspects of the intentional ecology of TESOL could be understood in terms of: (a) a linguistic dimension, including assumptions, beliefs, and practices about language in general, and the English language in particular; (b) a pedagogical dimension, encompassing thinking and practices about teaching and learning; and (c) a political dimension, which describes assumptions, values, and ideologies about the social contexts in which language education is embedded. Thus, normative assumptions may relate to any of these dimensions. In various chapters, we have alluded to different normative sociocultural aspects of TESOL intentional ecologies, such as the widespread belief that native speakers of English are better English language teachers, as well as the related beliefs that particular native speaker English varieties are more legitimate as 'target language', and that the English language has some inherent value that other local or global languages lack (see Holliday 2006).

In our model of intentional dynamics, normative assumptions, as an aspect of intentional ecologies, shape how we as learners, teachers, material designers, and so on think and act. Moreover, as argued at length throughout this book, our activity in TESOL also "changes" or "reproduces" the intentional ecology of TESOL. This means that the origin of normative assumptions, if it was practically possible to trace this back in time, is in the intentional dynamics of our individual and collective past activity. Once a normative assumption becomes an established part of the intentional ecology of TESOL, without or despite our awareness, our activity over time tends to reproduce this normative assumption. In such a situation of reproduction, the complex dynamic system of TESOL finds itself in an attractor state that may be difficult to escape. The normative assumption may be shared by a decisive number of stakeholders, may not be questioned, and will – as long as it is being reproduced – constrain affordances for thinking and acting. Once again, taking the example of the normative assumption that native varieties of English are somehow 'better', Kordt (2018: 144) points out that such a native-speaker ideal "can stand in the way of language learning as prospective learners despair in view of a native-speaker ideal they are not likely to attain. Giving up the native-speaker ideal would make the use of affordances for multilingualism that emerge in a globalised world much more likely."

Taking this one step further, since normative assumptions are generated by our activity-in-context, and since this activity is generated by intentional dynamics that includes individual, derived, and shared aspects of intentionality, it may be misleading to say that normative assumptions are sociocultural. Normative assumptions may appear, also, as individual and shared intentionality – imposed by the intentional ecology we are a part of – as well as in derived forms of intentionality, such as textbooks, curricular documents, and policy (see chapter 8). Crucially, it is through all our activity-in-context that normative assumptions remain a sociocultural aspect of the intentional ecology of TESOL. This means that if we want to understand how normative assumptions have the power to shape activity, how they are reproduced, and ultimately how they can be challenged, we must look at the entire intentional ecology of TESOL, its intentional dynamics, and the intentional activity which we ourselves engage in – across the many domains of TESOL.

11.2.2 The intentional dynamics of power, freedom, and agency

The critical-humanistic perspective suggests that we should always problematise the normative "givens" of TESOL (Pennycook 2001, 2004). More ideologically motivated critical action, such as those promoted by the philosophies of Marx and Freire, portray the challenge as a struggle against oppression. Thus, whether framed more neutrally or more ideologically, the theme of power runs deep in the critical-humanistic perspective. This includes, also, the related themes of freedom and agency; freedom and agency can be suppressed by normative assumptions. However, we believe that any discussion of power, freedom, and agency must address, also, how activity in a social ecology such as TESOL is multiply distributed, and how all this activity is constituted by a great many stakeholders with distinct roles, knowledge, and expertise. This social ecological view requires us to consider two fundamental issues. On the one hand, any individual stakeholder in any part of TESOL may struggle to understand the full social, economic, or political dynamics of oppression, or how it may have arisen. At the same time, however, we all have agency and power in TESOL; our collective activity is what shapes normative assumptions in the first place, and our collective activity is the greatest power we have to challenge such normative assumptions.

The intentional ecology of TESOL includes stakeholders across many domains of activity, who see and experience language education differently. In fact, TESOL as a profession is – we believe – becoming increasingly stratified. The expertise of a language teacher will be very different from that of an administrator or a materials writer. It seems clear, then, that in a large and diversified (or specialised) field such as TESOL, there are many different roles to be filled, and each role presupposes a different type of knowing. Moreover, the effect of specialized roles in a social system is that: (a) others, who fulfil a role different than ourselves, will shape/constrain our affordances for action, and this gives rise to (b) the feeling that those others have power over us. In this kind of system, there will be inevitable constellations of power, and unavoidable constraints on freedom and agency. We are reminded of Margaret Archer's (1995: 2) description of society as "that which nobody wants in exactly the form they find it and yet it resists both individual and collective efforts at transformation – not necessarily by remaining unchanged but altering to become something else which still conforms to no one's ideal". This is not to say that oppression of any sort, even if it is constituted by a stratified social system, is justified. However, what we want to argue is that the mechanisms for effectively challenging normative assumptions are only partially worked out by the existing critical literatures – the critical- cognitive, critical-contextual, and critical-humanistic perspectives. We do think that beliefs need "a firm basis of reasons", we fully accept that context "is a crucial determiner", and we believe that normative "givens" must be problematised. However, given the limits of our knowing, including ourselves as researchers, we are not sure that there is any one person, or any one group of people, who – by themselves – can challenge normative assumptions in an effective manner. As Sealey and Carter (2004: 175) point out, "among the properties of social structures [. . .] is their endurance beyond the actions or intentions of individuals".

Freire's (2005) critical pedagogy offers what is perhaps the most developed way forward. Freire proposes a dialogic process whereby "the oppressed" rise up to challenge their "oppressors", and then create a new and just order. Freire does concede that the oppressed may lack the necessary social and cultural capital to achieve this, but he suggests that they may receive help from "middle class" individuals, such as teachers. We believe this can indeed happen, locally, as suggested by Kumeravadivelu's (2006a) "liberatory autonomy", which teachers may encourage in their learners, or Allwright's (2005) "Exploratory Practice", which main aim is for teachers and learners to develop understanding and enhance the "quality of life" in their classrooms. We struggle to see, however, how the local activity of teachers and learners may, by itself, challenge normative assumptions that may be temporally and socially distributed. The point made by Stelma and Fay (2019: 59) is apposite in this regard.

> A language learner may have intimate knowledge of her own learning activity, perhaps also of her peers, and may even know something about what the teacher does in the classroom and why. However, the learner is less likely to know much about language teaching approaches, or curriculum design, or the policy reasons for why she is studying English or another language.

We believe the way forward is a better understanding of the "collective power" of the activity of learners, teachers, and the many other stakeholders in TESOL. Our argument includes the following elements: (a) the activity of all TESOL stakeholders is generated by intentional dynamics, and these intentional dynamics, as realised in intentional activity, is how the intentional ecology itself changes; (b) the activity of all TESOL stakeholders, whether in the classroom or in what may be perceived as 'offices of power', is genuine intentional activity. Thus, the activity of learners, teachers, and policy-makers is all governed by intentional dynamics, and *has the power to change* an intentional ecology; finally, (c) rather than focusing on the tendency of stakeholders to either impose their power, or conceding to the power of others, we must focus on the unique collective power that we together have – as learners, teachers, materials writers, or managers – to change the intentional ecologies that we are a part of. The next section addresses this in more detail, drawing on the ecological notion of *diversity* and the CDST concept of *emergence*.

11.2.3 The generative power of diversity and emergence

In this sub-section, we argue that the ecological notion of diversity, and the CDST concept of emergence – combined with the insights provided by the existing critical-cognitive, critical-contextual, and critical-humanistic perspectives – provides our best opportunity to disarm the power of existing normative assumptions, and to reduce the likelihood that any future normative assumptions go unchallenged.

Diversity is a central concept in ecological theory. In the natural ecological sciences, diverse ecologies are considered more able to withstand change, or more likely to "bounce back" when faced with external shocks. In these natural science origins, diversity is discussed in terms of "species richness" (number of unique species), "species evenness" (equal distribution of species) (see Peet 1974), or "species divergence" (inter-species difference) (see Lozupone and Knight 2008). The common focus of the natural ecological sciences, however, is preservation – reflecting a concern about the possible destabilizing effects of, e.g., human activity. Our focus, in this chapter, is different – we want to enhance rather than preserve diversity in TESOL. It seems possible, though, to conceive of intentional ecologies in terms of ideational richness (number of unique ideas), ideational evenness (equal distribution of ideas), and ideational divergence (inter-idea difference). An intentional ecology is an ecology of ideational intentionality (see chapter 4), or in plain language an 'ecology of ideas'. This includes individual, shared, derived, and sociocultural aspects, and our argument is that a greater diversity of ideational intentionality, including all the mentioned aspects, will enrich the intentional dynamics of TESOL. Affordances to act rely on our perception and interpretation of ideational intentionality, and an enhanced intentional ecology, then, will expand the affordances to act and extend the space for freedom and agency. This is consistent, we believe, with how cultural and linguistic diversity has been discussed in the fields of economics (Ottaviano and Peri 2006), cultural studies (Vertovec 2007), sociolinguistics (Aronin and Singleton 2010; Blommaert, Collins, and Slembrouck 2005; Piller 2016), education (Andrews and Yee 2006; Esteban-Guitart, and Moll 2014), educational research (Stelma et al. 2013), and TESOL (MacPherson 2003). For instance, linguistic diversity is valuable because each unique language indexes particular cultural practices and knowledge, and thus will support the well-being and vitality of the people using each unique language (Fill 2001; Phillipson and Skutnabb-Kangas 1996).

Furthermore, in an intentional ecology the diversity of ideas and affordances needs to extend to all domains of TESOL activity, whether it be learners learning, teachers teaching, materials writers designing materials, or policy-makers making policy. A brief return to the natural ecological sciences can help us understand why such diversity, both within and across the domains of the stratified intentional ecology of TESOL, has value. A recent proposal for measuring diversity in the natural sciences is "functional diversity", which captures the number of groups in an ecology that make a unique contribution (Mason et al. 2005). If each domain of activity in TESOL consisted of one functional group only - meaning that all learners were in the same group, and all teachers in another - the functional diversity of TESOL would be limited. By contrast, the affordances for action would expand greatly if there were functionally different groups of learners, teachers, and so on. Learners and teachers with unique individual intentionality, understanding the activities of learning and teaching differently, would dramatically extend diversity and expand the affordances for action in TESOL. With greater intentional diversity, there will be a reduced likelihood that a single "idea", or normative assumption, is shared and enacted by a decisive number of stakeholders. Moreover, the more recently developed conceptualisations of translingual practice (Canagarajah 2013) and translanguaging (García and Wei 2014) suggests that diversity must include, in addition, the various ways in which we, as teachers and learners, mix and move between languages for affective, social, and pedagogical purposes.

We have yet to address the CDST concept of emergence. We suggest that diversity and emergence can work hand-in-glove, in non-linear ways, to continually change the ideational make-up of intentional ecologies. A normative assumption is an emergent structure, as is the unjust order that the normative assumption underpins. Normative assumptions that we see in TESOL today are attractor states within the intentional ecology, with sometimes high levels of both historicity and adaptiveness. They are "present" in individual, shared, derived, and sociocultural aspects of an intentional ecology. Moreover, because a normative assumption is an emergent outcome of complex intentional dynamics, we cannot replace normative assumptions "by legislation". Rather, the emergence of new ideas needs to be encouraged, and these new ideas must then be allowed to challenge whatever may be the existing normative assumption. A new idea may be a compelling realisation about the injustice that the existing normative assumption engenders (which is the aim of the critical-humanistic perspective), or it may be the emergence of another equally powerful, but less oppressive, idea that can replace the earlier normative assumption.

We suggest, finally, that the emergence of new ideas, to challenge and replace normative assumptions, can be promoted by us - the stakeholders of TESOL. First, we have already argued that a diversity of ideas about learning, teaching, materials, policy, language, and more would enhance the affordances for action in TESOL. If we, at the same time, encourage creative and purposeful activity, wherever and whenever we have the opportunity, then the intentional dynamics of TESOL would be more non-linear, and the self-organisation of new ideas would be more likely. As Osberg (2008: 143) points out, "emergent processes are not fully determined - they contain within themselves the possibility of freedom". Thus, the freedom created by a diverse intentional ecology, with learners, teachers, managers, materials writers, and policymakers that all value being creative and purposeful, is – we believe – our best chance to challenge existing normative assumptions, and to promote the emergence of new and emancipatory ideas to guide TESOL into the future. Such a diverse intentional ecology would be in "motion", with new intentionality continually emerging. Locally, and occasionally globally, new intentional structures would emerge, and some of these might have the potential to become new normative structures. However, if we maintain the momentum towards greater levels of diversity and freedom, any single idea will have less time and opportunity to become "normative", and therefore less likely to underpin social, economic, and political injustices.

11.3 Conclusion

In this chapter, we have developed a critical-intentional perspective for TESOL. We have argued that normative assumptions, and the unjust orders that they underpin, may be understood using our model of the intentional dynamics of TESOL. This understanding accepts the stratified nature of TESOL ecologies, and that "no single individual can comprehend the full set of intentional dynamics at play" (Stelma and Fay 2019: 67). However, by harnessing the power of the collective activity of learners, teachers, policymakers, and all other stakeholders in TESOL we can challenge normative assumptions, and change the intentional ecology of TESOL for the better. This power to shape change can be enhanced if we value diversity, and encourage creative and purposeful activity, across all domains of activity in TESOL. This critical-intentional perspective has both local and global implications. It can provide the conditions for the continual emergence of new ideas, which may challenge existing normative assumptions, and reduce the opportunities for any new ideas to become "normative".

We propose this critical-intentional perspective as an addition to existing conceptualisations of being critical in TESOL. We accept the need to be rational, as stressed by the critical-cognitive perspective, but our definition of individual intentionality adds a variety of affective psychological states to the rational cognitive ones. We fully appreciate the need to consider the influence of context, but we include as context the totality of individual, shared, derived and sociocultural aspects of intentional ecologies. We support anyone determined to challenge normative assumptions and any unjust orders that these promote. However, we believe that the best way to counter such unjust orders is to harness the generative power of diversity and emergence, and to encourage creative and purposeful intentional activity across all domains of TESOL. No single group of TESOL stakeholders should be expected to do this alone – we are all in this together. Teachers may wish to reflect on how their teaching methods, or content focus, values and or encourages diverse learner styles and strategies, or more broadly whether they provide scope for learners to be creative and purposeful in the classroom and beyond. Teacher educators may encourage diverse developmental trajectories for the teachers whom they mentor, materials writers will need to reflect on the affordances for both teacher and learner action that they "design into" textbooks, and policy-makers – perhaps most challenging of all – need to question how the policies that they formulate are interpreted and enacted across the many domains of TESOL activity. Doing all this this requires extra effort that involves all of us, wherever we work in TESOL, and it may sometimes challenge the limits of our knowing.

Chapter 12
Researching intentional dynamics in TESOL

Throughout this book we have used the model of intentional dynamics to make sense of diverse contexts, activities, and outcomes in TESOL. In this chapter, we look at how we may research the intentional dynamics of TESOL. In part, this contributes to an ongoing shift in research methodology and thinking, in booth TESOL and the wider field of Applied Linguistics (Phakiti et al. 2018). This shift is away from variable-centred data collection and analysis, towards more synthetic, qualitative, and mixed-methods approaches (Dörnyei 2007; Hiver and Al-Hoorie 2020) designed to understand dynamic, interconnected, and meaningful entities and processes (Byrne 2002; Dörnyei 2009; Larsen-Freeman and Cameron 2008a, 2008b; MacIntyre et al. 2017). We need to note, though, that researching intentional dynamics is not necessarily about changing the research methods or forms of analysis that we employ. It is more fundamentally about selecting a focus consistent with our model of intentional dynamics, and to use existing research methods and analytical frames with a mind-set that is attuned to the intentional dynamics all around us in TESOL.

We start the chapter with a section (12.1) that develops a researcher mind-set that is sensitive to the interconnectivity of intentional ecologies, the adaptive, historically shaped, non-linear, and self-organised nature of intentional activity, and the particular challenge of understanding meaning and meaning-making. A second section (12.2) develops a typology for researching intentional dynamics in TESOL. In a final section (12.3), we reflexively engage with the empirical studies we have already presented in previous chapters, in order to exemplify how research may be designed, and how one may move from data collection to data analysis when investigating intentional dynamics.

12.1 A mind-set for researching intentional dynamics

As we have engaged with the ideas presented in this book, we have become increasingly attuned to the various aspects of intentionality that are present in, and shape, TESOL and wider linguistic and social phenomena. We have become attuned to contexts functioning as ideational intentional ecologies, we have come to notice how intentional ecologies shape activity, how this activity itself is intentional, and how the dynamic properties of intentional activity reproduce and/or change intentional ecologies. Finally, we have become attuned to how activity across different domains of TESOL may change intentional ecologies, and also how activity in one domain may affect activity in other domains. We have been helped by many years of reading and writing about ecological and complex dynamic systems theories, and with the addition of the concept of intentionality we have become alert to how meaning and meaning-making are interconnected and dynamic. What we have developed, then, is a mind-set that helps us to recognize and research the intentional dynamics of TESOL. Crucially, researching intentional dynamics is not necessarily about new or unique research methods or forms of analysis. Rather, it is in large part using existing research methods and analytical frames with a different mind-set. In this section, then, we detail this mind-set. The mind-set includes being attuned to the interconnected and dynamic natures of TESOL, and being always focused on meaning and meaning-making.

12.1.1 The "everything is connected" mind-set

A first part of the mind-set that we will describe in this section is related to our claim, in this book, that everything is connected. We have developed this claim in detail in chapter 3, and we will not rehearse the same theoretical detail again here. In research terms, however, if everything is indeed connected, then we have to leave behind the identification and analysis of discrete variables or other analytical constituents. Reducing phenomena to variables often produces logical dichotomies, such as the separation between learner and context, or disconnected social and cognitive explanations of linguistic development (Larsen-Freeman 2017). An obvious limitation of such separation is that when one element of the research problem is foregrounded it tends to generate partial explanations. A second shortcoming of this approach is that it fails to reveal how context, activity, and outcomes interconnect. In the view of Cilliers (1998: 2), to which we subscribe, this is a "fundamental flaw", because "in 'cutting up' a system, the [conventional] analytical method destroys what it seeks to understand". Similarly, Larsen-Freeman (2017: 29, emphasis added) notes that "it is from the components and *their relationships* that the system we are trying to understand emerges. If we isolate components artificially, we lose the essence of the phenomena we are attempting to describe". We do not dispute the multiple contributions that the analysis of discrete variables, and of selected observable relationships, has made to the advancement of human knowledge. Nevertheless, to understand intentional dynamics we need a different way of thinking. What we are suggesting, then, is that research to understand intentional dynamics should adopt a holistic mind-set. This part of the mind-set is not unique to research on intentional dynamics; it is shared with a range of recent contributions to researching complex and dynamic phenomena in TESOL (e.g., Hiver and Al-Hoorie 2020; Larsen-Freeman and Cameron 2008b; MacIntyre et al. 2017; Verspoor, de Bot, and Lowie 2011). In practical terms this means that, while data generation and analysis may focus on specific aspects or processes of intentional dynamics (see section 12.2), the research should foreground how these aspects and processes interconnect to generate a greater whole.

Closely related to a holistic perspective is the way context is understood. Some conventional approaches distinguish between the phenomena that are under investigation and the context in which they are situated – although there may, at times, be an acknowledgment that the lines demarcating the phenomenon and the context are "fuzzy". There are pragmatic reasons for such an approach, since after all, "it is humanly impossible to analyse everything at the same time" (Larsen-Freeman 2017: 32). However, ecological theory warns against severing theoretically significant relationships (e.g., Bateson 1972), and complexity-informed epistemology tells us that the intentional dynamics we seek to understand are, in fact, simply another perspective on context. In previous chapters, we noted how the intentional activity of participants in an MA course involved shifting between different ecologies (chapter 6), how the activity of Norwegian teenagers was shaped by intentional dynamics that straddled school years (chapter 7), and how the intentional ecology of a language school in Greece could be understood by taking into account the interplay between sociocultural aspects of the setting and the derived intentionality of the learning materials (chapter 8). Common to all of these research projects was a mind-set that equated intentional dynamics and context. Thus, an ecologically valid view on the interconnected nature of TESOL includes "context as part of the system(s) under investigation" (Larsen-Freeman and Cameron 2008b: 241).

Also related to the holistic perspective is the need to take a principled approach to identifying the system that we are investigating. This includes how this system may be "a nested reality that is composed of layered entities" (Reed and Harvey 1992: 358), and/or how the system may be an analytically defined sub-system of a larger over-arching system (see section 3.1). Some models that may be used as templates for such a systems perspective include Young et al.'s (2002) model of cascading constraints, or Davis and Sumara's (2006) hierarchical model, which posits that smaller structures are nested in larger ones – not unlike Russian dolls. Our own preference for using the model of intentional dynamics, including the individual, shared, derived, and sociocultural aspects of intentional ecologies, enables us to describe structural and/or analytical stratification, as well as intentional activity, which is stratified into different domains of activity in TESOL. More abstractly, intentional dynamics may describe functionally larger or smaller systems, such as the development of a national curriculum for language education (larger), syllabus development (in-between), or lesson planning (smaller). We should remain mindful, however, not to overly simplify the complex ecologies of TESOL, "where relationships cut across different hierarchies" (Cilliers 2001: 143). There is a need, then, for a transparent mind-set, clearly specifying the intentional dynamics being investigated, and how these intentional dynamics are nested, or act as sub-systems, of broader wholes. There is a need, also, to carefully detail possible interconnectivity between nested systems and/or sub-systems. One question to consider is co-adaptation (Larsen-Freeman and Cameron 2008a), i.e., how the intentional dynamics adapt to changes in the structures that surround them and vice versa. Another consideration is how deterministic the constraining links between the intentional dynamics and their surrounding structures are; e.g., can the system "break free" from the structures in which it is nested? Thus, any systems analysis, of intentional dynamics or other, needs to accept that the boundaries we draw are best conceptualized as interfaces that allow for the exchange of information between structures on either side of the boundary.

12.1.2 The "everything is dynamic" mind-set

Researching intentional dynamics must adopt a progressive understanding of causality. More conventional approaches to research aim to generate verifiable accounts of cause and effect (Larsen-Freeman 2017). In its simplest form, the conventional view holds that "all effects have a cause [. . .] if the cause is present, the effect always follows. If the cause is absent, then the effect never occurs" (Byrne 2002: 16). Again, this view has underpinned a great deal of valuable research, and in some fields it remains the "gold standard". However, the conventional view of cause and effect can be limiting, especially with regard to its ability to describe complex and dynamic phenomena. We noted, in chapter 3, that complex social structures, and this includes intentional ecologies, are assemblages of micro- and macro-structures "with causal powers running in all directions" (Byrne and Callaghan 2014: 45). These intricately interconnected causal pathways act as feedback loops within intentional ecologies, they amplify or cancel out intentional activity, and all of this challenges our ability to connect outcomes to specific causes (Cilliers 1998). Such non-linearity is easier to notice in open-ended situations, where creative intentional dynamics are likely to produce unexpected activity (for an extended example, see chapter 7), although it is important to note that non-linearity is a feature of all intentional ecologies. Moreover, CDST alerts us to the fact that phenomena are often shaped by "causes" that are too trivial to be measured and may be temporally removed from the effects they produce (Lorenz 1972). This could mean not only that causal attributions are hard to establish, but also that they could be of relatively little relevance to the situated reality of language education. What we suggest, instead, is a mind-set that foregrounds a holistic explanation of causality, using the notion of intentional dynamics as a frame of reference. Larsen-Freeman and Cameron (2008a) capture the difference between developing explanations and establishing causal attributions well, by alluding to an image of a sand pile to which additional sand is continually deposited, until an avalanche is formed and the sand pile collapses. They note that "the particular sand grain that produces the avalanche is a cause but not an explanation. Explanation is found at a higher level of organisation in terms of the structure and stability of the sand pile" (Larsen-Freeman and Cameron 2008a: 73). Applying this metaphor to TESOL, we believe that a focus on intentional dynamics is such a higher-level organisation, and a focus on intentional dynamics, therefore, can generate compelling explanations of TESOL contexts, activity, and outcomes.

Intricately linked to a more progressive understanding of causality is what kind of explanation we are seeking to construct as researchers. We have noted that conventional research is focused on generating verifiable accounts. The "acid test" for verifiability is replicability, and the ability of theoretical accounts to predict future activity (for more on the "predictive premise" of research, see Kostoulas 2018). However, as Larsen-Freeman and Cameron (2008a: 237) point out, "the position of complexity theorists, especially those preoccupied with the study of human behaviour, is that there can be no absolute replicability". Since complex dynamic systems are sensitive to minute differences in their internal structure and surroundings, and the relationships between outcomes and the events that triggered them are not linear, it is impossible to predict the long-term state of a system with any degree of certainty (see also Osberg and Biesta 2007). That said, there is a clear danger of falling into epistemological agnosticism, the view that "no knowledge system can describe reality" because of "the impossibility of prediction" (Byrne and Callaghan 2014: 61), or the unhelpful relativism encoded in the postmodernist view that "anything goes" (Cilliers 1998: 112). The challenge, therefore, is to find ways to use the intentional dynamics framework in order to build, from the trends and patterns that we do observe in TESOL, theoretical accounts that are locally and temporally contingent, while remaining relevant to a global profession.

A part of the dynamic mind-set that is closely related to the interconnected nature of phenomena is the notion of timescales. An identification of nested systems, including functionally larger and smaller systems, will reveal potentially different rates of change. Again, a larger scale system, such as the development of a national curriculum for language education, may "contain" smaller systems, such as syllabus development and lesson planning. When viewed from a temporal perspective, the larger system tends to change at a slower rate as compared the system that nests within it (Davis and Sumara 2006; Holling 2001). From the vantage point of an observer (e.g., a teacher or an administrator) larger systems tend to appear more static, whereas smaller systems are more dynamic. From this it follows that if we were to explore the intentional dynamics of teachers' lesson planning activity in a school, the larger-scale system of national curriculum development might appear as a static contextual backdrop. Even so, the development of national curricula has its own intentional dynamics that play out on a longer timescale. Thus, whether a phenomenon that interests us appears as real-time evolving or slow-moving, intentional dynamics will be a function of the timescale that we have chosen to work with. Maintaining a focus on how larger systems shape activity on shorter timescales, and how the activity on shorter timescales change the intentional dynamics of larger systems helps us to understand the reciprocal determination that gives coherence to a nested complex dynamic system such as TESOL. Such work is not always straightforward, however, because the change processes might not be directly observable. Sometimes what is perceived as (dynamic) stability in a system is the product of two or more change processes cancelling each other out. Also, unlike aspects of intentionality and the properties of intentional activity, which are in principle observable, the shaping and change processes that they constitute are not necessarily observable, and may not have psychological "reality" for the agents involved. For instance, hard-working and under-resourced teachers delivering English Medium Instruction in an international setting may not be aware of the ways in which their actions contribute towards strengthening inequalities between the western world and the Global South. Thus, identifying and describing the emergence and evolution of global intentional structures, like, e.g., linguistic imperialism (Phillipson 1992), requires analytical work that transcends the obvious.

12.1.3 The "meaning is primary" mind-set

So far, we have addressed that part of the mind-set that is shaped by ecological and complex dynamic systems theories. However, we must always remember that meaning and meaning-making is central to TESOL. There is a wealth of good advice, in the research methods literature, about how to take into account the meaningful dimension of phenomena, including research frames such as grounded theory (Charmaz 2008; Hadley 2017), ethnography (Blommaert 2013; Hammersley and Atkinson 2019; Pink 2013), interpretive phenomenological analysis (Smith

2004), narrative analysis (Cortazzi 1994), micro-history (Gray 2018), dairy studies (Bailey 2015), Action Research (Kemmis and McTaggart 2005), reflexivity (Etherington 2004), and many more. However, none of these existing frames fit with our own parallel concern with the interconnected and dynamic nature of TESOL, and the need to understand meaning in ways that are consistent with ecological and complex dynamic systems theories. Thus, this section takes us to more unfamiliar, but an equally important part, of the mind-set that we advocate for.

In chapter 3 we quoted Vickers, saying that "the dreams of men [sic] spread and colonize their inner world, clash, excite, modify, and destroy each other, or preserve their stability by making strange accommodations with their rivals" (Vickers 1968: 32). The mind-set that we encourage, here, is to imagine how dreams, or ideas, spread and colonize, clash, excite, modify, and destroy each other not only in our minds, but also throughout TESOL. Ideas clash, excite, and destroy each other in lesson planning, in classroom activity, in professional development, in policy-making, and more. Ideas flow from the intentional ecology, into intentional activity, and back again to the intentional ecology. This is the essence of the model of the intentional dynamics of TESOL. Ideas exist not only in our minds, they are present also in the shared, derived, and sociocultural ideational intentionality around us, and they are an inherent part of our intentional activity as teachers and learners, materials writers, policy-makers, and more. Thus, TESOL is an interconnected and dynamic ecology of ideas, which we have operationalized through the notions of intentional ecology and intentional activity. We accept that seeing TESOL as an ecology of ideas – our ideational intentionality – is a big change from the material world-views that so many of us have grown up with. However, it is an essential part of the mind-set required to research intentional dynamics.

Once we are able to view TESOL as an intentional whole, with ideas flowing and ebbing in interconnected and dynamic ways, the next step is to identify which part of the intentional dynamics we could fruitfully research. The key, we believe, is to identify intentional dynamics that generate the phenomena that we seek to explain, and this requires a consideration of ontological, intentional, and phenomenological validity. Ontological validity, we suggest, is the extent to which intentional dynamics generate an outcome. Hiver and Al-Hoorie (2016: 5), who take a CDST perspective, warn that some common objects of analysis are not really complex dynamic systems that generate outcomes. For example, "constellations (e.g., goals, interest) and abstract phenomena (e.g., L2 proficiency, L2 motivation) differ from systems because they do not produce an outcome by themselves, and must first be located within an agent who experiences and acts on them" (Hiver and Al-Hoorie 2016: 5). In terms of intentional dynamics, ontologically valid research aims may include the way that an intentional ecology, or some aspect of it, shapes the intentional activity that we seek to explain, or how some type of intentional activity reproduces or changes an intentional ecology, including one or more of its individual, shared, derived, and/or sociocultural aspects. Intentional validity, by contrast, is motivated by what Dennett (1987) has defined as an "intentional stance". The intentional stance eschews the exact specification of the components that make up a system, and instead foregrounds the purposeful outcomes of the system – or *what a system does*. For example, when researching the TESOL provision in a country's educational system, our starting point would be the desired outcome of the system; e.g., developing the students' linguistic competence, or more broadly, developing a country's economic competitiveness. Such an intentional stance, then, helps us to include and exclude aspects of an intentional ecology and types of intentional activity. Finally, phenomenological validity is whether an aspect of an intentional ecology, or type of intentional activity, is perceived as "real" by actual stakeholders in TESOL. Phenomenological reality might be established with reference to the discourses generated in a TESOL setting (e.g., when teachers self-identify as members of a social structure or participants in some activity), or empirically by establishing whether intentional structures appear to shape activity, or whether intentional activity appears to change participants' subsequent views (individual intentionality) or subsequent intentional activity.

Hiver and Al-Hoorie's (2016) suggestion that abstractly defined phenomena must "be located within an agent" (see previous paragraph) before we can determine outcomes, is a pertinent reminder of the key role of agents in any intentional dynamics. Agents may play a role as individuals, or they may act collectively as a group. In other words, the mind-set we advocate for must include a focus on human agency and meaning-making, and must include a focus on the role of individuals and groups in an intentional ecology and in intentional activity. This is an issue that has been raised, also, by Applied Linguistics researchers working within the complexity frame. For instance, Larsen-Freeman and Cameron (2008a: 75) note that "human intentionality and agency appear to be one of the most severe problems in applying a complex systems metaphor or analogy to the kinds of behaviors and processes that interest applied linguists". Since complex dynamic systems are deterministic, the theoretical accounts of CDST are "distancing" and the role of individual and collective decision- and meaning-making is unclear. Our intentional dynamics model goes some way towards addressing such concerns. For example, we have discussed the agentive potential of creative and purposeful intentional activity (chapter 5), while also tracing the constraints within which such action takes place. What is needed, then, is a mind-set that balances descriptions of derived and sociocultural aspects of intentional ecologies with analysis that foregrounds the role of individual and shared meaning-making. We must remember, also, that there will be agentive contributions across many different domains of activity in TESOL. In the classroom, the agents are teachers and learners, and this remains an ontologically valid focus. However, we need to account, also, for the agentive contribution of managers, materials writers, teacher trainers, policy-makers, and more (see also chapter 11).

Finally, the focus on meaning, including also the earlier discussion of ontological, intentional, and phenomenological validity, highlights that the researcher will have an impact on the research process. Ultimately, it is the researcher that determines what intentional dynamics have outcomes, what purposes have research value, and whether an aspect of an intentional ecology, or a type of intentional activity, is perceived as "real" by actual stakeholders in TESOL. As Underhill (1993: 183) suggests, we are always "confined to a version of reality that has been filtered through the subjectivity of [our] perception". In the qualitative research literature, the reflective stance that focuses on the influence of the researcher is called reflexivity (Etherington 2004). Writing in the context of teacher education, Edge (2011: 47) proposes a two-part heuristic for reflexivity. The first part is what he calls prospective reflexivity, which encourages reflection on what difference it makes that "I" conduct this research. When we are in the middle of doing research, the difference that we make is difficult to notice. For instance, we are now aware, in ways that were not obvious at the time, that the study of the language school that we reported in chapter 8 would have produced more nuanced findings if the principal researcher (Kostoulas) had been more attuned to his role as a powerful insider in the setting. Similarly, the interpretations of the Norwegian young learners' interaction, reported in chapter 7, may have been a function of the particular "liquid identity" (Thomson and Gunter 2011) of the researcher (Stelma), who experienced the Norwegian educational system first-hand, as a young person, but at the time of the research had been living in South Korea and the UK for about 20 years. Edge's second heuristic is retrospective reflexivity, and it involves problematizing how the research activity is changing us as researchers, and – one might add – how it is changing the participants in our research. Retrospective reflexivity has ethical and political implications. Research is not merely an act of description; rather, it has "constitutive and transformative potential" for everyone involved (Byrne and Callaghan 2014: 65). Finally, the model of intentional dynamics offers a unique view on researcher reflexivity. An awareness of the interplay between *the intentional dynamics that we are seeking to understand as researchers*, and *the intentional dynamics of our own research activity*, is what – in our view – defines a reflexive stance. Thus, the model of intentional dynamics highlights how our own research is intentional activity in its own right, and the associated intentional dynamics will affect the outcomes of our research (see Stelma and Fay 2014; Stelma, Fay, and Zhou 2013).

12.1.4 Summary

Table 9 provides a summary of the mind-set we suggest is needed to research intentional dynamics.

Table 9: A mind-set for researching intentional dynamics.

Everything is connected
– Adopting a holistic view
– Seeing intentional dynamics as both context and activity
– Being attuned to boundaries and nested levels, as well as co-adaptation with wider intentional dynamics
Everything is dynamic
– Adopting a progressive view of causality
– Seeing intentional dynamics as locally and temporally contingent
– Being attuned to timescale effects
Meaning is primary
– Seeing TESOL as an interconnected and dynamic ecology of ideas
– Being attuned to ontological, intentional, and phenomenological validity
– Being attuned to the role of individuals and groups in intentional dynamics
– Being attuned to the intentional dynamics of research activity, and its effect

12.2 Researchable aspects and processes of intentional dynamics

In this section, we outline what we believe are the researchable aspects and processes of the intentional dynamics of TESOL. We could define the scope of researching intentional dynamics by listing components and actors, such as teachers, learners, policy-makers, rules and traditions, structures, and more. However, with no component too small to be excluded, such an approach would quickly become unmanageable. Our preferred approach is to keep in mind the aspects and processes that comprise the model of the intentional dynamics of TESOL, which we show again in Figure 10 (but with shaping and change processes renamed as soft-assembly and morphogenesis, which are labels that we will use in this chapter).

Any empirical investigation of intentional dynamics should recognize, as a starting point, that there is an intentional ecology, and that this intentional ecology has individual, shared, derived, and sociocultural aspects; it should recognize that this intentional ecology shapes the affordances for intentional

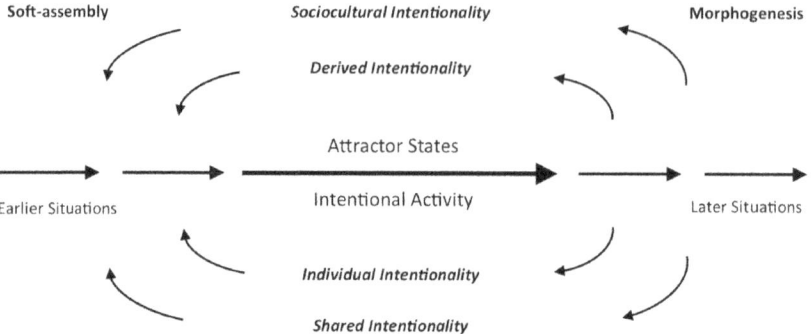

Figure 10: Researchable aspects and processes of the intentional dynamics of TESOL.

activity, sometimes resulting in attractor states; it should recognize that intentional activity has dynamic properties; and it should recognize how these dynamic properties will generate different outcomes, either reproducing or changing some aspects of the intentional ecology, or the intentional ecology as a whole. Finally, researchers need to recognize that researching all of these aspects and processes may be impossible. We are reminded of early social ecological researchers who established a "field-station" in some small town, and where a team of researchers would spend years meticulously documenting and analysing every possible aspect of the human ecology (see Barker 1968; Scott 2005). Such work- and time-intensive research is not realistic in the fast-paced world of TESOL. Our own analyses of intentional dynamics, in chapters 6, 7, 8, and 9, has illustrated how such a complete view is difficult or impossible to achieve. In this section, therefore, we look at the feasibility of researching one, or a few, of the aspects or processes suggested by the model of intentional dynamics shown in Figure 10, whilst foregrounding how these aspects and processes fit into a larger whole.

12.2.1 Understanding intentional ecologies

A central contribution of the model of intentional dynamics is that meaningful contexts of TESOL are composed of individual, shared, derived, and sociocultural aspects of intentionality – summarized in the notion of an intentional ecology (see chapter 5). Table 10 illustrates the aspects of intentional ecologies that our own studies, reported in the previous chapters, have described (bolding indicates the main focus of each respective study). Of the three studies listed in the table, the study of language teachers becoming researchers, reported in chapter 6,

Table 10: Aspects of intentional ecologies described in our own research.

Aspects of intentionality	Online MA TESOL course (chapter 6)	Norwegian EFL class (chapter 7)	Language school in Greece (chapter 8)
Sociocultural	UK academic UK research Local education	Norwegian society Norwegian education	Global TESOL Greek school Greek society
Derived	MA curriculum Course unit syllabus Tutor instructions	Textbook Task sheets Teacher instructions	**Learning materials** **Curriculum documents**
Shared	Participant-tutor Participant-participant	**Learner-learner** **Learner-teacher**	(not examined)
Individual	**Teacher aims** **Research aims** **Researcher development**	(not examined)	(not examined)

appears to have provided the fullest description of an intentional ecology. Moreover, this study detailed aspects of academic, research, and local pedagogical intentional ecologies, making the point that to become researchers the language teachers had to move between, or bridge, these distinct intentional ecologies. However, the main focus was on the development of the language teachers' individual intentionality as researchers, and hence the detail of the description of shared, derived, and sociocultural aspects of intentional ecologies was more restricted. By contrast, the study of a repeated task performance in a Norwegian classroom provided a more limited description of individual, derived, and sociocultural aspects of intentionality, but a detailed description of shared intentionality in the classroom. Finally, the study of the Greek private language school provided a great deal of detailed information about idiosyncratic intentional structures in the local sociocultural ecology, as well as a close analysis of derived intentionality evident in the learning materials of the school. In sum, no single study can be expected to provide a complete account of an intentional ecology; there may inevitably be a particular focus on one or more aspects of intentionality.

When aiming to describe an intentional ecology we need consider what Larsen-Freeman (2017: 32) calls the "boundary problem". Occasionally, the boundaries of a system might be suggested by the physical world. On this topic, Kostoulas (2018: 22) notes that:

> Schools have very unambiguous topological perimeters, in the form of building walls or schoolyard fences that separate the school from the community in which it is embedded. They also have recognizable temporal boundaries: we can, for example, decide to concern ourselves only with what teachers and learners do between the start and the end of the school day, or maybe our focus could be what happens to a child between their first and their last day at school.

Even in such seemingly unproblematic cases, however, boundaries are rarely airtight: in the example above, policy decisions made outside the school might influence its functioning, and it would be unhelpful to describe language teaching in the school without reference to prevailing language ideologies that transcend its boundaries. To provide another example, the boundaries of a language learner "self" are only partially suggested by the physical body, as the self is defined in terms of its relationship with other agents (Mercer 2011a). In other cases, defining boundaries in spatial and temporal terms is even harder: for example, Varela (1995, cited in Larsen-Freeman 2017), notes that the immune system does not have boundaries as such. Another such "distributed" system, which is closer to TESOL, is language policy in a community, defined as its linguistic ideologies, language management, and linguistic practices (Spolsky 2004), all of which are hard to assign to specific localities. In such cases, bounding the system may be approached with reference to its ontological, intentional, and phenomenological validity (see section 12.1.3). The research may gradually discover what part of the intentional ecology appears to generate outcomes (ontological validity), what parts of the intentional ecology appears to generate what the intentional system meaningfully does (intentional validity), and research participants may tell us – through data generation – what are the boundaries of the system (phenomenological validity).

12.2.2 Soft-assembly of intentional activity

Another central contribution of the model of intentional dynamics is how an intentional ecology, including its individual, shared, derived, and sociocultural aspects, shapes intentional activity in situations of TESOL. In chapter 6, we explored how a range of aspects of intentional ecologies shaped the researcher intentionality of language teachers. This included aspects from the intentional ecologies of research and the participants' professional contexts, as well as the academic intentional ecology that the language teachers were asked to engage with. The soft-assembly of such influences does not happen mechanically, or in any material way. Thus, the language teachers' activity on the research methods unit emerged from a process of synthesis; a range of different sources of ideational intentionality combined through the teachers' reflective engagement, giving rise to increasingly purposeful intentional researcher activity. Moreover, chapter 7 described a collaborative process of soft-assembly of intentional influences, giving rise to a shared intentionality that acted as an attractor state for the Norwegian young learners' task-based activity. We suggest, then, that to uncover the process of soft-assembly is another worth-while aim of research into the intentional dynamics of TESOL.

We have defined soft-assembly as the process by which multiple meaningful aspects of TESOL contexts constitute affordances and activity in situations (see section 3.1). More precisely, the presence of affordances is an indication of the potential for soft-assembly of activity taking place. Thus, the approach taken in chapter 8, where we identified how the derived intentionality of learning materials used in a Greek language school represented an affordance landscape, is another way to research the shaping influence of an intentional ecology. Also, in chapter 8, an additional step of soft-assembly was how derived intentionality combined with idiosyncratic intentional structures in this Greek context to generate attractor states for activity in the school. The identification of an affordance landscape, based on derived intentionality, suggested *potential* activity for teachers and learners in the school; the identification of attractor states, however, was based on observational data of what actually transpired in the school over time. Thus, the attractor states provided a picture of how intentional dynamics of resistance shaped activity over a temporally more extended timescale, with teaching and learning remaining much the same as before a curricular reform was attempted (Kostoulas and Stelma 2017). This research, then, identified a temporally more extended form of soft-assembly. However, and again, not all aspects of the intentional ecology were documented in chapter 8 (see Table 10), and this suggests a limitation of this research. Equally, the analysis of language teachers becoming researchers in chapter 6, and the analysis of the shifting shared intentionality in chapter 7, focused on particular shaping aspects of the respective intentional ecologies, and may therefore have included "gaps". In other words, as researchers try to establish how intentional activity is soft-assembled from the multiple meaningful aspects of TESOL contexts, there may invariably be a preferred perspective, or approach, which highlights the shaping influence of some aspects of an intentional ecology more than others. What may be missing from our own analyses in previous chapters is a sufficient consideration of co-adaptation (see section 12.1.1) across the boundaries of the system or systems defined using the data we had. In the case of the English language teachers becoming researchers, we could have generated more data on the intentional ecology of the teachers' professional contexts; in the Norwegian study we could have gathered more data on the sociocultural aspects of the context; and in the Greek study we could have gathered more data on individual and shared intentionality. Such additional data might have enabled a better view on co-adaptation across system boundaries.

12.2.3 Intentional activity as meaning-making

Looking at intentional activity in its own right (rather than how it is soft-assembled) is another possible focus that is consistent with the model of intentional dynamics. This focus is associated with the meaning-making that we believe is central to TESOL contexts, activity, and outcomes. In our own research, this focus on meaning-making is most clearly evident in chapters 6 and 7. In chapter 6, we explored language teachers making sense of the world of research, and in chapter 7 we explored the Norwegian young learner's meaning-making in a dialogue-writing and role-play task. These chapters focused on the interplay of aspects of intentional ecologies, thus retaining a concern for soft-assembly, but there was a parallel focus on the moment-to-moment, or diachronic, unfolding of the participants' activity. Broadly, this corresponds to what Hiver and Al-Hoorie (2016) designate as an analysis of a system's micro-structure. This, they suggest, may include "the aim, purpose or intention of the interaction; its directionality, intensity, frequency, and duration; its utility, and the rewards or costs that accrue from it" (2016: 9). We believe this describes the analyses provided in chapters 6 and 7 quite well. However, our analyses were guided, in addition, by our theoretical definition of different types of intentional activity (i.e. contingent, normative, creative, and purposeful), and their associated dynamic properties (i.e. adaptiveness, normativity, non-linearity, and self-organisation). What we suggest, then, is that the generative properties of the intentional activity types, which we defined in chapter 5, function as *causal signature dynamics* associated with system outcomes. This analysis was most clearly operationalized in chapter 7, were we showed how each of the four types of intentional activity, and their respective dynamic properties, contributed in unique ways to the emergence of a new shared intentionality in the classroom.

Taking this analysis of intentional activity one step further, we suggest that the generative properties of different types of intentional activity describe their "ability" to generate meaningful outcomes. The outcomes that we are focused on are not only microgenetic – meanings that become apparent in the micro-structure of situations. The outcomes of meaning-making include, in addition, change or reproduction of individual, shared, derived, and sociocultural aspects of intentional ecologies. In the Norwegian study, the most obvious outcome of the learners' meaning-making was a new shared intentionality. However, another outcome of their meaning-making was the derived intentionality assigned or sedimented in their role-play dialogues, including also the additional entertaining elements that were included when these were performed to the class. The Norwegian learners' intentional activity may also have resulted in enhanced individual intentionality of various sorts, including – we presume – becoming more intentional both as language users and learners (see chapter 10).

Finally, if a study of intentional activity in TESOL is able to establish the causal signature dynamics of meaning-making, and is able to point out the outcomes of this meaning-making activity, then we have evidence of the ontological and intentional validity of the research (see section 12.1.3). In addition, if the research participants are able to confirm that the meaning-making is taking place, through their observed behaviour in situations, through acting as co-researchers, or by confirming that meaning-making has taken place through personal identification in interviews or member checking processes (Lincoln and Guba 1985), researchers may, in addition, make claims about phenomenological validity.

12.2.4 Morphogenesis in intentional ecologies

A final research focus that is consistent with the model of intentional dynamics is the reproduction and/or change of intentional ecologies. In the previous section, we established that an outcome of meaning-making is such reproduction or change to an aspect of an intentional ecology. However, broader-based change in an intentional ecology may require more sustained and distributed meaning-making, and the resulting morphogenesis (Archer 1998) will take place on a temporally longer timescale. Chapter 6 looked at morphogenesis over the timescale of a semester, tracing the teachers developing individual researcher intentionality, and chapter 7 explored morphogenesis over a full year, but limited to the intentional activity of learners on five repeated task performances. Finally, chapter 8 explored the morphogenesis resulting from the interplay between the derived intentionality of the learning materials in a school, and idiosyncratic intentional structures in the local ecology. Moreover, with knowledge of an earlier curricular reform initiative, we were able to conclude that there were intentional dynamics of resistance – a form of morphogenesis – preventing change in this Greek school.

When researching morphogenesis, we need to consider the timescale effects across different nested levels of TESOL. As a complex dynamic system, TESOL is in a state of constant flux, and the rate at which different aspects of TESOL change is not uniform. It is likely that functionally smaller systems, like the individuals and groups whose intentional activity we described in chapters 6 and 7, tend to exhibit dynamic properties that play out on shorter timescales. Larger systems, such as the language school we described in chapter 8, and certainly the intentional ecology of TESOL world-wide, which we described in chapter 9, will exhibit change, which is still dynamic, but which plays out on longer timescales. For a researcher observing classroom interaction, any change will appear rapid. By contrast, when observing the ecology of international TESOL change will appear slow. What this suggests is that the study of intentional dynamics at different "focal timescales" (de Bot 2015) is likely to produce accounts with varying degrees of granularity. Shorter timescales can be observed in great detail, while research on longer timescales are subject to limitations of "sampling" (how often and at what points we observe the system). In sum, researchers wishing to explore morphogenesis in an intentional ecology will have to consider the timescale of this morphogenesis, and what may be the implications for data collection or generation.

If our interest is in longer timescales of reproduction or change, the focus is on what Hiver and Al-Hoorie (2016) have referred to as the macro-structure of a system. Researching the macro-structure of a system, they suggest, requires data on the overall trajectory of the system, changes in its configuration over time, and the patterns of stability and variability of the system as a whole. In our own terms, intentional activity, and the intentional dynamics driving the activity, may reproduce or change existing intentional structures of an intentional ecology. Such morphogenetic processes may gradually build, or reinforce, an attractor state in TESOL. We suggested the presence of such attractor states in chapters 8 and 9. In chapter 8, we suggested that the interplay between the derived intentionality evident in the learning materials of the Greek language school, and the idiosyncratic intentional structures of this context, constituted a form-focused attractor state for teaching and learning (see section 8.3). The broader discussion of international TESOL, in chapter 9, suggested that the transactional paradigm represented an attractor state. This latter observation was based on literature-based study and our own experience, and it included a chronological dimension. We were able to identify possible change to intentional structures, in part enabled by communicative approaches, but concluded that the transactional attractor state constrained the emergence (Deacon 2007) of what we suggested might be a more desirable transformative attractor state.

12.2.5 Summary

Table 11 provides a summary typology of the aspects and processes of the model of intentional dynamics that we believe can be researched.

At an earlier point we warned that researching all aspects and processes of intentional dynamics would be impossible. We would like to conclude with the converse warning; that researching a single aspect or process of intentional

Table 11: Typology of researchable aspects and processes of intentional dynamics.

Understanding intentional ecologies
– Describe the individual, shared, derived, and sociocultural aspects of an intentional ecology – Identify the boundaries of an intentional ecology – Identify interconnected intentional ecologies
Soft-assembly of intentional activity
– Describe how aspects of, and possible co-adaptation between, intentional ecologies shape activity – Identify affordances (or affordance landscapes) – Identify the intentional activity that is being soft-assembled
Intentional activity as meaning-making
– Describe the moment-to-moment unfolding of intentional activity – Identify the generative properties of intentional activity – Identify the meaningful outcomes of intentional activity
Morphogenesis in intentional ecologies and intentional dynamics
– Describe morphogenetic processes that reproduce or change intentional ecologies – Identify timescale effects, and appropriate degrees of granularity – Identify possible attractor states

dynamics, while possible, is undesirable. Looking at a single aspect or process in isolation is inconsistent with the holistic part of the mind-set outlined in section 12.1. Moreover, the nature of the model of intentional dynamics is that of an integrated whole. This means that whilst the focus of research may be on a specific aspect or process, there have to be frequent attempts at linking the analysis to the full model of intentional dynamics. The studies we have reported in chapters 6, 7, and 8 illustrate this point; whilst focused on a particular aspect or process of the model, they all sought to address other aspects and processes of intentional dynamics.

12.3 Reflecting on research design, methods, and analysis

In the final section of this chapter, we take a look at the research design, data generation, and data analysis we have employed in our own research on intentional dynamics in TESOL settings. We do so by taking another look at the three empirical studies which we have reported on in this book (see chapters 6, 7, and 8). We discuss each study in terms of the typology of researchable aspects of intentional dynamics, presented in Table 11. This is followed by a more general discussion of the research design, data generation, and data analysis used, as well as a few suggestions that expand on what may be related and promising methodological options. Our studies of intentional dynamics are exemplars only – they are not models of best practice. Rather, the discussion in this section illustrates how the mind-set that we argued for in section 12.1, as well as the typology developed in section 12.2, have shaped our own research on the intentional dynamics of TESOL.

12.3.1 Teacher development: The UK study

In chapter 6, we reported on a case study that focused on a UK-based, online MA course for language teachers (Stelma and Fay 2014). This study gathered naturalistic data in the form of email communications and online discussions between the two course tutors and 13 course participants. The study also had access to the course materials, a mid-term research plan, and the participants' final written assignments. This data was naturalistic in that none of it was generated for the purpose of the research. Rather, all the data was gathered from elements of the course unit pedagogy. This naturalistic data, which spanned the entire duration of the course, was qualitatively analysed, in order to identify common themes and idiosyncratic patterns in the development of the participants' researcher intentionality.

Using the frame provided by Table 11, the main focus of this study was to understand intentional activity as meaning-making, and specifically to:

– Identify the meaningful outcomes of intentional activity

The meaningful outcome we aimed to identify was the language teachers' developing researcher intentionality. The researchers, acting as course unit tutors, had taught the research methods course unit for a number of years, and knew that researcher competence was an outcome of the pedagogy. Moreover, as an intended learning outcome this researcher competence was a desired outcome. Hence, the focus on researcher competence, conceptualised as researcher intentionality, had ontological and intentional validity. However, given that the model of intentional dynamics is an integrated whole, and the associated need to maintain a holistic mind-set, the study also focused on understanding the intentional ecologies at play. Again following the frame provided by Table 11, this included:

- Describe the individual, shared, derived, and sociocultural aspects of an intentional ecology
- Identify the boundaries of an intentional ecology
- Identify interconnected intentional ecologies

Thus, the case study highlighted multiple aspects of the intentional ecology of the course. For example, the participants' postings revealed sociocultural aspects of intentionality, e.g., in the form of beliefs about research or expectations associated with their home educational contexts. In addition, derived intentionality was present in the form of instructions that were given by the course tutors, which reflected their own expectations as well as a cascade of constraints (Young et al. 2002) associated with University, School, programme, and course unit policies. Interactions between participants also showed evidence of developing shared intentionality, which was shaped by their own individual understandings, and the sociocultural and derived aspects of intentionality. There was great care, also, to identify the boundaries between the intentional ecologies of the teachers' home professional contexts, the academic context, and the world of research. In terms of the frame suggested by Table 11, this included consideration of how co-adaptation between the different intentional ecologies shaped the teachers' developing researcher intentionality. Finally, there was a focus on the generative properties of the language teachers' intentional activity (again see Table 11), so as to gain a better understanding of the outcomes of the teachers' meaning-making activity. In practical terms, this involved identifying the purposeful aspects of the interactions between participants, or tutors and participants, and how this purposeful intentional activity contributed to the emergence of the language teachers' developing researcher intentionality. Finally, the phenomenological validity of the study focus and findings was established through the participants' own final assessment of their researcher competence, in postings late in the semester, and though the personal reflections that were a part of their final written assignments.

More generally, we believe that the case study design employed by this study has considerable potential for informing research on intentional dynamics. A key strength of case-study design is that it seeks to develop in-depth understanding of how a bounded social grouping (e.g., an individual teacher or learner, a small group, a professional community, or other) operates in its context (Punch 2013; Yin 2003). In our case, the use of a case-study design helped us to connect the MA course unit participants' developing individual intentionality to the intentional ecologies which it straddled, namely the worlds of teaching and research. Another key affordance of case-study research is that it can generate findings that are of both practical and theoretical value (Stake 1994). By engaging with the data generated by the course participants and their tutors, we were able to generate insights that were useful both for subsequent iterations of the MA course (practical value), as well as for refining our understanding of how individual intentionality emerges (theoretical value).

Finally, we do not claim that this case study design was uniquely suited to investigating the development of individual intentionality, or even that it is necessarily superior to alternatives. A key limitation of this approach was that, much as it was suitable to understanding the idiosyncratic intentional ecologies at play in the course unit, it did not generate findings that could be generalized to other populations (Silverman 2006). The literature on how one might research complex dynamic systems in TESOL suggests ways to address this limitation. For example, Hiver and Al-Hoorie (2020: 85–94) suggest that a systematic comparison of different cases, or what they call qualitative comparative analysis, may be a way forward. Qualitative comparative analysis involves in-depth study of multiple individual cases (as in different cohorts of this MA course, or individual participants), identifying key variables, and comparing them in order to uncover patterns of causality and the conditions that are associated with individual outcomes. Another methodological option is Dörnyei's (2014) Retrodictive Qualitative Modeling, which would involve identifying "typical" trajectories of developing researcher intentionality among the MA participants, and then using the data to work backwards to trace the ways in which the intentional ecology shaped these trajectories.

12.3.2 Classroom research: The Norwegian study

The study that we reported on in chapter 7 focused on the emergence and shaping influence of shared intentionality among young learners doing repeated dialogue-writing and role-play tasks in a Norwegian primary classroom. The data we used included observation and audio-recordings of the teacher's instructions, learner pairs while writing their dialogues, and the subsequent role-play performances. There were post-observation interviews with both the learners and the teachers, and the study had access to relevant hand-outs and textbooks (Stelma 2003). Our overt analysis, however, focused mainly on the transcribed recordings of learner interaction, which were examined in order to trace how the shared intentionality of "being entertaining" emerged, bottom-up, from the learners' intentional activity. In terms of the frame offered by Table 11, the study was focused on intentional activity as meaning-making, including:
- Describe the moment-to-moment unfolding of intentional activity
- Identify the generative properties of intentional activity
- Identify the meaningful outcomes of intentional activity

The analysis of the moment-to-moment unfolding of intentional activity included some attention, also, to the derived and sociocultural aspects of the classroom intentional ecology, such as the impact of the textbooks, and the influence of popular culture. However, the main focus was on describing the learners' contingent, normative, creative, and purposeful intentional activity, how the balance of these four activity types shifted across the repeated task sequences, and how the dynamic properties of these activity types (see section 5.3) facilitated the bottom-up emergence of a meaningful outcome – i.e. the new shared intentionality. In terms of the typology offered by Table 11, there was a less direct, but still evident, focus on morphogenesis, including how the shared intentionality represented an attractor state for the learners' activity. Moreover, given the moment-to-moment timescale of the learner interaction, this analysis of morphogenesis included a finer level of granularity than, e.g., the analyses provided by chapters 8 and 9.

Research designs which rely on some form of observation or discourse analysis are fairly common in TESOL research, and with good reason. Larsen-Freeman and Cameron (2008b), for example, note that such methods may be useful for uncovering the dynamics of language patterns, or for generating "rich" descriptions of language learning activity. Observational and discourse analytic methods can be extended, also, by drawing on the broad methodological repertoire of Applied Linguistics . This may include the ethno-methodological orientation provided by Conversation Analysis (Seedhouse 2005), symbolic interactional analysis that may help to highlight how participants themselves shape the outcomes of talk-in-interaction (Kramsch 2008), or discourse analysis that takes into account movement and embodiment (Kasper and Wagner 2014). The co-construction of shared intentionality may also be observed in online collaboration spaces drawing on methods such as computer-mediated discourse analysis (Herring 2004). Finally, critical approaches to discourse analyses (e.g., Wodak and Meyer 2009) may be used to relate the development of shared intentionality to historical and political processes.

12.3.3 Investigating a school: The Greek study

The data that we presented in chapter 8 was generated by a mixed-methods case study, combining qualitative and quantitative procedures, in order to generate a "snapshot" of a private language school in Greece (Kostoulas 2015). The qualitative strand was loosely informed by ethnography, and it included classroom observations to record teaching practices and in-depth interviews with the school staff, so as to document beliefs about language, learning, and assessment. The

quantitative strand consisted of a content analysis of the textual content of the learning materials used by the school, coding according to specific variables (Krippendorff 2004; Neuendorf 2002), and then aggregation and cluster analysis (Field 2013). The focus of the study, as reported in chapter 8, was to describe derived and sociocultural aspects of the intentional ecology of the language school, and to identify how these aspects of intentionality shaped classroom teaching. In terms of the researchable aspects of intentional dynamics, outlined in Table 11, the main aims included:
- Describe the individual, shared, derived, and sociocultural aspects of an intentional ecology
- Identify affordances (or affordance landscapes)
- Identify possible attractor states

The description of the derived aspect of the intentional ecology, as evident in the learning materials, was used to generate an affordance landscape. This represented a first step towards identifying how intentional activity in the school might be soft-assembled. This was combined with the description of idiosyncratic intentional structures (credentialism, supplementation, and protectionism) that were a part of the sociocultural ecology of the school. Finally, the analysis identified intentional dynamics of resistance, manifest as a form-focused attractor state, to explain the limited success of the curricular reform that was attempted some time prior to the fieldwork (Kostoulas and Stelma 2017). The focus on derived intentionality and idiosyncratic intentional structures, and their synthesis into an attractor state that seemed to constrain teaching in the school, provided the study with ontological and intentional validity. More indirectly, in terms of the frame offered by Table 11, the description of derived intentionality and idiosyncratic intentional structures included an identification of the boundaries of the school's intentional ecology, as well as a consideration of how the idiosyncratic intentional structures of the school interconnected with the sociocultural aspects of international TESOL. Finally, in order to identify the attractor states that appeared to shape teaching in the school, there was a focus also on morphogenetic processes that reproduce or change intentional ecologies.

Research methods inspired by ethnography may be particularly useful to develop insights about intentional dynamics. The value of ethnographic methods is well documented in the CDST literature (e.g., Agar 2004; Larsen-Freeman and Cameron 2008b). Larsen-Freeman and Cameron (2008a: 243) suggest that ethnography can reveal "processes that apply iteratively and recursively at different patterns [and] variations which emerge from adaptation to contingencies and environment". Some ethnographic methods that seem particularly applicable to intentional dynamics research include observations of TESOL settings (Copland 2018) and qualitative interviewing of teachers and learners (Fielding 2008; Kvale and Brinkmann 2009). Ethnographically generated data can then be synthesized into descriptions of sociocultural aspects of intentional ecologies, perhaps employing procedures such as grounded theory (Hadley 2017).

Finally, the focal scale of the Greek study was the entire school, and this motivated the choice of ethnographic and content-analytical methods. Thus, combining these methods involved more than just selecting the methods that seemed to be intuitively more suitable for each type of data. It not only allowed the study to document both sociocultural and derived aspects of the school's intentional ecology. It also enabled the subsequent analytical synthesis of these two aspects, in the form of attractor states. In sum, the integration of two different methods allowed a more comprehensive explanation of how the intentional ecology in the Greek school may have shaped intentional activity. This kind of methodological integration may be appropriate, also, to researching intentional dynamics on other focal scales, such as individuals and small groups, and it could involve other aspects of intentionality. Some qualitative methods that could prove useful for researching other focal scales include introspective verbal reports, such as think-aloud or stimulated recall protocols during or immediately after learning events (Bowles 2018; Gass and Mackey 2016), diary studies spanning a bounded period of time (Bailey 2015), and life-history interviews (P. Benson 2011). These could be combined with quantitative approaches that involve repeated measurements of carefully chosen granularity and timescales, and the use of statistical models such as latent-growth curve modelling (Byrne and Crombie 2003) or idiodynamic research (MacIntyre et al. 2017).

12.4 Conclusion

In this chapter, we have developed our thoughts about researching intentional dynamics. The chapter has not presented a ready-made template, a list of "approved methods", or an exhaustive list of methodological options. We believe that such an attempt would be restrictive; the great diversity of settings in which our model of intentional dynamics might be employed precludes "one-size-fits-all" approaches, and favours flexibility and methodological pluralism (Moss and Haertel 2016). The intentional dynamics of TESOL will comprise infinite diversity in infinite combination, and this creates both challenges and opportunities for methodological innovation. We take a cue from the principle of equifinality from General Systems Theory (von Bertalanffy [1969] 2015), which holds that the same result can be reached in multiple different ways, and we therefore acknowledge that there are multiple empirical pathways to understanding intentional dynamics in TESOL. What the chapter has argued is that researchers wishing to understand the intentional dynamics of TESOL: (a) should adopt the mind-set that we developed in section 12.1; and (b) may benefit from focusing on some part of the typology of researchable aspects and processes of intentional dynamics, as outlined in section 12.2. In addition, we recognize an emerging research methods literature that develops methodological options for researchers who wish to understand TESOL as a complex dynamic system (e.g., Hiver and Al-Hoorie 2020; Larsen-Freeman and Cameron 2008b; MacIntyre at al. 2017; Verspoor, de Bot, and Lowie 2011). This literature, we believe, can be extended to the study of intentional dynamics, and our discussion in the present chapter has drawn on these sources. Beyond that, the chapter reflects our own methodological preferences, and we expect that other researchers similarly will rely on their own such preferences. A final piece of advice, perhaps, is that researchers should be creative and purposeful in making their methodological decisions (Stelma 2011; Stelma et al. 2013). As Larsen-Freeman and Cameron (2008b) observe, methodological innovation is both inevitable and welcome when the methodological principles of new perspectives are enacted in actual research projects.

Chapter 13
Intentional dynamics and the future of TESOL

We have arrived at a milestone on a longer journey. We have achieved the aims that we set ourselves for this book. Helped by the concept of intentionality, we have placed meaning and meaning-making at the heart of an ecological and complex dynamic systems account of TESOL. At the same time, with our model of intentional dynamics in place, there is much more we can see and do. In this final chapter, then, we first describe what we believe are the theoretical contributions of the book – at the end of our writing (section 13.1). Next, we offer a brief review of the practical implications of the model of intentional dynamics (section 13.2). Finally, we have a look at what we now see, as we scan a new horizon for opportunities (section 13.3).

Before we proceed, we must once again make clear that this book has focused on English language education, or TESOL. We have not explicitly addressed the teaching of other languages or translingual pedagogy; nor have we explicitly addressed the broader theoretical and empirical concerns of Applied Linguistics, which TESOL is a part of. Our strategy has been to ground our description in the realities of English language teaching and learning, as well as contexts, activities and outcomes that contribute to English language teaching and learning (i.e., materials design, management, policymaking, and more). We believe this clear focus on TESOL has value, as it counters trends that call for the increased professionalization of language teaching at the expense of intellectual development (Kramsch 2015). This final chapter is similarly focused on English language education, or TESOL. However, we do think that the metatheoretical qualities of our contribution, including our model of intentional dynamics, may have relevance to domains adjacent to TESOL, including mainstream education, Applied Linguistics and more.

13.1 Intentional dynamics as a contribution to TESOL

The primary contribution of this book is our model of the intentional dynamics of TESOL, which is designed to help understand the central role of meaning and meaning-making in TESOL contexts, activity, and outcomes. The model describes how TESOL is an "ecology of ideas", i.e., a meaningful context, comprised of intentional structures with individual, shared, derived, and sociocultural aspects. This intentional ecology shapes affordances for intentional activity, which collectively form what we have described as an "affordance landscape", and sometimes produce attractor states that constrain intentional activity. Drawing on CDST, the model further suggests that intentional activity has four distinct dynamic properties. These are adaptiveness, which we have associated with contingent activity; historicity, associated with normative activity; non-linearity, associated with creative activity; and self-organisation, which is associated with purposeful activity. Finally, the model suggests that intentional activity recursively shapes local and global intentional ecologies of TESOL, which it sometimes reproduces and sometimes changes. Change, when it happens, may be limited to specific aspects of an intentional ecology, such as individual, shared, derived, or sociocultural aspects, or it may affect the entirety of the intentional ecology. This conceptualisation of intentional dynamics, we believe, is a contribution with a number of theoretical and practical implications for TESOL.

The concept of an intentional ecology affords us a new way of looking at context in TESOL. It helps us to appreciate TESOL as a meaningful whole, comprising individuals, groups, resources, and social structures. Throughout this book, we have provided detailed descriptions of the different aspects that make up intentional ecologies. This conceptualisation is more than "an agent plus context" view. Rather, by way of their individual intentionality, agents are an integral part of the meaningful whole of the intentional ecology, which also includes shared, derived, and sociocultural aspects, all inextricably interlinked. In other words, the view of TESOL as an intentional ecology enables us to understand how agentive and collective phenomena co-adapt, and in doing so it transcends the "individual versus context" dichotomy. Furthermore, by thinking of TESOL as an intentional ecology, we can better understand how this ecology is multiply stratified, with distinct aspects of intentionality accounting for activity, ranging from the micro-level (e.g., small groups of learners engaging in specific learning activities) to the macro-level (e.g., language education as an international phenomenon). Finally, the concept of intentional ecologies is analytically helpful in highlighting how some aspects of intentionality are temporally and locally situated, whereas others may transcend the "here and now" of a specific learning context.

Our theoretical definition of different types of intentional activity, which leverages CDST in a new way, affords analyses of TESOL activity and change occurring over longer timescales. We have suggested that intentional activity, such as learning, teaching, materials writing, and more, is characterised by different dynamic properties, and (as we suggested in chapter 12) these properties act as signature dynamics, which can explain and broadly predict outcomes. Contingent activity, which is characterised by adaptiveness, tends to adjust to a changing environment and new situations, always maintaining sufficient flexibility to maintain an existing trajectory, and readiness to shift into new activity trajectories. Normative activity, which is characterised by historicity, acts as a stabilising influence. This provides TESOL with a sense of continuity, without which language teaching and learning might descend into a perpetual state of unrest or displacement. Creative activity, which is characterised by non-linearity, is key to evolving new possibilities, and when coupled with purposeful activity, which is associated with self-organisation, teaching and learning may contribute to the emergence of new and valuable future opportunities for TESOL. Crucially, the balance of these four dynamic properties will shift – we sometimes act habitually and at other times we are more creative – but there is always co-adaptation between these types of intentional activity. This is a unique view on activity in TESOL, which is informed by CDST, and it has a number of exciting new affordances for understanding the outcomes of what happens in TESOL classrooms, staffrooms, meeting rooms, and more.

Finally, our model of intentional dynamics provides a dynamic and interconnected view on how activity may shape the future of TESOL itself. We have used the concept of morphogenesis to understand macroscopic change in TESOL (although, as we suggested in chapter 12, it can be used to explain moment-to moment and individual change as well). We have argued that macroscopic change, including change to schools, educational systems, and more, is generated by intentional activity, as well as broader intentional dynamics. We have suggested, also, that macroscopic change may generate attractor states, which then enable and constrain activity within them. By way of example, in chapters 8 and 9 we discussed how teaching approaches and socio-professional paradigms might be understood as attractor states for teaching and learning in TESOL. We realise that these conceptualisations may be difficult to fully apprehend, and the fact that these attractor states are meaning-based structures heightens the conceptual challenge. In chapter 12, we argued that a particular mind-set is required to understand and research the intentional dynamics of TESOL, and this mind-set is perhaps even more important for appreciating macroscopic structures of TESOL, how these intentional structures evolve, how they may act as attractor states for meaning, and how they may enable and constrain what we do in TESOL.

Again, we accept that the model of intentional dynamics restates existing wisdoms in the social sciences and humanities, suggesting that context shapes activity and activity shapes context. However, with the addition of the concept of intentionality we have developed this existing insight further, providing us with the arguably more valuable proposition that *meaningful contexts shape meaningful activity, and meaningful activities shape meaningful contexts*. Thus, intentionality is the "connective tissue" that defines meaningful experience and activity in TESOL, and this is our unique contribution and milestone. We have achieved what we believe is a deep integration of a theory of meaning – provided by the concept of intentionality – with ecological and complex dynamic systems theories, which account for the interconnected and dynamic natures of TESOL. We are unaware of anyone prior to us attempting such a synthesis, either in TESOL or the broader informing literatures. This, we suggest, is a meta-theoretical contribution to TESOL (and perhaps also Applied Linguistics), with meaning as the central unit of analysis, and the interconnected and dynamic process of meaning-making as the central phenomenon to be investigated and understood.

In the introductory chapter, we said we could only highlight contributions in very general terms, and that an in-depth understanding of our model of the intentional dynamics of TESOL, including what has shaped this model and what it contributes, would require a committed engagement with the chapters that make up this book. This remains the case; the more specific contributions of our model are revealed by the detailed discussion in the preceding chapters. However, as a summary, the unique contributions that this book makes to TESOL scholarship include a new perspective on teachers becoming researchers, which we believe is relevant to teacher development (chapter 6). We have developed a new perspective on how collaborative activity develops in the language classroom, which has implications for understanding day-to-day teaching and learning (chapter 7). We have discussed how curriculum development, and change, in TESOL are shaped by the reciprocal relationship of learning resources and the idiosyncrasies of context, and we believe that these insights can inform administrative decisions in TESOL (chapter 8). We have also examined change in international TESOL (chapter 9), language learning as intentional becoming (chapter 10), a critical perspective based on diversity (chapter 11), and principles and options for researching the intentional dynamics of TESOL (chapter 12). All these specific contributions illustrate the potential of our model of intentional dynamics to challenge existing ways of thinking and doing. Yes, we have presented a challenging set of ideas, and what at first look may appear as a complicated synthesis. However, the model of intentional dynamics offers promising new avenues for research, scholarship, and practice, and as such the reward, we believe, is considerable.

13.2 Intentional dynamics and TESOL practice

In this section, we briefly review some of the practical implications of our model of intentional dynamics. These implications have been rehearsed by previous chapters – sometimes more overtly, and sometimes less so. This section offers a brief summary of some of the implications for practice that we have either rehearsed or alluded to.

13.2.1 The language classroom

A first implication for practice is an invitation, to teachers, to think of their language classrooms as interconnected and dynamic intentional ecologies, as sites of intentional activity, and as spaces that may transform themselves, their learners, and society. This is a critical-intentional view of the classroom, which encourages teachers to be open to diverse influences and diverse types of activity. This diversity should include individual, shared, derived, and sociocultural aspects. Teachers should value the diversity that their learners bring, they should encourage diverse shared practices, they should seek out learning materials representing diverse ideas and pedagogical approaches, and they should encourage engagement with wider sociocultural influences from a range of different sources. Practical ways in which such diversity may be acknowledged and fostered are readily available in the TESOL literature. To take one area only, methodological options that recognise the value of learners' individual intentionality include the proposal by Fay et al. (2010) to re-orient English language teaching from transmission of linguistic information to developing intercultural awareness, and to do so by harnessing the cultural capital (or what we might call the diverse "meanings") that learners bring to the classroom. Likewise, the concept of negotiated syllabuses (Breen and Littlewood 2000), in which teachers and learners make joint decisions about the purposes, content, methods, and assessment to be included, is another way to leverage the aspects of intentionality that learners bring into the classroom. Thus, our proposal for encouraging diversity is consistent with existing pedagogical suggestions in TESOL; what we add is a new theoretical rationale, in the form of the model of intentional dynamics, for encouraging such diversity.

At the same time, we invite teachers to encourage creative and purposeful activity in their classrooms. They may be creative in how they interact with their learners, and how they use tasks and learning materials. There should be clear, but open and inclusive, purposes for classroom activities and for studying the new language. Again, this is a very broad implication that resonates with existing contributions in the literature about language teaching and learning. For instance, one of the ways in which teachers can make their classrooms more purposeful is to develop a better understanding of their professional context and practices. Small-scale investigations, such as suggested by Action Research (Burns 2010; Wallace 1998), have the potential to help teachers to become more purposeful in their use of learning materials and activities. Similarly, Exploratory Practice, which brings teachers and learners together in collaborative meaning-making for and about language learning, is another way to make language learning more integrated and purposeful (Allwright 2003, 2005; Hanks 2015, 2017).

Finally, by fostering diverse and purposeful classrooms, teachers will be creating the conditions for language learning to take place. As argued in chapter 10, creative and purposeful intentional activity may enhance language learners' intrinsic motivation for learning the new language, leading to their intentional becoming as language users and language learners. We would like to suggest, in addition, that a diverse and purposeful classroom, where language learning outcomes may emerge through the process of intentional becoming, will be beneficial also for language teachers' own professional development. Just as language learners become more intentional, as language users and learners, language teachers will become more intentional as well. Thus, if language teachers become habitually more creative and purposeful, their own development as teachers will benefit (see, e.g., Constantino 2019).

13.2.2 Materials development

The next implication for practice that we wish to highlight is the intentional activity of developing learning materials of various kinds. Whether developing materials for a local class, or producing a course book commissioned by a publisher, materials writers need to understand how their activity is shaped by their own individual intentionality, by intentionality they may share with colleagues, by the derived intentionality of other materials they consult, and by sociocultural aspects of the intentional ecologies that they are part of. These influences will determine the derived intentionality that they embed in the textbooks and other resources that they design. A failure to reflect on these shaping influences may lead to what has been referred to as a "hidden curriculum" (Auerbach and Burgess 1985; Sayer 2019), which may index undesirable normative assumptions, and thereby be unreflective of the realities and needs of the learners for which the materials are intended. Moreover, the hidden curriculum can extend to less political pedagogical affordances. For instance, Hadfield's (2018) notion of a "covert syllabus" highlights how an unreflective materials development process may be shaped by the materials writer's unconscious preferences, and result in over- or under-representation of particular topics and activity types. Our own advice is consistent with these warnings; we suggest that by critically reflecting on the diverse shaping influences of intentional ecologies, including the materials writers' own individual intentionality – their conscious and/or unconscious preferences – the derived intentionality of the materials that are written will be purposefully *assigned* rather than unreflectively *sedimented*. Sedimented derived intentionality may "point" in widely different directions, and it may lead to unintended pedagogical consequences. A better way forward is for the materials developer to be aware of the derived intentionality that she has assigned to the materials, and what affordances for teacher and learner activity this derived intentionality promotes (see chapter 8). This would reduce the possibility of unintended pedagogical consequences.

At the same time, the model of intentional dynamics views materials development as an intentional activity which may have a range of different dynamic properties. If the materials development activity is normative, and thus unreflectively guided by the dynamic property of historicity, the resulting materials will likely adhere to normative assumptions, with the attendant possibility of reinforcing unjust orders. Alternatively, the materials may reflect the idiosyncratic preference of the materials writer herself, favouring – as Hadfield warned against – covert over- or under-representation of particular topics or activity types. A more desirable scenario is for the materials writer to be creative, so to expand not only the affordances for the materials development process itself, but also the affordances for language use and language learning activity in the resulting learning materials. Moreover, a materials designer should be purposeful in what she includes in the materials she develops. In chapter 10, where we reconceptualised language learning as intentional becoming, we argued that this intentional becoming will benefit from learners engaging in diverse intentional ecologies and a diversity of intentional activity. The learning materials used will play a significant part in enabling this diversity, and a materials writer may need to engage in their own creative and purposeful process to achieve materials with the right kind of affordances – affordances that encourage diversity in the language classroom.

13.2.3 Policy and decision-making

Another implication that we wish to highlight is policy and decision-making in TESOL. We believe that individuals in positions of power, including school managers and administrators, individuals that occupy influential roles in non-governmental organisations, and government education officials, would benefit from being attuned to the intentional dynamics of the TESOL contexts which they seek to impact. We include this implication because, somewhat surprisingly we think, TESOL does not have a developed literature on policy and policymaking. There is some TESOL scholarship focused on school-based decision-making, e.g., in the form of curriculum development (Graves 2008; Kostoulas and Stelma 2017), but there is no developed scholarship on understanding the role of TESOL policy-making that happens on "higher" levels of educational systems (Al-Senafi 2020).

Looking at the broader discipline of education, there is a highly developed policy literature, and this literature describes policymaking in education as values-driven (Fischer [1980] 1999; Jung 2018; Sant and Hanley 2018), as dynamic and complex (Ball 1993; Fullan 2006), and, as viewed from the perspective of policymakers, it is a process that is often subverted by stakeholders on other levels of the educational system. In a rare study of policymaking in TESOL, Al-Senafi (2020) investigated how government policy-making in Kuwait affected primary English teaching and assessment. She observed how government policy changed, as it filtered through successive levels of the educational system; in her words,

> In the journey from [policy] being produced at the government level, to reaching the classroom level, it passes by different levels of stakeholders in the process. On each of these levels, the policy is interpreted based on the values that the stakeholders, on the different levels, have. As this happens, the values written into policy documents may either impose themselves on the next lower levels, the values may actually be espoused in similar form by the stakeholders on the lower levels, or the values may be reinterpreted or challenged. (Al-Senafi 2020: 51)

Thus, the wider educational policy literature, which seems to have had a minimal impact on TESOL scholarship, already includes developed views of policymaking. Our intentional dynamics highlights that a more developed view of policymaking is needed, also, in TESOL. We believe that policymaking in TESOL is similarly values-driven, dynamic and complex, and subject to "subversive" influences. From a macro-perspective, TESOL may appear homogenous (see our discussion in chapter 9). However, language classrooms, schools, and school systems each constitute unique intentional ecologies, with unique intentional dynamics. Within these ecologies, each individual learner and teacher will bring their own unique individual intentionality, the "small culture" (Holliday 1999) and shared intentionality of teachers and learner groups will be diverse, the learning materials will shape the affordances for activity, and each language school may be shaped by idiosyncratic sociocultural intentional structures (see chapter 8). Thus, there is a constant danger, in TESOL, that policy initiatives may fail, and this most often happens because of lack of consultation with the stakeholders that were meant to implement the policy. We believe that it would be misguided, therefore, for policymakers to believe that their position at the top of an educational system relieves them of the responsibility to develop and understand the intentional ecologies they seek to impact.

We suggest that our model of intentional dynamics provides a frame that can help policy-makers to understand the idiosyncrasies of different intentional ecologies of TESOL, how these emerge, and what kinds of intentional activity the idiosyncrasies may generate. Thus, the model of intentional dynamics may inform policy and decision-makers about how policy (as process) may be "tested" as it makes the "journey" from their government (or other) office to local schools and classrooms. We believe that an awareness of intentional dynamics is helpful, in addition, to more local decision-making in TESOL. In fact, it is probably more realistic for a local manager, with some insider knowledge, to have, or to develop, an understanding of the intentional dynamics at play in a specific TESOL setting. At such a local level, therefore, we expect that our model might help raise awareness of the sociocultural and derived aspects of intentionality already present, in what ways these aspects of the intentional ecology shape teaching and learning, and how any proposed intervention is meant to replace or co-exist with existing influences and practices. Without such a good understanding of possibly idiosyncratic aspects of an intentional ecology, local managers and administrators may, when trying to change curricula or procedures, experience intentional dynamics of resistance of the kind we documented in chapter 8.

13.2.4 Research in TESOL

One final practical implication of this book is the new understanding of TESOL contexts, activity, and outcomes that research focused on intentional dynamics may generate. In chapter 12, we presented a typology of researchable aspects of intentional dynamics, including a focus on understanding intentional ecologies, soft-assembly of intentional activity, intentional activity as meaning-making, and morphogenesis in intentional ecologies. We believe such a research agenda may contribute new and valuable understanding of a range of TESOL phenomena.

Research on intentional ecologies may generate new understandings of language classrooms, language schools, educational systems, and perhaps also linguistically defined settings of various sorts, as meaningful ecological and complex dynamic systems. Such research would extend beyond physical, material, or organisational descriptions, and instead contribute understanding of TESOL contexts as shaped by social norms and expectations, as well as individual and group perspectives and beliefs. The distinction between individual, shared, derived, and sociocultural aspects of intentional ecologies provides a coherent frame for such research, and the understandings of context would be unique by including – as part of the context – the individual agents (by way of their individual intentionality). Moreover, an understanding of the intentional aspects of a TESOL context could pave the way for subsequent research to understand how affordances and activity in the context are shaped, or soft-assembled. This could include how intentional ecologies shape both classroom activity and a range of other activity in TESOL, including, e.g., materials writing, teacher development, curriculum innovation, and policymaking. The model of intentional dynamics considers all of these activities as ecological, dynamic and complex, as well as intentional.

Research focused on intentional activity as meaning-making could, similarly, extend beyond the language classroom, and contribute valuable new understanding of meaning-making across the full range of domains of activity in TESOL. To this end, we believe that understanding the interplay between contingent, normative, creative, and purposeful activity, the possibility that the balance between these forms of activity may shift over time, and the generative properties of activity that such an analysis can reveal – as demonstrated by our analysis of classroom interaction in chapter 7 – offers exciting analytical affordances to understand meaning-making across TESOL. We can imagine researchers looking at intentional activity, and its generative properties, in a variety of formal and informal, pedagogical, multilingual, professional, and managerial TESOL settings. This could contribute new understanding of previously under-researched areas of TESOL, increase our awareness of how meaning is made across and between parts of TESOL, and what might be the outcomes of meaning-making in these broader domains.

Research on morphogenetic change in TESOL, as informed by the model of intentional dynamics, represents a particularly promising new area of research for TESOL. This might include change in classroom and school settings, as well as broader change in, e.g., educational systems or the professional world of TESOL. Understanding change on longer timescales offers particular challenges for researchers, and the use of CDST in chapter 12, as well as the analyses of morphogenetic change offered by chapters 8 and 9, provide principles and options that may guide such research. Focusing on morphogenetic change can increase our understanding of the continuity of practices and social structures in TESOL, how such practices and structures may be underpinned by normative or other assumptions, and how new practices and social structures may emerge from the intentional ecology of, and intentional activity in, TESOL. When understanding morphogenetic change from the perspective of the model of intentional dynamics, research may also develop new insight into the recursive and structuring relationship between TESOL contexts, activity, and outcomes. CDST offers an abstract conceptualisation of this recursive relationship, and the model of intentional dynamics makes this recursive relationship more concrete. The model understands context as an intentional ecology, this context shapes intentional activity, and the outcome of this intentional activity may include change in an intentional ecology – or some aspect of this intentional ecology. This, then, provides researchers with a coherent framework, with new affordances, for understanding the role and impact of meaning and meaning-making across TESOL.

13.3 Intentional dynamics and new horizons for TESOL

We believe that the model of intentional dynamics widens the horizons for TESOL scholarship. We have explored a range of possibilities in this book; this final section highlights a few possibilities that we believe may be especially promising for advancing TESOL scholarship.

13.3.1 Using ecological and complex dynamic systems theories in TESOL

The first possibility we would like to highlight is the further use of ecological and complex dynamic systems theories in TESOL. These theories have enabled new ways of viewing a number of otherwise intractable theoretical challenges for TESOL. However, we need to address, once more, the reservations about using theories originally developed in, and for, the natural sciences.

Of the two theory sets, we believe ecological theory has received less critical scrutiny by TESOL scholars. Ecological theory has emerged quite gradually in TESOL. It has appeared in different guises, beginning with van Lier's (2000) suggestion that we replace the concern for input in SLA research with the concept of affordances. A number of other authors have also picked up on the analytical potential of affordances to describe a range of phenomena in language education (see Kordt 2018). Ecological thinking has also been used to understand language teaching and language classrooms (e.g., Kramsch 2008; Tudor 2001, 2003); Pennington and Hoekje (2010) have described a language programme as an ecology; MacPherson (2003) has used ecological thinking to understand the threat of English language teaching to the viability of indigenous languages; Blommaert et al. (2005) have developed sociolinguistic views of language teaching inspired by ecological thinking; Zheng et al. (2009) have provided ecological analyses of virtual language learning; and we have, ourselves, used ecological theory to frame earlier versions of our model of the intentional dynamics (Stelma et al. 2015). Despite the potential reservations about the "transfer" of this theory, originally developed in and for the natural sciences, to TESOL (see chapter 2), the use of ecological theory in TESOL has been relatively uncontested.

By contrast, the influence of CDST on TESOL has been more visible, and – we will argue – more contested. An important landmark in the development of complexity-informed thinking in TESOL was Larsen-Freeman's (1997) seminal discussion of how the theoretical composite of Chaos and Complexity theories could provide new ways of looking at otherwise "enduring SLA conundrums" (p. 141). There were additional contributions which explored the linkages between language and complexity-related concepts (e.g., N. C. Ellis 1998; Larsen-Freeman 2002, 2006) and the theory also inspired book-length contributions, including monographs by Tudor (2001), van Lier (2004), and Herdina and Jessner (2002). Roughly ten years later – perhaps corresponding to the period of time needed for the theory to "mature" in TESOL – uses of CDST appeared with increased frequency and covering a broader range of phenomena. This included complex dynamic systems views of language use and language learning (de Bot, Lowie, and Verspoor 2007; Five Graces Group 2009; Hohenberger and Peltzer-Karpf 2009); the publication of a special issue in *Applied Linguistics* exploring language learning, use, and change from the perspective of emergentism (Ellis and Larsen-Freeman 2006); and a comprehensive monograph entitled *Complex Systems and Applied Linguistics* (Larsen-Freeman & Cameron 2008a). We consider this point in time to be the "coming of age" of CDST in TESOL. From this point forward CDST was used to theorise and research an increasingly diverse set of phenomena in TESOL, including language learner agency (S. Mercer 2011c), language classroom spoken interaction (Seedhouse 2010), language learner motivation (Dörnyei, Henry, and Muir 2015; Dörnyei, MacIntyre, and Henry 2015; Sampson 2016), language schools (Kostoulas 2015; 2018), language pedagogy (S. Mercer 2013), language teacher cognition and identity (Ell et al. 2017; Feryok 2010; Henry 2016), connecting research and practice (Kostoulas et al. 2018), and culminating in more refined principles and options for researching complex dynamic systems in TESOL (Hiver and Al-Hoorie 2020; MacIntyre et al. 2017; Verspoor, de Bot, and Lowie 2011).

Despite this coming of age for CDST in TESOL, however, we believe that the use of CDST remains contested in TESOL. This is due to the inherent challenges of making native to language education a set of ideas that originated in the natural sciences. In chapter 1, we quoted Larsen-Freeman and Cameron (2008a: 201), who suggest that there is a "material difference between applied linguistics and the natural sciences with respect to objects of inquiry" (for a similar point, see also Hiver and Al-Hoorie 2020: 6). We quoted them again in chapter 12, with their warning that "human intentionality and agency appear to be one of the most severe problems in applying a complex systems metaphor or analogy to the kinds of behaviors and processes that interest applied linguists" (Larsen-Freeman and Cameron 2008a: 75). We believe that this compatibility challenge extends into TESOL as well. We have ourselves alluded to such concerns, in chapter 3, and have also voiced similar reservations about the use of ecological theory, in chapter 2. In both chapters, we have described how TESOL scholarship has made great strides in using these theories in ways that have value to the field, but the concern about their origins – we believe – has lingered.

We believe that the present book, and the model of intentional dynamics, may move us a step forward in this regard. We have taken steps to use ecological and complex dynamic systems theories in a manner that does not compromise the inherently meaningful nature of TESOL contexts, activity, and outcomes. The model of intentional dynamics that we have developed retains the analytical affordances of both ecological and complex dynamic systems theory, but – with the addition of intentionality – it also becomes more than the sum of these components. With the addition of the concept of intentionality, as the "connective tissue" of our meaningful experience in TESOL, we have placed meaning and meaning-making at the heart of an ecological and complex dynamic systems account of TESOL. This combination of theoretical influences has given us a theoretical framework – the model of intentional dynamics – that makes use of ecological and complex dynamic systems theories in a new way. Each of the concepts that we have taken from these theories – including affordances, attractor states, and more – have been "cast" in the new light offered by intentionality. We believe this furnishes us with a new use of ecological and complex systems theories, and that this new use begins to put to rest the concerns about the natural and hard science origins of these theories. The model of intentional dynamics is developed within TESOL, for TESOL, and the aspects and processes the model is designed to understand are all inherently focused on the meaningful nature of TESOL. Thus, we believe that the addition of intentionality enables us to use ecological and complex dynamic systems theories without the customary "apology" about their origins.

13.3.2 Locating the individual in intentional dynamics

A next possibility that we wish to highlight is how an intentional ecology and intentional dynamics may be unique to individuals. To claim the opposite – that intentional ecologies and intentional dynamics do not depend on individuals' perception, interpretation, and other forms of agency – is counter to what we have argued for in this book. Thus, the individual nature of intentional dynamics has been an implicit part of our argument and the examples we have provided.

In order to understand exactly how intentional dynamics may be unique to individuals, it is useful to distinguish between intentional dynamics being uniquely *experienced*, which is a very narrow phenomenological position, and the *influences* and *outcomes* of intentional dynamics being unique to individuals, and this is an ontological position. The narrow phenomenological position may be summarised as follows: a language teacher's intentional activity in, say, the language classroom will be consciously (or unconsciously) experienced, and this experience cannot be compared to the experience of any other teacher, or the same teacher in any subsequent intentional activity in the same or different classroom. The ontological position, by contrast, suggests that every individual brings something different to a situation, and gets something different out of a situation. Each teacher will contribute unique individual intentionality, and the resulting intentional dynamics of a classroom situation will therefore be unique, and the change in the teacher, and perhaps also the broader intentional ecology, will be unique.

We have not overtly addressed the possibility and consequences of uniquely experienced, or actually unique, intentional dynamics in the chapters of this book. However, it has been always on our mind. It is implicit in our thinking and research that individuals do bring something unique to situations, that they do react and reflect on what happens in situations, that these cognitive, and perhaps also affective, individual, and sometimes collective, mental processes have their own intentional dynamics that will make a difference. Moreover, the reflective and emotive processes of individuals will, as intentional activity in its own right, co-adapt with the "larger" complex dynamic system of activity, and thus have a unique impact on current and future situations. Thus, we take the more encompassing ontological position, but also reject any suggestion that experience is epiphenomenal. In fact, as researchers and teacher educators, we see affordances in teachers and other TESOL stakeholders being able to report on their unique experience.

13.3.3 Extending the notion of intentional becoming

Another possibility that we believe needs to be highlighted is how the notion of "intentional becoming", which we developed in chapter 10, may be extended. In chapter 10, intentional becoming was used to reconceptualise language learning, and we defined it as a process of becoming part of a new intentional ecology, which reflects the new language and its use, and engaging in new intentional dynamics. Moreover, we described intentional becoming as a journey towards being more interconnected and purposeful. We proposed, also, that language development as intentional becoming would be facilitated by engaging in a diverse range of contingent, normative, creative, and purposeful intentional activity, and that teachers and learners needed to work together, without short-cuts, to sustain this intentional becoming.

We see two possible ways in which the notion of intentional becoming may be extended. First, we believe that the notion resonates with research on language learner motivation. For example, self-determination theory (Ryan and Deci 2000), which has been used to understand language learner motivation (Jones, Llacer-Arrastia, and Newbill 2009; Muñoz and Ramirez 2015), highlights how learners may initially experience language learning behaviours as disconnected, or extrinsic, from their own selves. However, over time, and provided that the language learning activity they engage in nurtures and satisfies their basic psychological needs, they may come to identify with the new language and what happens in the language classroom. If this happens, they will be more intrinsically motivated, or as the theory suggests, they will be self-determined learners. This, we believe, resonates with our notion of intentional becoming. Just as our model of intentional dynamics, self-determination theory highlights how the social environment shapes the process of becoming self-determined. There are a couple of divergences, however, from our model. Self-determination theory maintains an analytical separation between the individual and the environment, and there is no allowance in self-determination theory for more collective forms of developing motivation. Even so, the overlap with self-determination theory suggest it may be possible to extend our intentional becoming to describe language learner motivation, and the ways in which our model diverges from self-determination theory suggests that motivation as intentional becoming might extend the analytical and explanatory affordances of, at least this one, existing theory of motivation.

A second way in which we believe the notion of intentional becoming might be extended is to language teaching and language teacher professional development. This possibility is overtly suggested by the model of language teacher professional development put forward by Edge (2011), which describes teacher development as a process of becoming increasingly purposeful and engaged with the world of TESOL through the stages of copying, applying theoretical knowledge, theorising, reflecting, and acting in a transformative way. Indeed, any activity which is purposeful somehow in TESOL, whether this be learning, teaching, materials development, administration, policy-making, and more, is generated by intentional dynamics, and hence may be understood as a process of intentional becoming. Such a view of the broad range of activities in TESOL would recognise how each stakeholder is interconnected with the rest of TESOL, and that all intentional activity in TESOL is dynamic and complex. This would prevent static views of stakeholder roles, and emphasise that development can and should occur right across TESOL.

13.3.4 Towards an intentional dynamics of language?

One more, very tentative, possibility that we have alluded to in some parts of this book, but which we have not developed in any detail, is a possible connection between intentionality and linguistic aspects of language use. In chapter 4, we talked about speech acts (Austin 1975; Searle 1969) as prototypical examples of derived intentionality, and we also suggested that linguistic constructs such as indexicality (Hughes and Tracy 2015) and intertextuality (Pecorari and Shaw 2012) tells us something about how language "points" or "connects" to intentional structures present in social, political, and professional contexts (see section 4.2). Our instinct is that since language use is deeply meaningful, the model of intentional dynamics should, in principle, extend to a wider range of skills and aspects of language. The skills of reading, writing, listening, and speaking all involve some type of engagement with derived intentionality, and our discussion of speech acts in chapter 4 may offer clues as to how the intentional dynamics of these language skills could be understood.

On the other hand, an analysis of aspects such as semantics, prosody, syntax, and pragmatics poses more significant conceptual challenges. It may be possible to view these components of language as analytical sub-systems of an over-arching complex dynamic system of language use. However, how they may be understood as intentional is less clear. Semantics seem relatively straightforward in this regard, as words represent information, or ideational intentionality, and although word forms are allocated meaning in an arbitrary way, historicity offers a possible "hook" for an intentional analysis. Prosody may be analysed in terms of the interconnection between thinking and speaking, such as, e.g., Chafe's (1994) hypothesised relationship between consciousness and features of intonation units in speech. In such an analysis, well-formed and/or truncated intonation units, prominences of various sorts, or the appearance of given and new information across intonation units, might be used as evidence of intentional aspects of speech. The nature of syntax, which may be rooted deeply in the unconscious (at least in a Chomskyan perspective) may defy an intentional analysis; however, if we were to take a usage-based perspective, Larsen-Freeman's (2002) dynamic and meaning-based notion of "grammaring" might enable an analysis of the syntax of speech as intentional activity. Finally, pragmatics may be approached from a speech act perspective, as rehearsed in chapter 4 (see section 4.2). Moreover, and given its link to meaning and action, pragmatics might also be integrated into an analysis of intentional activity.

In sum, our thinking in this regard is clearly embryonic, and in time we may regret suggesting this possibility. However, our instinct, at this junction, is that it should be possible to use our model of intentional dynamics to understand language use as a form of meaning-making and intentional activity.

13.3.5 Promoting change in TESOL

As we conclude this book, we would like to comment on the new possibilities for understanding and action that are enabled by the critical-intentional perspective that we presented in chapter 11. This perspective argues that we can challenge normative assumptions in TESOL by harnessing the power of the collective activity of learners, teachers, policymakers, and all other stakeholders, and that in doing so, we can change the intentional ecology of TESOL for the better. We also suggested that this collective potential to change TESOL can be enhanced if we foster diversity, and encourage creative and purposeful activity, across all domains of activity in TESOL. On one level, this perspective complements existing conceptualisations of being critical in TESOL. There will always be a need to be rational, to consider the influence of context, and to challenge normative assumptions and unjust orders that such normativity promotes. However, the critical-intentional perspective challenges the underlying ideas of the previous critical perspectives, which foreground cognitive, contextual, and humanistic considerations (see section 11.1). As we suggested in chapter 11, it is misguided to consider rationality without reference to the affective aspects of human activity. It is also limiting to consider context without looking at the totality of intentional ecologies, i.e., their individual, shared, derived, and sociocultural aspects. And finally, it is unhelpful to consider normative assumptions and unjust orders without attempting to understand how such normative assumptions appear in the first place.

The new possibilities that we wish to highlight, here, relate particularly to challenging normative assumptions, unjust orders, and different forms of oppression in TESOL. Normative assumptions and unjust orders do indeed result in what appears as a powerful set of entities (e.g., Western publishers and thinking), or what we have called intentional structures, which may be oppressing a large class of less influential stakeholders (e.g., teachers and learners world-wide). However, addressing this imbalance in adversarial terms, such as "class-struggle", may not be the best way forward; rather, a better solution, we believe, is to build on an understanding of how social orders emerge, and then to disrupt such social orders at the point of their emergence. We believe that our concept of intentional dynamics is helpful in developing such understandings. Our perspective posits that normative structures emerge from the entirety of activity in TESOL, and not just the activity of a small number of powerful stakeholders. We are aware that this is a potentially dangerous claim to make, because "where all are guilty, no one is" (Arendt 1987: 43), but our point here is not to absolve those who benefit from the imbalanced distribution of power. Rather, our intention is to highlight the potential for collective change; for all of us to benefit, we should all be part of the solution. We believe that the best way to counter unjust orders is to harness the generative power of diversity and emergence, and we suggest that this can be done by encouraging creative and purposeful intentional activity by all stakeholders in TESOL, including those that are associated with disproportionate power and influence. Our aims are the same as those of Marxist and Freirian critical scholars. Our solution, however, is to maximise diversity and the potential for emergence of new intentional structures. We want *all* stakeholders in TESOL, regardless of their power or role, to become more intentional.

References

Agar, Michael. 2004. We have met the other and we're all non-linear: Ethnography as a non-linear dynamic system. *Complexity* 10 (2). 16–24.
Alderson, Charles J., Caroline Clapham & Dianne Wall. (1995). *Language test construction and evaluation*. Cambridge: Cambridge University Press.
Alfaro, María Jesús Martínez. 1996. Intertextuality: Origins and development of the concept. *Atlantis* 18 (1/2). 268–285.
Allwright, Dick. 2003. Exploratory Practice: Rethinking practitioner research in language teaching. *Language Teaching Research* 7 (2). 113–141.
Allwright, Dick. 2005. Developing principles for practitioner research: The case of Exploratory Practice. *The Modern Language Journal* 89 (3). 353–366.
Allwright, Dick & Rosa Lenzuen. 1997. Exploratory Practice: Work at the Cultura Inglesa, Rio de Janeiro, Brazil. *Language Teaching Research* 1 (1). 73–79.
Al-Senafi, Basemah S. 2020. Policy and decision-making about assessment of English language for young learners in Kuwait. Manchester, UK: The University of Manchester doctoral thesis.
Alptekin, Cem. 2002. Towards intercultural communicative competence in ELT. *ELT Journal* 56 (1). 57–64.
Anderson, Jason. 2015. Affordance, learning opportunities, and the lesson plan pro forma. *ELT Journal* 69 (3). 228–238.
Anderson, John R. 1996. *The architecture of cognition*. Mahwah, NJ: Lawrence Erlbaum.
Anderson, Phil W. 1972. More is different. *Science* 177. 393–396.
Andrews, Jane & Wan Chin Yee. 2006. Children's "funds of knowledge" and their real life activities: Two minority ethnic children learning in out-of-school contexts in the UK. *Educational Review* 58 (4). 435–449.
Aneja, Geeta A. 2016. (Non) native speakered: Rethinking (non) nativeness and teacher identity in TESOL teacher education. *TESOL Quarterly* 50 (3). 572–596.
Angouri, Jo, Marina Mattheoudakis & Maria Zigrika. 2010. Then how will they get the 'much-wanted paper'?: A multifaceted study of English as a foreign language in Greece. *Advances in research on language acquisition and teaching: Selected papers (Proceedings of the 14th International Conference of Greek Applied Linguistics Association)*, 179–194. Athens: GALA.
Antón, Marta & Frederick DiCamilla. 1998. Socio-cognitive functions of L1 collaborative interaction in the L2 classroom. *Canadian Modern Language Review* 54 (3). 314–342.
Archer, Margaret S. 1995. *Realist social theory: The morphogenetic approach*. Cambridge: Cambridge University Press.
Archer, Margaret S. 1998. Realism and morphogenesis. In Margaret Archer, Roy Bashkar, Andrew Collier, Tony Lawson & Alan Norrie (eds.), *Critical realism: Essential readings*, 356–383. London: Routledge.
Arendt, Hannah. 1987. Collective responsibility. In James W. Bernauer (ed.), *Amor Mundi: Explorations in the faith and thought of Hannah Arendt*, 43–50. Dordrecht: Martinus Nijhoff.
Aronin, Larissa & David Singleton. 2010. Affordances and the diversity of multilingualism. *International Journal of the Sociology of Language* 205. 105–129.

Aspbury, Edmund. 2018. Learner authenticity: An ecological and Heideggerian perspective on authenticity in classroom tasks. Manchester, UK: The University of Manchester MA dissertation.

Atkinson, Dwight. 1997. A critical approach to critical thinking in TESOL. *TESOL Quarterly* 31 (1). 71–94.

Auerbach, Elsa R. & Denise Burgess. 1985. The hidden curriculum of survival ESL. *TESOL Quarterly* 19 (3). 475–495.

Austin, John L. 1975. *How to do things with words*. Oxford: Oxford University Press.

Awwad, Anas, Parvaneh Tavakoli & Clare Wright. 2017. "I think that's what he's doing": Effects of intentional reasoning on second language (L2) speech performance. *System* 67. 158–169.

Bailey, Kathleen M. 2015. Conducting diary studies. In James D. Brown & Christine Coombe (eds.), *The Cambridge guide to research in teaching and learning*, 247–252. Cambridge: Cambridge University Press.

Bakhtin, Mikhail M. 1981. *The dialogic imagination: Four essays*, edited by Michael Holquist, translated by Caryl Emerson & Michael Holquist. Austin, TX: University of Texas Press.

Barker, Roger G. 1968. *Ecological psychology: Concepts and methods for studying the environment of human behavior*. Stanford, CA: Stanford University Press.

Barkhuizen, Gary. 2009. Topics, aims, and constraints in English teacher research: A Chinese case study. *TESOL Quarterly* 43 (1). 113–125.

Bateson, Gregory. 1987 [1972]. *Steps to an ecology of mind*. Northvale, NJ: Jason Aronson.

Baum, William M. 2002. From molecular to molar: A paradigm shift in behavior analysis. *Journal of the Experimental Analysis of Behavior* 78 (1). 95–116.

Bax, Stephen. 2003. The end of CLT: A context approach to language teaching. *ELT Journal* 57 (3). 278–287.

Bazerman, Charles. 2004. Intertextuality: How texts rely on other texts. In Charles Bazerman & Paul Prior (eds.), *What writing does and how it does it: An introduction to analysing texts and textual practices*, 83–96. Mahwah, NJ: Lawrence Erlbaum.

Ball, Stephen J. 1993. What is policy? Texts, trajectories and toolboxes. *The Australian Journal of Education Studies* 13 (2). 10–17.

Benesch, Sarah. 1993. Critical thinking: A learning process for democracy. *TESOL Quarterly* 27 (3). 545–548.

Benetka, Gerhard & Amrei C. Joerchel. 2016. Psychology as a phenomenological science. In Jaan Valsiner, Giuseppina Marsico, Nandita Chaudhary, Tatsuya Sato & Virginia Dazzani (eds.), *Psychology as the Science of Human Being: The Yokohama Manifesto*, 17–32. Cham: Springer.

Benson, Carol. 2014. Adopting a multilingual habitus: What north and south can learn from each other about the essential role of non-dominant languages in education. In Durk Gorter, Victoria Zenotz & Jasone Cenoz (eds.), *Minority languages and multilingual education: Bridging the local and the global*, 11–28. Dordrecht: Springer.

Benson, Phil. 2011. Language learning careers as units of analysis in narrative research. *TESOL Quarterly* 45 (3). 545–553.

Bernstein, Katie A., Emily A. Hellmich, Noah Katznelson, Jaran Shin & Kimberly Vinall (eds.). 2015. Critical perspectives on neoliberalism in second/foreign language education. *L2 Journal* 7 (3).

Birch, Barbara M. 2009. *The English language teacher in global civil society*. Abingdon: Routledge.

Blackledge, Adrian & Angela Creese (eds.). 2014. *Heteroglossia as practice and pedagogy*. Dordrecht: Springer.

Block, David. 2008. Language education and globalisation. In Stephen May & Nancy Hornberger (eds.), *Encyclopedia of language and education: Language policy and political issues in education*, 2nd edn, 1: 31–43. New York: Springer.

Block, David. 2009. *Second language identities*. London: Continuum.

Blommaert, Jan. 2007. Sociolinguistics and discourse analysis: Orders of indexicality and polycentricity. *Journal of Multicultural Discourses* 2 (2). 115–130.

Blommaert, Jan. 2013. *Ethnography, superdiversity and linguistic landscapes: Chronicles of complexity*. Clevendon: Multilingual Matters.

Blommaert, Jan, James Collins & Stef Slembrouck. 2005. Spaces of multilingualism. *Language & Communication* 25 (3). 197–216.

Bloom, Benjamin S. (ed.). 1956. *Taxonomy of educational objectives: The classification of educational goals. Handbook 1: Cognitive domain*. New York: David McKay.

Blumer, Herbert. 1969. *Symbolic interactionism: Perspective and method*. Berkley, CA: University of California Press.

Blumer, Herbert. 2005. Society as symbolic interaction. In Sean P. Hier (ed.), *Contemporary sociological thought: Themes and theories*, 91–100. Toronto, ON: Canadian Scholars' Press.

Bocking, Stephen. 1994. Visions of nature and society: A history of the ecosystem concept. *Alternatives* 20 (3). 12–18.

Boers, Frank. 2018. Intentional versus incidental learning. In John I. Liontas (ed.), *The TESOL Encyclopedia of English Language Teaching*. Hoboken, NJ: Wiley-Blackwell. doi: 10.1002/9781118784235.eelt0074

Borg, Simon. 2003. Teacher cognition in language teaching: A review of research on what language teachers think, know, believe, and do. *Language Teaching* 36 (2). 81–109.

Borg, Simon. 2010. Language teacher research engagement. *Language Teaching* 43 (4). 391–429.

Bourdieu, Pierre. 1988. *Homo academicus*, translated by Peter Collier. Stanford, CA: Stanford Academic Press.

Bourdieu, Pierre. 2005. *The social structures of the economy*. Cambridge: Cambridge University Press.

Bowles, Melissa A. 2018. Introspective verbal reports: Think alouds and stimulated recall. In Aek Phakiti, Peter De Costa, Luke Plonsky & Sue Starfield (eds.), *The Palgrave handbook of applied linguistics research methodology*, 339–358. Houndmills: PalgraveMacmillan.

Bratman, Michael E. 1999. *Faces of intention: Selected essays on intention and agency*. Cambridge: Cambridge University Press.

Breen, Michael. 1989. The evaluation cycle for language learning tasks. In Robert K. Johnson (ed.), *The second language curriculum*, 187–206. Cambridge: Cambridge University Press.

Breen, Michael & Andrew Littlejohn. 2000. *Classroom decision: Making negotiation and process syllabuses in practice*. Cambridge: Cambridge University Press.

Brentano, Franz. 2015 [1874]. *Psychology from an empirical standpoint*, translated by Antos C. Rancurello, D. Burnham Terrell & Linda L. McAlister. London: Routledge Classics.

Bronfenbrenner, Urie. 1977. Toward an experimental ecology of human development. *American Psychologist* 32 (7). 513–531.

Bronfenbrenner, Urie. 1979. *The ecology of human development: Experiments by nature and design*. Cambridge, MA: Harvard University Press.

Brumfit, Chris J. 1980. From defining to designing: Communicative specifications versus communicative methodology in foreign language teaching. *Studies in Second Language Acquisition* 3 (1). 1–9.
Bruner, Jerome S. 1981. Intention in the structure of action and interaction. *Advances in Infancy Research* 1. 41–56.
Burns, Anne. 2010. *Doing action research in English language teaching: A guide for practitioners*. New York: Routledge.
Bygate, Martin. 1999. Quality of language and purpose of task: Patterns of learners' language on two oral communication tasks. *Language Teaching Research* 3 (3). 185–214.
Byram, Michael. 1997. *Teaching and assessing intercultural communicative competence*. Clevedon: Multilingual Matters.
Byrne, David. 1998. *Complexity theory and the social sciences*. London: Routledge.
Byrne, David. 2002. *Interpreting quantitative data*. Thousand Oaks, CA: SAGE.
Byrne, Barbara M. & Gail Crombie. 2003. Modeling and testing change: An introduction to the latent growth curve model. *Understanding Statistics* 2 (3). 177–203.
Byrne, David & Gill Callaghan. 2014. *Complexity theory and the social sciences: The state of the art*. London: Routledge.
Cameron, Lynne. 2001. *Teaching languages to young learners*. Cambridge: Cambridge University Press.
Cameron, Lynne. 2003. Challenges for ELT from the expansion in teaching children. *ELT Journal* 57 (2). 105–112.
Canagarajah, Suresh A. 1993. Critical ethnography of a Sri Lankan classroom: Ambiguities in student opposition to reproduction through ESOL. *TESOL Quarterly* 27 (4). 601–626.
Canagarajah, Suresh A. 1999. *Resisting linguistic imperialism in English language teaching*. Oxford: Oxford University Press.
Canagarajah, Suresh A. 2013. *Translingual practice: Global Englishes and cosmopolitan relations*. Abingdon, Oxon: Routledge.
Canagarajah, Suresh A. 2015. TESOL as a professional community: A half-century of pedagogy, research, and theory. *TESOL Quarterly* 50 (1). 7–41.
Canagarajah, Suresh A. (ed.). 2018. *The Routledge handbook of migration and language*. London: Routledge.
Canale, Michael & Merrill Swain. 1980. Theoretical bases of communicative approaches to second language teaching and testing. *Applied Linguistics* 1 (1). 1–47.
Carr, Wilfred & Stephen Kemmis. 1986. *Becoming critical: Education, knowledge and action research*. London: RoutledgeFalmer.
Carter, Ronald. 2004. *Language and creativity: The art of common talk*. London: Routledge.
Cenoz, Jasone & Durk Gorter (eds.). 2011. Toward a multilingual approach in the study of multilingualism in school contexts [Special Issue]. *The Modern Language Journal* 95 (3).
Chafe, Wallace. 1994. *Discourse, consciousness, and time: The flow and displacement of conscious experience in speaking and writing*. Chicago: Chicago University Press.
Chang, Lilian Ya-Hui. 2010. Group processes and EFL learners' motivation: A study of group dynamics in EFL classrooms. *TESOL Quarterly* 44 (1). 129–154.
Chappell, Philip. 2016. Creativity through inquiry dialogue. In Rodney H. Jones & Jack C. Richards (eds.), *Creativity in language teaching: Perspectives from research and practice*, 130–145. London: Routledge.

Charmaz, Kathy. 2008. Constructionism and the grounded theory method. In James A. Holstein & Jaber F. Gubrium (eds.), *Handbook of constructionist research*, 397–412. New York, NY: Guilford Press.
Chemero, Anthony. 2003. An outline of a theory of affordances. *Ecological Psychology* 15 (2). 181–195.
Chomsky, Noam. 1986. *Knowledge of language: Its nature, origin, and use*. Westport, CT: Praeger.
Chomsky, Noam. 1993 [1981]. *Lectures on government and binding*, 7th edn. The Hague: Mouton de Gruyter.
Cilliers, Paul. 1998. *Complexity and postmodernism: Understanding complex systems*. London: Routledge.
Cilliers, Paul. 2001. Boundaries, hierarchies and networks in complex systems. *International Journal of Innovation Management* 5 (2). 135–147.
Clark, Elizabeth & Amos Paran. 2007. The employability of non-native-speaker teachers of EFL: A UK survey. *System* 35 (4). 407–430.
Clarke, Andy. 1997. *Being there: Putting brain, body, and the world together again*. Cambridge, MA: Bradford/MIT Press.
Cochran-Smith, Marilyn & Susan L. Lytle. 1990. Research on teaching and teacher research: The issues that divide. *Educational Researcher* 19 (2). 2–11.
Codd, John. A. 1988. The construction and deconstruction of educational policy documents. *Journal of Education Policy* 3 (3). 235–247.
Costantino, Anna. 2019. Space and time for understanding(s): The recursive cycle of language education and classroom enquiry. In Achilleas Kostoulas (ed.), *Challenging boundaries in language education*, 71–86. Cham: Springer.
Cook, Guy. 2000. *Language play, language learning*. Oxford: Oxford University Press.
Copland, Fiona. 2018. Observation and fieldnotes. In Aek Phakiti, Peter De Costa, Luke Plonsky & Sue Starfield (eds.), *The Palgrave handbook of applied linguistics research methodology*, 249–268. Houndmills: PalgraveMacmillan.
Copland, Fiona, Sue Garton & Anne Burns. 2013. Challenges in teaching English to young learners: Global perspectives and local realities. *TESOL Quarterly* 48 (4). 738–762.
Corbin, Juliet & Anselm Strauss. 2008. *Basics of qualitative research: Techniques and procedures for developing grounded theory*, 3rd edn. Thousand Oaks, CA: SAGE.
Cortazzi, Martin. 1994. Narrative analysis. *Language Teaching* 27 (3). 157–170.
Costall, Alan. 1995. Socializing affordances. *Theory & Psychology* 5 (4). 467–481.
Coughlan, Peter & Patricia A. Duff. 1994. Same task, different activities: analysis of SLA task from an activity theory perspective. In James P. Lantolf & Gabriela Appel (eds.), *Vygotskian approaches to second language research*, 173–193. Norwood, NJ: Ablex.
Council of Europe. 2001. *Common European frame of reference for languages: Learning, teaching, assessment*. Cambridge: Cambridge University Press.
Cromdal, Jakob. 2005. Bilingual order in collaborative word processing: On creating an English text in Swedish. *Journal of Pragmatics* 37 (3). 329–353.
Crystal, David. 2003. *English as a global language*, 2nd edn. Cambridge: Cambridge University Press.
Davies, Alan. 1999. Standard English: Discordant voices. *World Englishes* 18 (2). 171–186.
Davis, Brent. 2008. Complexity and education: Vital simultaneities. In Mark Mason (ed.), *Complexity theory and the philosophy of education*, 46–61. Oxford: Wiley-Blackwell.

Davis, Brent & Dennis Sumara. 2006. *Complexity and education: Inquiries into learning, teaching, and research*. London: Laurence Erlbaum Associates.

Davis, Brent & Dennis Sumara. 2012. Fitting teacher education in/to/for an increasingly complex world. *Complicity: An International Journal of Complexity and Education* 9 (1). 30–40.

de Bot, Kees. 2015. Rates of change: Timescales in second language development. In Zoltán Dörnyei, Peter D. MacIntyre & Alastair Henry (eds.), *Motivational dynamics in language learning*, 29–37. Bristol: Multilingual Matters.

de Bot, Kees. 2017. Complexity theory and dynamic systems theory: Same or different? In Lourdes Ortega & ZhaoHong Han (eds.), *Complexity theory and language development: In celebration of Diane Larsen-Freeman*, 51–58. Amsterdam: John Benjamins.

de Bot, Kees, Wander Lowie & Marjolijn Verspoor. 2007. A dynamic systems theory approach to second language acquisition. *Bilingualism: Language and Cognition* 10 (1). 7–21.

de Bot, Kees, Wander Lowie, Steven L. Thorne & Marjolijn Verspoor. 2013. Dynamic systems theory as a comprehensive theory of second language development. In María del Pilar García Mayo, María Junkal Gutierrez Mangado & María Martínez Adrián (eds.), *Contemporary approaches to second language acquisition*, 199–220. Amsterdam: John Benjamins.

Deacon, Terrence W. 2007. Three levels of emergent phenomena. In Nancy Murphy & William R. Stoeger (eds.), *Evolution and emergence: Systems, organisms, persons*, 88–110. Oxford: Oxford University Press.

Dearden, Julie. 2014. *English as a medium of instruction: A growing global phenomenon*. London: British Council.

Deci, Edward L. & Richard M. Ryan. 1980. Self-determination theory: When mind mediates behavior. *The Journal of Mind and Behavior* 1 (1). 33–43.

Deci, Edward L. & Richard M. Ryan. 2008. Self-determination theory: A macrotheory of human motivation, development, and health. *Canadian Psychology/Psychologie Canadienne* 49 (3). 182–185.

Dekeyser, Robert & Raquel Criado. 2012. Automatization, skill acquisition, and practice in second language acquisition. In Carol A. Chapelle (ed.), *The encyclopedia of applied linguistics*. Oxford: Wiley-Blackwell. doi:10.1002/9781405198431.wbeal0067

Dendrinos, Bessie. 2009. Comment 3 to 'Lingua franca or lingua frankensteinia'. In Robert Phillipson (ed.), *Linguistic imperialism continued*, 181–182. Abingdon: Routledge.

Dennett, Daniel. 1987. *The intentional stance*. Cambridge, MA: MIT Press.

Denzin, Norman K. 2004. Symbolic interactionism. In Uwe Flick, Ernst von Kardoff & Ines Steinke (eds.), *Companion to qualitative research*, 81–87. London: SAGE.

Descartes, René. 1966 [1637]. *Discours de la méthode pour bien conduire sa raison, et chercher la vérité dans les sciences (avec introduction et notes par Étienne Gilson)*. Paris: Librairie Philosophique J. Vrin.

Dewey, John. 1910. *How we think*. Boston, MA: D. C. Heath.

Díaz Maggioli, Gabriel. 2017. Ideologies and discourses in the standards for language teachers in South America: A corpus-based analysis. In Lía D. Kamhi-Stein, Gabriel Díaz Maggioli & Luciana C. de Oliveria (eds.), *English language teaching in South America*, 31–54. Bristol: Multilingual Matters.

DiCamilla, Frederick J. & Marta Anton. 1997. Repetition in the collaborative discourse of L2 learners: A Vygotskian perspective. *Canadian Modern Language Review* 53 (4). 609–633.

Donato, Richard. 1994. Collective scaffolding in second language learning. In James P. Lantolf & Gabriella Appel (eds.), *Vygotskian approaches to second language research*, 33–56. Norwood, NJ: Ablex.

Dörnyei, Zoltán. 2007. *Research methods in applied linguistics*. Oxford: Oxford University Press.

Dörnyei, Zoltán. 2009. The L2 motivational self system. In Zoltán Dörnyei & Emma Ushioda (eds.), *Motivation, language identity and the L2 self*, 9–11. Clevedon: Multilingual Matters.

Dörnyei, Zoltán. 2014. Researching complex dynamic systems: "Retrodictive qualitative modelling" in the language classroom. *Language Learning* 47 (1). 80–91.

Dörnyei, Zoltán. 2019. Towards a better understanding of the L2 Learning Experience, the Cinderella of the L2 Motivational Self System. *Studies in Second Language Learning and Teaching*, 9 (1). 19–30.

Dörnyei, Zoltán, Alastair Henry & Christine Muir. 2015. *Motivational currents in language learning: Frameworks for focused interventions*. Abingdon, Oxon: Routledge.

Dörnyei, Zoltán, Peter D. MacIntyre & Alastair Henry (eds.). 2015. *Motivational dynamics in language learning*. Bristol: Multilingual Matters.

Dörnyei, Zoltán & István Ottó. 1998. Motivation in action: A process model of L2 motivation. *Working Papers in Applied Linguistics, Thames Valley University, London* 4. 43–69.

Doughty, Catherine & Teresa Pica. 1986. "Information gap" tasks: Do they facilitate second language acquisition? *TESOL Quarterly* 20 (2). 305–325.

Eckert, Penelope. 2003. Language and adolescent peer groups. *Journal of Language and Social Psychology* 22 (1). 112–118.

Edge, Julian. 1993. The dance of Shiva and the linguistics of relativity. *Applied Linguistics* 14 (1). 43–55.

Edge, Julian (ed.). 2006. *(Re)locating TESOL in an age of Empire*. Houndmills: Palgrave-Macmillan.

Edge, Julian. 2007. Action research as attitude. *Research: Newsletter of the IATEFL Research Special Interest Group* 20. 14–16.

Edge, Julian. 2011. *The reflexive teacher educator in TESOL: Roots and wings*. London: Routledge.

Edwards, Emily & Anne Burns. 2016. Action research to support teachers' classroom materials development. *Innovation in Language Learning and Teaching* 10 (2). 106–120.

Ell, Fiona, Mavis Haigh, Marilyn Cochran-Smith, Lexie Grudnoff, Larry Ludlow & Mary F. Hill. 2017. Mapping a complex system: What influences teacher learning during initial teacher education? *Asia-Pacific Journal of Teacher Education* 45 (4). 327–345.

Ellis, Nick C. 1998. Emergentism, connectionism and language learning. *Language Learning*. 48 (4). 631–664.

Ellis, Nick C. 2007. Dynamics systems in SLA: The wood and the trees. *Bilingualism: Language and Cognition* 10 (1). 23–25.

Ellis, Nick C. & Diane Larsen-Freeman (eds.). 2006. Special issue on Language and Emergence. *Applied Linguistics* 27 (4).

Ellis, Rod. 1982. Informal and formal approaches to communicative language teaching. *ELT Journal* 36 (2). 73–81.

Ellis, Rod. 2003. *Task-based language learning and teaching*. Oxford: Oxford University Press.

Ellis, Rod. 2016. Creativity and language learning. In Rodney H. Jones & Jack C. Richards (eds.), *Creativity in language teaching: Perspectives from research and practice*, 32–48. Abingdon, Oxon: Routledge.

Elman, Jeffrey L. 1995. Language as a dynamical system. In Robert F. Port & Timothy Van Gelder (eds.), *Mind as motion: Explorations in the dynamics of cognition*, 195–223. Cambridge, MA: MIT Press.

Elman, Jeffrey L., Elizabeth A. Bates, Mark H. Johnson, Annette Karmiloff-Smith, Domenico Parisi & Kim Plunkett. 1996. *Rethinking innateness: A connectionist perspective on development*. Cambridge, MA: MIT Press.

Enever, Janet (ed.). 2011. *ELLiE: Early language learning in Europe*. London: British Council.

Enever, Janet & Eva Lindgren (eds.). 2017. *Early language learning: Complexity and mixed methods*. Bristol: Multilingual Matters.

Esteban-Guitart, Moisès & Luis C. Moll. 2014. Funds of identity: A new concept based on the funds of knowledge approach. *Culture & Psychology* 20 (1). 31–48.

Etherington, Kim. 2004. *Becoming a reflexive researcher: Using ourselves in research*. London: Jessica Kingsley.

Fairclough, Norman. 2001. *Language and power*, 2nd edn. Harlow: Pearson.

Fairclough, Norman. 2013. *Critical discourse analysis: The critical study of language*. London: Routledge.

Farrell, Thomas S. C. 2014. *Promoting teacher reflection in second language education: A framework for TESOL professionals*. New York: Routledge.

Farrell, Thomas S. C. 2016. Anniversary article: The practices of encouraging TESOL teachers to engage in reflective practice: An appraisal of recent research contributions. *Language Teaching Research* 20 (2). 223–247.

Fay, Richard & Juup Stelma. 2016. Criticality, intentionality and intercultural action. In Maria Dasli & Adriana Raquel Diaz (eds.), *The critical turn in language and intercultural communication pedagogy*, 126–139. London: Routledge.

Fay, Richard, Vally Lytra & Maria Ntavaliagkou. 2010. Multicultural awareness through English: A potential contribution of TESOL in Greek schools. *Intercultural Education* 21 (6). 581–595.

Feryok, Anne. 2010. Language teacher cognitions: Complex dynamic systems? *System* 38 (2). 272–279.

Field, Andy. 2013. *Discovering statistics using IBM SPSS statistics*, 4th edn. Thousand Oaks, CA: SAGE.

Fielding, Nigel. 2008. Ethnography. In Nigel Gilbert (ed.), *Researching social life*, 3rd edn, 245–265. Thousand Oaks, CA: SAGE.

Fill, Alwin F. 2001. Language and ecology: Ecolinguistic perspectives for 2000 and beyond. *AILA Review* 14. 60–75.

Fill, Alwin F. 2018. Introduction. In Alwin F. Fill & Hermine Penz (eds.), *The Routledge handbook of ecolinguistics*, 1–7. London: Routledge.

Fischer, Frank. 2019 [1980]. *Politics, values, and public policy: The problem of methodology*. Abingdon, Oxon: Routledge.

"Five Graces Group": Clay Beckner, Richard Blythe, Joan Bybee, Morten H. Christiansen, William Croft, Nick C. Ellis, John Holland, Jinyun Ke, Diane Larsen-Freeman & Tom Schoenemann. 2009. Language is a complex adaptive system: Position paper. *Language Learning* 59 (s1). 1–26.

Flores, Nelson & Geeta Aneja. 2017. "Why needs hiding?" Translingual (re)orientations in TESOL teacher education. *Research in the Teaching of English* 51 (4). 441.

Flores, Nelson & Jamie L. Schissel 2014. Dynamic bilingualism as the norm: Envisioning a heteroglossic approach to standards-based reform. *TESOL Quarterly* 48 (3). 454–479.

Flubacher, Mi-Cha & Alfoso Del Percio (eds.). 2017. *Language, education, and neoliberalism*. Bristol: Multilingual Matters.

Freeman, Donald. 2016. *Educating second language teachers: The same things done differently*. Oxford: Oxford University Press.

Freire, Paulo. 2005 [1968]. *Pedagogy of the oppressed*, 30th anniversary edn, translated by Myra Bergman Ramos. New York: Continuum.

Fullan, Michael. 2006. The future of educational change: System thinkers in action. *Journal of Educational Change* 7 (3). 113–122.

Fuster, Carles & Hannah Neuser. 2019. Exploring intentionality in lexical transfer. *International Journal of Multilingualism*, 1–19. doi: 10.1080/14790718.2018.1559845

García, Ofilia & Li Wei. 2013. *Translanguaging: Language, bilingualism and education*. Houndsmills, Basingstoke: Palgrave MacMillan.

García Mayo, Maria del Pillar (ed.). 2017. *Learning foreign languages in primary school: Research insights*. Bristol: Multilingual Matters.

Garner, Mark. 2004. *Language: An ecological view*. Bern: Peter Lang.

Garton, Sue. 2002. Learner initiative in the language classroom. *ELT Journal* 56 (1). 47–56.

Gass, Susan M. & Alison Mackey. 2016. *Stimulated recall methodology in applied linguistics and L2 research*, 2nd edn. Abingdon, Oxon: Routledge.

Gibbons, Pauline. 2003. Mediating language learning: Teacher interactions with ESL students in a content-based classroom. *TESOL Quarterly* 37 (2). 247–273.

Gibbs, Raymond W. 2001. Intentions as emergent products of social interactions. In Bertram F. Malle, Louis J. Moses & Dare A. Baldwin (eds.), *Intentions and intentionality: Foundations of social cognition*, 105–122. Cambridge, MA: MIT Press.

Gibson, James J. 1979. *The ecological approach to visual perception*. Boston, MA: Houghton Mifflin.

Giddens, Anthony. 1976. *New rules of sociological method*. London: Hutchinson.

Giddens, Anthony. 1979. *Central problems in social theory: Action, structure and contradiction in social analysis*. London: Macmillan.

Giroux, Henry A. 1992. *Border crossings: Cultural workers and the politics of education*. New York: Routledge.

Gleick, James. 1987. *Chaos: Making a new science*. New York: Penguin Books.

Gogolin, Ingrid. 2002. Linguistic and cultural diversity in Europe: A challenge for educational research and practice. *European Educational Research Journal* 1 (1). 123–138.

Golombek, Paula & Meredith Doran. 2014. Unifying cognition, emotion, and activity in language teacher professional development. *Teaching and Teacher Education* 39. 102–111.

Good, James M. M. 2007. The affordances for social psychology of the ecological approach to social knowing. *Theory & Psychology* 17 (2). 265–295.

Gorniak, Peter & Deb Roy. 2007. Situated language understanding as filtering perceived affordances. *Cognitive Science* 31 (2). 197–231.

Gottesman, Isaac. 2010. Sitting in the waiting room: Paulo Freire and the critical turn in the field of education. *Educational Studies* 46 (4). 376–399.

Goulah, Jason. 2017. Climate change and TESOL: Language, literacies, and the creation of eco-ethical consciousness. *TESOL Quarterly* 51 (1). 90–114.

Graves, Kathleen. 2008. The language curriculum: A social contextual perspective. *Language Teaching* 41 (2). 147–181.

Graves, Kathleen. 2000. *Designing language courses: A guide for teachers*. Boston, MA: Heinle & Heinle.

Gray, Benedict C. M. 2018. A micro-history of an in-service teacher training programme in post-Revolutionary Libya. Manchester, UK: The University of Manchester doctoral thesis.

Gregg, Kevin R. 2010. Shallow draughts: Larsen-Freeman and Cameron on complexity. *Second Language Research* 26 (4). 549–560.

Guerrettaz, Anne Marie & Bill Johnston. 2013. Materials in the classroom ecology. *The Modern Language Journal* 97 (3). 779–796.

Gunderson, Lee. 2007. *English-only instruction and immigrant students in secondary schools: A critical examination*. New York: Routledge.

Habermas, Jürgen. 1976. *Legitimation crisis*, translated by Thomas McCarthy. London: Heinemann.

Hadfield, Jill. 2018. Covert syllabuses. *Folio* 18 (2). 25–29.

Hadley, Gregory. 2017. *Grounded theory in applied linguistics research: A practical guide*. London: Routledge.

Halliday, Michael A. K. 1978. *Language as social semiotic: The social interpretation of language and meaning*. London: Edward Arnold.

Hammersley, Martyn & Paul Atkinson. 2019. *Ethnography: Principles in practice*, 4th edn. Abingdon, Oxon: Routledge.

Hanks, Judith. 2015. Language teachers making sense of Exploratory Practice. *Language Teaching Research* 19 (5). 612–633.

Hanks, Judith. 2017. Integrating research and pedagogy: An Exploratory Practice approach. *System* 68, 38–49.

Harvey, Lou. 2017. Language learning motivation as ideological becoming. *System* 65. 69–77.

Haugen, Einar I. 1972. *The ecology of language*. Stanford, CA: Stanford University Press.

Hawkins, Margaret & Bonnie Norton. 2009. Critical language teacher education. In Anne Burns & Jack Richards (eds.), *Cambridge guide to second language teacher education*, 30–39. Cambridge: Cambridge University Press.

Heller, Monica. 2010. Language as a resource in the new globalised economy. In Nicholas Coupland (ed.), *Handbook of language and globalisation*, 349–365. London: Blackwell.

Henry, Alastair. 2016. Conceptualizing teacher identity as a complex dynamic system: The inner dynamics of transformations during a practicum. *Journal of Teacher Education* 67 (4). 291–305.

Herdina, Philip & Ulrike Jessner. 2002. *A dynamic model of multilingualism*. Clevedon: Multilingual Matters.

Herring, Susan H. 2004. Computer-mediated discourse analysis: An approach to researching online behaviour. In Sasha A. Barab, Rob Kling & James H. Gray (eds.), *Designing for virtual communities in the service of learning*, 338–376. Cambridge: Cambridge University Press.

Hiver, Phil & Ali Al-Hoorie. 2016. A dynamic ensemble for second language research: Putting complexity theory into practice. *The Modern Language Journal* 100 (4). 1–16.

Hiver, Phil & Ali Al-Hoorie. 2020. *Research methods for complexity theory in applied linguistics*. Bristol: Multilingual Matters.

Hoey, Michael. 2005. *Lexical priming: A new theory of words and language*. Abingdon, Oxon: Routledge.

Hohenberger, Annette. 2002. *Functional categories in language acquisition: Self-organization of a dynamical system*. Tübingen: Niemeyer.

Hohenberger, Annette & Annemarie Peltzer-Karpf. 2009. Language learning from the perspective of nonlinear dynamic systems. *Linguistics* 47 (2). 481–511.

Holborow, Marnie. 2012. What is neoliberalism? Discourse, ideology and the real world. In David Block, John Grey & Marnie Holborow (eds.), *Neoliberalism and applied linguistics*, 14–32. London: Routledge.

Holborow, Marnie. 2015. *Language and neoliberalism*. Abingdon, Oxon: Routledge.

Holliday, Adrian. 1992. Tissue rejection and informal orders in ELT projects: Collecting the right information. *Applied Linguistics* 13 (4). 403–424.

Holliday, Adrian. 1994. *Appropriate methodology and social context*. Cambridge: Cambridge University Press.

Holliday, Adrian. 1999. Small cultures. *Applied Linguistics* 20 (2). 237–264.

Holliday, Adrian. 2005. *The struggle to teach English as an international language*. Oxford: Oxford University Press.

Holliday, Adrian. 2006. Native-speakerism. *ELT Journal* 60 (4). 385–387.

Holliday, Adrian. 2010. *Intercultural communication and ideology*. Thousand Oaks, CA: SAGE.

Holliday, Adrian R. & Terence Cooke. 1982. An ecological approach to ESP. In Alan Waters (ed.), *Issues in ESP*, 124–143. Oxford: Pergamon Press.

Holling, Crawford S. 2001. Understanding the complexity of economic, ecological, and social systems. *Ecosystems* 4. 390–405.

Hornberger, Nancy H. 2002. Multilingual language policies and the continua of biliteracy: an ecological approach. *Language Policy* 1. 27–51.

Hornberger, Nancy H. (ed.). 2003. *Continua of biliteracy: An ecological framework for educational policy, research, and practice in multilingual settings*. Clevedon: Multilingual Matters.

Howatt, Anthony P. R. (with Henry G. Widdowson). 2004. *A history of ELT*. Oxford: Oxford University Press.

Hua, Zhu. 2008. Duelling languages, duelling values: Codeswitching in bilingual intergenerational conflict talk in diasporic families. *Journal of Pragmatics* 40 (10). 1799–1816.

Hughes, Jessica M. F. & Karen Tracy. 2015. Indexicality. In Karen Tracy, Cornelia Ilie & Todd Sandel (eds.), *The international encyclopedia of language and social interaction*, 2: 788–793. Oxford: Wiley-Blackwell.

Hymes, Dell. 1972. On communicative competence. In John Bernard Pride & Janet Holmes (eds.), *Sociolinguistics: Selected readings*, 269–293. Harmondsworth: Penguin.

Javier, Eljee A. 2015. Narratively performed role identities of visible ethnic minority, native English-speaking teachers in TESOL. Manchester, UK: The University of Manchester doctoral thesis.

Jessner, Ulrike. 2003. A dynamic approach to language attrition in multilingual systems. In Vivian Cook (ed.), *Effects of the second language on the first*, 234–246. Clevedon: Multilingual Matters.

Jessner, Ulrike. 2014. On multilingual awareness or why the multilingual learner is a specific language learner. In Mirosław Pawlak & Larissa Aronin (eds.), *Essential topics in applied linguistics and multilingualism*, 175–184. Cham: Springer.

Johnson, Karen E. 2009. *Second language teacher education: A sociocultural perspective*. London: Routledge.

Jones, Brett D., Sonia Llacer-Arrastia & Paula B. Newbill. 2009. Motivating foreign language students using self-determination theory. *International Journal of Innovation in Language Learning and Teaching* 3 (2). 171–189.

Juarrero, Alicia. 1999. *Dynamics in action: Intentional behavior as a complex system*. Cambridge, MA: MIT Press.

Jung, Jisun. 2018. Higher education in Korea: Western influences, Asian values and indigenous processes. *Journal of Asian Public Policy* 11 (1). 1–13.

Kabel, Ahmed. 2009. Native-speakerism, stereotyping and the collusion of applied linguistics. *System* 37 (1). 12–22.

Kachru, Braj B. 2017. *World Englishes and culture wars*. Cambridge: Cambridge University Press.

Kant, Immanuel. 2013 [1874]. *An answer to the question: "What is enlightenment?"*, translated by H. B. Nisbet. London: Penguin UK.

Kaplan, Robert B. 2018. Ecolinguistic aspects of language planning. In Alwin F. Fill & Hermine Penz (eds.), *The Routledge handbook of ecolinguistics*, 89–105. London: Routledge.

Karavas, Evdokia. 2010. How satisfied are Greek EFL teachers with their work? Investigating the motivation and job satisfaction levels of Greek EFL Teachers. *Porta Linguarum* 14. 59–78.

Kasper, Gabriele & Johannes Wagner. 2014. Conversation analysis in applied linguistics. *Annual Review of Applied Linguistics* 34. 171–212.

Kauffman, Stuart. 1996. *At home in the universe: The search for the laws of self-organization and complexity*. Oxford: Oxford University Press.

Ke, Jinyun, James W. Minett, Ching-Pong Au & William S.-Y. Wang. 2002. Self-organization and natural selection in the emergence of vocabulary. *Complexity* 7. 41–54.

Kemmis, Stephen & Robin McTaggart. 2005. *Participatory action research: Communicative action and the public sphere*. Thousand Oaks, CA: SAGE.

Kerr, Philip. 2016. Questioning "English-only" classrooms: Own language use in ELT. In Graham Hall (ed.), *The Routledge handbook of English language teaching*, 513–526. London: Routledge.

Kinginger, Celeste. 1994. Learner initiative in conversation management: An application of van Lier's pilot coding scheme. *The Modern Language Journal* 78 (1). 29–40.

Kissine, Mikhail. 2008. Locutionary, illocutionary, perlocutionary. *Language and Linguistics Compass* 2 (6). 1189–1202.

Kitsiou, Roula, Maria Papadopoulou, George Androulakis, Roula Tsokalidou & Eleni Skourtou. 2019. Beyond conventional borders of second language teacher education: A digital, interdisciplinary, and critical postgraduate curriculum. In Achilleas Kostoulas (ed.), *Challenging boundaries in language education*, 229–246. Cham: Springer.

Kohonen, Viljo, Riitta Jaatinen, Pauli Kaikkonen & Jorma Lehtovaara. 2014. *Experiential learning in foreign language education*. Harlow, Essex: Pearson.

Köpke, Barbara. 2017. A neuropsycholinguistic approach to complexity: Bi/multilingual attrition and aphasia as destabilisation. In Lourdes Ortega & ZhaoHang Han (eds.), *Complexity theory and language development*, 191–208. Amsterdam: John Benjamins.

Kordt, Birgit. 2018. Affordance theory and multiple language learning and teaching. *International Journal of Multilingualism* 15 (2). 135–148.

Kostoulas, Achilleas. 2014. A Greek tragedy: Understanding and challenging "the Known" from a complexity perspective. In Damian Rivers (ed.), *Resistance to the known: Counter-conduct in language education*, 47–70. Houndmills: MacmillanPalgrave.

Kostoulas, Achilleas. 2015. A complex systems perspective on English language teaching: A case study of a language school in Greece. Manchester, UK: The University of Manchester doctoral thesis.

Kostoulas, Achilleas. 2018. *A language school as a complex system: Complex systems theory in English language teaching.* Berlin: Peter Lang.
Kostoulas, Achilleas. 2019a. Conceptualizing and problematizing boundaries in language education. In Achilleas Kostoulas (ed.), *Challenging boundaries in language education.* Cham: Springer.
Kostoulas, Achilleas. 2019b. Repositioning language education theory. In Achilleas Kostoulas (ed.), *Challenging boundaries in language education.* Cham: Springer.
Kostoulas, Achilleas & Juup Stelma. 2016. Intentionality and complex systems theory: A new direction for language learning psychology. In Christina Gkonou, Dietmar Tatzl & Sarah Mercer (eds.), *New directions in language learning psychology,* 7–23. Cham: Springer.
Kostoulas, Achilleas & Juup Stelma. 2017. Understanding curriculum change in an ELT school in Greece. *ELT Journal* 71 (3). 354–363.
Kostoulas, Achilleas, Juup Stelma, Sarah Mercer, Lynne Cameron & Susan Dawson. 2018. Complex systems theory as a shared discourse space for TESOL. *TESOL Journal* 9 (2). 246–260.
Kowal, Maria & Merrill Swain. 1994. Using collaborative language production tasks to promote students' language awareness. *Language Awareness* 3 (2). 73–93.
Kramsch, Claire. 2006. From communicative competence to symbolic competence. *The Modern Language Journal* 90 (2). 249–252.
Kramsch, Claire. 2008. Ecological perspectives on foreign language education. *Language Teaching* 41 (3). 389–408.
Kramsch, Claire. 2011. The symbolic dimensions of the intercultural. *Language Teaching* 44 (3). 354–367.
Kramsch, Claire. 2012. Why is everyone so excited about complexity theory in applied linguistics? *Mélanges Crapel* 33. 10–24.
Kramsch, Claire. 2015. Applied linguistics: A theory of the practice. *Applied Linguistics* 36 (4). 454–465.
Kramsch, Claire & Anne Whiteside. 2008. Language ecology in multilingual settings. Towards a theory of symbolic competence. *Applied Linguistics* 29 (4). 645–671.
Krashen, Stephen D., Michael A. Long & Robin C. Scarcella. 1979. Age, rate and eventual attainment in second language acquisition. *TESOL Quarterly* 13 (4). 573–582.
Krathwohl, David R. 2002. A revision of Bloom's taxonomy: An overview. *Theory into Practice* 41 (4). 212–218.
Krippendorff, Klaus. 2004. *Content analysis: An introduction to its methodology,* 2nd edn. Thousand Oaks, CA: SAGE.
Kristeva, Julia. 1986. Word, dialogue and novel. In Toril Moi (ed.), *The Kristeva reader,* 34–61. Oxford: Basil Blackwell.
Kubanyiova, Maggie & Anne Feryok. 2015. Language teacher cognition in applied linguistics research: Revisiting the territory, redrawing the boundaries, reclaiming the relevance. *The Modern Language Journal* 99 (3). 435–449.
Kubota, Ryuko. 2011. Questioning linguistic instrumentalism: English, neoliberalism and language tests in Japan. *Linguistics and Education* 22 (3). 248–260.
Kubota, Ryuko. 2016. The multi/plural turn, postcolonial theory, and neoliberal multiculturalism: Complicities and implications for applied linguistics. *Applied Linguistics* 37 (4). 474–494.
Kumaravadivelu, Bala. 1991. Language-learning tasks: Teacher intention and learner interpretation. *ELT Journal* 45 (2). 98–107.

Kumaravadivelu, Bala. 2003a. *Beyond methods: Macrostrategies for language teaching*. New Haven, CT: Yale University Press.
Kumaravadivelu, Bala. 2003b. A postmethod perspective on English language teaching. *World Englishes* 22. 539–550.
Kumaravadivelu, Bala. 2006a. Dangerous liaison: Globalisation, empire and TESOL. In Julian Edge (ed.), *(Re-)Locating TESOL in an age of Empire*, 1–26. Houndmills: PalgraveMacmillan.
Kumaravadivelu, Bala. 2006b. TESOL methods: Changing tracks, challenging trends. *TESOL Quarterly* 40 (1). 59–81.
Kumaravadivelu, Bala. 2006c. *Understanding language teaching: From method to postmethod*. Abingdon, Oxon: Routledge.
Kvale, Steinar & Svend Brinkmann. 2009. *InterViews: Learning the craft of qualitative research interviewing*. Thousand Oaks, CA: SAGE.
Lamb, Martin. 2007. The impact of school on EFL learning motivation: An Indonesian case study. *TESOL Quarterly* 41 (4). 757–780.
Lamb, Terry. 2015. Towards a plurilingual habitus: Engendering interlinguality in urban spaces. *International Journal of Pedagogies and Learning* 10 (2). 151–165.
Larsen-Freeman, Diane. 1997. Chaos/complexity science and second language acquisition. *Applied Linguistics* 18 (2). 141–165.
Larsen-Freeman, Diane 2002. Language acquisition and language use from a chaos/complexity perspective. In Claire Kramsch (ed.), *Language acquisition and language socialization: Ecological perspectives*, 33–46. London: Continuum.
Larsen-Freeman, Diane. 2003. *Teaching language: From grammar to grammaring*. Boston, MA: Thomson Heinle.
Larsen-Freeman, Diane. 2006. The emergence of complexity, fluency and accuracy in the oral development of five Chinese learners of English. *Applied Linguistics* 27 (4). 590–619.
Larsen-Freeman, Diane. 2017. Complexity theory: The lessons continue. In Lourdes Ortega & ZhaoHang Han (eds.), *Complexity theory and language development*, 11–50. Amsterdam: John Benjamins.
Larsen-Freeman, Diane. 2018. Second Language Acquisition, WE, and language as a complex adaptive system (CAS). *World Englishes* 37 (1). 80–92.
Larsen-Freeman, Diane & Lynne Cameron. 2008a. *Complex systems and applied linguistics*. Oxford: Oxford University Press.
Larsen-Freeman, Diane & Lynne Cameron. 2008b. Research methodology on language development from a complex systems perspective. *The Modern Language Journal* 92 (2). 200–213.
Lewin, Kurt. 1935. *A dynamic theory of personality: Selected papers*, translated by Donald K. Adams & Karl E. Zener. New York, NY: McGraw-Hill.
Lewin, Kurt. 1946. Action research and minority problems. *Journal of Social Issues* 2 (4). 34–46.
Lincoln, Yvonna S. & Egon, S. Guba. 1985. *Naturalistic inquiry*. Newbury Park, CA: SAGE.
Littlewood, William. 2011. Communicative language teaching: An expanding concept for a changing world. In Eli Hinkel (ed.), *Handbook of research in second language teaching and learning*, 2: 541–557. Abingdon, Oxon: Routledge.
Littman, Richard A. & Ephraim Rosen. 1950. Molar and molecular. *Psychological Review* 57 (1). 58–65.

Long, Michael H. 1983. Native speaker/non-native speaker conversation and the negotiation of comprehensible input. *Applied Linguistics* 4 (2). 126–141.

Long, Michael H. 1990. Maturational constraints on language development. *Studies in Second Language Acquisition* 12 (3). 251–285.

Lorenz, Edward. 1972. Does the flap of a butterfly's wings in Brazil set off a tornado in Texas? Paper presented at the 139th Annual Meeting of the American Association for the Advancement of Science, Washington, D.C.

Lothe Flemmen, Randi & Bjørn Sørheim. 1997. *Scoop 6: Engelsk for 6. klasse*. Oslo: Det Norske Samlaget.

Lothe Flemmen, Randi & Bjørn Sørheim. 1998. *Scoop 6: Engelsk for 6. klasse (workbook)*. Oslo: Det Norske Samlaget.

Lothe Flemmen, Randi & Bjørn Sørheim. 1999a. *Scoop 7: Engelsk for 7. klasse*. Oslo: Det Norske Samlaget.

Lothe Flemmen, Randi & Bjørn Sørheim. 1999b. *Scoop 7: Engelsk for 7. klasse (workbook)*. Oslo: Det Norske Samlaget.

Lozupone, Catherine A. & Rob Knight. 2008. Species divergence and the measurement of microbial diversity. *FEMS Microbiology Reviews* 32 (4). 557–578.

Lütge, Christiane. 2015. *Global education: Perspectives for English language teaching*. Münster: LIT Verlag.

Macaro, Ernesto, Samantha Curle, Jack Pun, Jiangshan An & Julie Dearden. 2018. A systematic review of English medium instruction in higher education. *Language Teaching* 51 (1). 36–76.

MacIntyre, Peter D., Richard Clément, Zoltán Dörnyei & Kimberly A. Noels. 1998. Conceptualizing willingness to communicate in a L2: A situational model of L2 confidence and affiliation. *The Modern Language Journal* 82 (4). 545–562.

MacIntyre, Peter D., Emily MacKay, Jessica Ross & Esther Abel. 2017. The emerging need for methods appropriate to study dynamical systems: Individual differences in motivational dynamics. In Lourdes Ortega & ZhaoHong Han (eds.), *Complexity theory and language development*, 11–50. Amsterdam: John Benjamins.

MacIntyre, Peter D. & Alicia Serroul. 2015. Motivation on a per-second timescale: Examining approach-avoidance motivation during L2 task performance. In Zoltán Dörnyei, Peter D. MacIntyre & Alastair Henry (eds.), *Motivational dynamics in language learning*, 109–138. Bristol: Multilingual Matters.

MacPherson, Seonaigh. 2003. TESOL for biolinguistic sustainability: The ecology of English as a lingua mundi. *TESL Canada Journal* 20 (2). 1–22.

MacWhinney, Brian. 1999. *The emergence of language*. Hillsdale, NJ: Lawrence Erlbaum Associates.

Malle, Bertram F., Louis J. Moses & Dare A. Baldwin (eds.). 2001. *Intentions and intentionality: Foundations of social cognition*. Cambridge, MA: Bradford/MIT.

Marshall, Steve & Danièle Moore. 2018. Plurilingualism amid the panoply of lingualisms: Addressing critiques and misconceptions in education. *International Journal of Multilingualism* 15 (1). 19–34.

Marginson, Simon. 2006. Dynamics of national and global competition in higher education. *Higher Education* 52 (1). 1–39.

Marx, Karl. 2010 [1859]. A contribution to the critique of political economy. In John F. Sitton (ed.), *Marx today: Selected works and recent debates*, 91–94. New York: Palgrave Macmillan.

Mason, Mark (ed.). 2008. *Complexity theory and the philosophy of education* Oxford: Wiley-Blackwell.

Mason, Norman W., David Mouillot, William G. Lee & J. Bastow Wilson. 2005. Functional richness, functional evenness and functional divergence: The primary components of functional diversity. *Oikos* 111 (1). 112–118.

Matthaioudakis, Marina. 2007. Tracking changes in pre-service EFL teacher beliefs in Greece: A longitudinal study. *Teaching and Teacher Education* 23 (8). 1272–1288.

May, Stephen (ed.). 2014. *The multilingual turn: Implications for SLA, TESOL and bilingual education*. London: Routledge.

McDonough, Jo & Christopher Shaw. 1993. *Materials and methods in ELT: A teacher's guide*. Oxford: Blackwell.

McLaughlin, Barry, Tammy Rossman & Beverly McLeod. 1983. Second language learning: An information-processing perspective. *Language Learning* 33 (2). 135–158.

Meara, Paul. 2004. Modelling vocabulary loss. *Applied Linguistics* 25 (2). 137–155.

Mercer, Neil. 1995. *The guided construction of knowledge: Talk amongst teachers and learners*. Clevendon: Multilingual Matters.

Mercer, Neil. 1996. The quality of talk in children's collaborative activity in the classroom. *Learning and Instruction* 6 (4). 359–377.

Mercer, Sarah. 2011a. *Towards an understanding of language learner self-concept*. Dordrecht: Springer.

Mercer, Sarah. 2011b. Language learner self-concept: Complexity, continuity and change. *System* 39 (3). 335–346.

Mercer, Sarah. 2011c. Understanding learner agency as a complex dynamic system. *System* 39 (4). 427–436.

Mercer, Sarah. 2012. The complexity of learner agency. *Apples – Journal of Applied Language Studies* 6 (2). 41–59.

Mercer, Sarah. 2013. Towards a complexity-informed pedagogy for language learning. *Revista Brasileira de Linguística Aplicada* 13 (2). 375–398.

Mewald, Claudia. 2019. Across languages and cultures: Modelling teaching and learning with intercomprehension. In Achilleas Kostoulas (ed.), *Challenging boundaries in language education*, 141–164. Cham: Springer.

Miller, John H. & Scott E. Page. 2007. *Complex adaptive systems: An introduction to computational models of social life*. Princeton, NJ: Princeton University Press.

Mitchell, Melanie. 2009. *Complexity: A guided tour*. New York: Oxford University Press.

Moran, Dermot. 2000. Heidegger's critique of Husserl's and Brentano's accounts of intentionality. *Inquiry* 43 (1). 39–65.

Morin, Edgar. 2006. Restricted complexity, general complexity. Paper presented at the *Colloquium "Intelligence de la complexité : Épistémologie et pragmatique"*. Cerisy-La-Salle, France. http://cogprints.org/5217/1/Morin.pdf.

Moss, Pamela A. & Edward H. Haertel. 2016. Engaging methodological pluralism. In Drew H. Gitomer & Courtney A. Bell (eds.), *Handbook of research on teaching*, 5th edn, 127–247. Washington D.C.: American Educational Research Association.

Muñoz, Ana & Marta Ramirez. 2015. Teachers' conceptions of motivation and motivating practices in second-language learning: A self-determination theory perspective. *Theory and Research in Education* 13 (2). 198–220.

Muñoz, Carmen. 2006. *Age and rate of foreign language learning*. Clevedon: Multilingual Matters.

Neisser, Ulric. 1994. Multiple systems: A new approach to cognitive theory. *European Journal of Cognitive Psychology* 6 (3). 225–241.
Neuendorf, Kimberly A. 2002. *The content analysis guidebook*. Thousand Oaks, CA: SAGE.
Nicolis, Gregoire. 1995. *Introduction to non-linear science*. Cambridge: Cambridge University Press.
Nikula, Tarja, Emma Dafouz, Pat Moore & Ute Smit (eds.). 2016. *Conceptualising integration in CLIL and multilingual education*. Bristol: Multilingual Matters.
Noels, Kimberly A., Luc G. Pelletier, Richard Clément & Robert J. Vallerand. 2000. Why are you learning a second language? Motivational orientations and self-determination theory. *Language Learning* 50 (1). 57–85.
Norton, Bonny. 2013. *Identity and language learning: Extending the conversation*. Clevedon: Multilingual Matters.
Norton, Bonny. 2016. Identity and language learning: Back to the future. *TESOL Quarterly* 50 (2). 475–479.
Nunan, David. 1990. *Learner-centred curriculum*. Cambridge: Cambridge University Press.
Nunan, David. 2004. *Task-based language teaching*. Cambridge: Cambridge University Press.
Odlin, Terence. 1989. Language transfer: Cross-linguistic influence in language learning. Cambridge: Cambridge University Press.
Oliver, Rhonda. 1998. Negotiation of meaning in child interactions. *The Modern Language Journal* 82 (3). 372–386.
Ollerhead, Sue & Anne Burns. 2016. Creativity as resistance: Implications for language teaching and teacher education. In Rodney H. Jones & Jack C. Richards (eds.), *Creativity in language teaching: Perspectives from research and practice*, 227–240. Abingdon, Oxon: Routledge.
Orr, William F. & Stephen C. Cappannari. 1964. The emergence of language. *American Anthropologist* 66 (2). 318–324.
Ortega, Lourdes & ZhaoHong Han (eds.). 2017. *Complexity theory and language development*, 11–50. Amsterdam: John Benjamins.
Osberg, Deborah. 2008. The logic of emergence: An alternative conceptual space for theorizing critical education. *Journal of the Canadian Association for Curriculum Studies* 6 (1). 133–161.
Osberg, Deborah & Gert J. J. Biesta. 2007. Beyond presence: Epistemological and pedagogical implications of "strong" emergence. *Interchange* 38 (1). 31–51.
Osberg, Deborah & Gert Biesta. 2010. *Complexity theory and the politics of education*. Rotterdam: Sense.
Otha, Amy S. 1995. Applying sociocultural theory to an analysis of learner discourse: Learner-learner collaborative interaction in the Zone of Proximal Development. *Issues in Applied Linguistics* 6 (2). 93–121.
Ottaviano, Gianmarco I. & Giovanni Peri. 2006. The economic value of cultural diversity: Evidence from US cities. *Journal of Economic Geography* 6 (1). 9–44.
Overton, Willis F. 2007. A coherent metatheory for dynamic systems: Relational organicism-contextualism. *Human Development* 50 (2–3). 154–159.
Park, Joseph. 2014. Cartographies of language: Making sense of mobility among Korean transmigrants in Singapore. *Language and Communication* 39. 83–91.
Pauwels, Paul. 2018. How advanced students approach intentional vocabulary study. *The Language Learning Journal* 46 (3). 293–310.
Pecorari, Diane & Philip Shaw. 2012. Types of student intertextuality and faculty attitudes. *Journal of Second Language Writing* 21 (2). 149–164.

Pedersen, Sofie & Jytte Bang. 2016. Historicizing affordance theory: A rendezvous between ecological psychology and cultural-historical activity theory. *Theory & Psychology* 26 (6). 731–750.
Peet, Robert K. 1974. The measurement of species diversity. *Annual Review of Ecology and Systematics* 5 (1). 285–307.
Peltzer-Karpf, AnneMarie. 1990. *Selbstorganizsationsprozesse in der sprachlichen Ontogennese: Erst- und Fremdsprache(n)*. Tübingen: Narr.
Peng, Jian-E. 2012. Towards an ecological understanding of willingness to communicate in EFL classrooms in China. *System* 40 (2). 203–213.
Peng, Jian-E. 2015. L2 motivational self system, attitudes, and affect as predictors of L2 WTC: An imagined community perspective. *The Asia-Pacific Education Researcher* 24 (2). 433–443.
Pennington, Martha C. & Barbara J. Hoekje. 2010. Language program as ecology: A perspective for leadership. *RELC Journal* 41 (3). 213–228.
Pennycook, Alastair (ed.). 1999. Critical approaches to TESOL [Special Issue]. *TESOL Quarterly* 33 (3).
Pennycook, Alastair. 2001. *Critical applied linguistics: A critical introduction*. New York: Routledge.
Pennycook, Alastair. 2004. Critical applied linguistics. In Alan Davies & Catherine Elder (eds.), *The handbook of applied linguistics*, 784–807. Oxford: Blackwell.
Pennycook, Alastair. 2018a. Posthumanist applied linguistics. *Applied Linguistics* 39 (4). 445–461.
Pennycook, Alastair. 2018b. *Posthumanist applied linguistics*. London: Routledge.
Pfenninger, Simone E. & David Singleton. 2017. *Beyond age-effects in instructional L2 learning: Revisiting the age factor*. Bristol: Multilingual Matters.
Phakiti, Aek, Peter De Costa, Luke Plonsky & Sue Starfield. 2018. Applied linguistics research: Current issues, methods and trends. In Aek Phakiti, Peter De Costa, Luke Plonsky & Sue Starfield (eds.), *The Palgrave handbook of applied linguistics research methodology*, 5–29. Houndmills: PalgraveMacmillan.
Phillipson, Robert & Tove Skutnabb-Kangas. 1996. English-only worldwide or language ecology? *TESOL Quarterly* 30 (3). 429–452.
Phillipson, Robert (ed.). 2009. *Linguistic imperialism revisited*. London: Routledge.
Phillipson, Robert. 1992. *Linguistic imperialism*. Oxford: Oxford University Press.
Piller, Ingrid. 2016. *Linguistic diversity and social justice: An introduction to applied sociolinguistics*. Oxford: Oxford University Press.
Piller, Ingrid & Jynhyun Cho. 2013. Neoliberalism as language policy. *Language in Society* 42 (1). 23–44.
Pim, Chris. 2013. Emerging technologies, emerging minds: Digital innovations within the primary sector. In Gary Motteram (ed.), *Innovations in learning technologies for English Language Teaching*, 15–42. London: British Council.
Pink, Sarah. 2013. *Doing visual ethnography*. Thousand Oaks, CA: SAGE.
Pozzi, Rebecca. 2017. Examining teacher perspectives on language policy in Buenos Aires. In Lía D. Kamhi-Stein, Gabriel Díaz Maggioli & Luciana C. de Oliveria (eds.), *English language teaching in South America*, 141–157. Bristol: Multilingual Matters.
Prabhu, Nagore S. 1990. There is no best method – Why? *TESOL Quarterly* 24 (2). 161–176.
Prabhu, Nagore S. 1992. The dynamics of a language lesson. *TESOL Quarterly* 26 (2). 225–241.
Price, Bob. 1997. The myth of postmodern science. In Raymond A. Eve, Sara Horesefall & Mary E. Lee (eds.), *Chaos, complexity, and sociology: Myths, models, and theories*, 3–14. Thousand Oaks, CA: SAGE.

Punch, Keith. 2013. *Introduction to social research: Quantitative and qualitative approaches*, 3rd edn. Thousand Oaks, CA: SAGE.
Quirk, Randolph. 1985. The English language in a global context. In Randolph Quirk & Henry G. Widdowson (eds.), *English in the world: teaching and learning of language and literature*, 1–6. Cambridge: Cambridge University Press.
Quirk, Randolph. 1990. Language varieties and standard language. *English Today* 21 (1). 3–10.
Ramanathan, Vai. 2002. *The politics of TESOL education: Writing, knowledge, critical pedagogy*. London: RoutledgeFalmer.
Ramanathan, Vaidehi & Brian Morgan. 2009. Global warning? West-based TESOL, class blindness, and the challenge for critical pedagogies. In Farzan Sharifian (ed.), *English as an international language: Perspectives and pedagogical issues*, 153–168. Clevedon: Multilingual Matters.
Reed, Edward, S. 1996. *Encountering the world*. New York, NY: Oxford University Press.
Reed, Michael & David L. Harvey. 1992. The new science and the old: Complexity and realism in the social sciences. *Journal for the Theory of Social Behaviour* 22. 356–379.
Reis-Jorge, José M. 2005. Developing teachers' knowledge and skills as researchers: A conceptual framework. *Asia-Pacific Journal of Teacher Education* 33 (3). 303–319.
Richards, Jack C. & Theodore S. Rodgers. 2014. *Approaches and methods in language teaching*, 3rd edn. Cambridge: Cambridge University Press.
Rietveld, Erik. 2008. Situated normativity: The normative aspect of embodied cognition in unreflective action. *Mind* 117 (468). 973–1001.
Rivers, Damian J. (ed.). 2014. *Resistance to the Known: Counter-conduct in language education*. Houndmills: Palgrave-Macmillan.
Robertson, Roland. 1995. Glocalisation: Time-space and homogeneity-heterogeneity. In Mike Featherston, Scott Lash & Roland Robertson (eds.), *Global modernities*. 24–44. Thousand Oaks, CA: SAGE.
Rommetveit, Ragnar. 1976. On the architecture of intersubjectivity. In Lloyd H. Strickland (ed.), *Social psychology in transition*, 201–214. Boston, MA: Springer.
Rotabi, Karen S. 2007. Ecological theory origin from natural to social science of vice versa? A brief conceptual history for social work. *Advances in Social Work* 8 (1). 113–129.
Ruecker, Todd. 2011. Challenging the native and nonnative English speaker hierarchy in ELT: New directions from race theory. *Critical Inquiry in Language Studies* 8 (4). 400–422.
Ruecker, Todd & Lindsey Ives. 2015. White native English speakers needed: The rhetorical construction of privilege in online teacher recruitment spaces. *TESOL Quarterly* 49 (4). 733–756.
Ryan, Richard M. & Edward L. Deci. 2000. Self-determination theory and the facilitation of intrinsic motivation, social development, and well-being. *American Psychologist* 55 (1). 68–78.
Sant, Edda & Chris Hanley. 2018. Political assumptions underlying pedagogies of national education: The case of student teachers teaching "British values" in England. *British Educational Research Journal* 44 (2). 319–337.
Sampson, Richard J. 2016. *Complexity in classroom foreign language motivation: A practitioner perspective from Japan*. Bristol: Multilingual Matters.
Sauvignon, Sandra J. 1983. *Communicative competence: Theory and classroom practice*. Reading, MA: Addison-Wesley.
Sayer, Peter. 2019. The hidden curriculum of work in English language education: Neoliberalism and early English programs in public schooling. *AILA Review* 32. 36–63.

Scarantino, Andrea. 2003. Affordances explained. *Philosophy of Science* 70 (5). 949–961.
Schön, Donald A. 1991 [1983]. *The reflective practitioner: How professionals think in action.* Farnham: Asgate Publishing.
Schwarzl, Lena, Eva Vetter & Miroslav Janík. 2019. Schools as a linguistic space: Multilingual realities at schools in Vienna and Brno. In Achilleas Kostoulas (ed.), *Challenging boundaries in language education*, 211–228. Cham: Springer.
Scott, Myrtle M. 2005. A powerful theory and a paradox: Ecological psychologists after Barker. *Environment and Behavior* 37 (3). 295–329.
Sealey, Alison & Bob Carter. 2004. *Applied linguistics as social science.* London: Continuum.
Seargeant, Phillip. 2005. "More English than England itself": The simulation of authenticity on English language practice in Japan. *International Journal of Applied Linguistics* 15 (3). 326–345.
Seargeant, Phillip & Elizabeth J. Erling. 2018. Introduction: English and development. In Elizabeth J. Erling & Phillip Seargeant (eds.), *English and development: Policy, pedagogy and globalisation*, 1–20. Bristol: Multilingual Matters.
Searle, John R. 1969. *Speech acts: An essay in the philosophy of language.* Cambridge: Cambridge University Press.
Searle, John R. 1979. What is an intentional state? *Mind* LXXXVIII (1). 74–92.
Searle, John R. 1980. The intentionality of intention and action. *Cognitive Science* 4 (1). 47–70.
Searle, John R. 1983. *Intentionality: An essay in the philosophy of mind.* Cambridge: Cambridge University Press.
Searle, John R. 1984. Intentionality and its place in nature. *Dialectica* 38 (2–3). 87–99.
Searle, John R. 2002. *Consciousness and language.* Cambridge: Cambridge University Press.
Seedhouse, Paul. 2005. Conversation analysis as research methodology. In Keith Richards & Paul Seedhouse (eds.), *Applying conversation analysis*, 251–266. London: PalgraveMacmillan.
Seedhouse, Paul. 2010. Locusts, snowflakes and recasts: Complexity theory and spoken interaction. *Classroom Discourse* 1 (1). 4–24.
Seidlhofer, Barbara. 2011. *Understanding English as a lingua franca.* Oxford: Oxford University Press.
Selinker, Larry. 1972. Interlanguage. *International Review of Applied Linguistics in Language Teaching* 10 (1–4). 209–232.
Selinker, Larry. 2013. *Rediscovering interlanguage.* London: Routledge.
Selvi, Ali F. 2011. The non-native speaker teacher. *ELT Journal* 65 (2). 187–189.
Semetsky, Inna. 2008. Rereading Dewey through the lens of complexity science, or: On the creative logic of education. In Mark Mason (ed.), *Complexity theory and the philosophy of education*, 79–90. Oxford: Wiley-Blackwell.
Shapiro, Shawna, Raichle Farrelly & Mary J. Curry (eds.). 2018. *Educating refugee-background students: Critical issues and dynamic contexts.* Bristol: Multilingual Matters.
Sharkey, Judy. 2004. ESOL teachers' knowledge of context as critical mediator in curriculum development. *TESOL Quarterly* 38 (2). 279–299.
Shin, Ji-Eun & David Kellogg. 2007. The novice, the native, and the nature of language teacher expertise. *International Journal of Applied Linguistics* 17 (2). 159–177.
Shotter, John. 1983. "Duality of structure" and "intentionality" in an ecological psychology. *Journal for the Theory of Social Behaviour* 13 (1). 19–44.
Sifakis, Nikos. 2009. Challenges in teaching ELF in the periphery: The Greek context. *ELT Journal* 63 (3). 230–237.

Silverman, David. 2006. *Interpreting qualitative data*, 3rd edn. Thousand Oaks, CA: SAGE.
Singleton, David. 2005. The critical period hypothesis: A coat of many colours. *International Review of Applied Linguistics in Language Teaching* 43 (4). 269–285.
Singleton, David M. & Lisa Ryan. 2004. *Language acquisition: The age factor*, 2nd edn. Clevedon: Multilingual Matters.
Skehan, Peter. 1996. A framework for the implementation of task-based instruction. *Applied Linguistics* 17 (1). 38–62.
Skehan, Peter & Pauline Foster. 1997. Task type and task processing conditions as influences on foreign language performance. *Language Teaching Research* 1 (3). 185–211.
Skela, Janez. 2019. A journey through the landscapes of teacher education. In Achilleas Kostoulas (ed.), *Challenging boundaries in language education*, 15–32. Cham: Springer.
Skutnabb-Kangas, Tove. 2000. Linguistic human rights and teachers of English. In Joan K. Hall & William G. Egginton (eds.), *The sociopolitics of English language teaching*, 22–44. Clevedon: Multilingual Matters.
Slobin, Dan I. 1996. From "thought and language" to "thinking for speaking." In John J. Gumperz & Stephen C. Levinson (eds.), *Rethinking linguistic relativity*, 70–96. Cambridge: Cambridge University Press.
Smith, Eliot R. & Sarah Queller. 2001. Mental representations. In Abraham Tesser & Norbert Schwarz (eds.), *Blackwell handbook of social psychology: Intraindividual processes*, 111–133. Malden, MA: Blackwell.
Smith, Jonathan A. 2004. Reflecting on the development of interpretative phenomenological analysis and its contribution to qualitative research in psychology. *Qualitative Research in Psychology* 1 (1). 39–54.
Smith, Larry E. & Cecil L. Nelson. 1985. International intelligibility of English: Directions and resources. *World Englishes* 4 (3). 333–342.
Snow, Catherine E. & Marian Hoefnagel-Höhle. 1978. The critical period for language acquisition: Evidence from second language learning. *Child Development* 49 (4). 1114–1128.
Soherwardy, Manal A. A. 2019. *Teachers' perspectives regarding contextualized teaching in an underprivileged environment, Pakistan*. Manchester, UK: The University of Manchester MA Thesis.
Søndergaard, Bent. 1991. Switching between seven codes within one family – A linguistic resource. *Journal of Multilingual & Multicultural Development* 12 (1–2). 85–92.
Spolsky, Bernard. 2004. *Language policy*. Cambridge: Cambridge University Press.
Stake, Robert E. 1994. Case studies. In Norman K. Denzin & Yvonna S. Lincoln (eds.), *Handbook of qualitative research*, 236–247. Thousand Oaks, CA: SAGE.
Stauffer, Robert C. 1957. Haeckel, Darwin, and ecology. *The Quarterly Review of Biology* 32 (2). 138–144.
Stelma, Juup. 2003. *Visualising the dynamics of learner interaction: Cases from a Norwegian language classroom*. Leeds, UK: University of Leeds doctoral thesis.
Stelma, Juup. 2010. What is communicative language teaching? In Susan Hunston & David Oakey (eds.), *Introducing applied linguistics: Concepts and skills*, 53–59. Abingdon, Oxon: Routledge.
Stelma, Juup. 2011. An ecological model of developing researcher competence: The case of software technology in doctoral research. *Instructional Science* 39 (3). 367–385.
Stelma, Juup. 2014. Developing intentionality and L2 classroom task-engagement. *Classroom Discourse* 5 (2). 119–137.

Stelma, Juup H. & Lynne J. Cameron. 2007. Intonation units in spoken interaction: Developing transcription skills. *Text & Talk – An Interdisciplinary Journal of Language, Discourse Communication Studies* 27 (3). 361–393.

Stelma, Juup & Richard Fay. 2014. Intentionality and developing researcher competence on a UK master's course: An ecological perspective on research education. *Studies in Higher Education* 39 (4). 517–533.

Stelma, Juup & Richard Fay. 2019. An ecological perspective for critical action in applied linguistics. In Achilleas Kostoulas (ed.), *Challenging boundaries in language education*, 51–69. Cham: Springer.

Stelma, Juup, Richard Fay & Xiaowei Zhou. 2013. Developing intentionality and researching multilingually: An ecological and methodological perspective. *International Journal of Applied Linguistics* 23 (3). 300–315.

Stelma, Juup, Zeynep Onat-Stelma, WooJoo Lee & Achilleas Kostoulas. 2015. Intentional dynamics in TESOL: An ecological perspective. *Teachers College, Columbia University Working Papers in TESOL & Applied Linguistics* 15 (1). 14–32.

Stern, Hans. 1983. *Fundamental concepts of language teaching: Historical and interdisciplinary perspectives on applied linguistic research*. Oxford: Oxford University Press.

Sternberg, Robert J. 1986. *Critical thinking: Its nature, measurement, and improvement*. Washington, DC: National Institute of Education.

Stevick, Earl. 1980. *Teaching languages: A way and ways*. Boston, MA: Heinle & Heinle.

Stevick, Earl W. 1990. *Humanism in language teaching*. Oxford: Oxford University Press.

Storch, Neomy. 1998. Comparing second language learners' attention to form across tasks. *Language Awareness* 7 (4). 176–191.

Storch, Neomy. 2002. Patterns of interaction in ESL pair work. *Language Learning* 52 (1). 119–158.

Swain, Merrill. 2000. The output hypothesis and beyond: Mediating acquisition through collaborative dialogue. In James Lantolf (ed.), *Sociocultural theory and second language acquisition*, 97–114. Oxford: Oxford University Press.

Swain, Merrill & Sharon Lapkin. 1995. Problems in output and the cognitive processes they generate: a step towards second language learning. *Applied Linguistics* 16 (3). 371–391.

Swales, John M. 1990. *Genre analysis: English in academic and research settings*. Cambridge: Cambridge University Press.

Thelen, Esther & Linga B. Smith. 1994. *A dynamic systems approach to the development of cognition and action*. Cambridge, MA: MIT Press.

Thomson, Pat & Helen Gunter. 2011. Inside, outside, upside down: The fluidity of academic researcher "identity" in working with/in school. *International Journal of Research & Method in Education* 34 (1). 17–30.

Titchener, Edward B. 1921. Brentano and Wundt: Empirical and experimental psychology. *American Journal of Psychology* 32 (1). 108–120.

Tolman, Edward C. 1949 [1932]. *Purposive behavior in animals and men*. Berkeley, CA: University of California Press.

Tomasello, Michael. 2003. *Constructing a language: A usage-based theory of language acquisition*. Cambridge, MA: Harvard University Press.

Tomasello, Michael & Malinda Carpenter. 2007. Shared intentionality. *Developmental Science* 10 (1). 121–125.

Tomasello, Michael, Malinda Carpenter, Josep Call, Tanya Behne & Henrike Moll. 2005. Understanding and sharing intentions: The origins of cultural cognition. *Behavioral and Brain Sciences* 28 (5). 675–735.

Tsagari, Dina & Spiros Papageorgiou (eds.). 2012. Special issue on language testing and assessment in the Greek educational context. *Research Papers in Language Teaching and Learning* 3 (1).

Tudge, Jonathan R. H, Irina Mokrova, Bridget E. Hatfield & Rachana B. Karnik. 2009. Uses and misuses of Bronfenbrenner's bioecological theory of human development. *Journal of Family Theory & Review* 1 (4). 198–210.

Tudor, Ian. 2001. *The dynamics of the language classroom*. Cambridge: Cambridge University Press.

Tudor, Ian. 2003. Learning to live with complexity: Towards an ecological perspective on language teaching. *System* 31. 1–12.

Underhill, Adrian. 1993. Awareness: The instrument and the aim of experiential research. In Julian Edge & Keith Richards (eds.), *Teachers develop teachers research: Papers on classroom research and teacher development*, 183–187. Oxford: Heinemann.

Ushioda, Ema. 2009. A person-in-context relational view of emergent motivation, self and identity. In Zoltán Dörnyei & Ema Ushioda (eds.), *Motivation, language identity and the L2 self*, 215–228. Clevedon: Multilingual Matters.

Ushioda, Ema. 2015. Context and complex dynamic systems theory. In Zoltán Dörnyei, Peter D. MacIntyre & Alastair Henry (eds.), *Motivational dynamics in language learning*, 47–54. Bristol: Multilingual Matters.

Van Dijk, Teun A. 2006. Ideology and discourse analysis. *Journal of Political Ideologies* 11 (2). 115–140.

van Ginkel, Agatha J. 2017. Early language learning in complex linguistic settings: Insights from Africa. In Janet Enever & Eva Lindgren (eds.), *Early language learning: Complexity and applied methods*, 9–23. Bristol: Multilingual Matters.

van Lier, Leo. 2000. From input to affordance: Social-interactive learning from an ecological perspective. In James Lantolf (ed.), *Sociocultural theory and second language learning*, 245–259. Oxford: Oxford University Press.

van Lier, Leo. 2002. An ecological-semiotic perspective on language and linguistics. In Claire Kramsch (ed.), *Language acquisition and language socialization: Ecological perspectives*, 140–164. London: Continuum.

van Lier, Leo. 2004. *The ecology and semiotics of language learning: A sociocultural perspective*. Boston, MA: Kluwer.

van Lier, Leo. 2007. Action-based teaching, autonomy and identity. *International Journal of Innovation in Language Learning and Teaching* 1 (1). 46–65.

van Riel, Raphael & Robert Van Gulick. 2019. Scientific reduction. In Edward N. Zalta (ed.), *The Stanford Encyclopedia of Philosophy*. Available from https://plato.stanford.edu/archives/spr19/entries/scientific-reduction Accessed on 1st March 2020.

Varela, Francisco. 1995. The emergent self. In John Brockman (ed.), *The third culture: Beyond the scientific revolution*, 209–222. New York: Simon & Schuster.

Verspoor, Marjolijn, Kees de Bot & Wander Lowie (eds.). 2011. *A dynamic approach to second language development: Methods and techniques*. Amsterdam: John Benjamins.

Verspoor, Marjolijn, Wander Lowie & Marjin van Dijk. 2008. Variability in second language development from a dynamic systems perspective. *The Modern Language Journal* 92 (2). 214–231.

Vertovec, Steven. 2007. Super-diversity and its implications. *Ethnic and Racial Studies* 30 (6). 1024–1054.
Vickers, Geoffrey (ed.). 1968. *Value systems and social process*. London: Tavistock Publications.
von Bertalanffy, Ludwig. 2015 [1969]. *General system theory: Foundations, development, applications*, revised edn. New York, NY: George Braziller.
Vygotsky, Lev S. 1978. *Mind in society: The development of higher psychological processes*. Cambridge, MA: Harvard University Press.
Wallace, Michael J. 1998. *Action research for language teachers*. Cambridge University Press.
Waring, Hansun Zhang. 2011. Learner initiatives and learning opportunities in the language classroom. *Classroom Discourse* 2 (2). 201–218.
Watts, Richard J. 2011. *Language myths and the history of English*. Oxford: Oxford University Press.
Wee, Lionel. 2008. Linguistic instrumentalism in Singapore. In Peter Tan & Rani K. W. Rubdy (eds.), *Language as a commodity: Global structures, local marketplaces*, 31–43. London: Continuum.
Wehrmann, Jürgen. 2019. Beyond the Garrison: Global education and teaching (Canadian) literature in the EFL classroom. In Achilleas Kostoulas (ed.), *Challenging boundaries in language education*, 107–120. Cham: Springer.
Whiteman, Natasha & Martin Oliver. 2008. Engaging with the research methods curriculum. *Reflecting Education* 4 (1). 63–71.
Widdowson, Henry G. 2003. *Defining issues in English language teaching*. Oxford: Oxford University Press.
Widdowson, Henry G. 2004. A perspective on recent trends. In Anthony P. R. Howatt (with Henry G. Widdowson), *A history of English language teaching*, 2nd edn, 353–372. Oxford: Oxford University Press.
Williams, Dylan G. 2015. A systematic review of EMI and implications for the South Korean HE context. *ELT World Online* (Special Issue on CLIL). 1–23.
Willis, Dave & Jane Willis. 2007. *Doing task-based teaching*. Oxford: Oxford University Press.
Winn, Sandra. 1995. Learning by doing: Teaching research methods through student participation in a commissioned research project. *Studies in Higher Education* 20 (2). 203–214.
Wodak, Ruth & Michael Meyer. 2009. *Methods of critical discourse analysis*, 2nd edn. Thousand Oaks, CA: SAGE.
Wu, Xinyi. 2003. Intrinsic motivation and young language learners: The impact of the classroom environment. *System* 31 (4). 501–517.
Yin, Robert K. 2003. *Case study research: Design and methods*, 3rd edn. Thousand Oaks, CA: SAGE.
Young, Michael, Andrew DePalma & Steven Garrett. 2002. Situations, interaction, process and affordances: An ecological psychology perspective. *Instructional Science* 30 (1). 47–63.
Zheng, Dongping, Michael F. Young, Manuela Maria Wagner & Robert A. Brewer. 2009. Negotiation for action: English language learning in game-based virtual worlds. *The Modern Language Journal* 93 (4). 489–511.
Zheng, Yongyan. 2016. The complex, dynamic development of L2 lexical use: A longitudinal study on Chinese learners of English. *System* 56. 40–53.

Index

aboutness 4, 9, 55, 63–64, 67, 75, 83, 183
Action Research 90–91, 93, 104, 229
action-perception cycles 71–72, 81
action-present 90, 102, 104
activation 167, 170, 172–173, 175, 182
affordance landscape 135–141, 143, 213, 222
affordances 2, 11, 22, 26, 29, 32, 42, 70, 72, 75, 77, 81–82, 123, 135–136, 138, 143, 193–194, 196–197, 209, 213, 231, 234–235
– goal 30, 78
– happening 30, 74
– immediate 28–29, 74
– mediated 28–29, 71, 169
agency 15, 31, 49, 60, 65, 82, 178, 180, 189, 191, 193–194, 196, 207, 236–237
Al-Hoorie, Ali 15, 206–207, 214, 216, 220, 224
applied linguistics 15, 36, 166, 185–187, 221, 225, 236
appreciative system 90–91, 101, 103
Archer, Margaret 41
attractor state 9, 11, 40, 42, 51, 72, 75, 77, 79, 81, 124–125, 143, 153, 159, 167–168, 175, 182, 193, 197, 210, 213, 216, 221–223, 227
– communicative 139, 142
– form-focused 139–143, 216, 222

Bateson, Gregory 8, 19–20, 31, 38, 190
Blommaert, Jan 172
Blumer, Herbert 19, 31, 169
Brentano, Franz 4, 55
Bronfenbrenner, Urie 8, 23–26, 29
Byrne, David 15, 37, 46–47, 204

Callaghan, Gill 15, 37, 46–47, 204
Cameron, Lynne 15, 36, 41, 75, 132, 148, 166, 168, 170, 172, 176, 181, 204, 207, 222, 224, 236
Canagarajah, Suresh A. 152, 180
cascading constraints hierarchy 30, 202
case study 219, 221
causality 203–204

Cilliers, Paul 35, 37, 41–42, 47
co-adaptation 123, 132, 203, 213, 219, 226–227, 238
communicative competence 156–158
Communicative Language Teaching 129, 132, 135, 137, 141–142, 149–150, 156–157, 161, 173, 178
Complex Adaptive System 48
Complex Dynamic System (CDS) 36, 204
– boundaries 37–38, 50, 82, 168–169, 203, 211, 213, 219, 222
– elements 37, 39, 50
– L2 development 174–175, 177, 181
– language learning 173–174, 177
– language school 41, 139
– language use 166, 168–169, 174, 176, 240
Complex Dynamic Systems Theory (CDST) 1–2, 8, 14, 35, 45, 73, 144, 161, 203, 226, 228, 234, 236–237
complexity paradigm 15, 45
connectionism 166
context 64–65, 187–189, 202, 226, 233
critical
– critical-cognitive 186–187
– critical-contextual 188
– critical-humanistic 158, 161, 189, 193
– critical-intentional 12, 185, 191–192, 229, 241
curriculum 127–128, 131, 139–141, 143, 155, 205, 222

Davis, Brent 44, 48, 205
Dennett, Daniel 9, 53
design stance 53
developing researcher competence 93
direct perception 27, 29, 70
discourse community 170
diversity 12, 147, 151, 158, 161, 178–180, 182–183, 192, 196–198, 229, 231, 241–242
dynamic properties 39–40, 42, 50, 72–73, 122, 168, 173–174, 176, 180, 210, 214–215, 221, 231

– adaptiveness 9, 40, 75, 79, 116, 123, 141–142, 168, 173–174, 181, 197
– historicity 9, 32, 41, 76, 79, 112, 123, 139, 142, 160–161, 167–168, 173, 175, 181, 197
– non-linearity 9, 41, 78–79, 112, 116, 123, 167–168, 173, 175, 181, 197
– self-organisation 9, 41, 79, 123, 175, 181, 197
Dynamic Systems Theory 46
dynamics of intentions 96

ecolinguistics 152
Ecological Psychology 2, 70, 81
Ecological theory 1–2, 7, 14, 19, 168, 196, 228, 235, 237
ecology
– as system 8, 21, 66
– natural vs. social 20
– of activity 8, 22, 25
– of ideas 31, 196, 206, 225
– of meaning 31, 33, 64
Edge, Julian 91, 152, 166, 171, 208, 239
emergence 44, 117, 122–123, 125, 165, 167, 172, 177, 182, 192, 197, 205, 214, 216, 219–221, 227, 230, 234, 242
English as a Lingua Franca 147
equifinality 223
equilibrium 40
ethnography 221–222
Exploratory Practice 90, 93, 104, 178, 195, 230

Fay, Richard 54, 89, 191, 195, 229
Feryok, Anne 14, 58
Five Graces Group 48, 165, 168, 176
folk-psychology 53, 59
form-focused teaching 135–137, 155–156
freedom 186, 189, 191, 193–194, 196–197
Freire, Paulo 190, 194

generative potential 9–10, 38–39, 46, 55, 73, 77, 79, 192, 195–198, 214, 219, 234, 242
Gibson, James J. 2, 8, 22, 26
grammaring 240
grounded theory 128, 223

Harvey, Lou 183
heterogeneity 37, 39
Hiver, Phil 15, 206–207, 214, 216, 220, 224
Holliday, Adrian 16, 109, 129, 149, 170, 187, 192
Holling, Crawford S. 43, 45, 47, 205

identity 125, 178–179, 183, 236, 239
ideological becoming 183
indexicality 62, 158, 171, 240
information 27
– as intentionality 71, 169
– meaningful 21, 33, 38, 96
intention 2, 4, 9, 29–30, 56, 58, 82
intentional activity 9, 14, 53, 70, 81–82, 210, 226, 234
– contingent 11, 74, 113, 116–117, 121, 123, 142, 160, 181, 226
– creative 11, 77, 116, 121, 123, 161, 181, 227, 229, 241
– normative 76, 112, 139, 142, 161, 179, 181, 227
– purposeful 10, 78, 94, 96, 98–99, 123, 161, 174–175, 181, 219, 227, 229, 241
intentional becoming 12, 97, 165, 177, 182–183, 230–231, 238–239
intentional dynamics 5, 14, 30, 47, 82, 109, 122, 232, 238
– mind-set 13, 201, 203, 205, 208, 227
– model of 1, 68, 80, 96, 103, 169, 176, 182, 192, 206–209, 217, 225, 227, 233, 237
– resistance 128, 138–140, 161, 213, 222
intentional ecologies 65, 89, 91–92, 101, 103, 105, 171, 188, 211, 219, 232–233
intentional ecology 14, 71, 81–82, 124, 169, 173, 209, 211, 226
– idiosyncratic 96, 132, 143, 220, 233
– of TESOL 9, 64, 67
– pedagogical 102, 177
– professional 90, 95–96, 104
– research 96, 100, 105
intentional stance 53, 57, 207
intentional structure 5, 12, 64, 145, 198, 205, 240–241
– "earlier is better" 148, 151, 157
– authenticity 148, 157

- credentialism 129, 141–142
- critical-humanistic 152–153, 157–158
- diversity 151–152
- English as development 146, 148, 157
- English-only 147
- hegemony 150, 157–158, 161
- idiosyncratic 11, 142, 211, 213, 222
- language as social action 147, 153, 157–158, 161
- language as system 145, 153, 155–156, 160
- learning group 149, 157, 161
- linguistic instrumentalism 146–148, 150, 161
- neoliberalism 151, 153, 155–156, 160
- postmethod 150, 153, 157–159
- protectionism 131–132, 139–142
- standard language 145, 147, 149, 157–158, 161
- supplementation 130, 132, 141–142
- technicalisation 149, 151, 153, 155–156, 160
intentionality 4, 9, 14–15, 227, 237, 240
- assigned 61–62, 123, 139, 231
- derived 5, 11, 61–62, 65, 67, 76, 80, 83, 93, 100, 123, 133–139, 142, 171, 177, 187, 193, 211, 213, 219, 222, 230
- ideational 9, 55–57, 65–66, 83, 174, 196, 206, 213, 240
- individual 10, 67, 79–80, 93, 99–100, 125, 170, 177–178, 182, 187, 193, 197, 211, 220, 232
- intrinsic 61
- ordinary 9, 55, 57, 67, 78
- sedimented 61–62, 139, 231
- shared 4, 11, 59–61, 64, 67, 80, 83, 98, 106–108, 112, 116, 121–125, 129, 170, 177, 179, 193, 211, 213, 219–221, 232
- sociocultural aspects of 11, 62, 64–65, 67, 76, 80, 83, 114, 129–130, 132, 153, 159, 171, 177, 179–180, 192–193, 219, 222
intersubjectivity 59
intertextuality 62, 171, 240
isomorphic processes 167, 172, 174

Juarrero, Alicia 3, 78, 82

Kramsch, Claire 32, 176, 182
Kubanyiova, Maggie 14, 58
Kumaravadivelu, Bala 56, 150, 159, 188–189

Larsen-Freeman, Diane 15, 36, 41, 45–46, 48, 75, 132, 166–168, 170, 172, 176, 204, 207, 222, 224, 236, 240
lexical priming 167
linguistic human rights 152

Marx, Karl 190
materials development 231
meaning-making 1, 5, 14–15, 21, 25, 27, 32, 83, 109, 124–125, 169, 175–178, 181, 207, 214–215, 218–220, 225, 228, 234, 237
meta-theory 7, 10, 13–14, 16, 47, 51, 183, 225, 228
microgenesis 214
molar activity 19, 26, 29
molecular activity 29–30
Morin, Edgar 47
morphogenesis 14, 41–42, 51, 73, 97, 209, 215, 221–222, 227, 234
motivation 54, 124, 183, 230, 236, 239
- self-determination theory 54, 239
mutuality 28–29, 71, 81

Neisser, Ulric 27
normative assumptions 13, 63, 145, 147, 151, 159, 161, 190, 192–194, 197–198, 241
normative consensus 11, 109, 111, 113, 116, 118, 121–122, 124, 166

object theory 48

paradigm
- transactional 153, 155, 157, 159, 162, 216
- transformative 153, 159
Pennycook, Alastair 16, 146–147, 152, 189
perturbations 41, 168
phenomenology 55
Phillipson, Robert 150, 190
physical stance 53
Piaget, Jean 170
policy-making 231–232
postmethod 159, 190
power 82, 150, 171, 179–180, 189–191, 194–195, 231, 242

professional development 90, 92, 131–132, 230, 239
psychological states 28, 55–57, 59, 66, 75, 81, 83, 170

rationalities 56, 63
reflection 90–91, 101, 188
reflexivity 208
representation
– mental 55, 59
– process 168, 170
researcher intentionality 54, 93–94, 96–97, 99–101, 103, 218–219

Scarantino, Andrea 30
Schön, Donald 90
Searle, John 5, 56, 59, 61, 82
semiotic budget 32
signature dynamics 214–215, 226
small culture 109, 129, 232
Smith, Linga B. 41
social structures 64, 124–125, 145, 147, 151, 180, 226, 234
sociocultural theory 60, 124, 169, 179
soft-assembly 14, 41, 51, 73, 81, 174, 209, 212–213, 234
Speech Act theory 61, 240–241
stability 40, 75, 82, 205, 216

stratification 23–26, 34, 43, 50, 80, 180, 194, 202
– activity (domains of) 25, 64, 81, 194, 196, 208, 241
– analytical (sub-systems) 9, 44, 47, 49, 65, 173
– structural (nested) 8, 10, 23, 43, 47–49, 64, 129, 215
Sumara, Dennis 48, 205
symbolic interactionism 32, 169, 176

teacher development 91, 239
Thelen, Esther 41
time 167, 182
timescales 6, 76, 177, 204, 213, 215–216, 221, 226, 234
Tolman, Edward C. 19, 29
Tomasello, Michael 4
Tudor, Ian 56, 63, 149

validity 206–207, 212, 215, 218–219, 222
van Lier, Leo 15, 20, 22, 28, 32
Vygotsky, Lev 60, 125

World Englishes 147, 158

Young, Michael 2, 30, 71, 82, 96

www.ingramcontent.com/pod-product-compliance
Lightning Source LLC
Chambersburg PA
CBHW031423150426
43191CB00006B/377